Hitsuji Gondaira

This self-portrait is a fox in sheep's clothing. I like foxes because they're cool. And I like sheep because they're delicious. Volume 2 is about to start!

Hitsuji Gondaira's first series, *Demon Prince Poro's Diaries,* was published in *Weekly Shonen Jump* in 2017. He started work on *Mission: Yozakura Family* in 2019.

D1502006

MISSION: YOZAKURA FAMILY
VOL. 2
SHONEN JUMP Edition

STORY AND ART BY
HITSUJI GONDAIRA

TRANSLATION AND LETTERING
PINKIE-CHAN

DESIGN
JIMMY PRESLER

RETOUCH LETTERER
JOHN HUNT

EDITOR
RAE FIRST

YOZAKURA-SANCHI NO DAISAKUSEN © 2019 by Hitsuji Gondaira
All rights reserved. First published in Japan in 2019 by SHUEISHA Inc., Tokyo.
English translation rights arranged by SHUEISHA Inc.

The stories, characters, and incidents mentioned
in this publication are entirely fictional.

No portion of this book may be reproduced or transmitted in any form or
by any means without written permission from the copyright holders.

Printed in Canada

Published by VIZ Media, LLC
P.O. Box 77010
San Francisco, CA 94107

10 9 8 7 6 5 4 3 2 1
First printing, December 2022

PARENTAL ADVISORY
MISSION YOZAKURA FAMILY is rated T for Teen
and is recommended for ages 13 and up for
realistic and fantasy violence.

viz.com

MISSION:
Yozakura Family

2 — Date

Story and Art by
Hitsuji Gondaira

Mission: Yozakura Family Characters

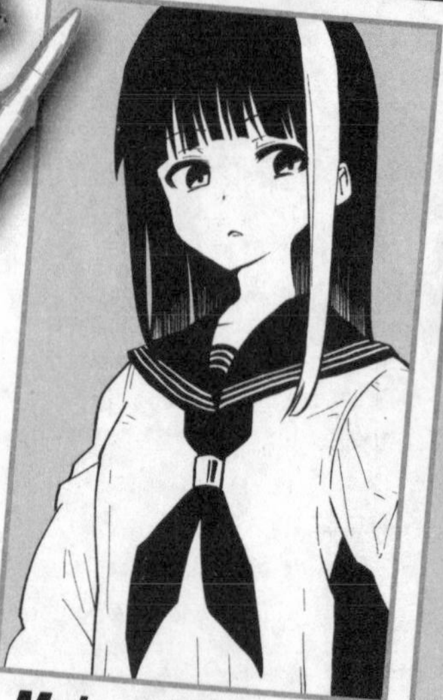

Mutsumi Yozakura

The third daughter of the Yozakura family. She has the ability to birth superhumans as the head of the household and is protected by her siblings.

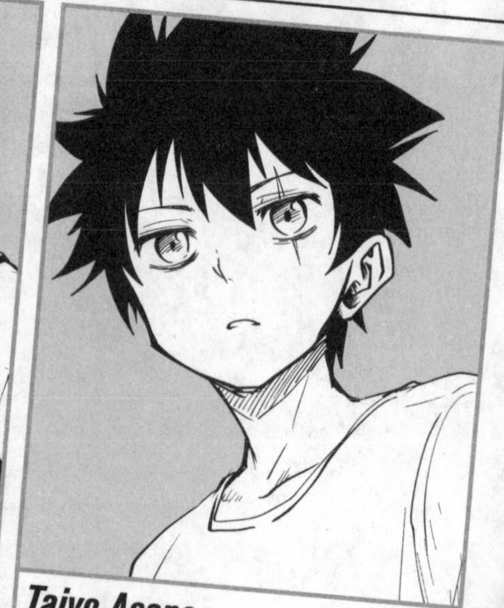

Taiyo Asano

A high school student who lost his family in an accident, causing him to retreat emotionally from others. He married the only person he could talk to—his childhood friend Mutsumi Yozakura.

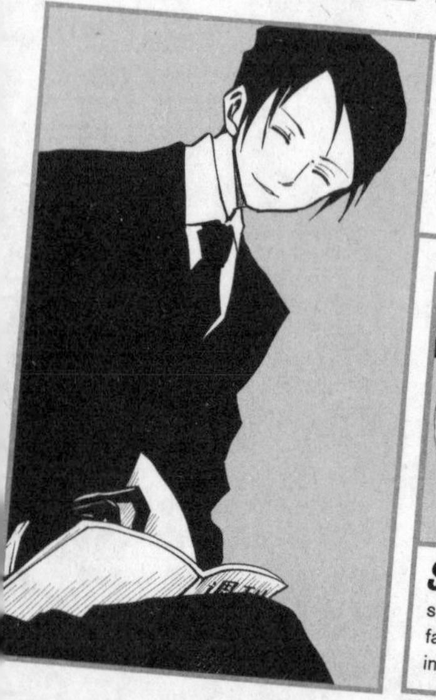

Kyoichiro Yozakura

The eldest son of the Yozakura family. He's the top spy in both skills and popularity. He uses the alias "Hirukawa" when he works as the high school vice principal.

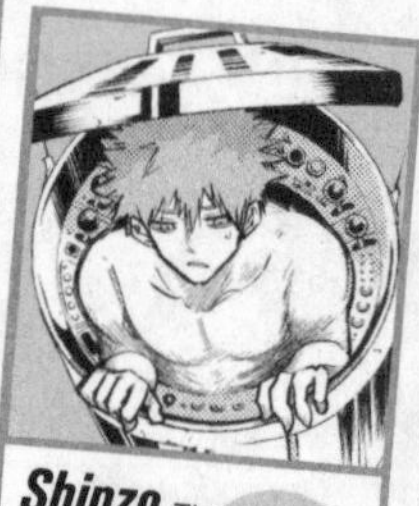

Shinzo The second son of the Yozakura family. He specializes in weapons.

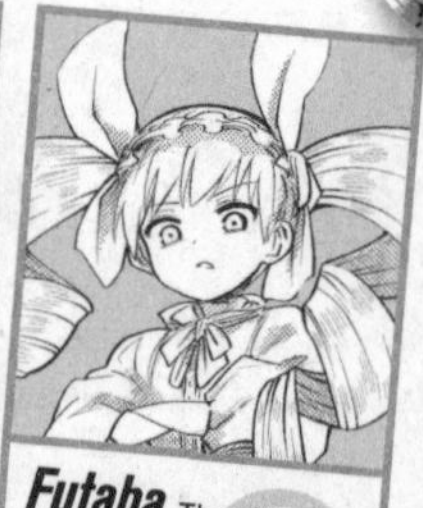

Futaba The eldest daughter of the Yozakura family. She's an expert at aikido and jujitsu.

Nanao The fourth son of the Yozakura family. He has super-human strength and specializes in drugs and poisons.

Kengo The third son of the Yozakura family. An expert in disguise, he can transform into anyone.

Shion The second daughter of the Yozakura family. She's a gamer and a genius computer hacker.

Hanawa The president of the Flower Bin Delivery Service and the spy who kidnapped Mutsumi.

Ritsu Katai A teacher at Taiyo and Mutsumi's high school. She's super strict.

Goliath The Yozakura family's pet dog.

Story.

When Taiyo Asano loses his family in a car accident, he becomes a shell of a person and extremely anxious around other people. The only person he feels comfortable enough to talk to is his childhood friend Mutsumi Yozakura. But one day, Mr. Hirukawa, the vice principal of their high school, decides to break up their relationship.

It turns out that Hirukawa is actually Mutsumi's older brother and Mutsumi's family are all spies descended from ninjas!

Even though Mutsumi doesn't possess any spy skills herself, as the head of the household she is the only one who can produce children with superhuman abilities. Her siblings are there to protect Mutsumi from outsiders, Kyoichiro is also trying to eliminate Taiyo! efforts to protect Mutsumi from outsiders, Kyoichiro is also trying to eliminate Taiyo! The only way to escape Kyoichiro's wrath is for Taiyo to marry Mutsumi. With the help of Mutsumi's other siblings, Taiyo receives the Cherry Blossom ring, making him a member of the Yozakura family. Taiyo's new life as a member of a spy family has just begun when Hanawa the Courier kidnaps Mutsumi. It's now up to Taiyo and the Yozakura family to get her back!

Mission: Yozakura Family Vol. 2

Date
Mission Objectives

Mission:
Yozakura Family

MISSION 8: THREE MINUTES

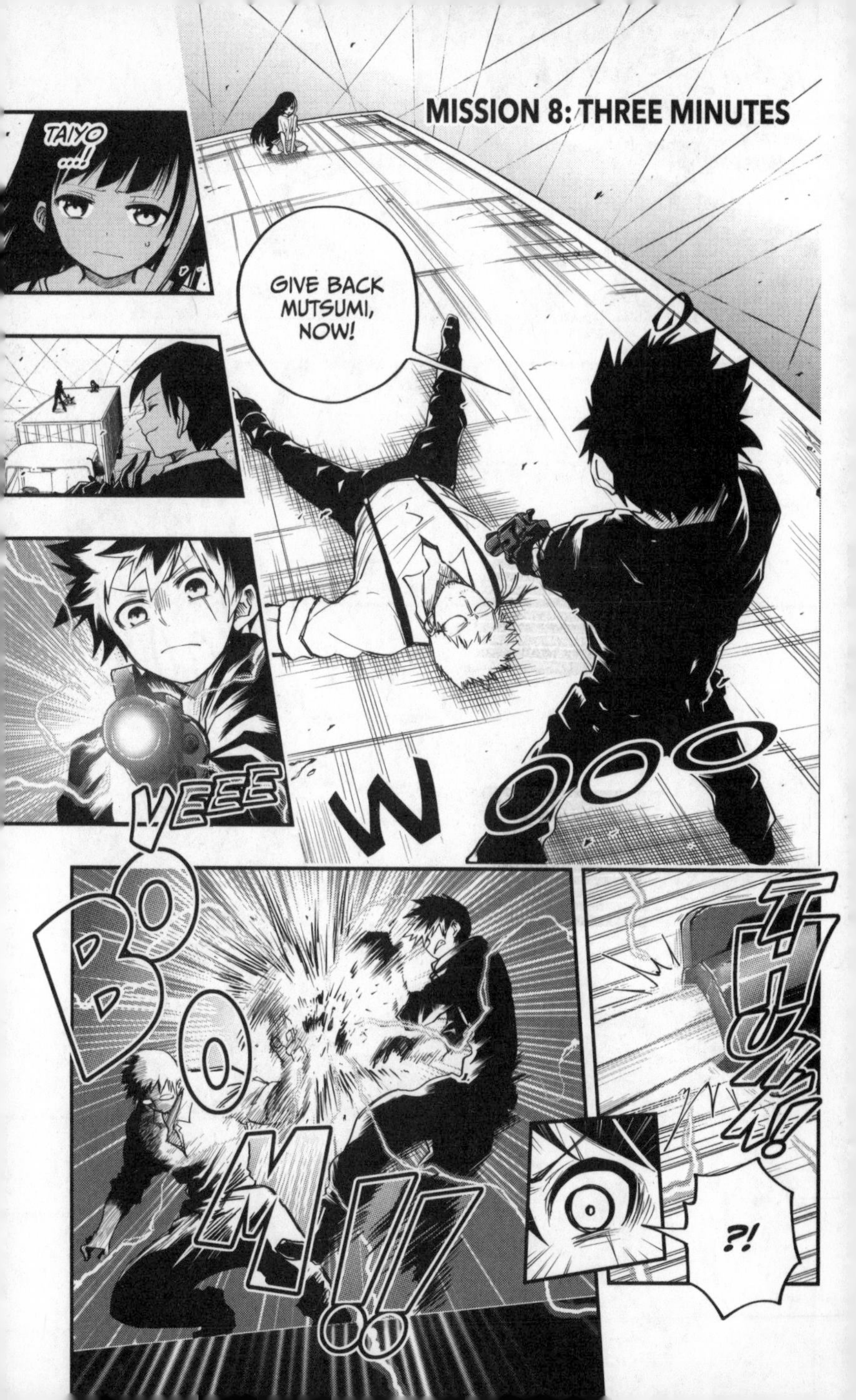
GIVE BACK MUTSUMI, NOW!
TAIYO ...!
VEEEE
WOOOO
THUNK!!
?!
BOOM!!

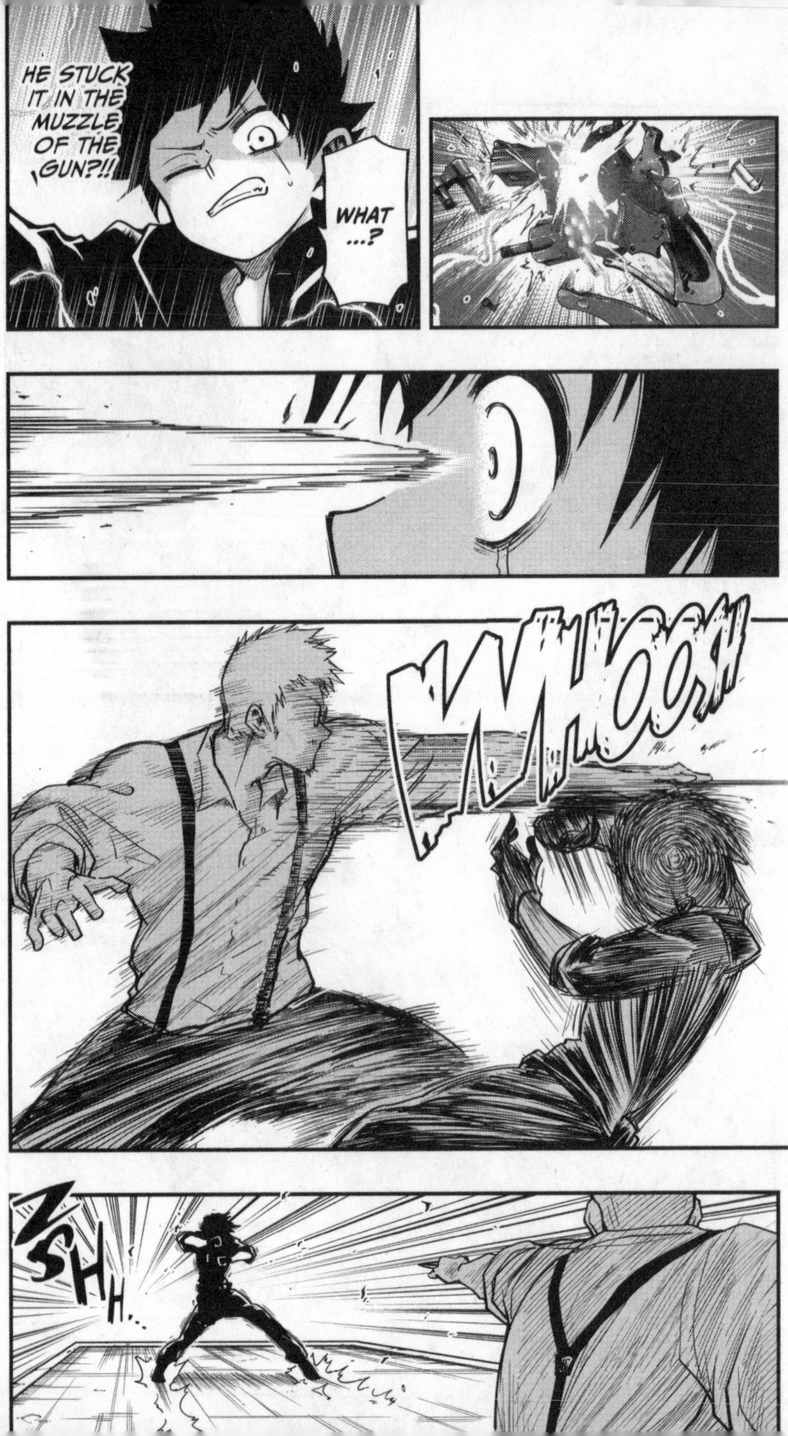
WHAT ...?
HE STUCK IT IN THE MUZZLE OF THE GUN?!!
WHOOSH
SHH...

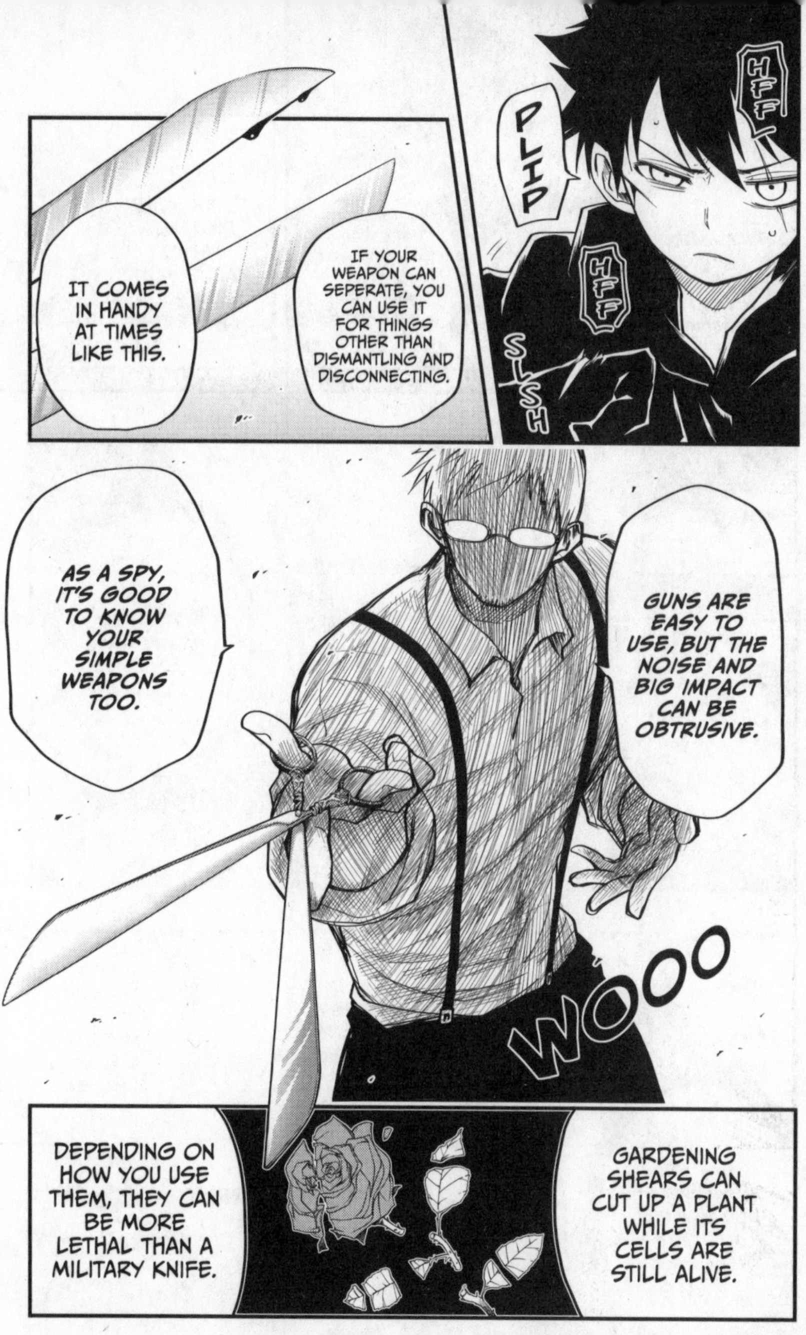
HFF
PLIP
HFF
SLSH
IF YOUR WEAPON CAN SEPERATE, YOU CAN USE IT FOR THINGS OTHER THAN DISMANTLING AND DISCONNECTING.
IT COMES IN HANDY AT TIMES LIKE THIS.
GUNS ARE EASY TO USE, BUT THE NOISE AND BIG IMPACT CAN BE OBTRUSIVE.
AS A SPY, IT'S GOOD TO KNOW YOUR SIMPLE WEAPONS TOO.
WOOO
GARDENING SHEARS CAN CUT UP A PLANT WHILE ITS CELLS ARE STILL ALIVE.
DEPENDING ON HOW YOU USE THEM, THEY CAN BE MORE LETHAL THAN A MILITARY KNIFE.

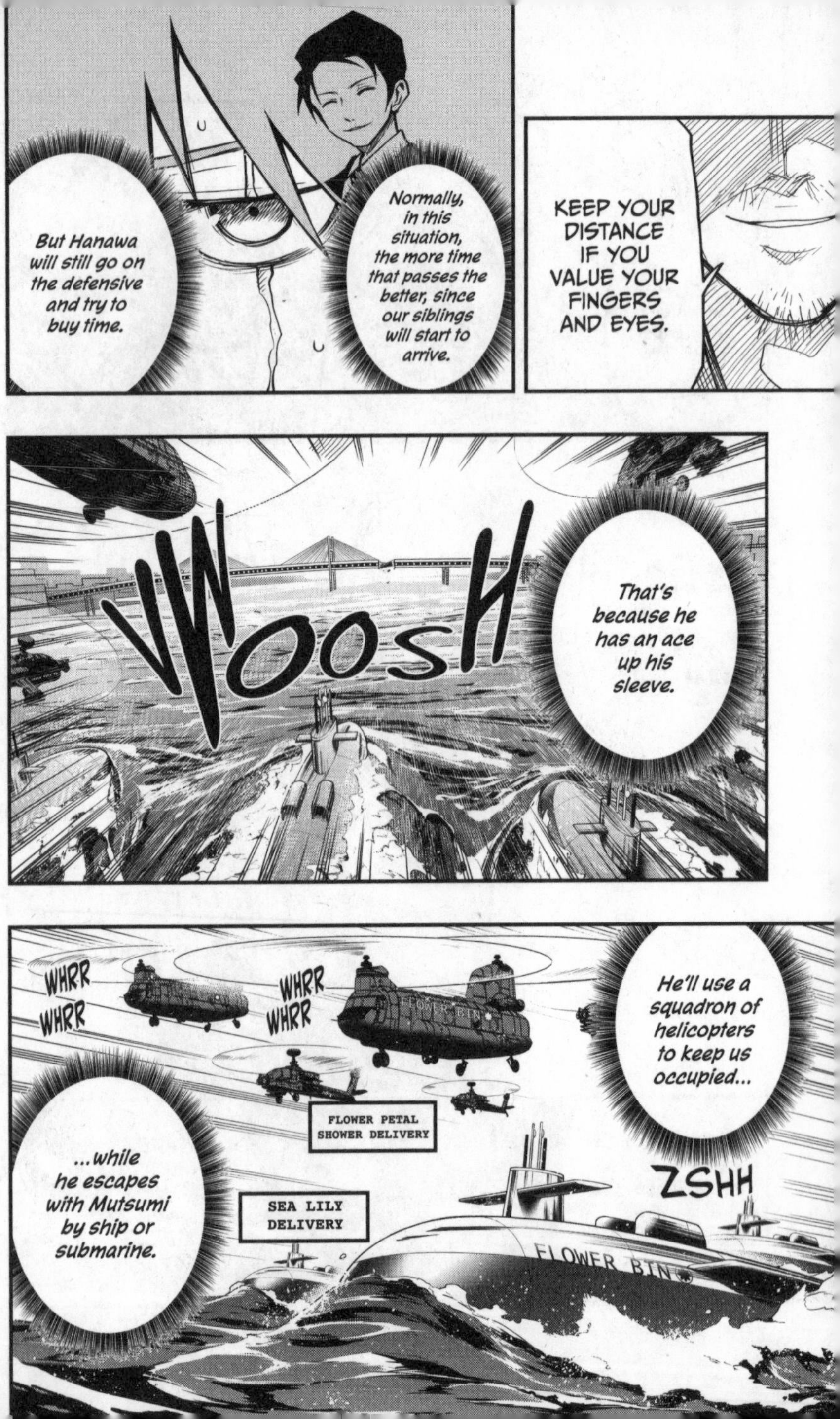
KEEP YOUR DISTANCE IF YOU VALUE YOUR FINGERS AND EYES.
Normally, in this situation, the more time that passes the better, since our siblings will start to arrive.
But Hanawa will still go on the defensive and try to buy time.
That's because he has an ace up his sleeve.
WOOSH
He'll use a squadron of helicopters to keep us occupied...
WHRR WHRR
WHRR WHRR
FLOWER PETAL SHOWER DELIVERY
ZSHH
SEA LILY DELIVERY
...while he escapes with Mutsumi by ship or submarine.

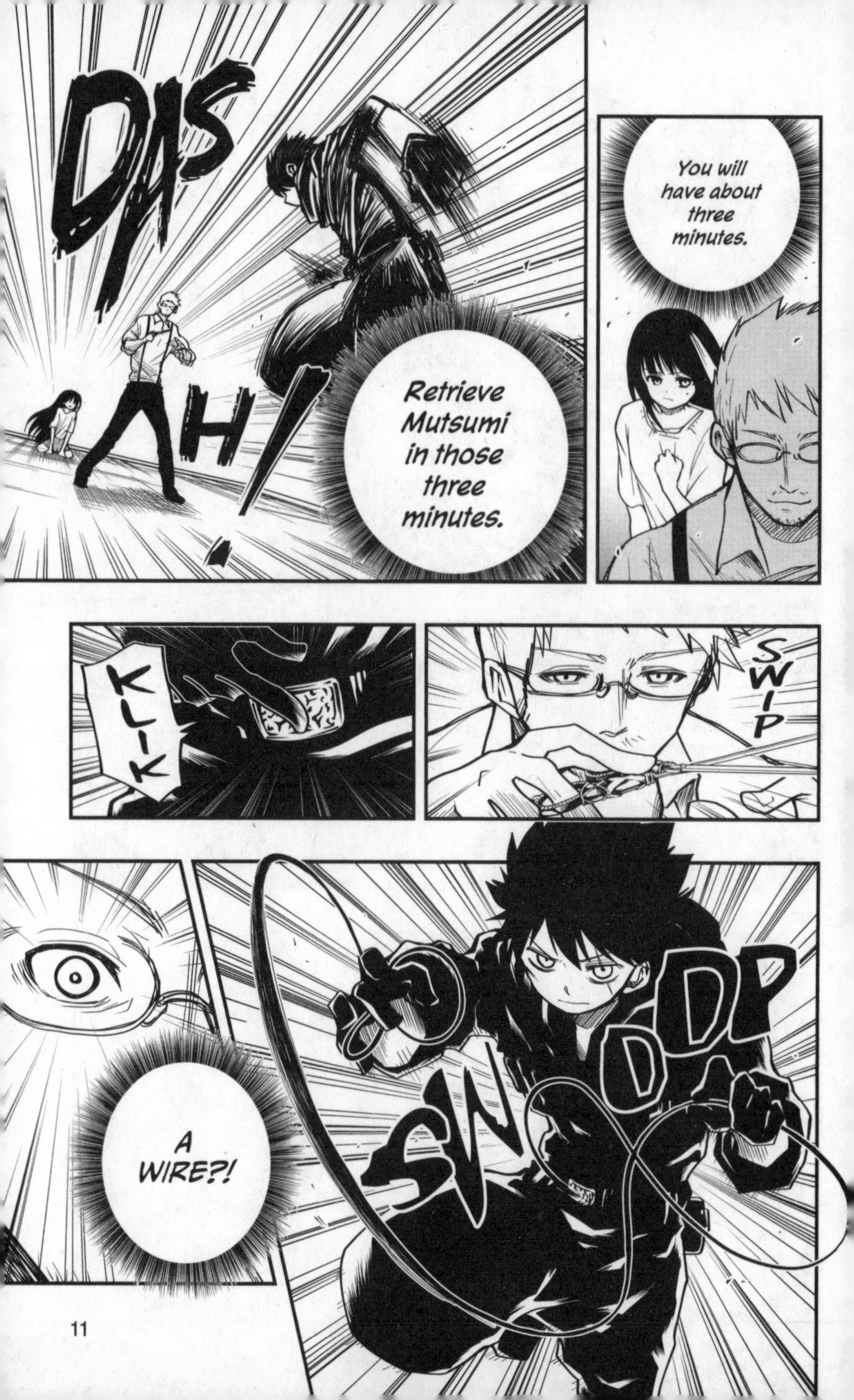
You will have about three minutes.
DASH!
Retrieve Mutsumi in those three minutes.
SWIP
KLIK
SWDDDP
A WIRE?!

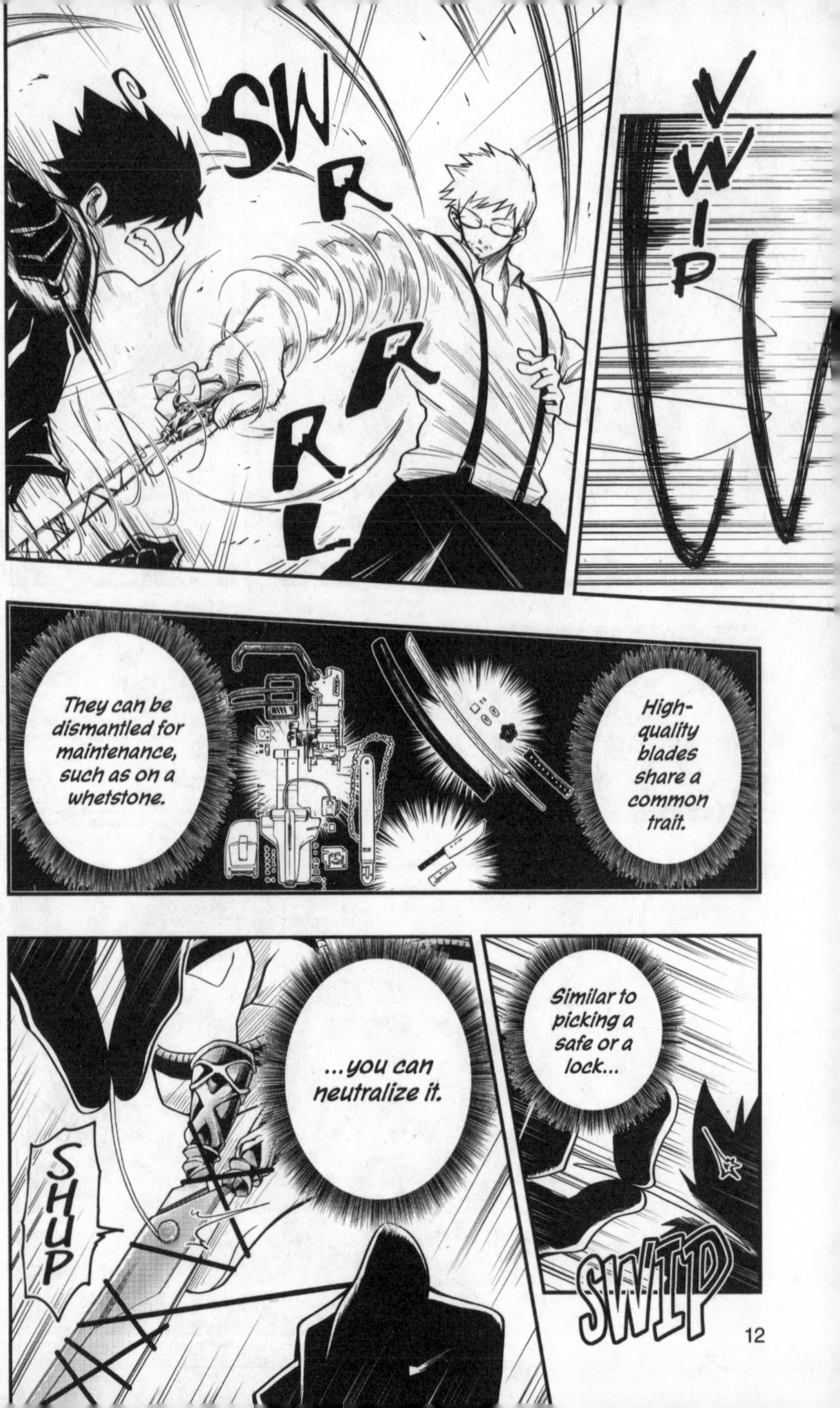
VWIP
SWRRRRL
High-quality blades share a common trait.
They can be dismantled for maintenance, such as on a whetstone.
Similar to picking a safe or a lock...
SWIP
...you can neutralize it.
SHUP

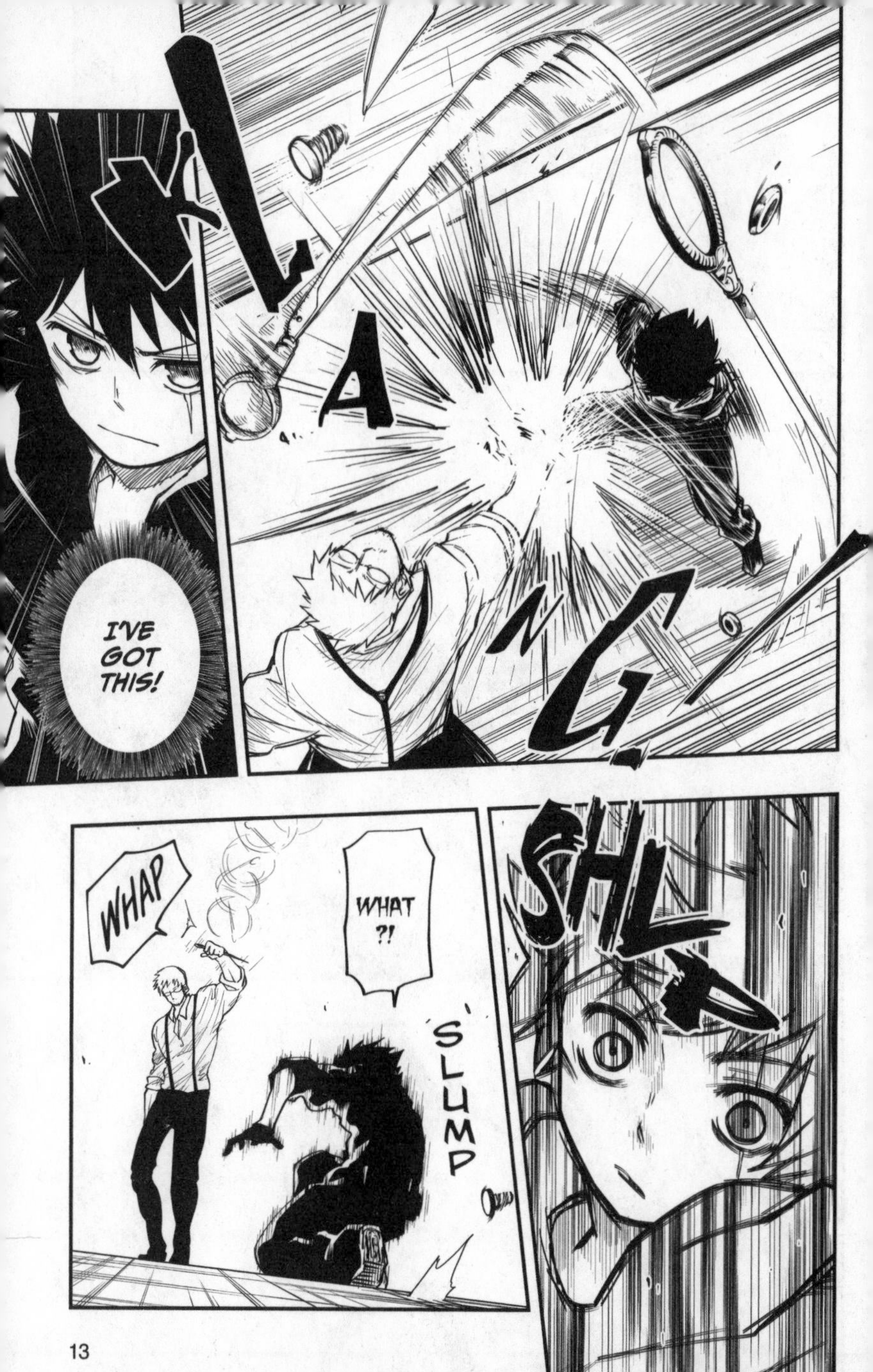
CLANG
I'VE GOT THIS!
SHLK
WHAT ?!
WHAP
SLUMP

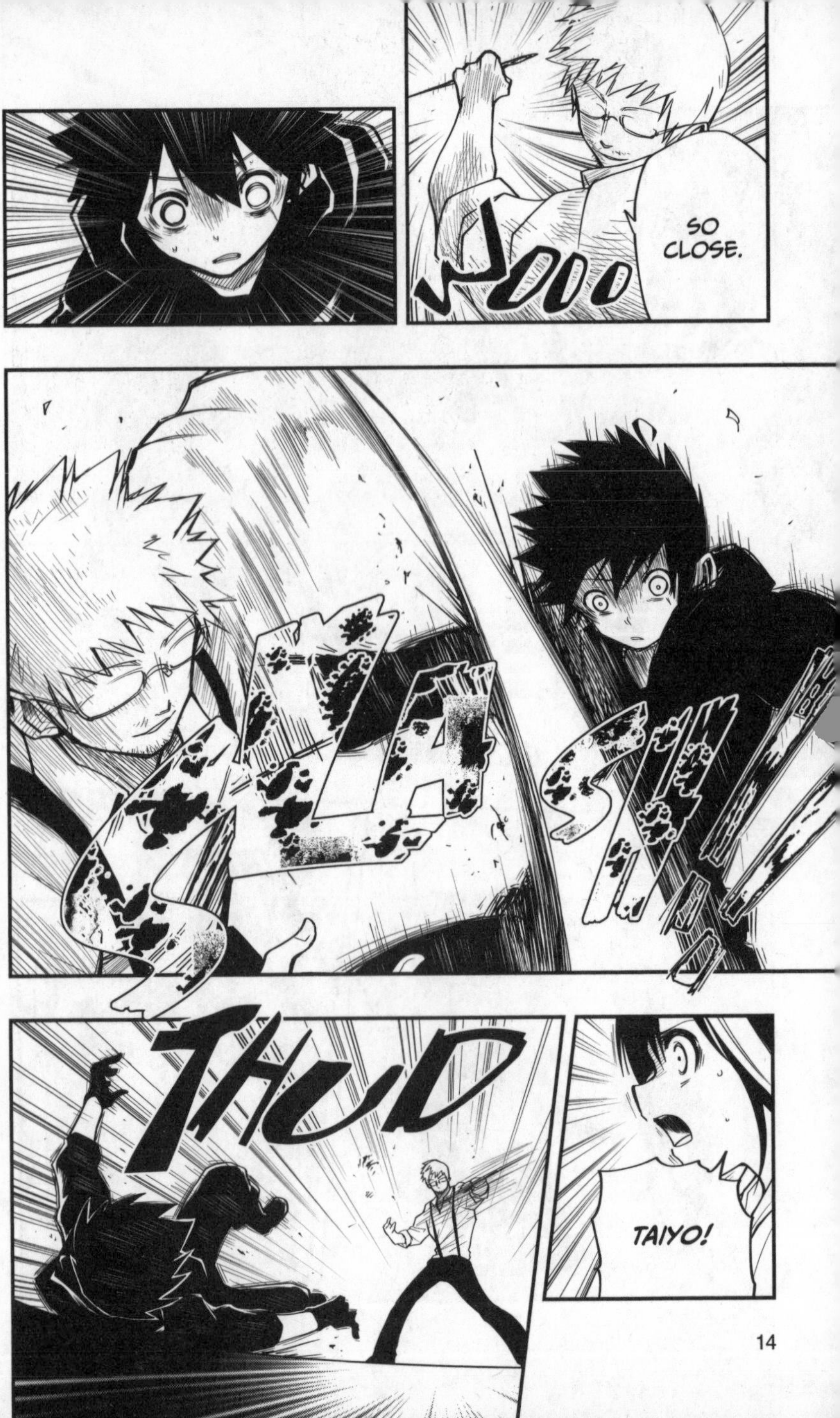
SO CLOSE.
SLASH
THUD
TAIYO!

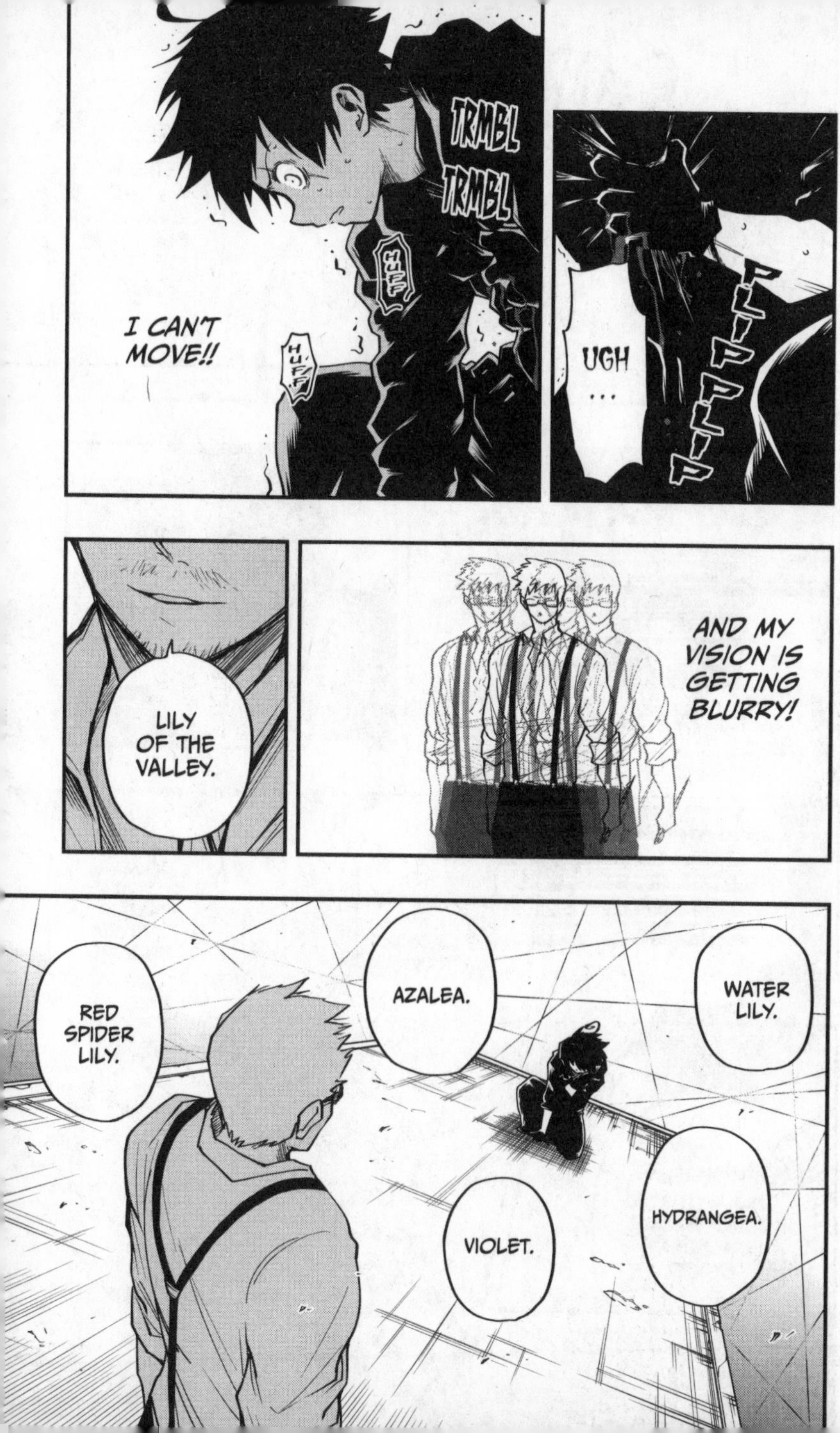
UGH ...
PLIP PLIP
TRMBL TRMBL
HUFF
HUFF
I CAN'T MOVE!!
AND MY VISION IS GETTING BLURRY!
LILY OF THE VALLEY.
WATER LILY.
AZALEA.
RED SPIDER LILY.
HYDRANGEA.
VIOLET.

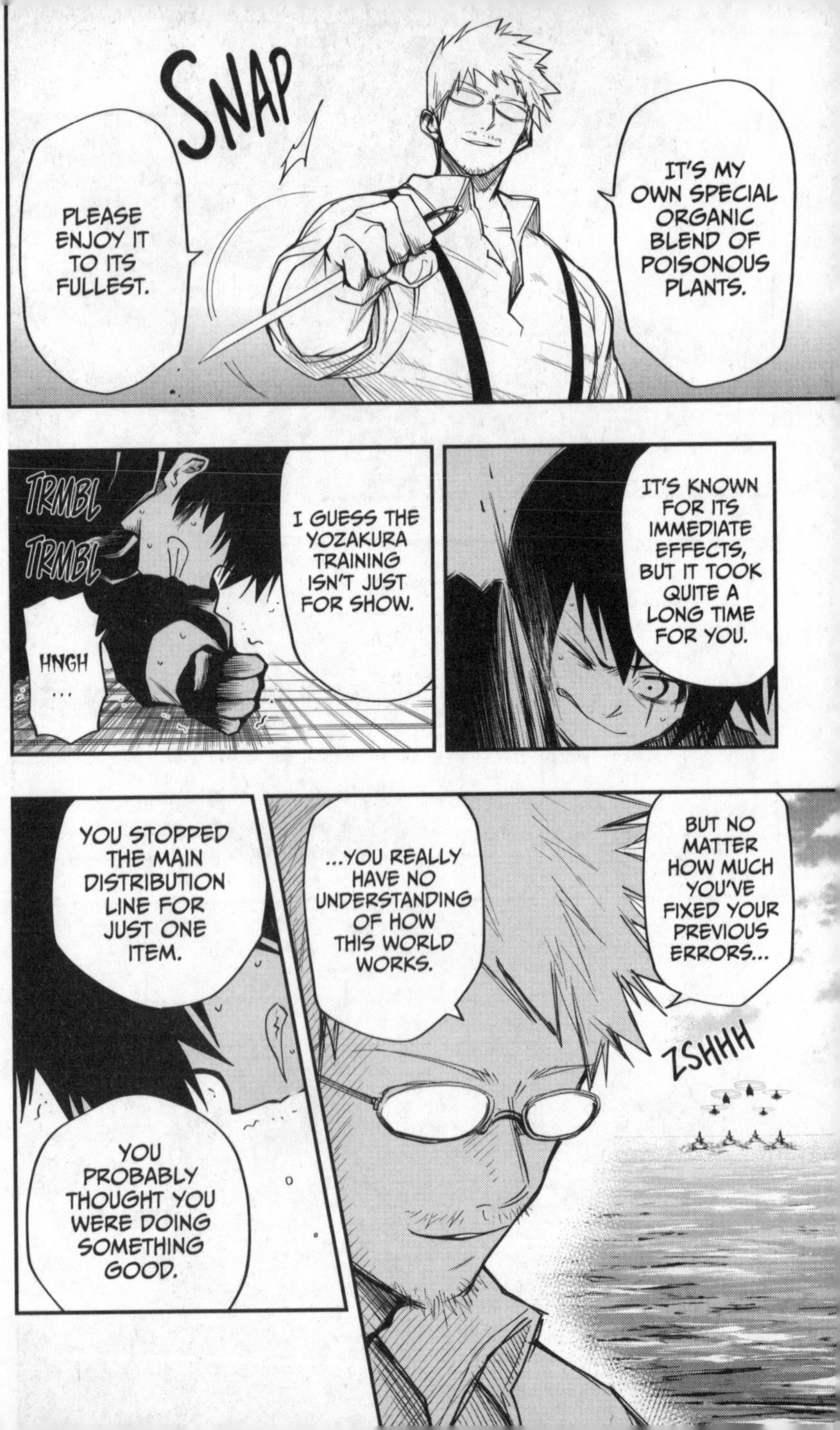
IT'S MY OWN SPECIAL ORGANIC BLEND OF POISONOUS PLANTS.
SNAP
PLEASE ENJOY IT TO ITS FULLEST.
IT'S KNOWN FOR ITS IMMEDIATE EFFECTS, BUT IT TOOK QUITE A LONG TIME FOR YOU.
I GUESS THE YOZAKURA TRAINING ISN'T JUST FOR SHOW.
TRMBL
TRMBL
HNGH ...
BUT NO MATTER HOW MUCH YOU'VE FIXED YOUR PREVIOUS ERRORS...
...YOU REALLY HAVE NO UNDERSTANDING OF HOW THIS WORLD WORKS.
ZSHHH
YOU STOPPED THE MAIN DISTRIBUTION LINE FOR JUST ONE ITEM.
YOU PROBABLY THOUGHT YOU WERE DOING SOMETHING GOOD.

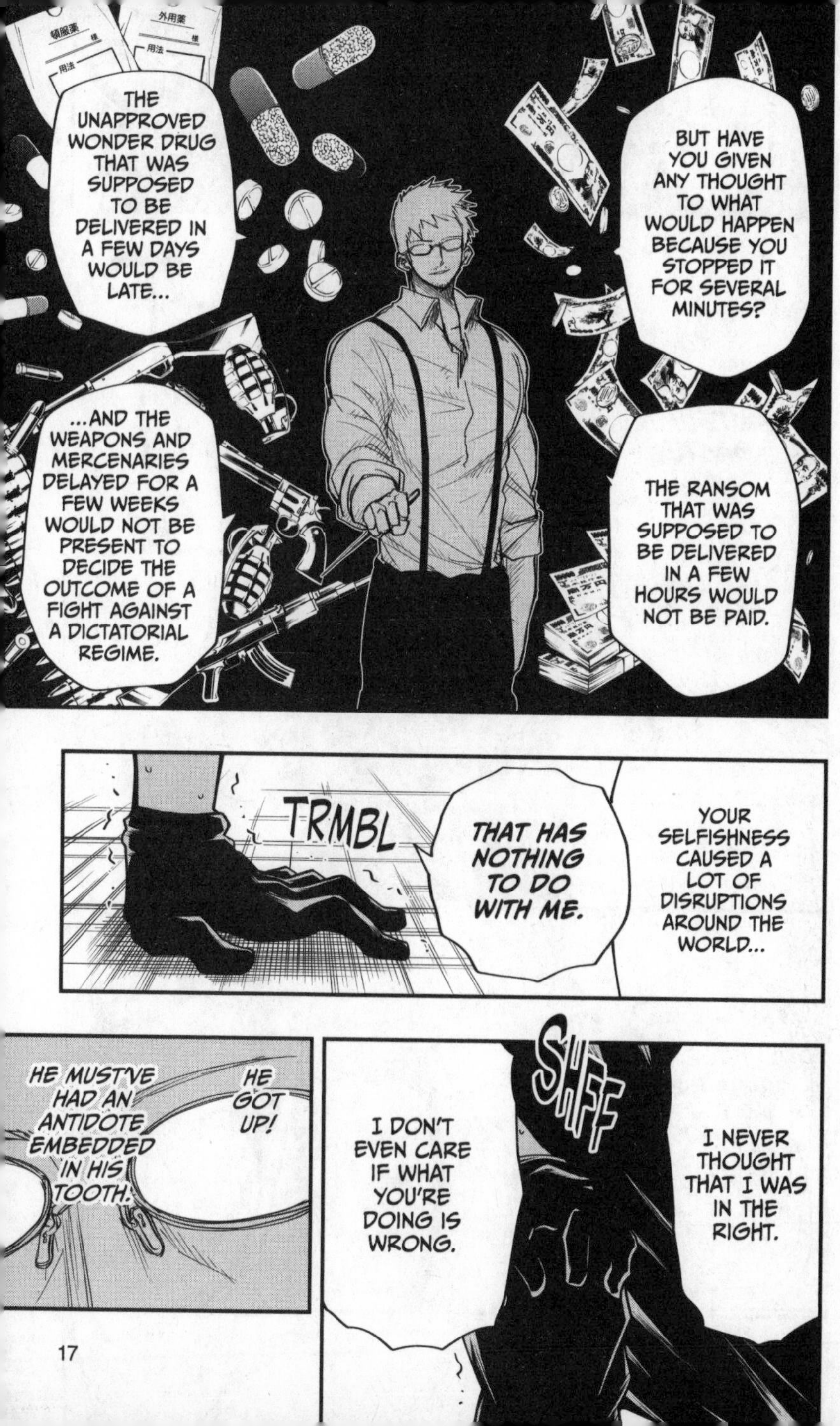
BUT HAVE YOU GIVEN ANY THOUGHT TO WHAT WOULD HAPPEN BECAUSE YOU STOPPED IT FOR SEVERAL MINUTES?
THE UNAPPROVED WONDER DRUG THAT WAS SUPPOSED TO BE DELIVERED IN A FEW DAYS WOULD BE LATE...
...AND THE WEAPONS AND MERCENARIES DELAYED FOR A FEW WEEKS WOULD NOT BE PRESENT TO DECIDE THE OUTCOME OF A FIGHT AGAINST A DICTATORIAL REGIME.
THE RANSOM THAT WAS SUPPOSED TO BE DELIVERED IN A FEW HOURS WOULD NOT BE PAID.
YOUR SELFISHNESS CAUSED A LOT OF DISRUPTIONS AROUND THE WORLD...
THAT HAS NOTHING TO DO WITH ME.
TRMBL
SHFF
I NEVER THOUGHT THAT I WAS IN THE RIGHT.
I DON'T EVEN CARE IF WHAT YOU'RE DOING IS WRONG.
HE GOT UP!
HE MUST'VE HAD AN ANTIDOTE EMBEDDED IN HIS TOOTH.

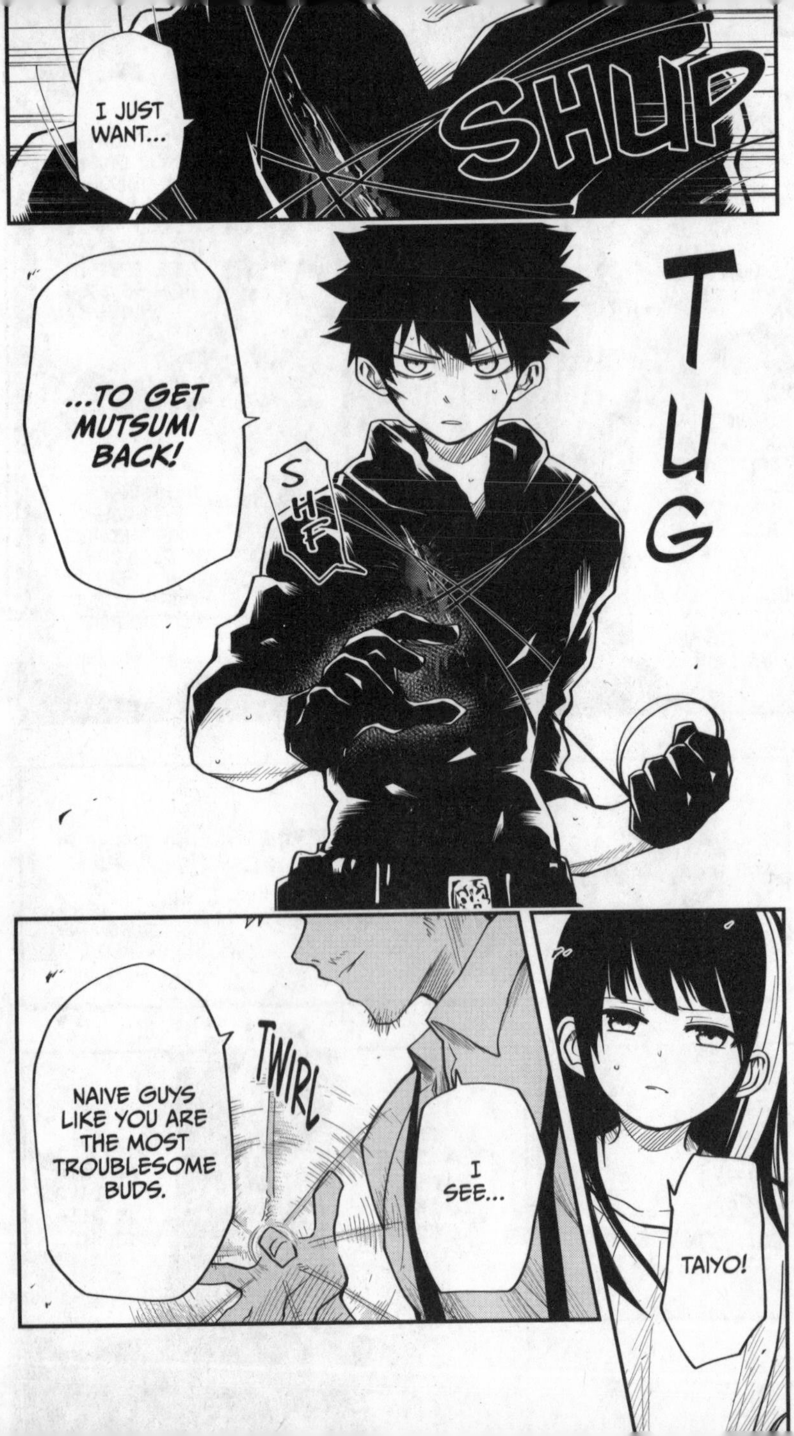
SHUP
I JUST WANT...
TUG
...TO GET MUTSUMI BACK!
SHF
TAIYO!
I SEE...
TWIRL
NAIVE GUYS LIKE YOU ARE THE MOST TROUBLESOME BUDS.

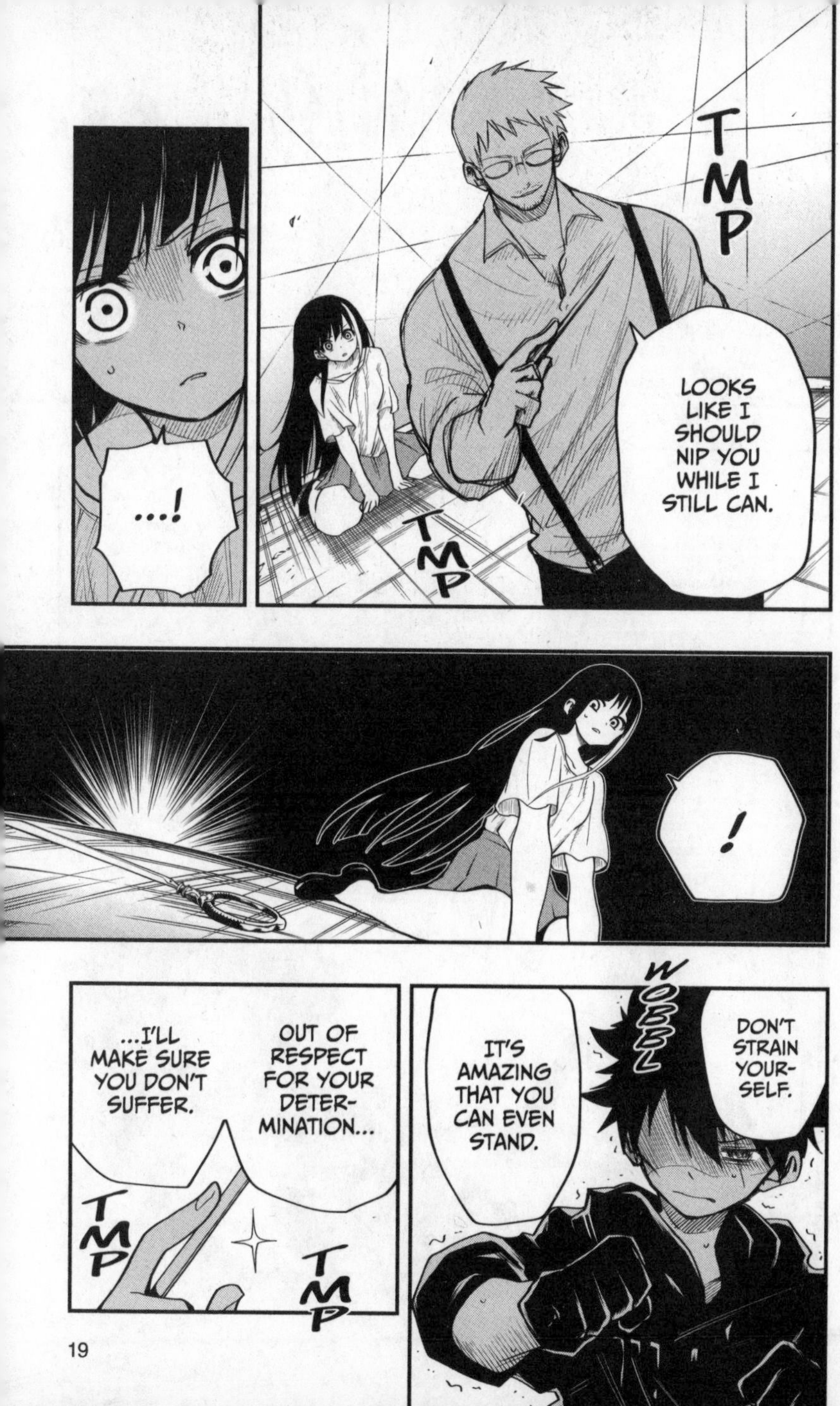
TMP
LOOKS LIKE I SHOULD NIP YOU WHILE I STILL CAN.
TMP
...!
!
WOBBL
DON'T STRAIN YOUR-SELF.
IT'S AMAZING THAT YOU CAN EVEN STAND.
OUT OF RESPECT FOR YOUR DETER-MINATION...
...I'LL MAKE SURE YOU DON'T SUFFER.
TMP
TMP

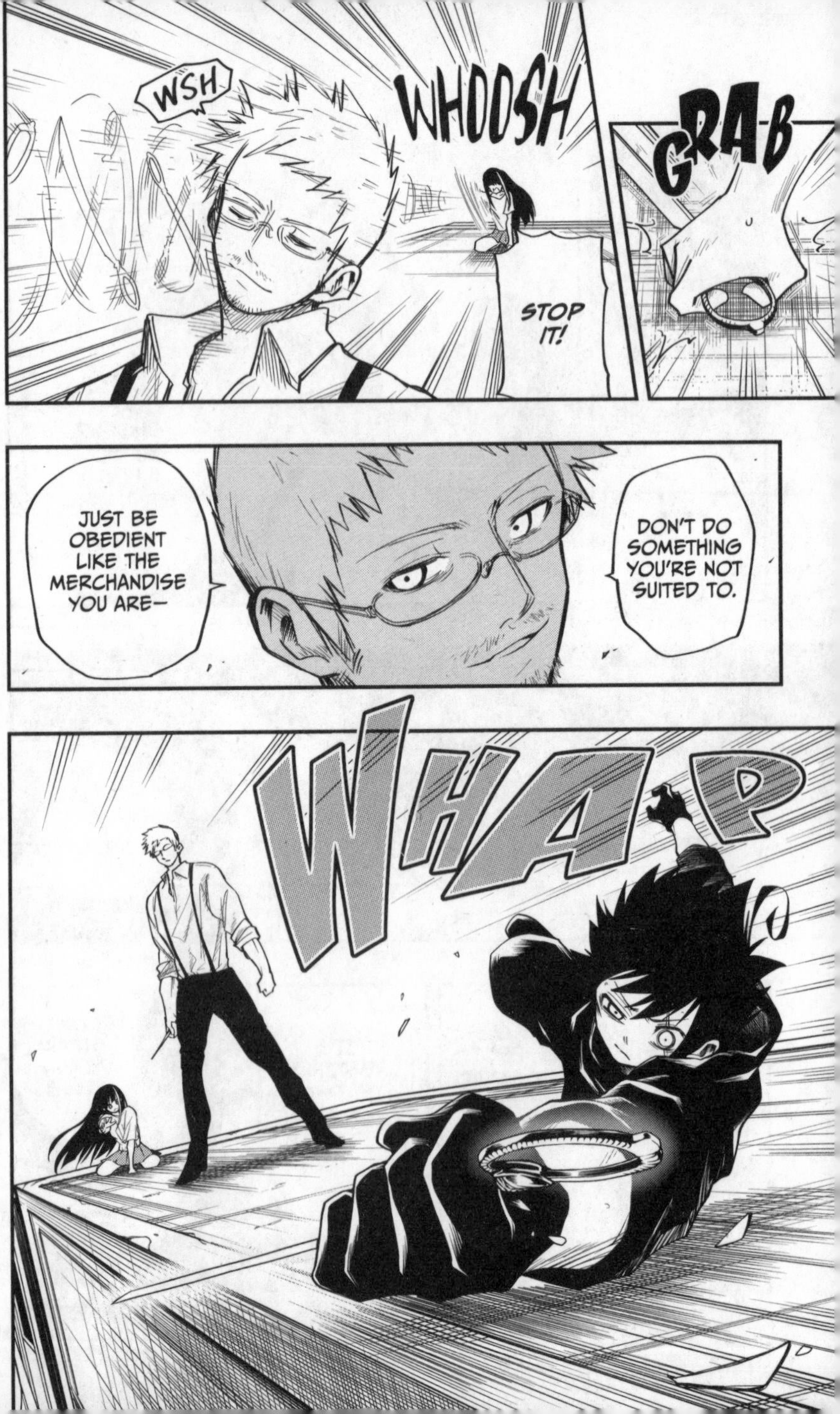
GRAB
WHOOSH
STOP IT!
WSH
DON'T DO SOMETHING YOU'RE NOT SUITED TO.
JUST BE OBEDIENT LIKE THE MERCHANDISE YOU ARE—
WHAP

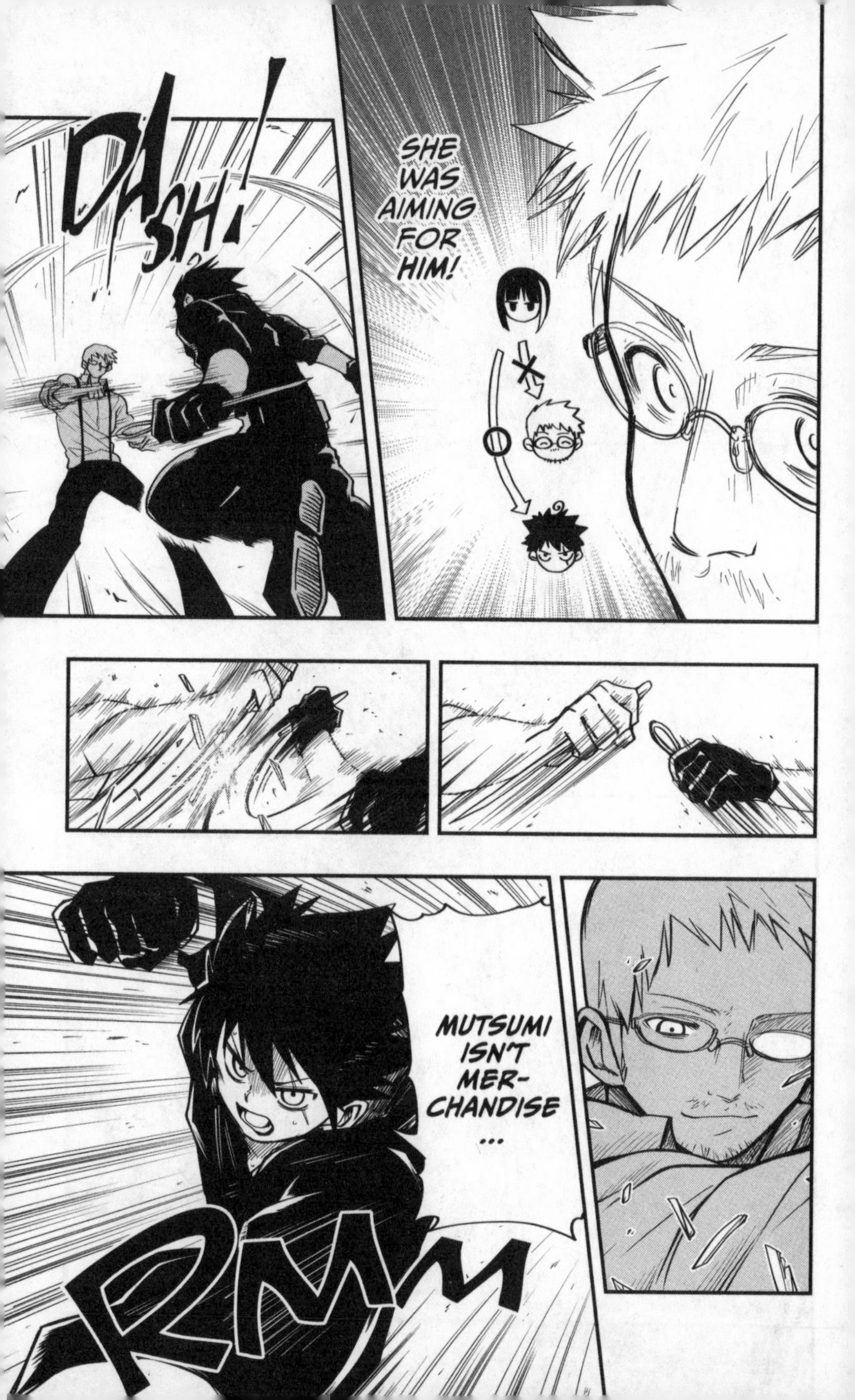
SHE WAS AIMING FOR HIM!
DASH!
MUTSUMI ISN'T MER-CHANDISE ...
RMM

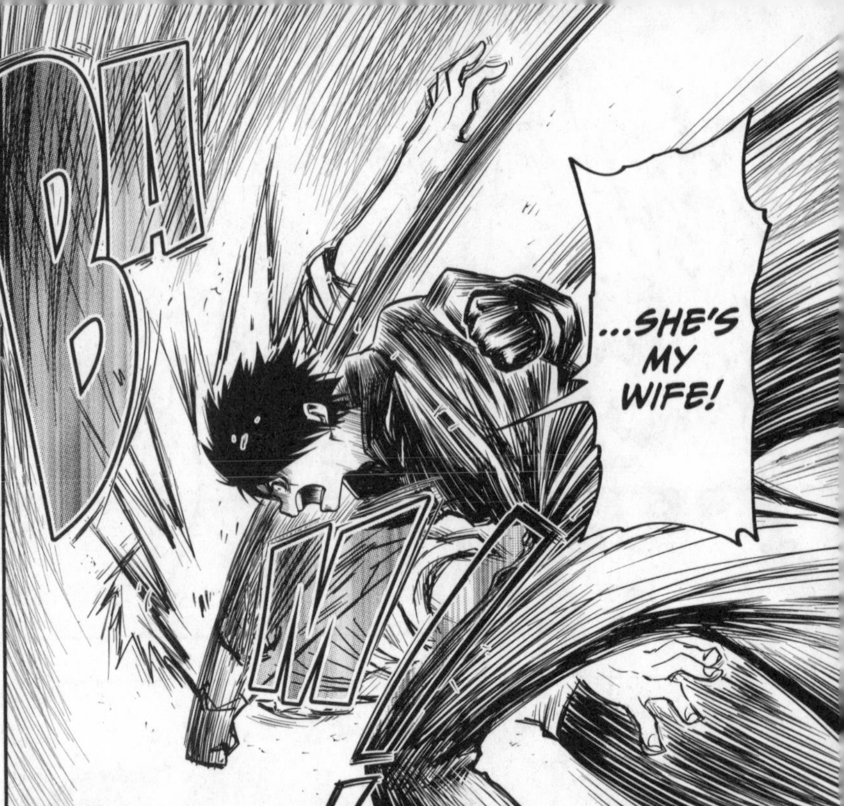
...SHE'S MY WIFE!
BAM

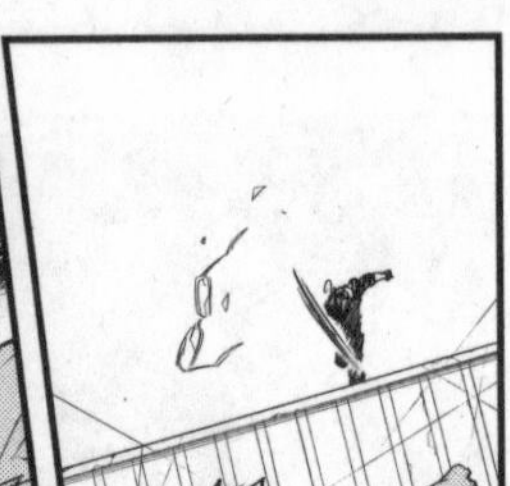

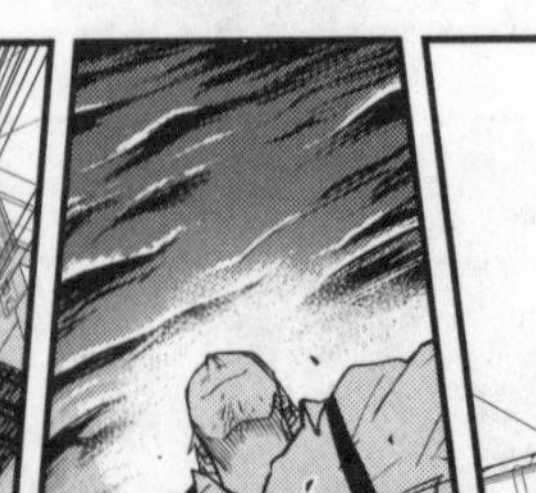

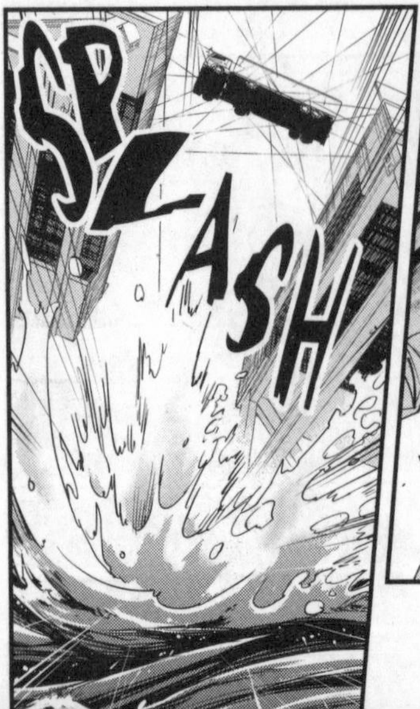
SPLASH

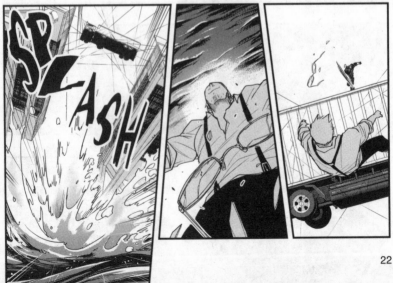

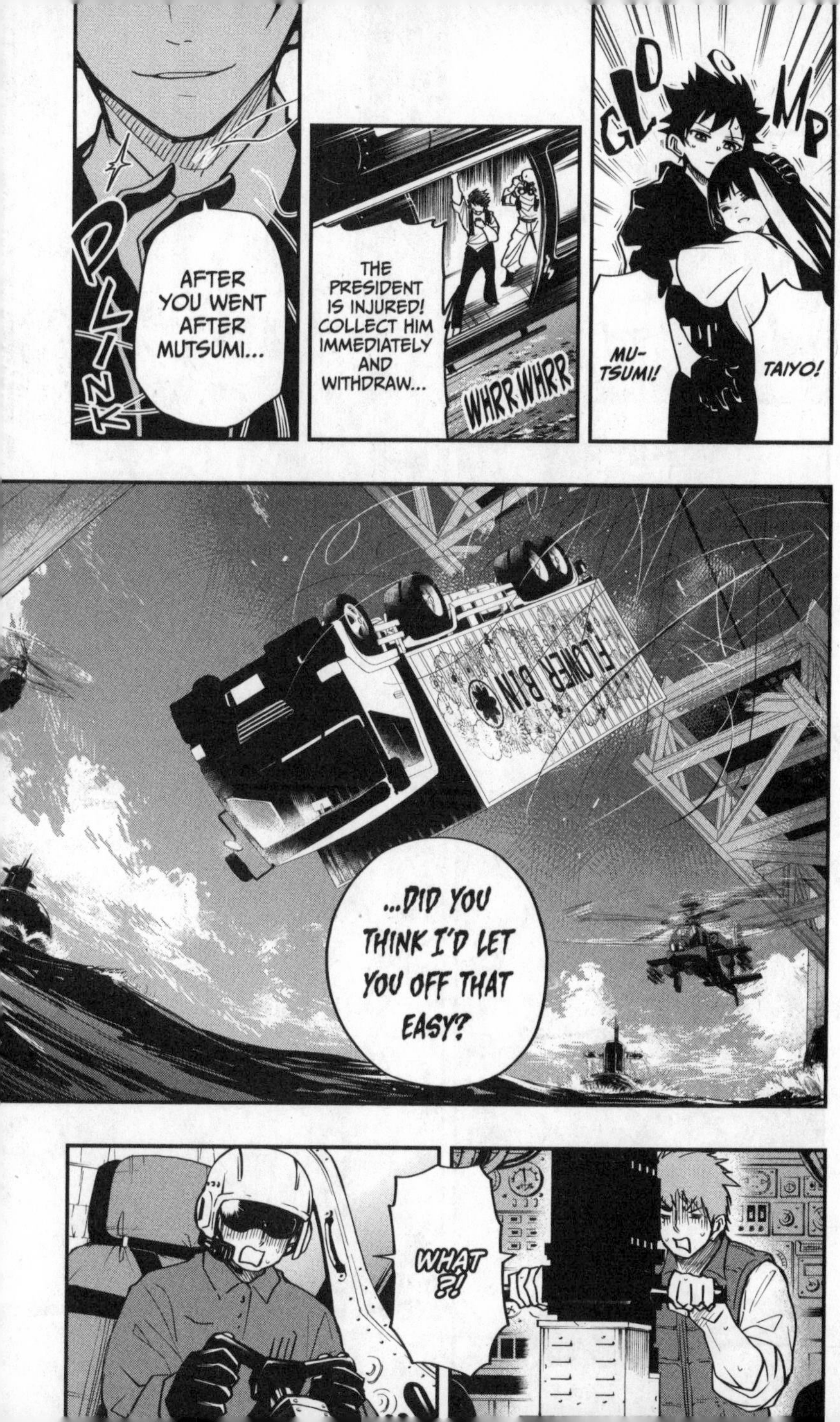
GLOMP
TAIYO!
MU-
TSUMI!
THE PRESIDENT IS INJURED! COLLECT HIM IMMEDIATELY AND WITHDRAW...
WHRR WHRR
AFTER YOU WENT AFTER MUTSUMI...
PLINK
FLOWER BIN
...DID YOU THINK I'D LET YOU OFF THAT EASY?
WHAT?!

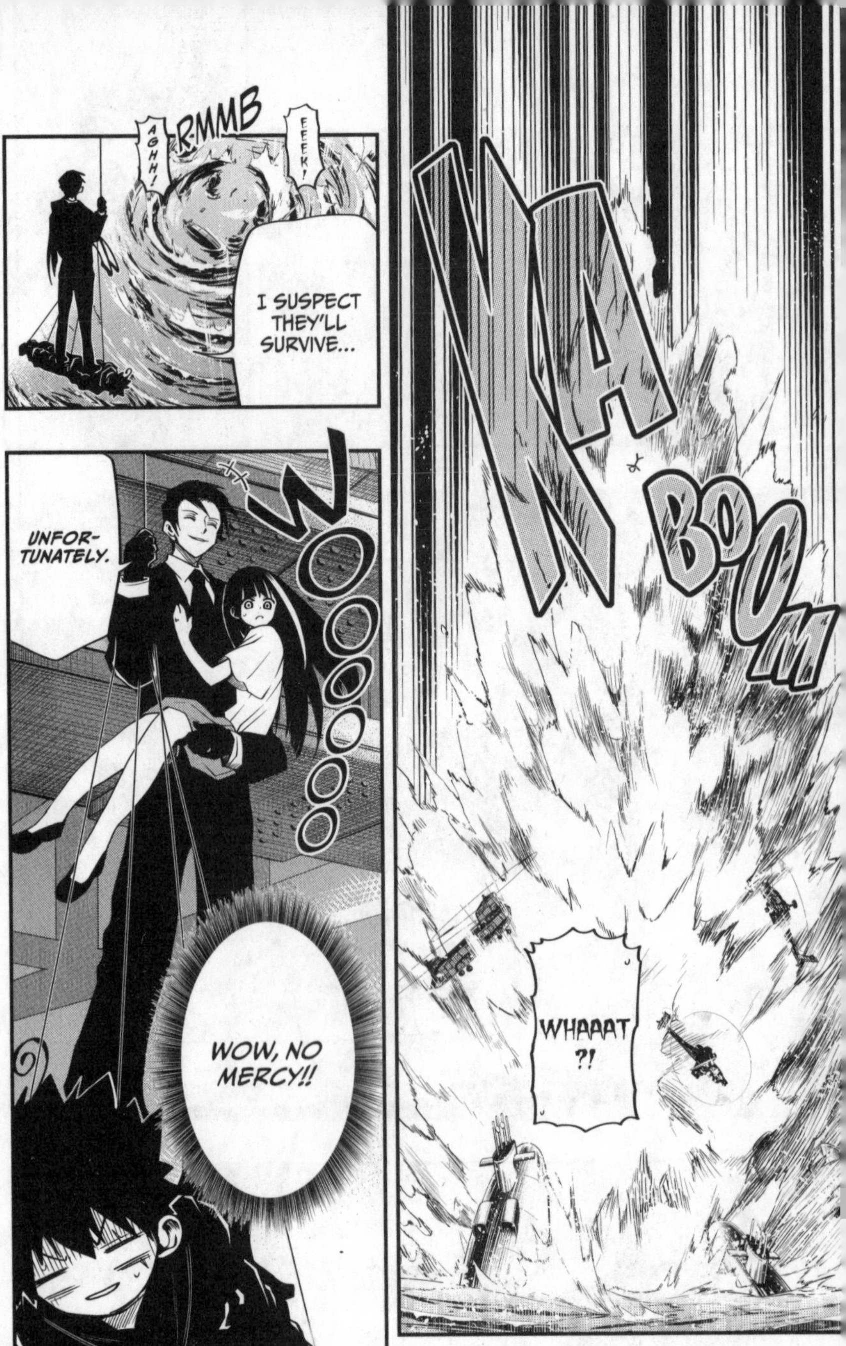
KA
BOOM
WHAAAT ?!
EEEK!
R-MMB
AGHH!
I SUSPECT THEY'LL SURVIVE...
WOOOOOO
UNFOR-TUNATELY.
WOW, NO MERCY!!

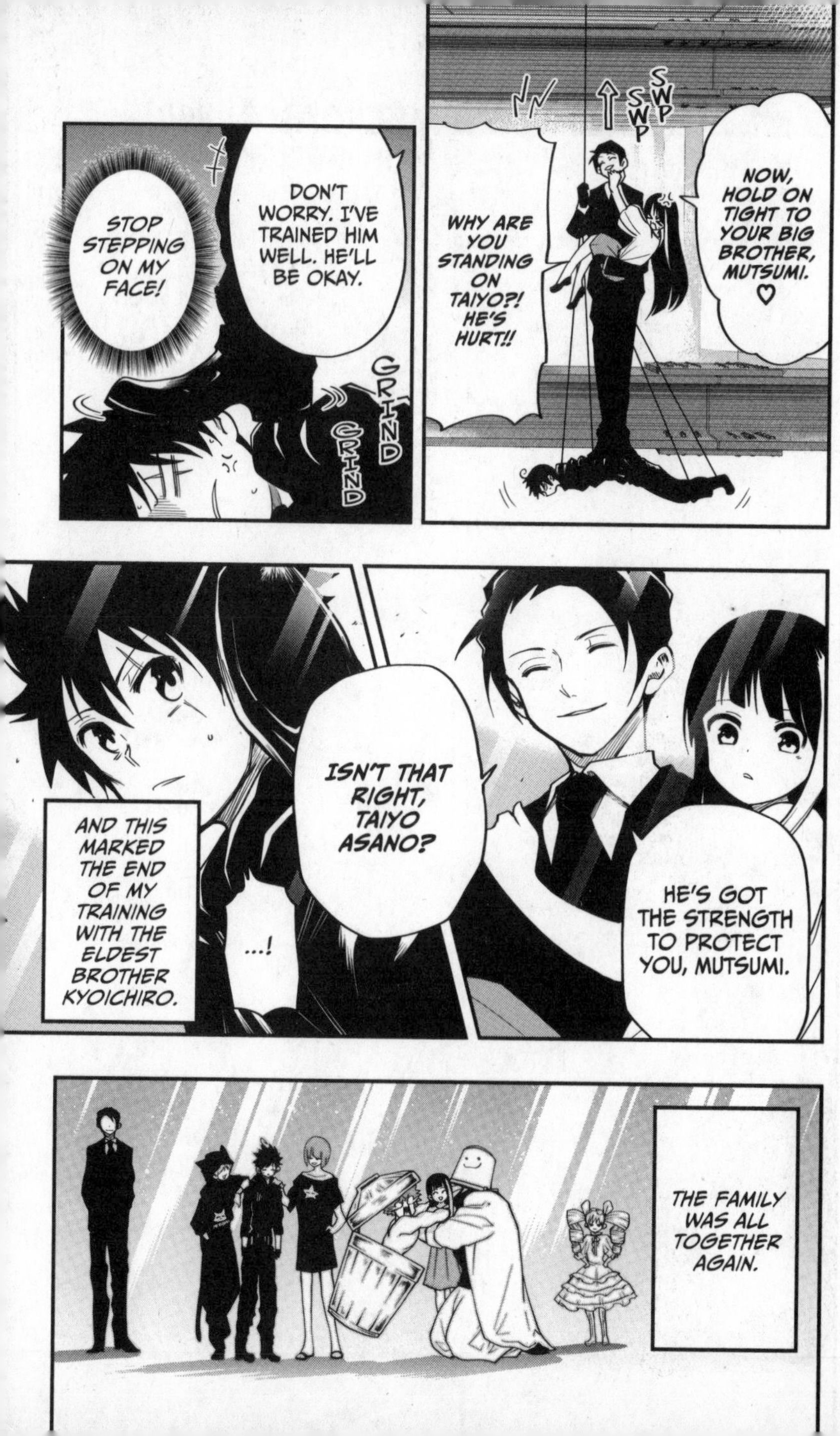
SWP SWP
NOW, HOLD ON TIGHT TO YOUR BIG BROTHER, MUTSUMI. ♡
WHY ARE YOU STANDING ON TAIYO?! HE'S HURT!!
DON'T WORRY. I'VE TRAINED HIM WELL. HE'LL BE OKAY.
STOP STEPPING ON MY FACE!
GRIND GRIND
HE'S GOT THE STRENGTH TO PROTECT YOU, MUTSUMI.
ISN'T THAT RIGHT, TAIYO ASANO?
...!
AND THIS MARKED THE END OF MY TRAINING WITH THE ELDEST BROTHER KYOICHIRO.
THE FAMILY WAS ALL TOGETHER AGAIN.

KYOICHIRO'S MEDICAL CLINIC

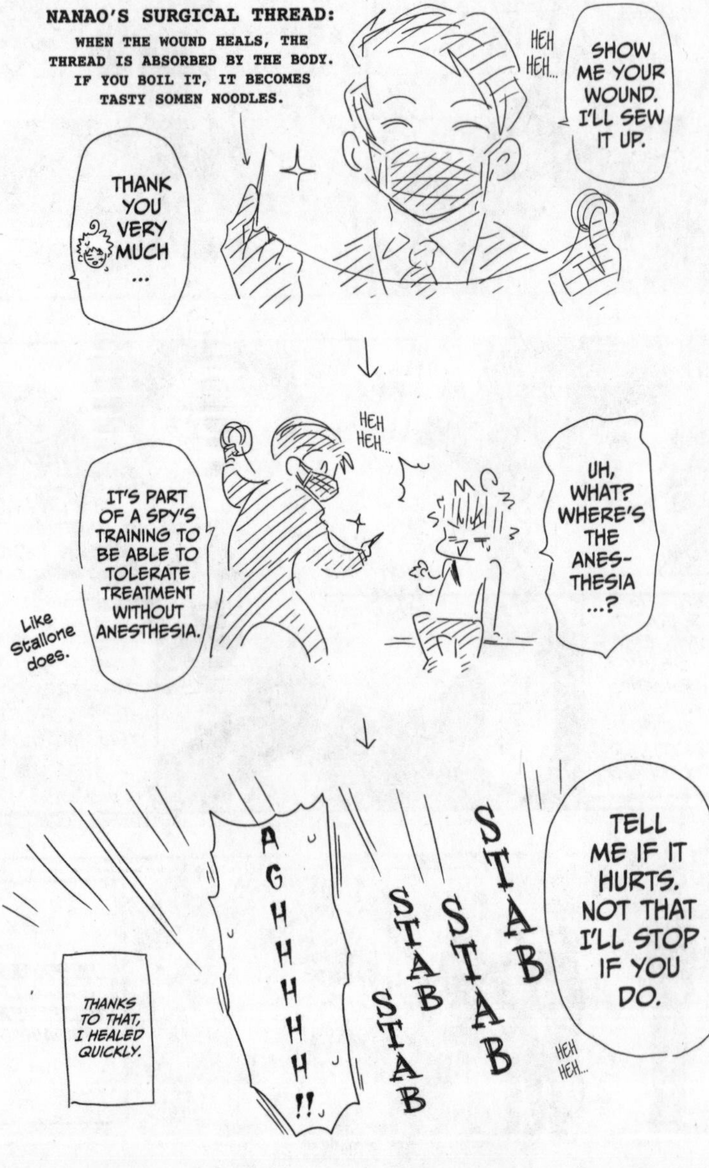

SHOW ME YOUR WOUND. I'LL SEW IT UP.
HEH HEH...
NANAO'S SURGICAL THREAD:
WHEN THE WOUND HEALS, THE THREAD IS ABSORBED BY THE BODY. IF YOU BOIL IT, IT BECOMES TASTY SOMEN NOODLES.
THANK YOU VERY MUCH ...
UH, WHAT? WHERE'S THE ANES-THESIA ...?
HEH HEH...
IT'S PART OF A SPY'S TRAINING TO BE ABLE TO TOLERATE TREATMENT WITHOUT ANESTHESIA.
Like Stallone does.
TELL ME IF IT HURTS. NOT THAT I'LL STOP IF YOU DO.
HEH HEH...
STAB
STAB
STAB
STAB
AGHHHHH!!
THANKS TO THAT, I HEALED QUICKLY.

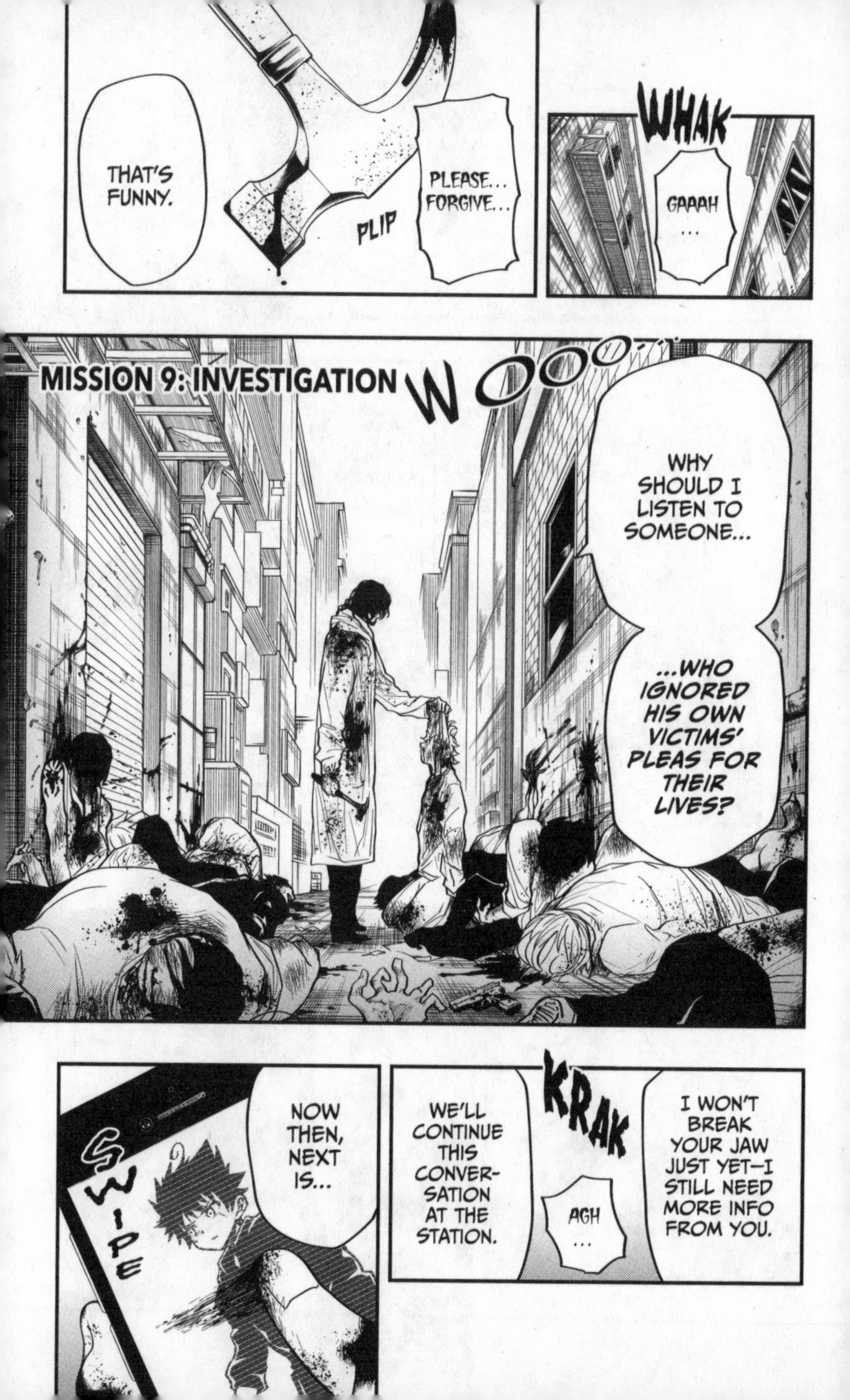
WHAK
GAAAH...
PLEASE... FORGIVE...
PLIP
THAT'S FUNNY.
MISSION 9: INVESTIGATION
WOOO...
WHY SHOULD I LISTEN TO SOMEONE...
...WHO IGNORED HIS OWN VICTIMS' PLEAS FOR THEIR LIVES?
KRAK
I WON'T BREAK YOUR JAW JUST YET—I STILL NEED MORE INFO FROM YOU.
AGH...
WE'LL CONTINUE THIS CONVER-SATION AT THE STATION.
NOW THEN, NEXT IS...
SWIPE

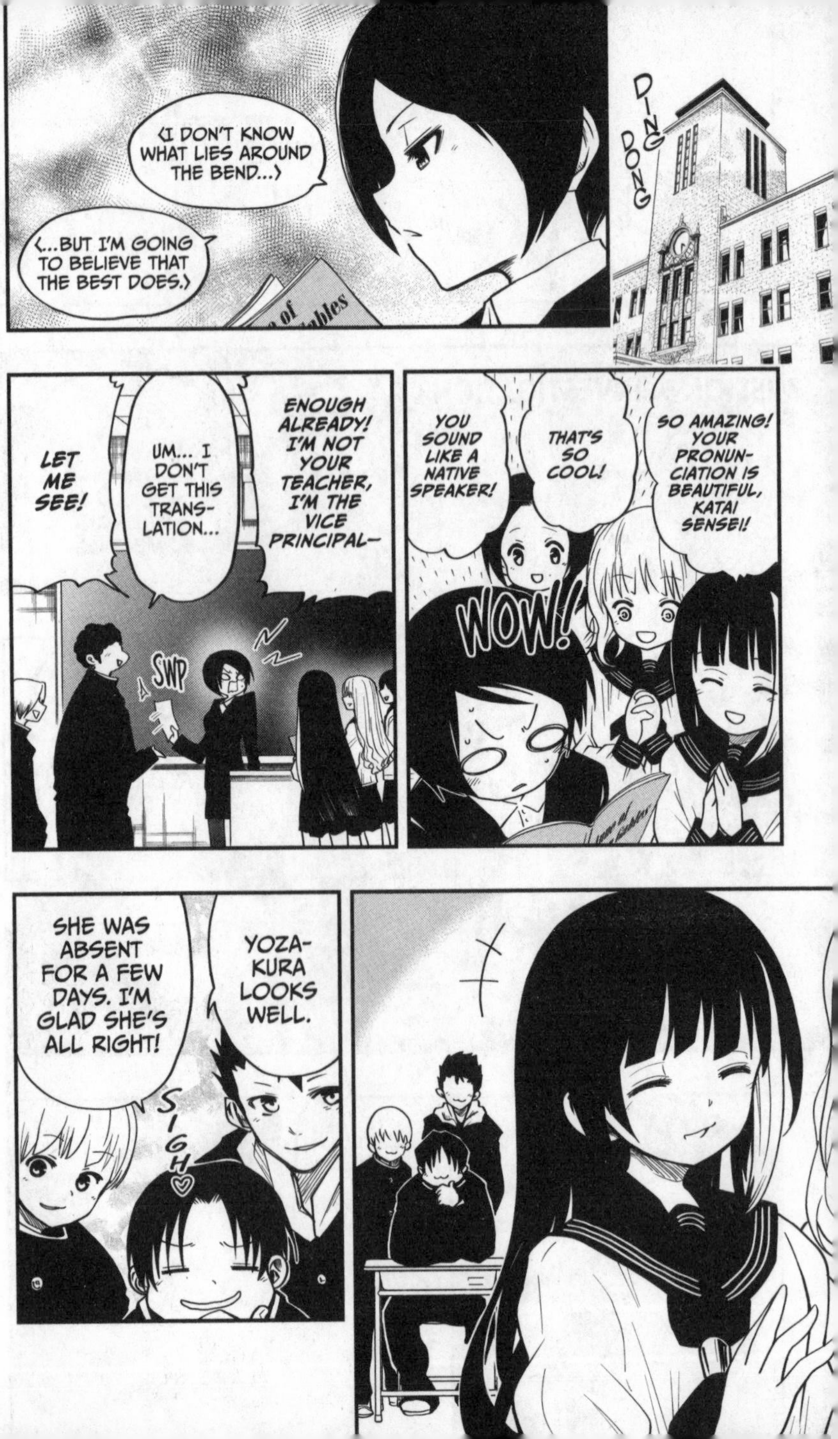
DING DONG
〈I DON'T KNOW WHAT LIES AROUND THE BEND...〉
〈...BUT I'M GOING TO BELIEVE THAT THE BEST DOES.〉
SO AMAZING! YOUR PRONUNCIATION IS BEAUTIFUL, KATAI SENSEI!
THAT'S SO COOL!
YOU SOUND LIKE A NATIVE SPEAKER!
WOW!!
ENOUGH ALREADY! I'M NOT YOUR TEACHER, I'M THE VICE PRINCIPAL—
UM... I DON'T GET THIS TRANSLATION...
LET ME SEE!
SWP
YOZA-KURA LOOKS WELL.
SHE WAS ABSENT FOR A FEW DAYS. I'M GLAD SHE'S ALL RIGHT!
SIGH♡

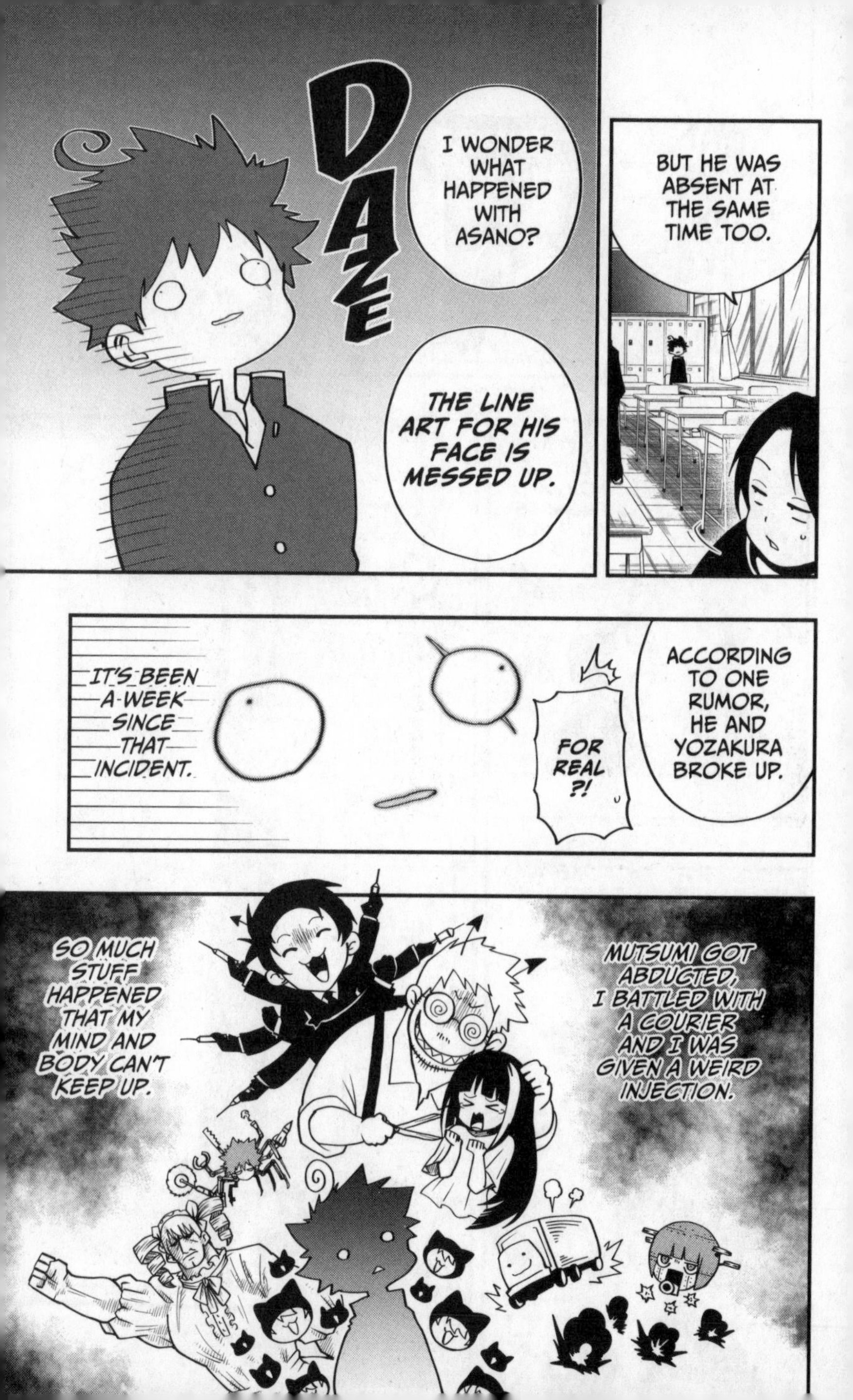
BUT HE WAS ABSENT AT THE SAME TIME TOO.
I WONDER WHAT HAPPENED WITH ASANO?
THE LINE ART FOR HIS FACE IS MESSED UP.
DAZE
ACCORDING TO ONE RUMOR, HE AND YOZAKURA BROKE UP.
FOR REAL?!
IT'S BEEN A WEEK SINCE THAT INCIDENT.
MUTSUMI GOT ABDUCTED, I BATTLED WITH A COURIER AND I WAS GIVEN A WEIRD INJECTION.
SO MUCH STUFF HAPPENED THAT MY MIND AND BODY CAN'T KEEP UP.

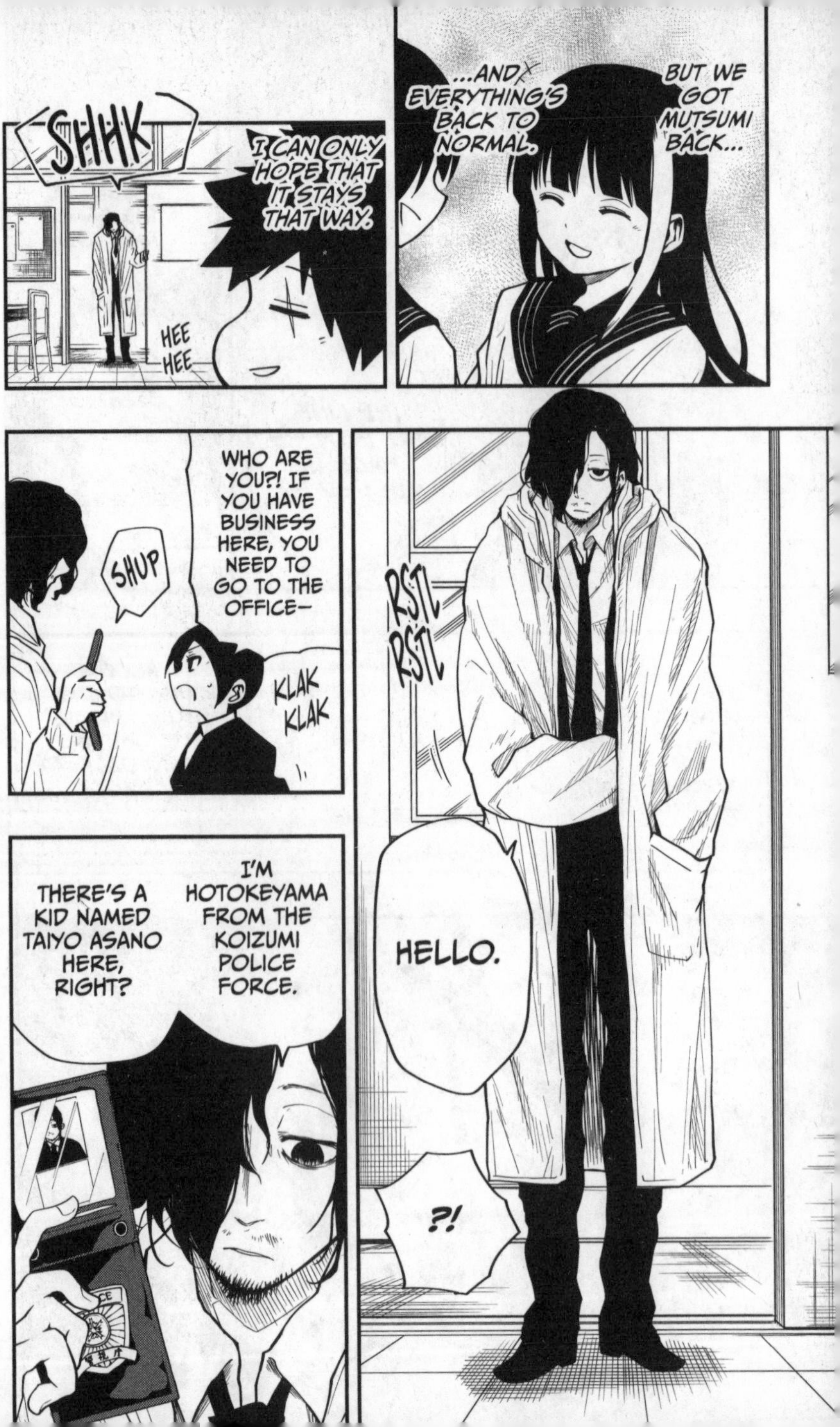
BUT WE GOT MUTSUMI BACK...
...AND EVERYTHING'S BACK TO NORMAL.
I CAN ONLY HOPE THAT IT STAYS THAT WAY.
SHHK
HEE HEE
RSTL RSTL
HELLO.
?!
WHO ARE YOU?! IF YOU HAVE BUSINESS HERE, YOU NEED TO GO TO THE OFFICE—
SHUP
KLAK KLAK
I'M HOTOKEYAMA FROM THE KOIZUMI POLICE FORCE.
THERE'S A KID NAMED TAIYO ASANO HERE, RIGHT?

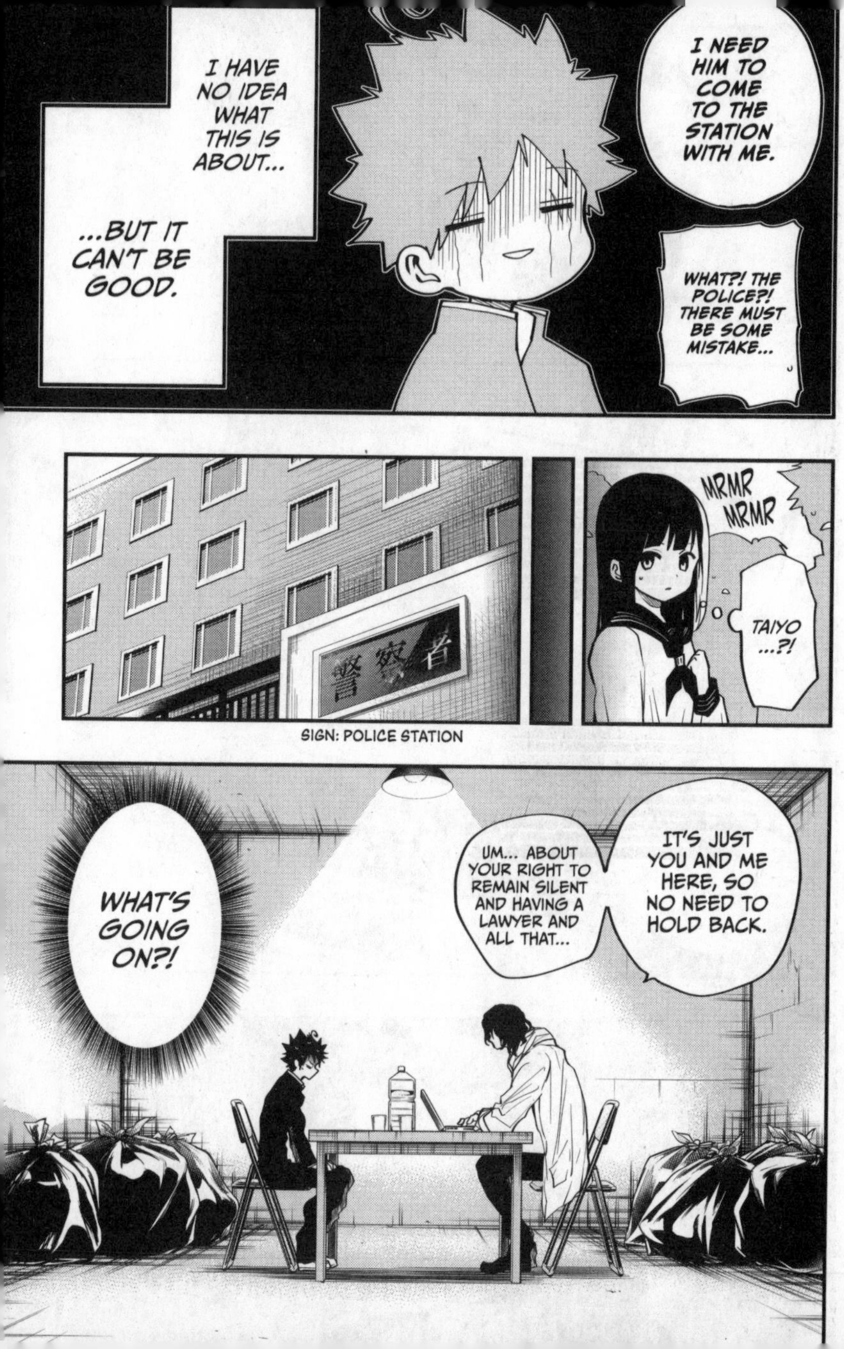
I NEED HIM TO COME TO THE STATION WITH ME.
WHAT?! THE POLICE?! THERE MUST BE SOME MISTAKE...
I HAVE NO IDEA WHAT THIS IS ABOUT...
...BUT IT CAN'T BE GOOD.
MRMR MRMR
TAIYO ...?!
SIGN: POLICE STATION
IT'S JUST YOU AND ME HERE, SO NO NEED TO HOLD BACK.
UM... ABOUT YOUR RIGHT TO REMAIN SILENT AND HAVING A LAWYER AND ALL THAT...
WHAT'S GOING ON?!

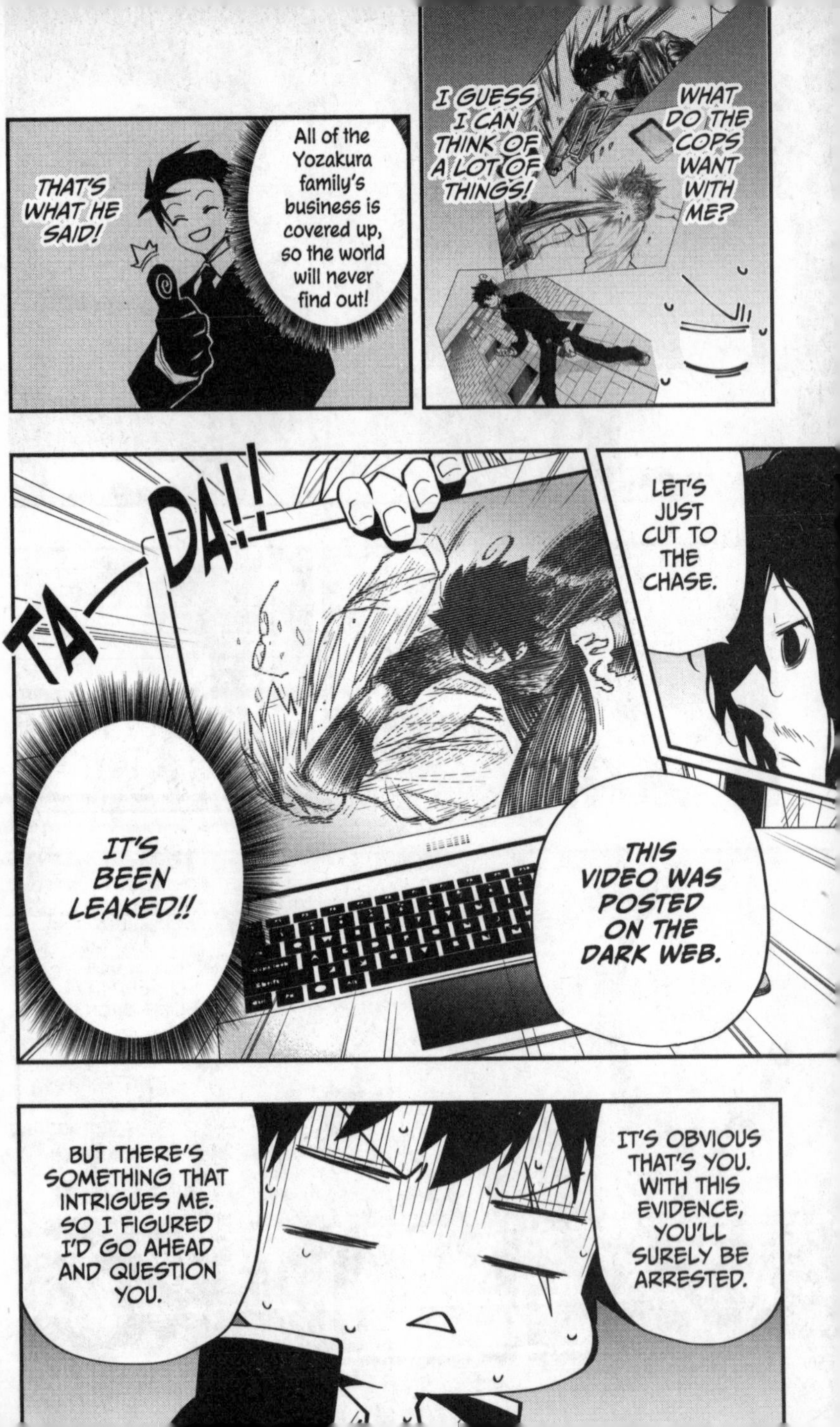
WHAT DO THE COPS WANT WITH ME?
I GUESS I CAN THINK OF A LOT OF THINGS!
All of the Yozakura family's business is covered up, so the world will never find out!
THAT'S WHAT HE SAID!
LET'S JUST CUT TO THE CHASE.
TA—DA!!
THIS VIDEO WAS POSTED ON THE DARK WEB.
IT'S BEEN LEAKED!!
IT'S OBVIOUS THAT'S YOU. WITH THIS EVIDENCE, YOU'LL SURELY BE ARRESTED.
BUT THERE'S SOMETHING THAT INTRIGUES ME. SO I FIGURED I'D GO AHEAD AND QUESTION YOU.

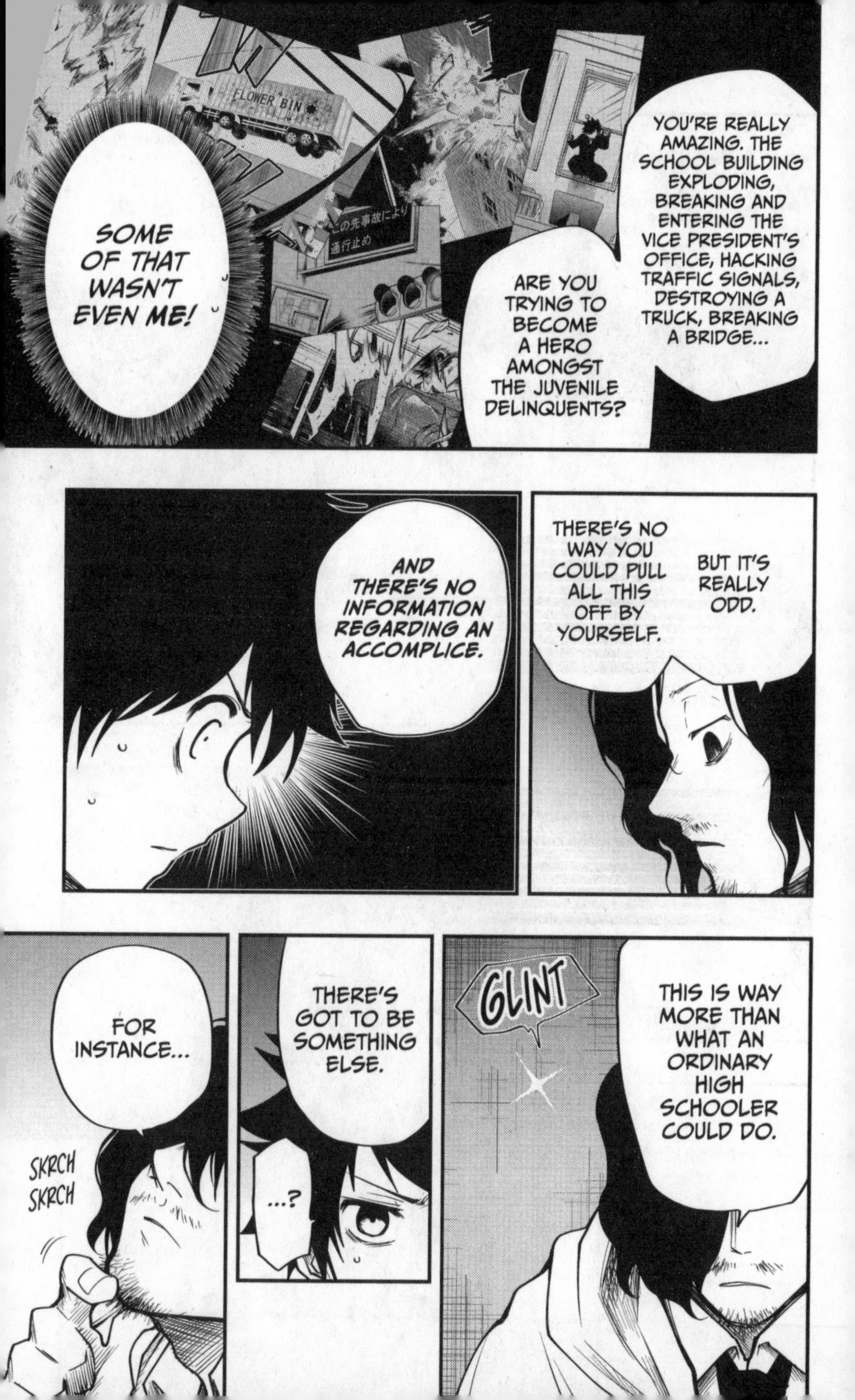
YOU'RE REALLY AMAZING. THE SCHOOL BUILDING EXPLODING, BREAKING AND ENTERING THE VICE PRESIDENT'S OFFICE, HACKING TRAFFIC SIGNALS, DESTROYING A TRUCK, BREAKING A BRIDGE...
ARE YOU TRYING TO BECOME A HERO AMONGST THE JUVENILE DELINQUENTS?
FLOWER BIN
この先事故により
通行止め
SOME OF THAT WASN'T EVEN ME!
BUT IT'S REALLY ODD.
THERE'S NO WAY YOU COULD PULL ALL THIS OFF BY YOURSELF.
AND THERE'S NO INFORMATION REGARDING AN ACCOMPLICE.
THIS IS WAY MORE THAN WHAT AN ORDINARY HIGH SCHOOLER COULD DO.
GLINT
THERE'S GOT TO BE SOMETHING ELSE.
...?
FOR INSTANCE...
SKRCH SKRCH

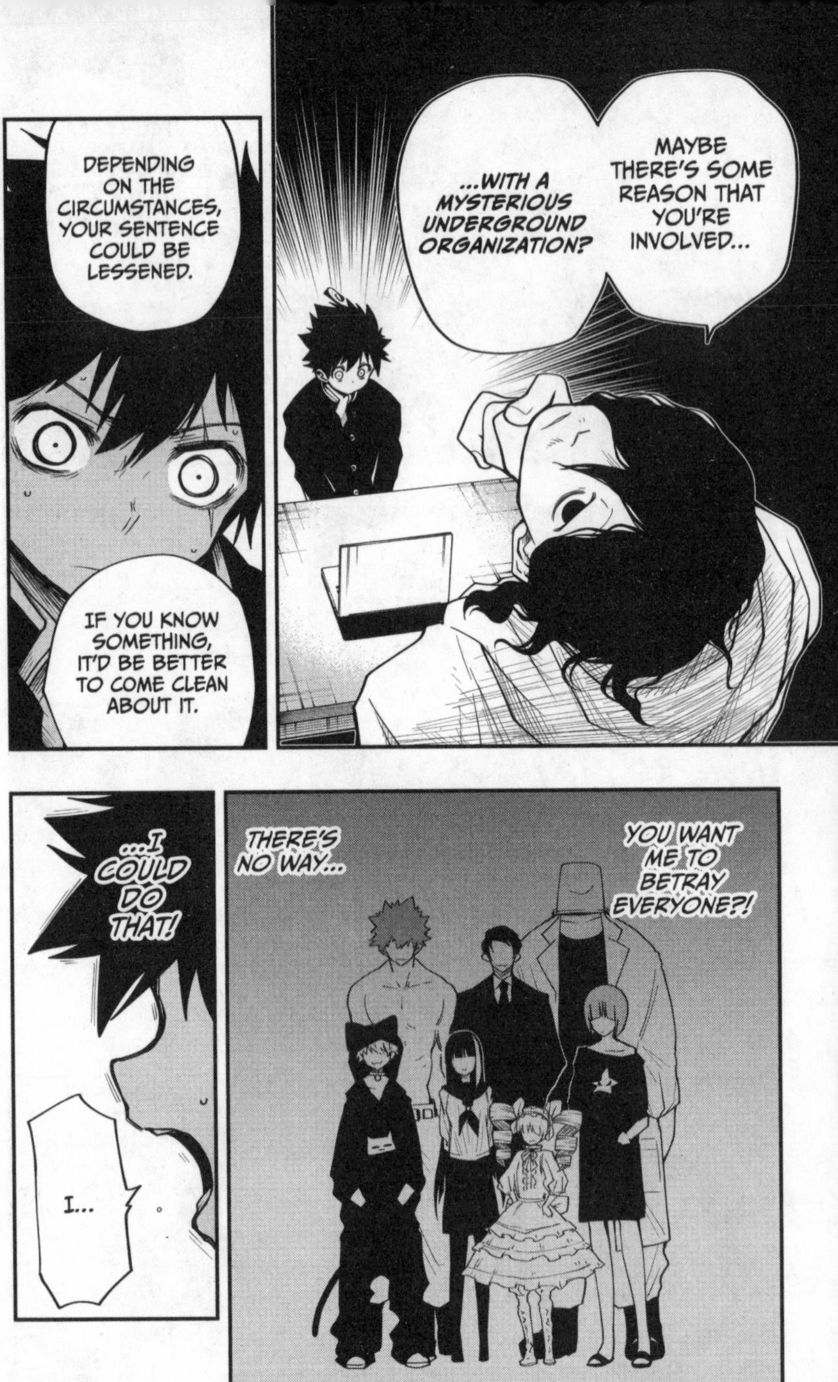
MAYBE THERE'S SOME REASON THAT YOU'RE INVOLVED...
...WITH A MYSTERIOUS UNDERGROUND ORGANIZATION?
DEPENDING ON THE CIRCUMSTANCES, YOUR SENTENCE COULD BE LESSENED.
IF YOU KNOW SOMETHING, IT'D BE BETTER TO COME CLEAN ABOUT IT.
YOU WANT ME TO BETRAY EVERYONE?!
THERE'S NO WAY...
...I COULD DO THAT!
I...

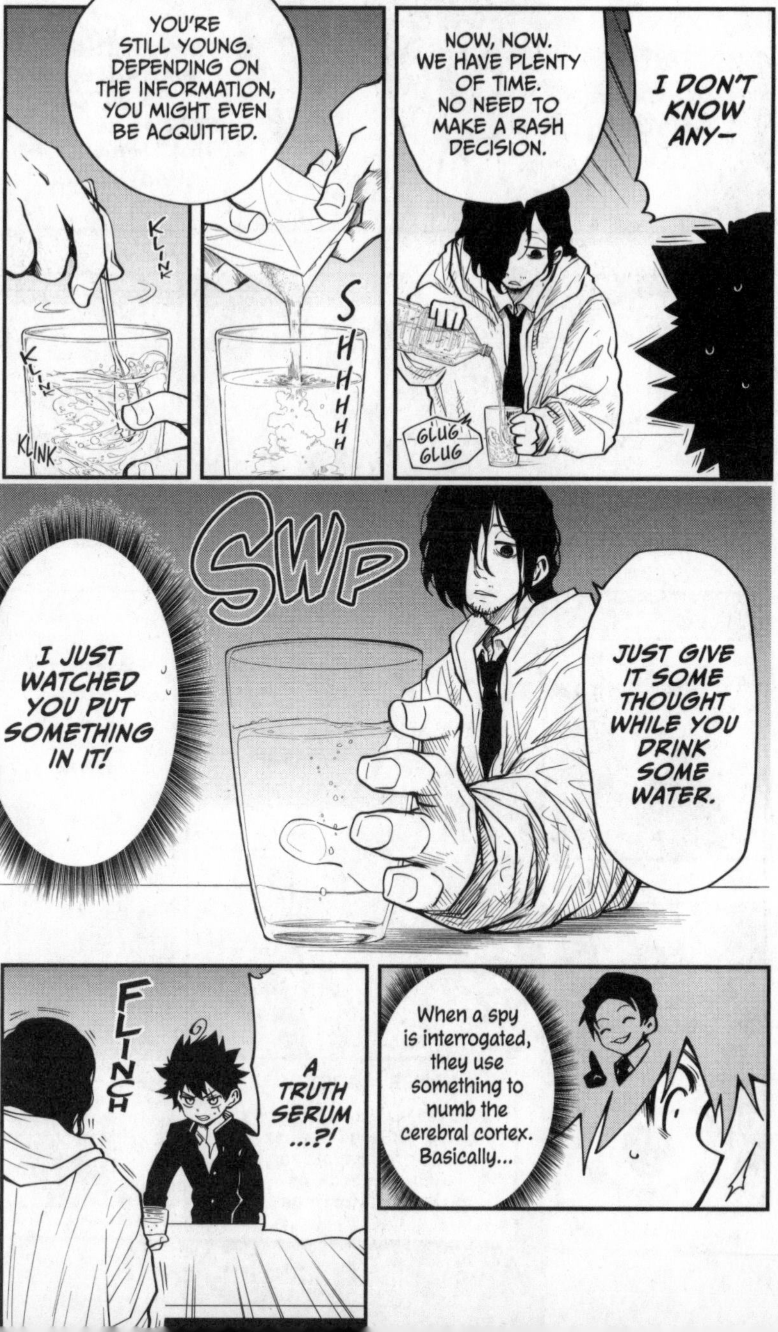
I DON'T KNOW ANY—
NOW, NOW. WE HAVE PLENTY OF TIME. NO NEED TO MAKE A RASH DECISION.
GLUG GLUG
SHHHHHH
YOU'RE STILL YOUNG. DEPENDING ON THE INFORMATION, YOU MIGHT EVEN BE ACQUITTED.
KLINK
KLINK
KLINK
JUST GIVE IT SOME THOUGHT WHILE YOU DRINK SOME WATER.
SWP
I JUST WATCHED YOU PUT SOMETHING IN IT!
When a spy is interrogated, they use something to numb the cerebral cortex. Basically...
A TRUTH SERUM ...?!
FLINCH

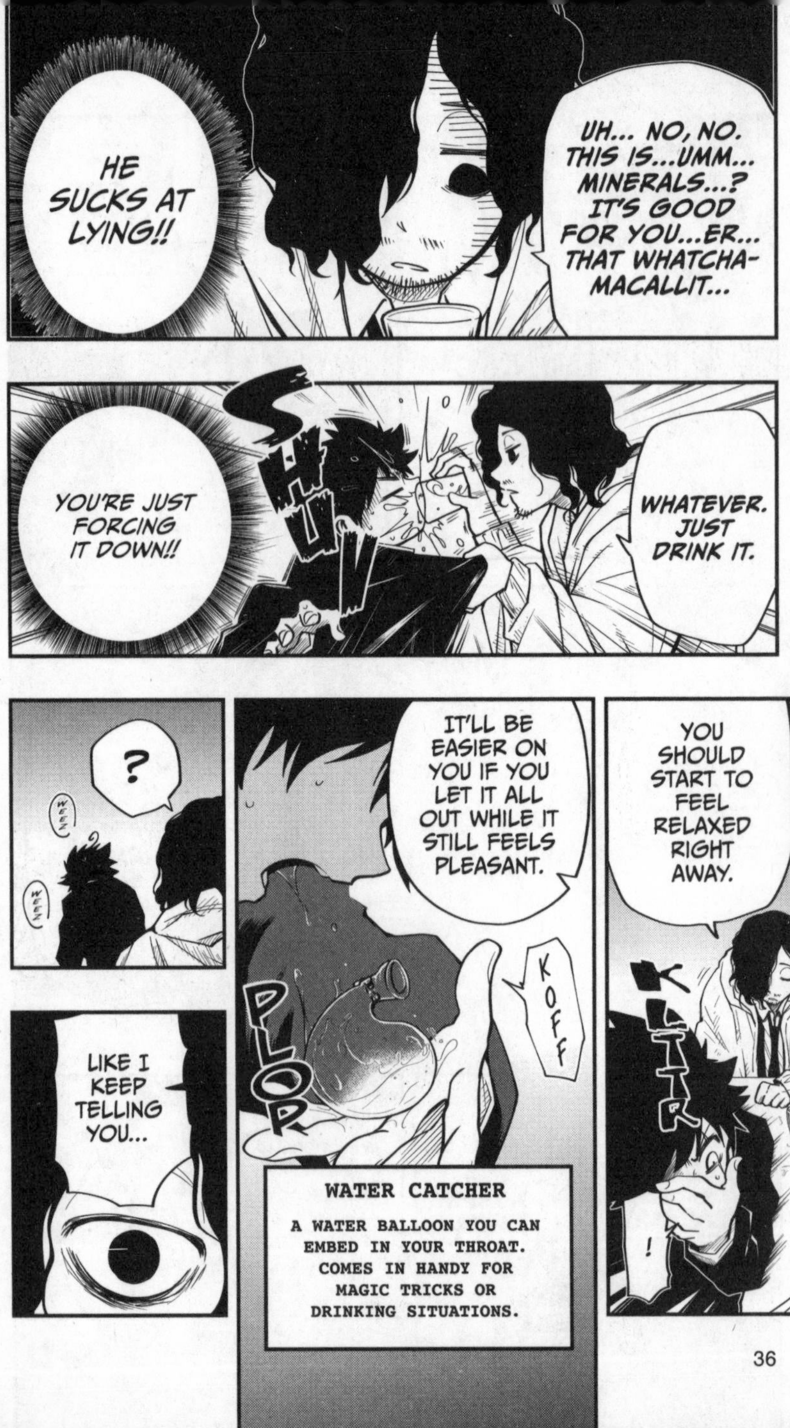
UH... NO, NO. THIS IS...UMM... MINERALS...? IT'S GOOD FOR YOU...ER... THAT WHATCHAMACALLIT...
HE SUCKS AT LYING!!
WHATEVER. JUST DRINK IT.
YOU'RE JUST FORCING IT DOWN!!
YOU SHOULD START TO FEEL RELAXED RIGHT AWAY.
!
IT'LL BE EASIER ON YOU IF YOU LET IT ALL OUT WHILE IT STILL FEELS PLEASANT.
KOFF
PLOP
WATER CATCHER
A WATER BALLOON YOU CAN EMBED IN YOUR THROAT. COMES IN HANDY FOR MAGIC TRICKS OR DRINKING SITUATIONS.
?
WEEZ
WEEZ
LIKE I KEEP TELLING YOU...

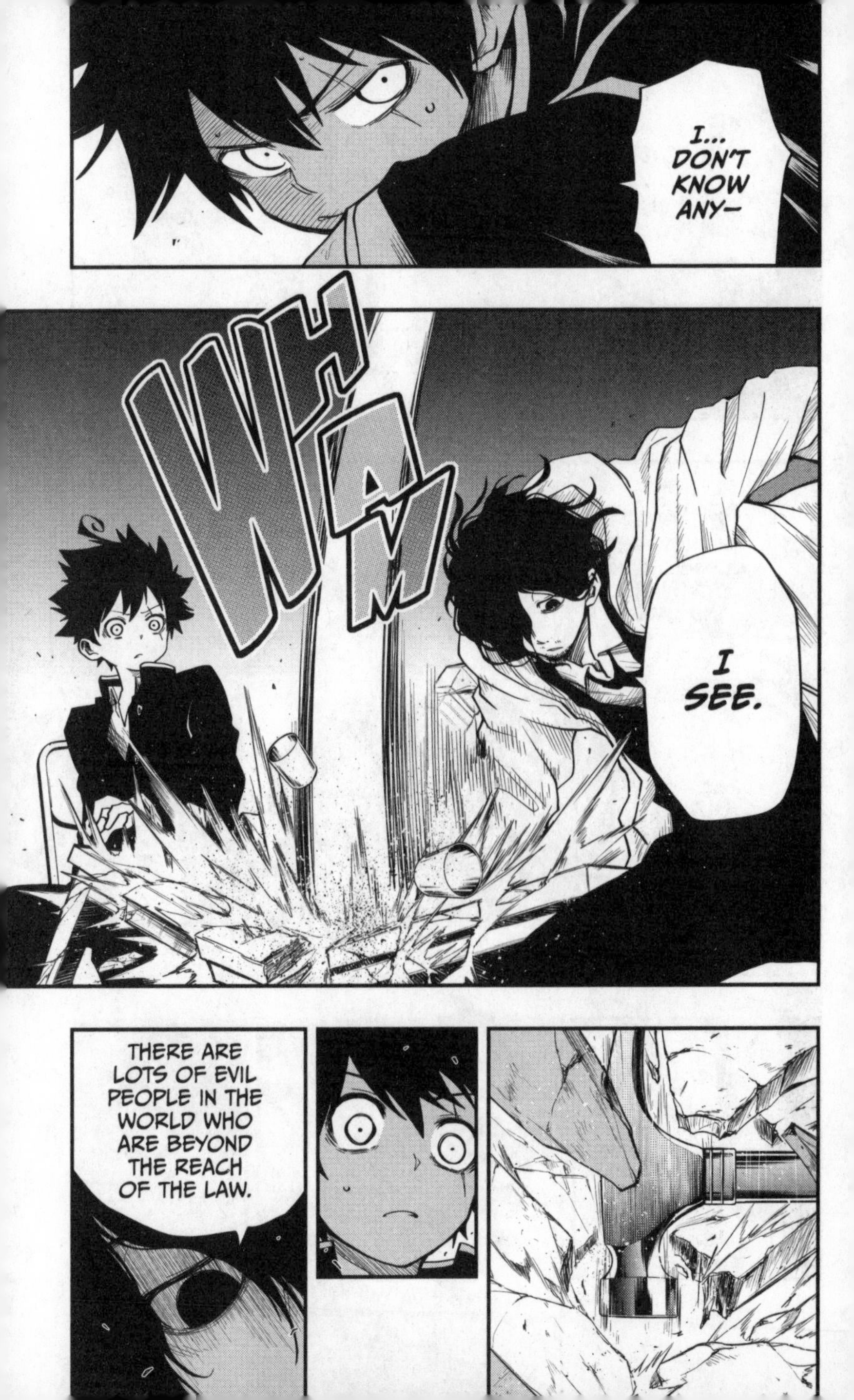
I... DON'T KNOW ANY—
WHAM
I SEE.
THERE ARE LOTS OF EVIL PEOPLE IN THE WORLD WHO ARE BEYOND THE REACH OF THE LAW.

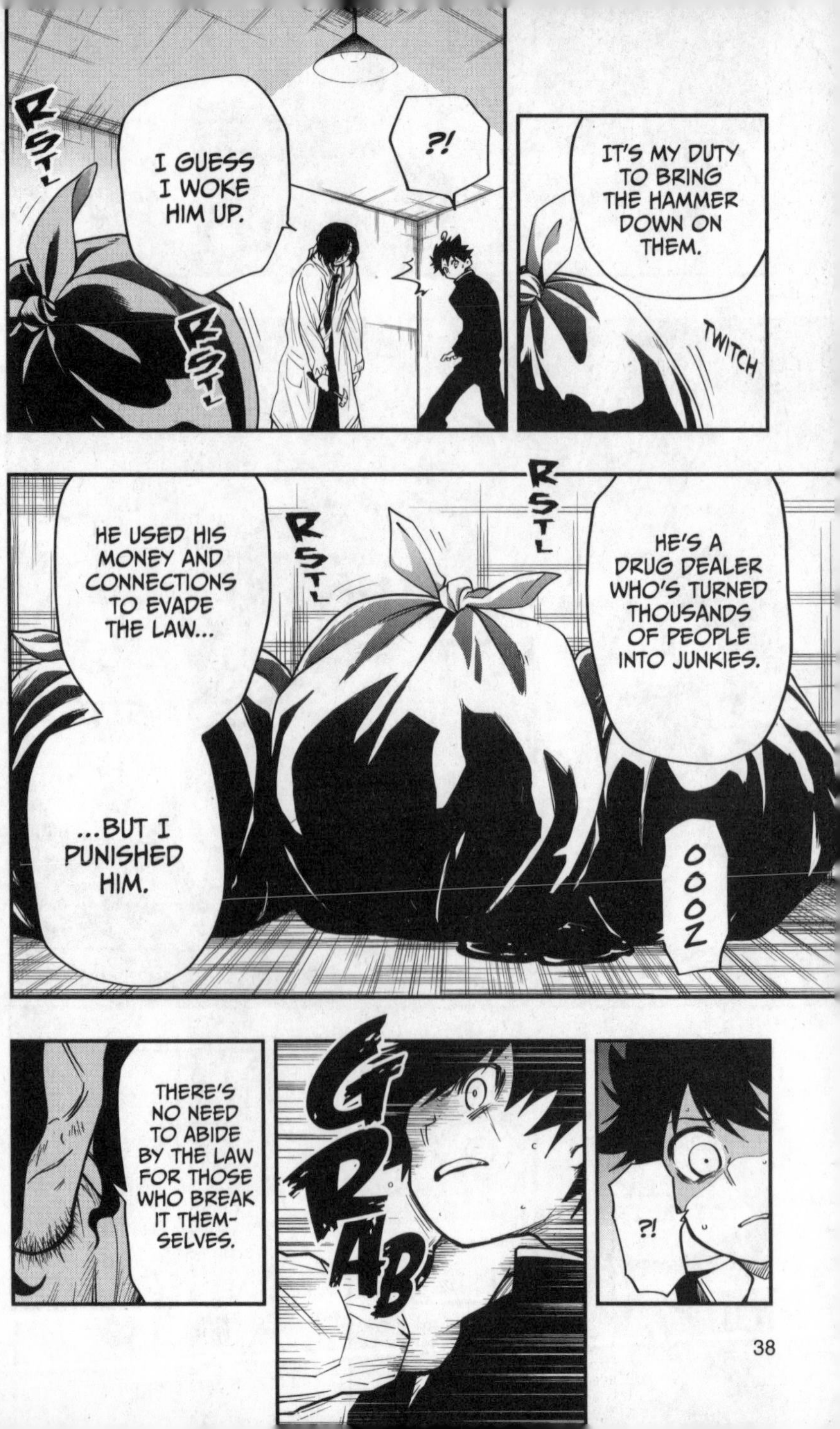
IT'S MY DUTY TO BRING THE HAMMER DOWN ON THEM.
TWITCH
?!
I GUESS I WOKE HIM UP.
RSTL
RSTL
RSTL
HE'S A DRUG DEALER WHO'S TURNED THOUSANDS OF PEOPLE INTO JUNKIES.
RSTL
HE USED HIS MONEY AND CONNECTIONS TO EVADE THE LAW...
OOOZ
...BUT I PUNISHED HIM.
?!
GRAB
THERE'S NO NEED TO ABIDE BY THE LAW FOR THOSE WHO BREAK IT THEM-SELVES.

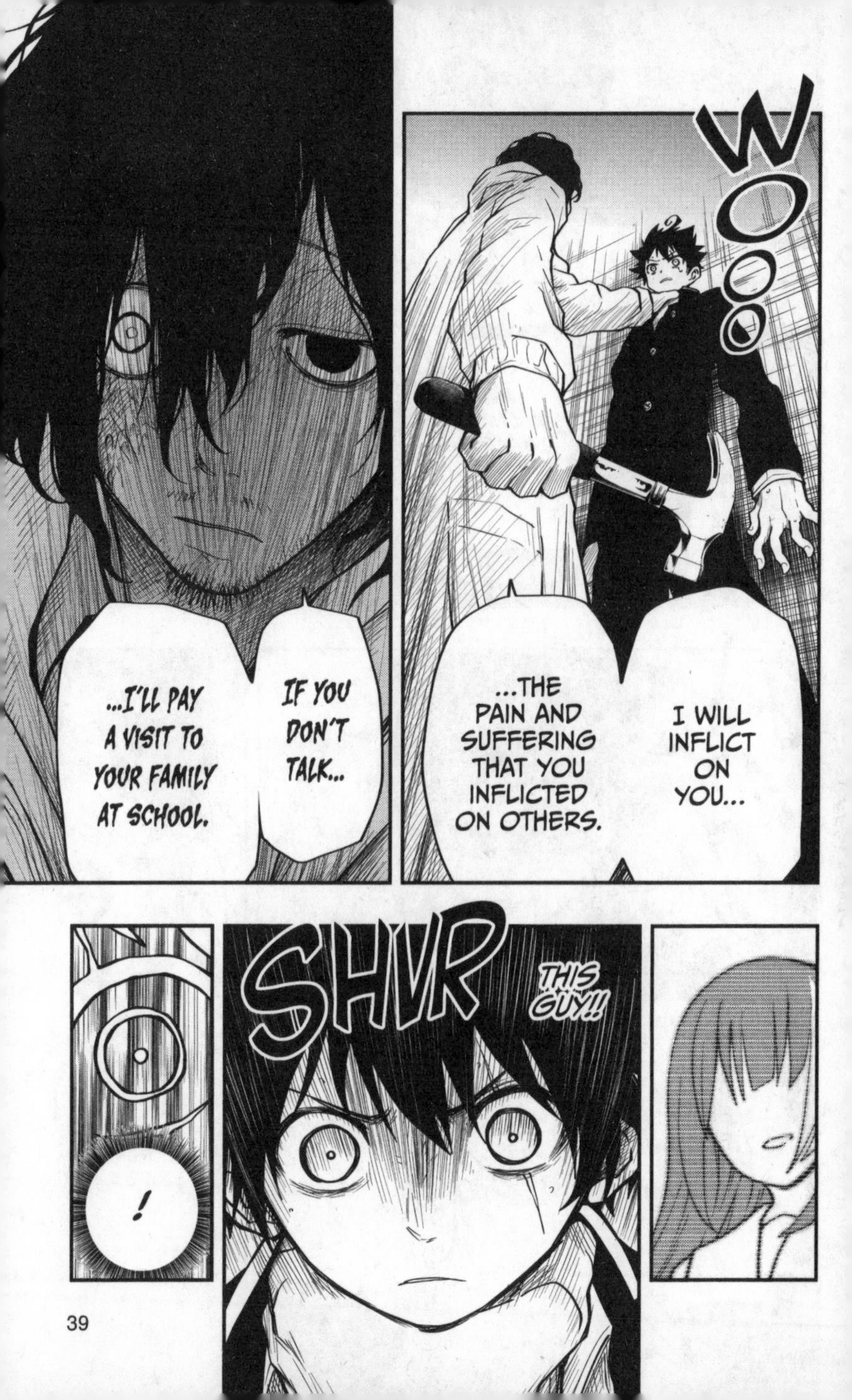
WOOO
I WILL INFLICT ON YOU...
...THE PAIN AND SUFFERING THAT YOU INFLICTED ON OTHERS.
IF YOU DON'T TALK...
...I'LL PAY A VISIT TO YOUR FAMILY AT SCHOOL.
SHVR
THIS GUY!!
!

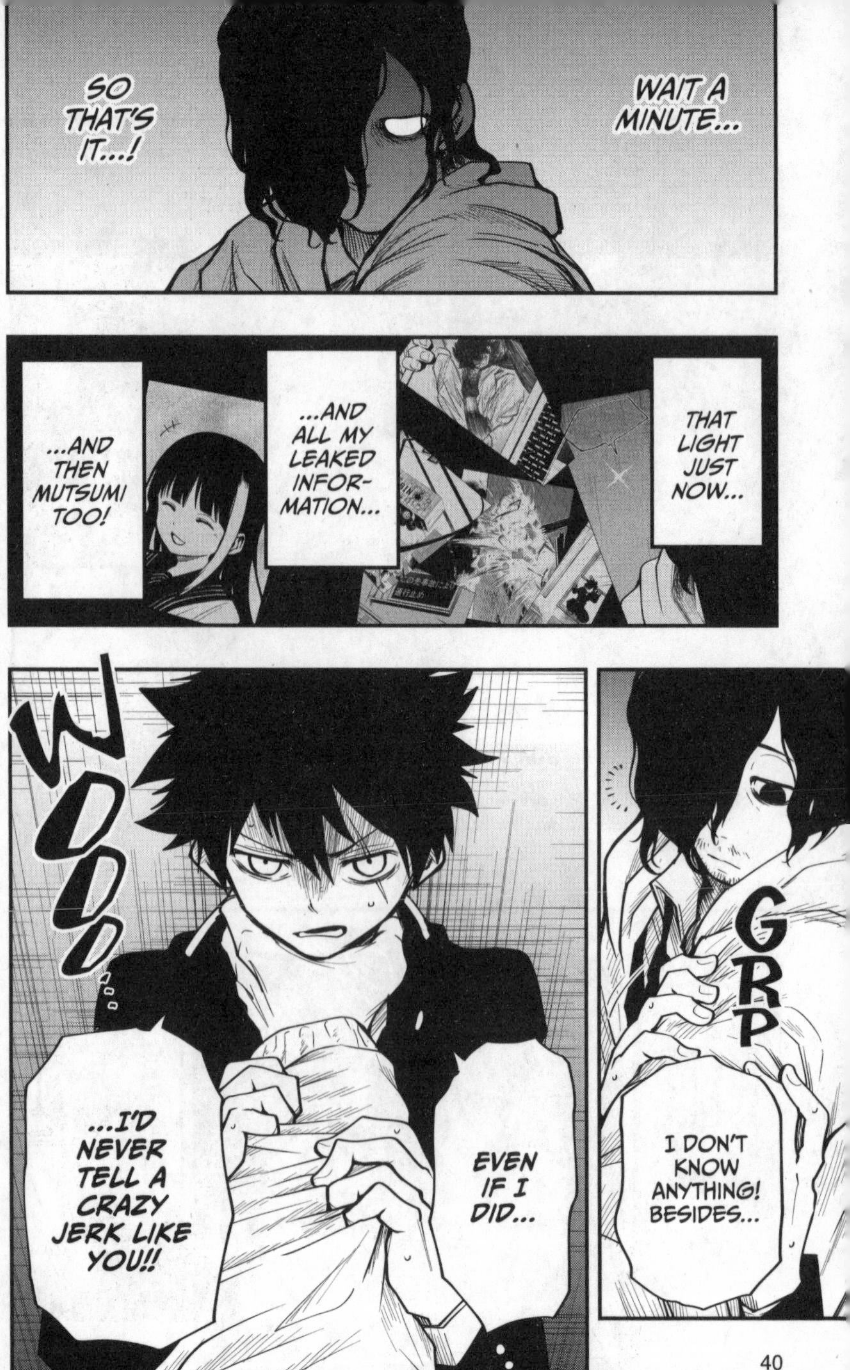
WAIT A MINUTE...
SO THAT'S IT...!
THAT LIGHT JUST NOW...
...AND ALL MY LEAKED INFOR-MATION...
...AND THEN MUTSUMI TOO!
I DON'T KNOW ANYTHING! BESIDES...
GRP
EVEN IF I DID...
...I'D NEVER TELL A CRAZY JERK LIKE YOU!!

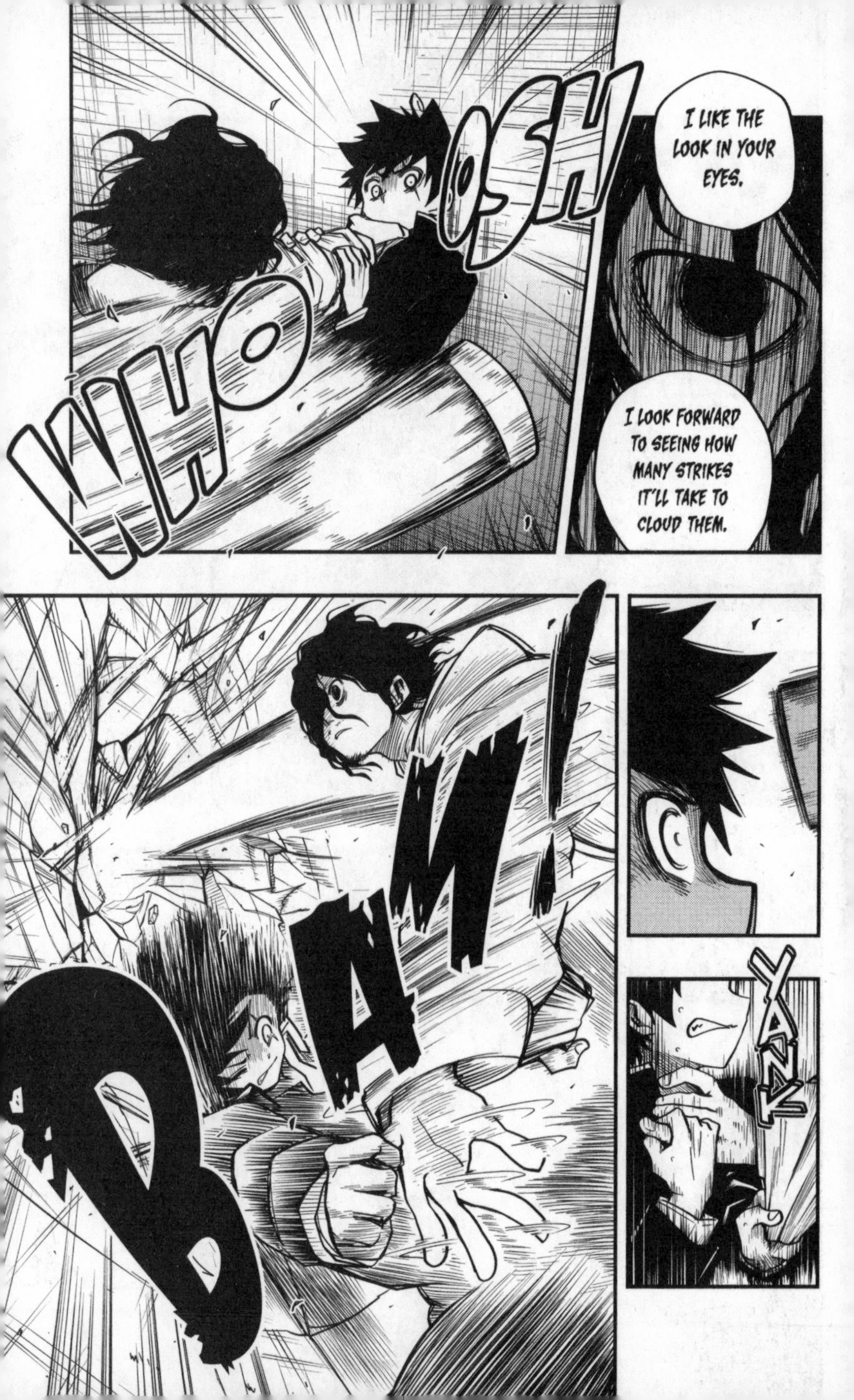
I LIKE THE LOOK IN YOUR EYES.
I LOOK FORWARD TO SEEING HOW MANY STRIKES IT'LL TAKE TO CLOUD THEM.
WHOOSH
YANK
BAM!

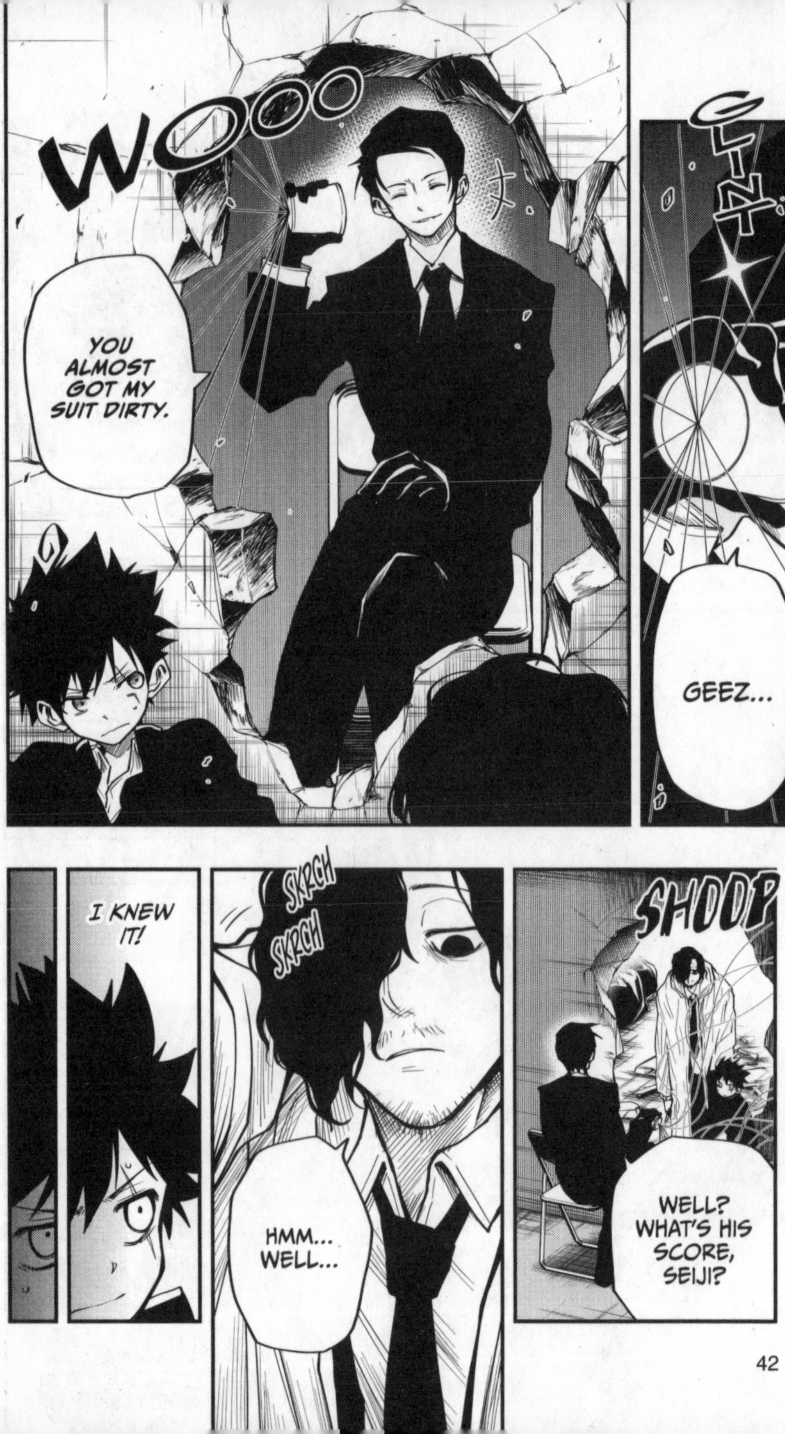
GLINT
GEEZ...
WOOOO
YOU ALMOST GOT MY SUIT DIRTY.
SHOOP
WELL? WHAT'S HIS SCORE, SEIJI?
SKRCH
SKRCH
HMM... WELL...
I KNEW IT!

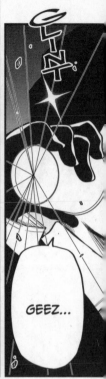

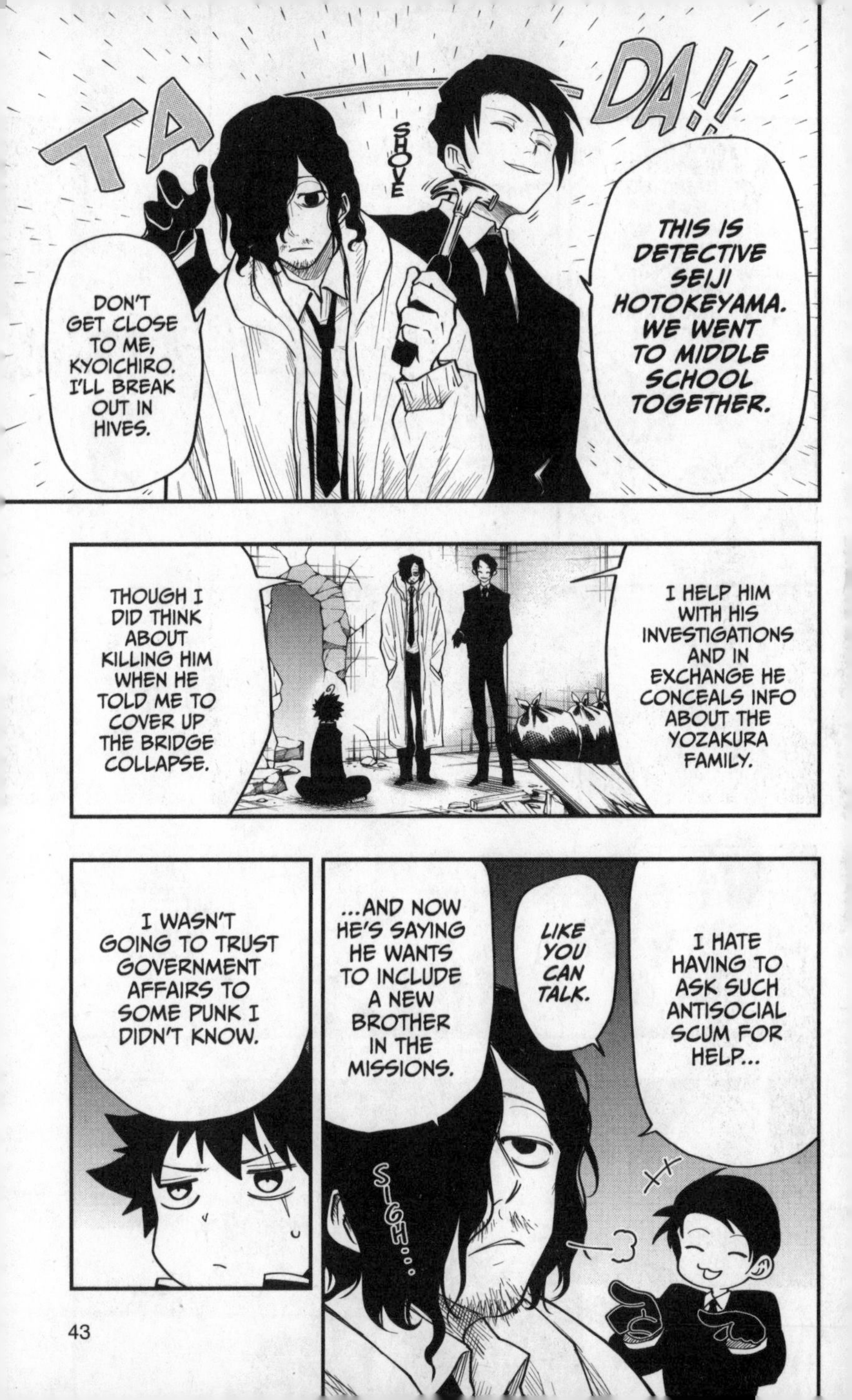
TA-DA!!
SHOVE
THIS IS DETECTIVE SEIJI HOTOKEYAMA. WE WENT TO MIDDLE SCHOOL TOGETHER.
DON'T GET CLOSE TO ME, KYOICHIRO. I'LL BREAK OUT IN HIVES.
I HELP HIM WITH HIS INVESTIGATIONS AND IN EXCHANGE HE CONCEALS INFO ABOUT THE YOZAKURA FAMILY.
THOUGH I DID THINK ABOUT KILLING HIM WHEN HE TOLD ME TO COVER UP THE BRIDGE COLLAPSE.
I HATE HAVING TO ASK SUCH ANTISOCIAL SCUM FOR HELP...
LIKE YOU CAN TALK.
...AND NOW HE'S SAYING HE WANTS TO INCLUDE A NEW BROTHER IN THE MISSIONS.
SIGH...
I WASN'T GOING TO TRUST GOVERNMENT AFFAIRS TO SOME PUNK I DIDN'T KNOW.

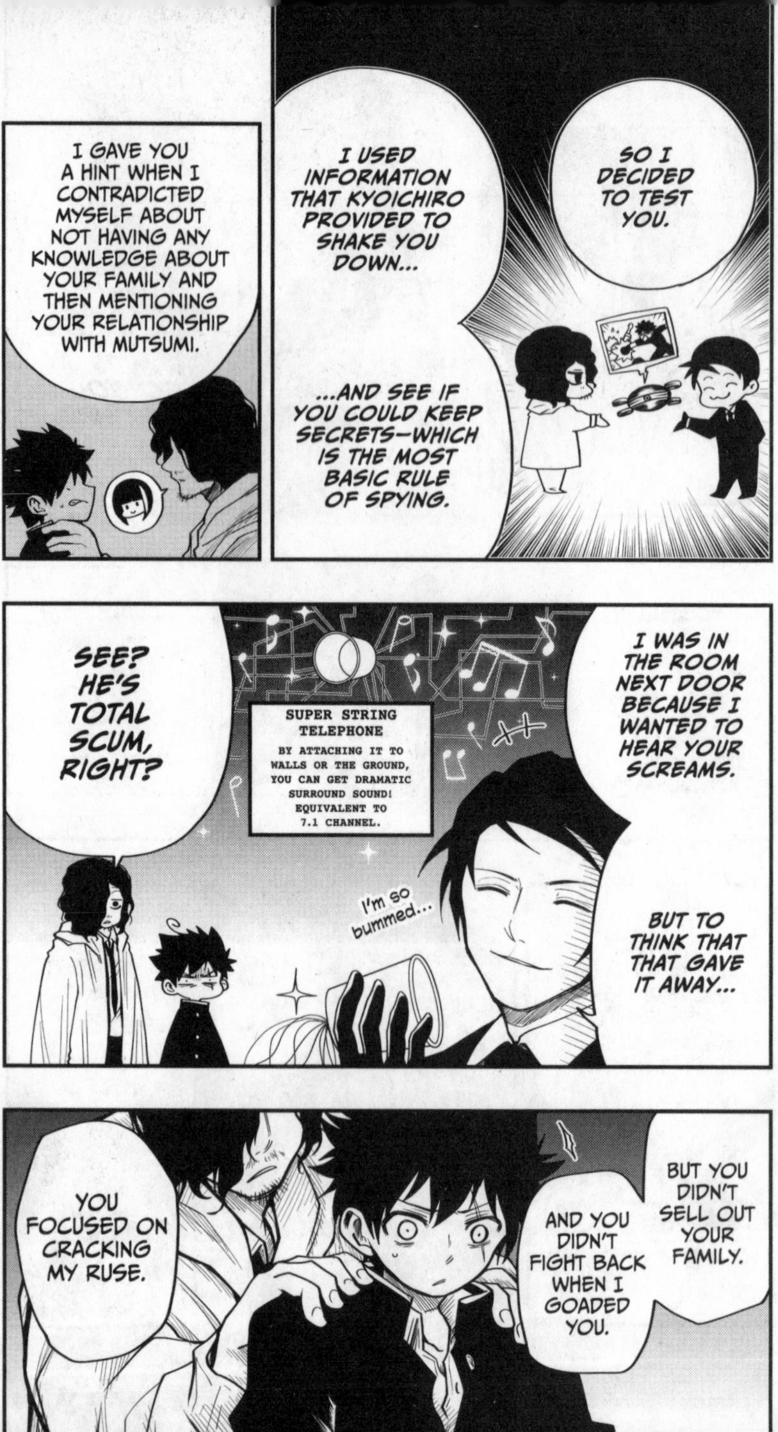
SO I DECIDED TO TEST YOU.
I USED INFORMATION THAT KYOICHIRO PROVIDED TO SHAKE YOU DOWN...
...AND SEE IF YOU COULD KEEP SECRETS—WHICH IS THE MOST BASIC RULE OF SPYING.
I GAVE YOU A HINT WHEN I CONTRADICTED MYSELF ABOUT NOT HAVING ANY KNOWLEDGE ABOUT YOUR FAMILY AND THEN MENTIONING YOUR RELATIONSHIP WITH MUTSUMI.
I WAS IN THE ROOM NEXT DOOR BECAUSE I WANTED TO HEAR YOUR SCREAMS.
BUT TO THINK THAT THAT GAVE IT AWAY...
SUPER STRING TELEPHONE
BY ATTACHING IT TO WALLS OR THE GROUND, YOU CAN GET DRAMATIC SURROUND SOUND! EQUIVALENT TO 7.1 CHANNEL.
I'm so bummed...
SEE? HE'S TOTAL SCUM, RIGHT?
BUT YOU DIDN'T SELL OUT YOUR FAMILY.
AND YOU DIDN'T FIGHT BACK WHEN I GOADED YOU.
YOU FOCUSED ON CRACKING MY RUSE.

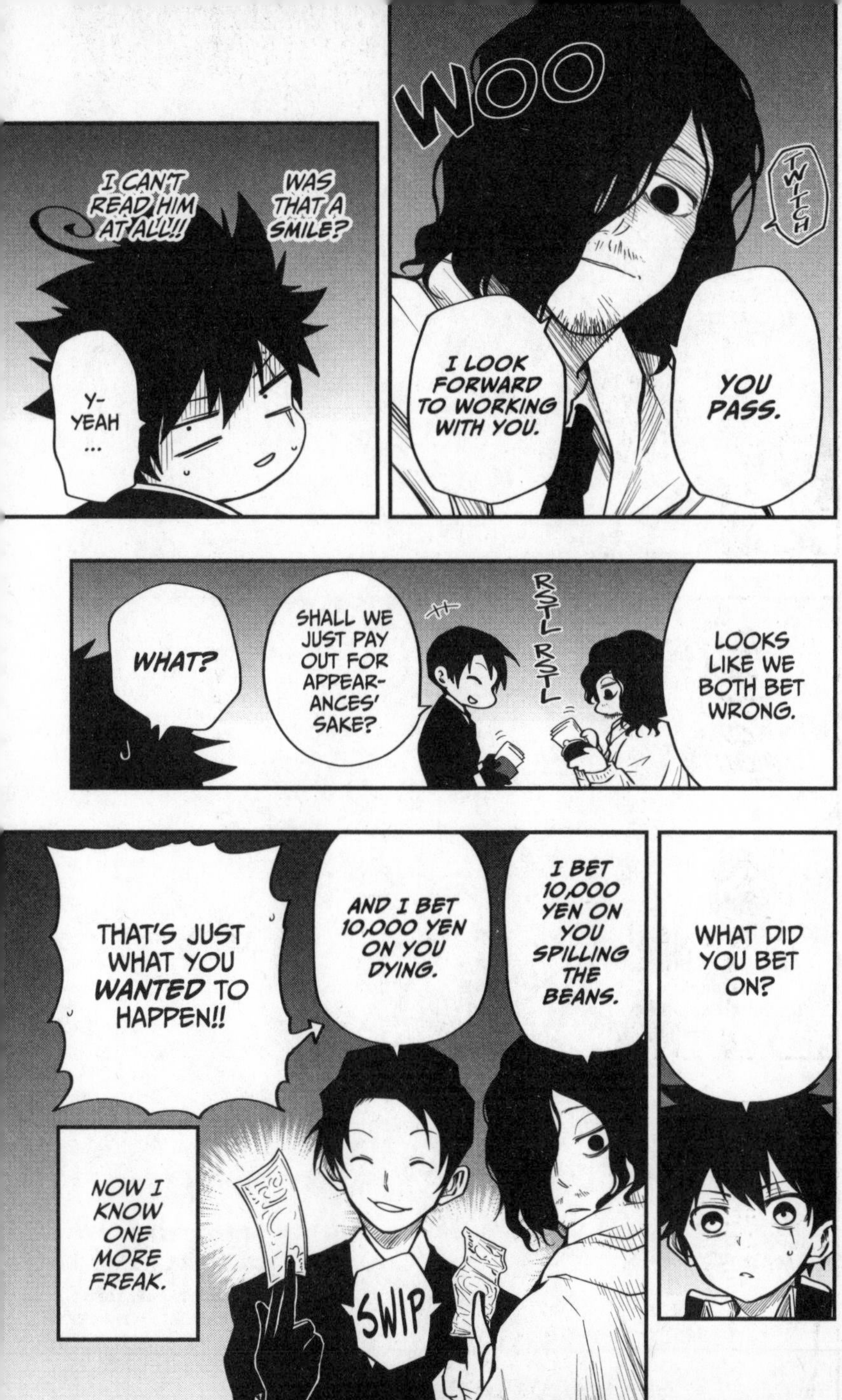
WOO
TWITCH
YOU PASS.
I LOOK FORWARD TO WORKING WITH YOU.
WAS THAT A SMILE?
I CAN'T READ HIM AT ALL!!
Y-YEAH...
LOOKS LIKE WE BOTH BET WRONG.
RSTL RSTL
SHALL WE JUST PAY OUT FOR APPEARANCES' SAKE?
WHAT?
WHAT DID YOU BET ON?
I BET 10,000 YEN ON YOU SPILLING THE BEANS.
AND I BET 10,000 YEN ON YOU DYING.
THAT'S JUST WHAT YOU WANTED TO HAPPEN!!
SWIP
NOW I KNOW ONE MORE FREAK.

SEIJI AND KYOICHIRO'S YOUTH

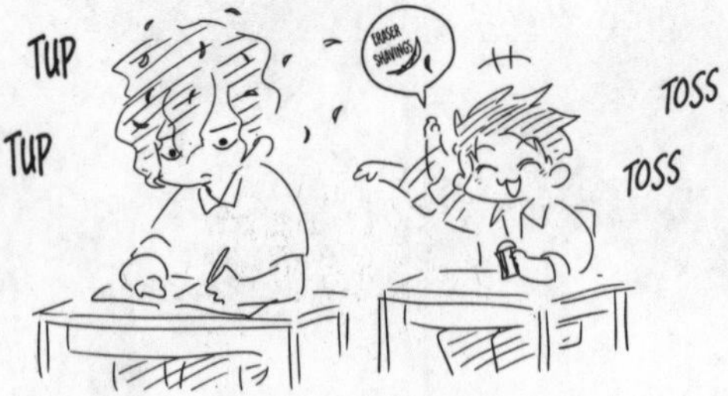
TOSS
TOSS
ERASER SHAVINGS
TUP
TUP

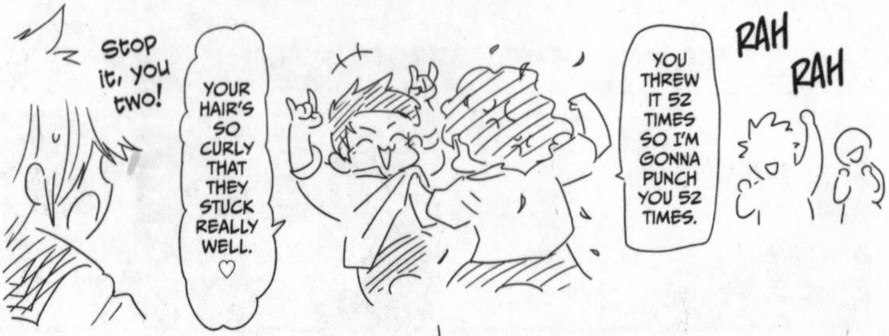
RAH
RAH
YOU THREW IT 52 TIMES SO I'M GONNA PUNCH YOU 52 TIMES.
YOUR HAIR'S SO CURLY THAT THEY STUCK REALLY WELL. ♡
Stop it, you two!

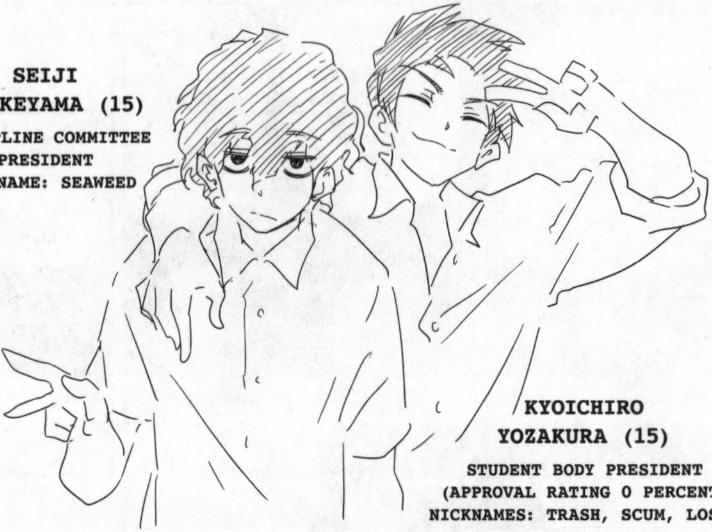

KYOICHIRO YOZAKURA (15)
STUDENT BODY PRESIDENT (APPROVAL RATING 0 PERCENT)
NICKNAMES: TRASH, SCUM, LOSER

SEIJI HOTOKEYAMA (15)
DISCIPLINE COMMITTEE PRESIDENT
NICKNAME: SEAWEED

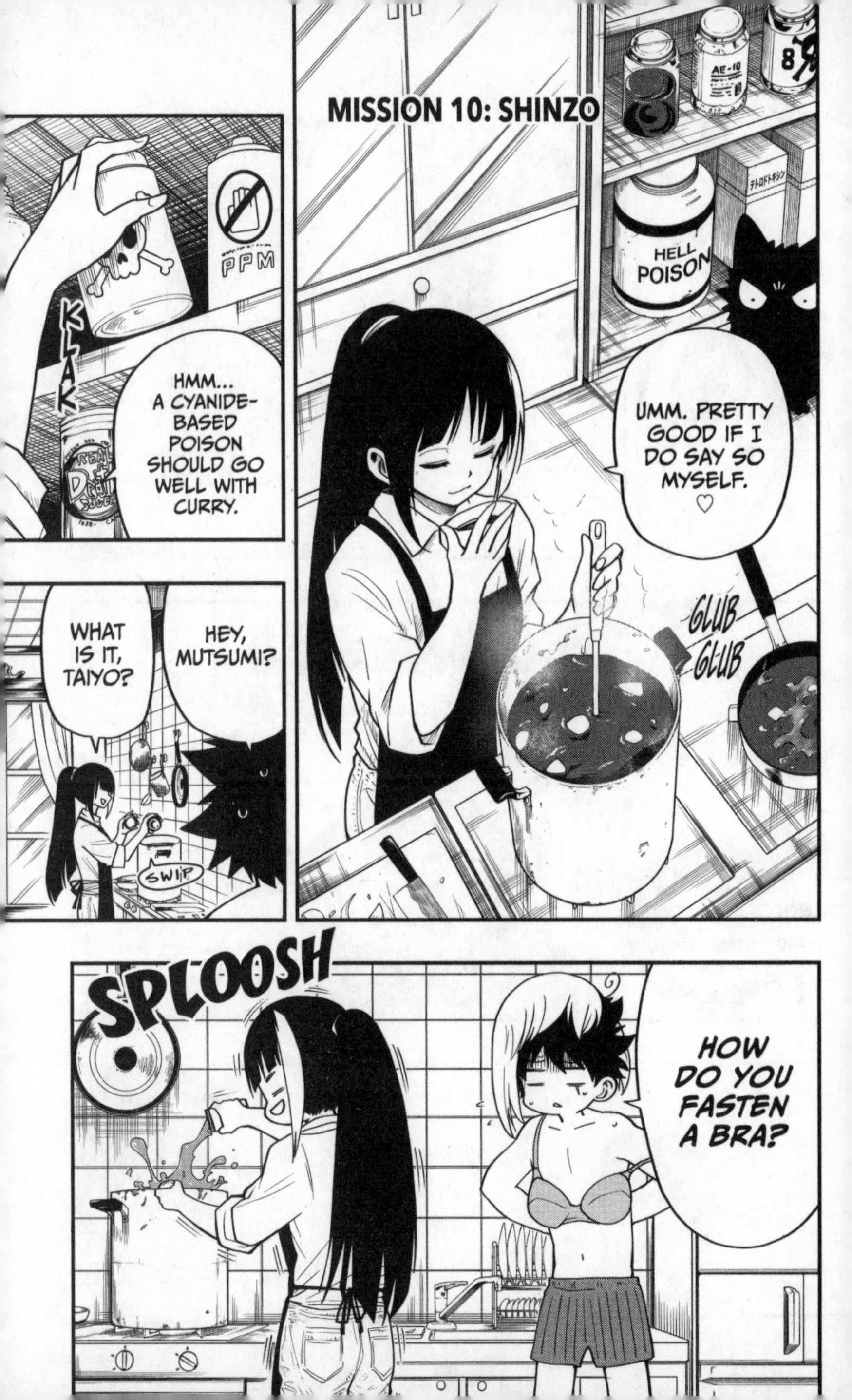
MISSION 10: SHINZO
AE-10
テトロドトキシン
HELL POISON
UMM. PRETTY GOOD IF I DO SAY SO MYSELF. ♡
GLUB GLUB
PPM
KLAK
HMM... A CYANIDE-BASED POISON SHOULD GO WELL WITH CURRY.
HEY, MUTSUMI?
WHAT IS IT, TAIYO?
SWIP
SPLOOSH
HOW DO YOU FASTEN A BRA?

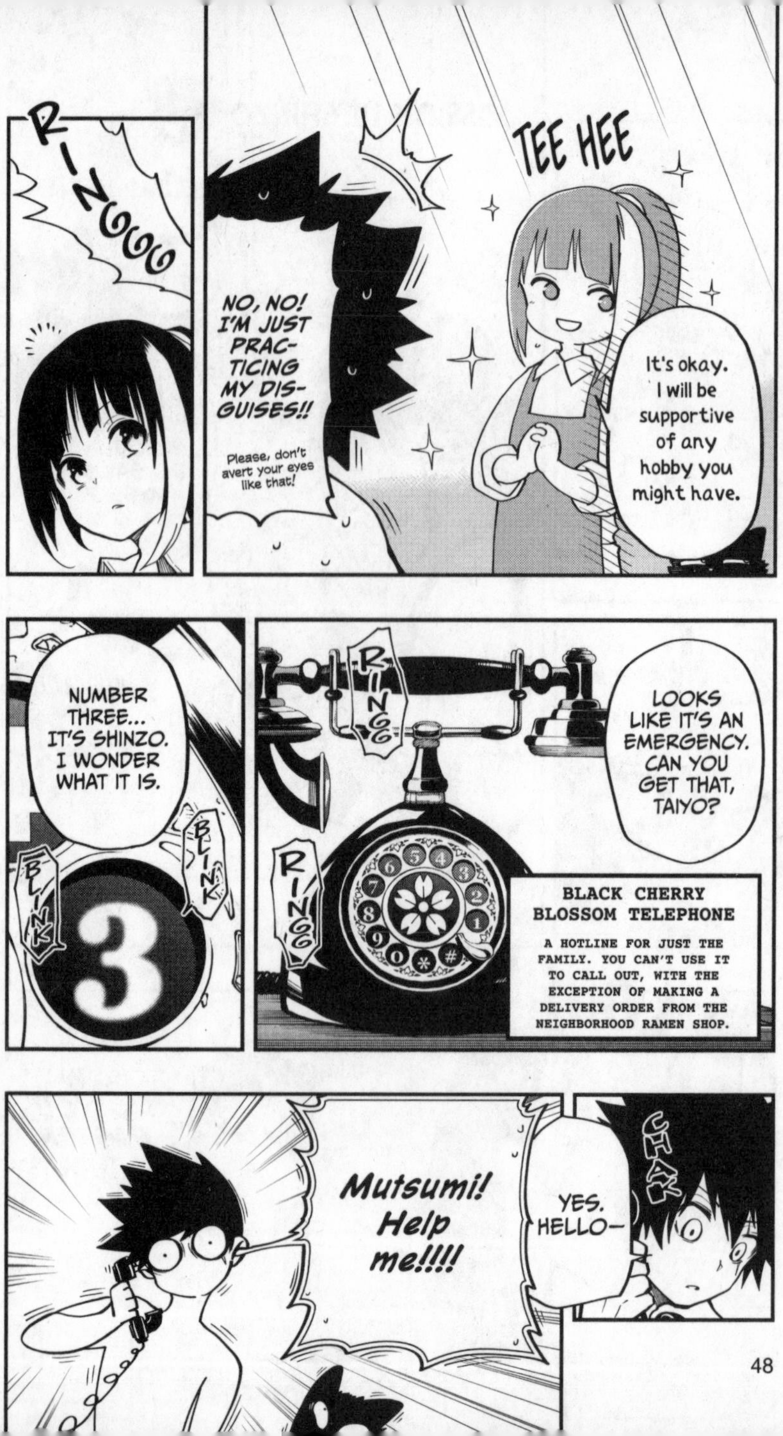
TEE HEE
It's okay. I will be supportive of any hobby you might have.
NO, NO! I'M JUST PRAC-TICING MY DIS-GUISES!!
Please, don't avert your eyes like that!
RINGGG
LOOKS LIKE IT'S AN EMERGENCY. CAN YOU GET THAT, TAIYO?
RINGG
RINGG
BLACK CHERRY BLOSSOM TELEPHONE
A HOTLINE FOR JUST THE FAMILY. YOU CAN'T USE IT TO CALL OUT, WITH THE EXCEPTION OF MAKING A DELIVERY ORDER FROM THE NEIGHBORHOOD RAMEN SHOP.
NUMBER THREE... IT'S SHINZO. I WONDER WHAT IT IS.
BLINK
BLINK
3
CHAK
YES. HELLO—
Mutsumi! Help me!!!!

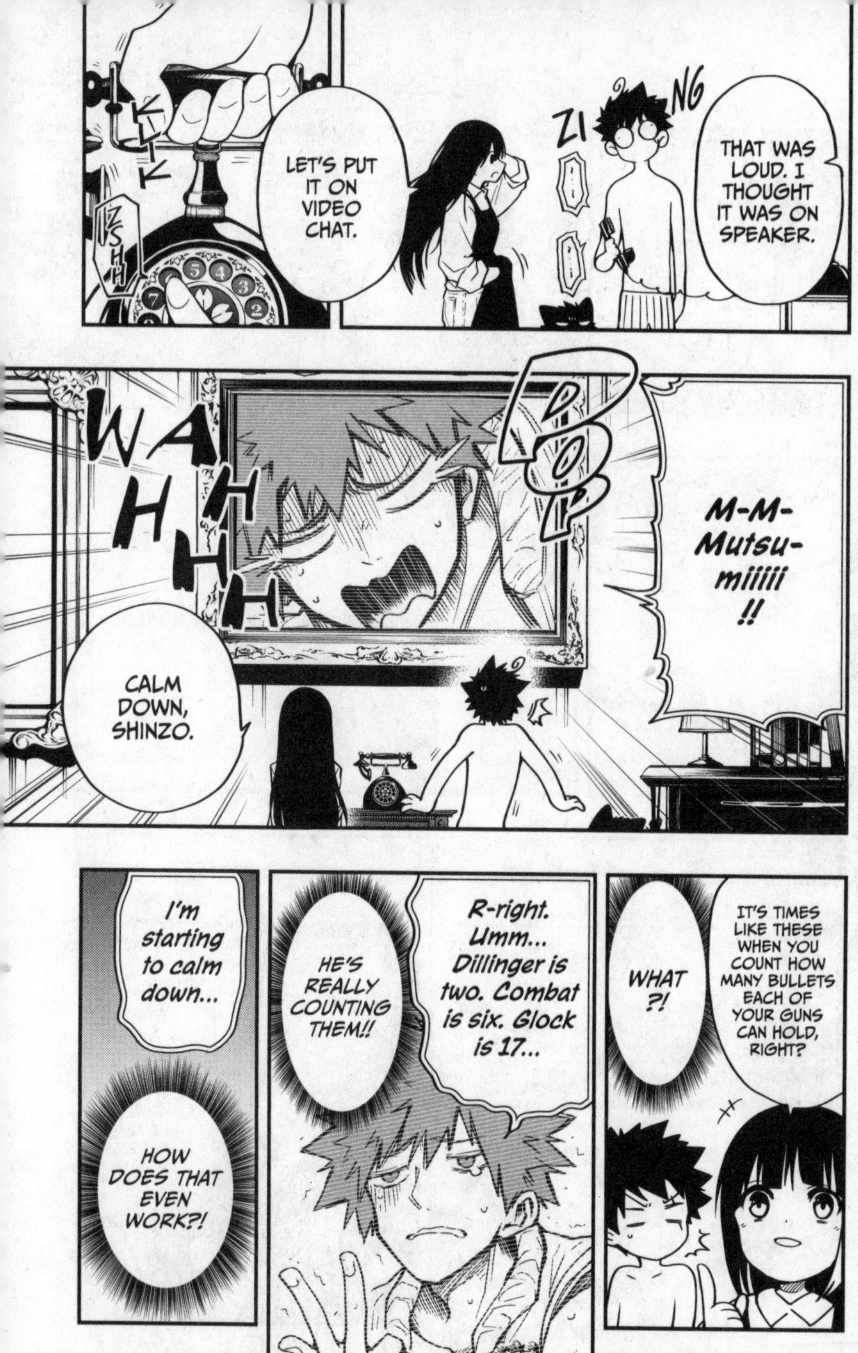
ZING
THAT WAS LOUD. I THOUGHT IT WAS ON SPEAKER.
LET'S PUT IT ON VIDEO CHAT.
ZSHH
M-M-Mutsu-miiiii!!
WAHHHH
CALM DOWN, SHINZO.
IT'S TIMES LIKE THESE WHEN YOU COUNT HOW MANY BULLETS EACH OF YOUR GUNS CAN HOLD, RIGHT?
WHAT?!
R-right. Umm... Dillinger is two. Combat is six. Glock is 17...
HE'S REALLY COUNTING THEM!!
I'm starting to calm down...
HOW DOES THAT EVEN WORK?!

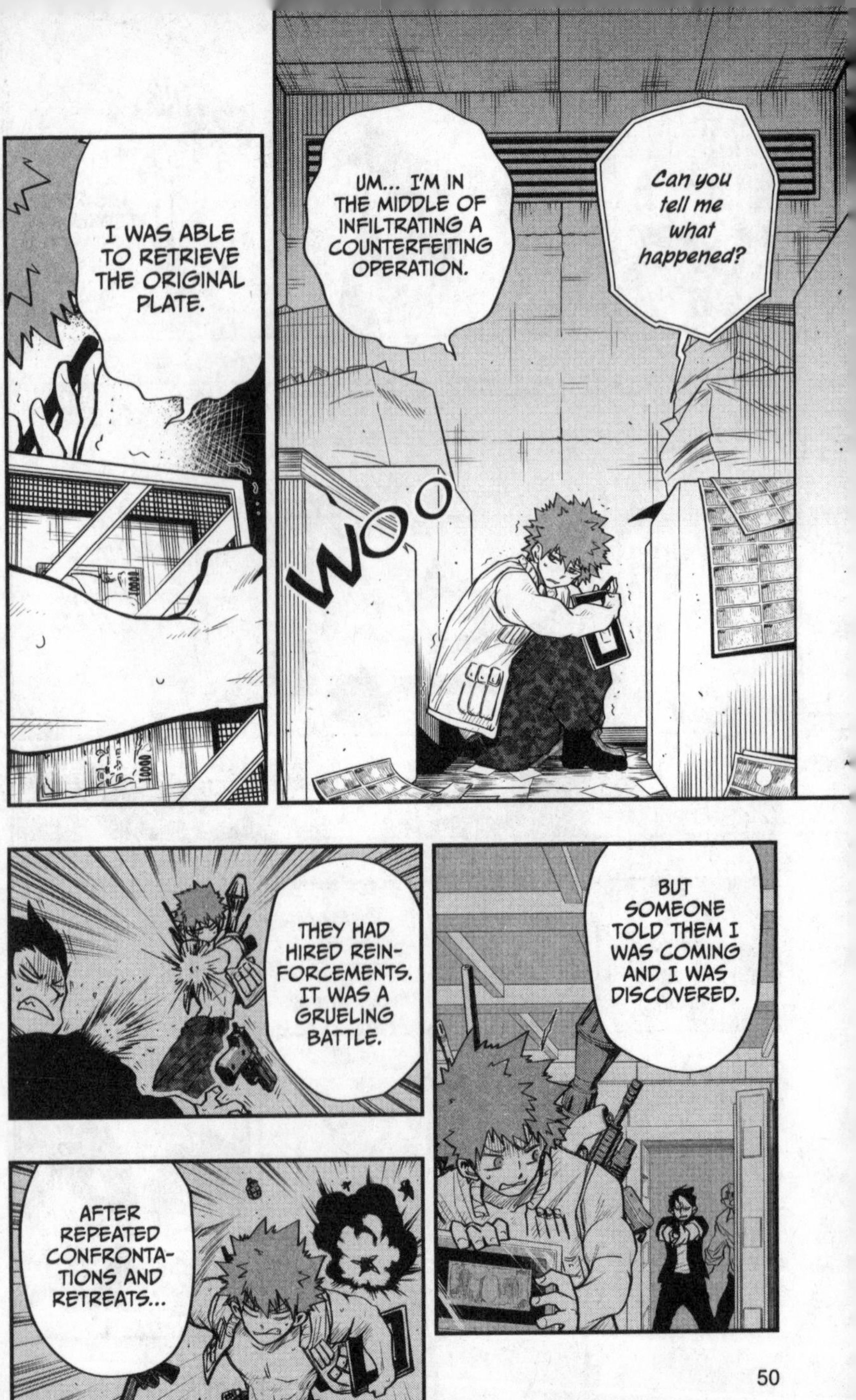
Can you tell me what happened?
UM... I'M IN THE MIDDLE OF INFILTRATING A COUNTERFEITING OPERATION.
WOO
I WAS ABLE TO RETRIEVE THE ORIGINAL PLATE.
BUT SOMEONE TOLD THEM I WAS COMING AND I WAS DISCOVERED.
THEY HAD HIRED REIN-FORCEMENTS. IT WAS A GRUELING BATTLE.
AFTER REPEATED CONFRONTA-TIONS AND RETREATS...

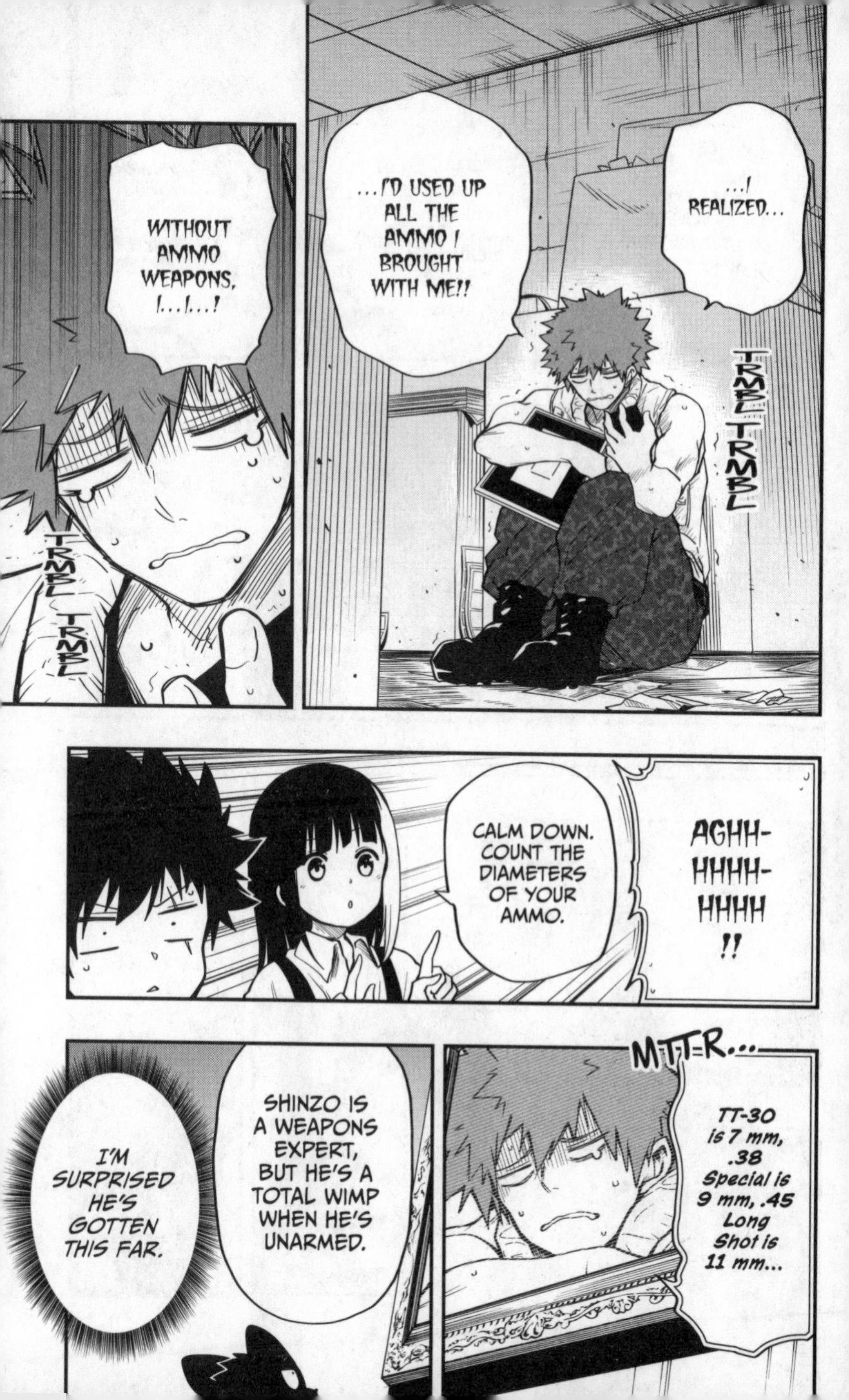
...I REALIZED...
...I'D USED UP ALL THE AMMO I BROUGHT WITH ME!!
TRMBL TRMBL
WITHOUT AMMO WEAPONS, I...I...!
TRMBL TRMBL
AGHH-HHHH-HHHH!!
CALM DOWN. COUNT THE DIAMETERS OF YOUR AMMO.
MTTR...
TT-30 is 7 mm, .38 Special is 9 mm, .45 Long Shot is 11 mm...
SHINZO IS A WEAPONS EXPERT, BUT HE'S A TOTAL WIMP WHEN HE'S UNARMED.
I'M SURPRISED HE'S GOTTEN THIS FAR.

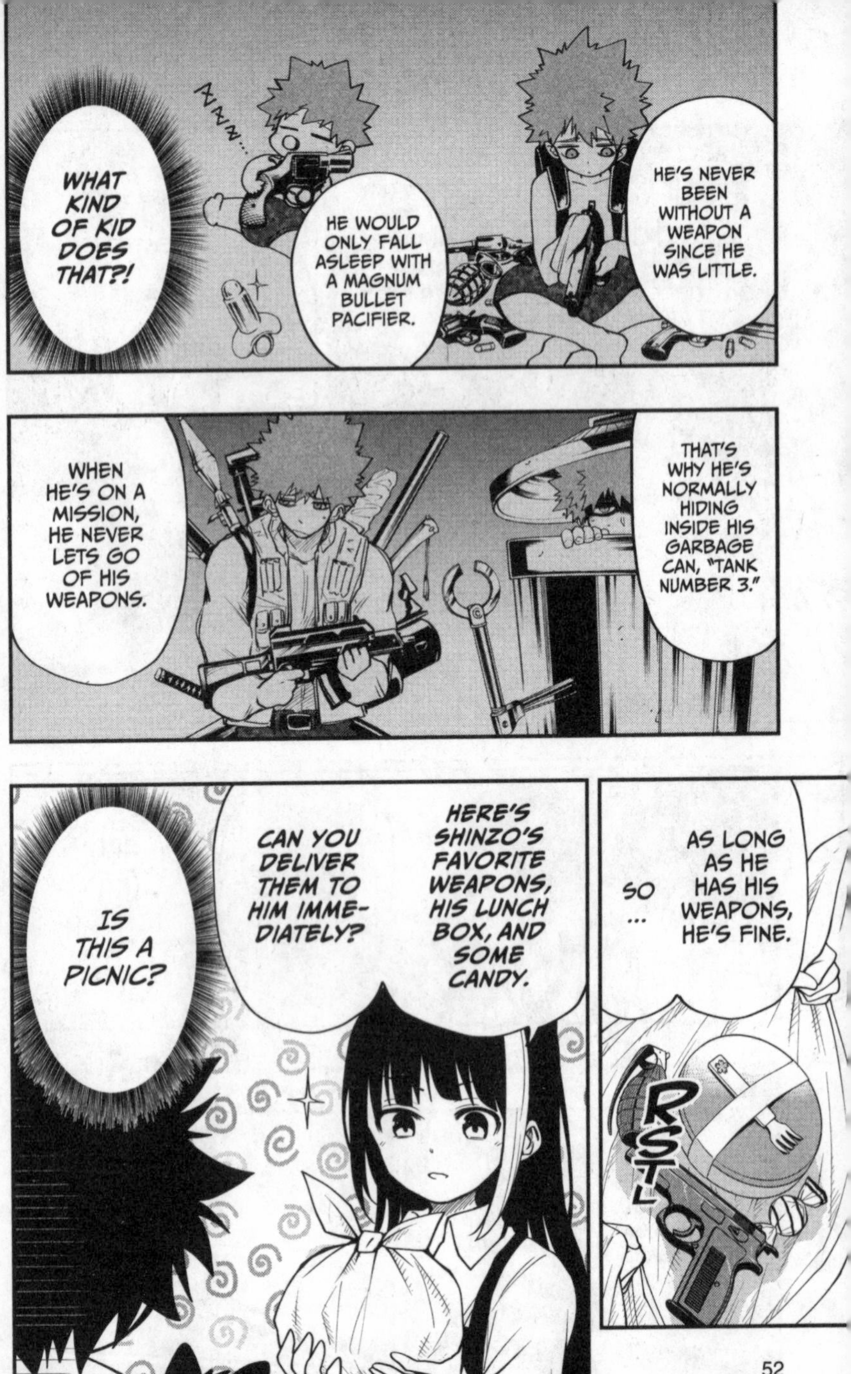
HE'S NEVER BEEN WITHOUT A WEAPON SINCE HE WAS LITTLE.
HE WOULD ONLY FALL ASLEEP WITH A MAGNUM BULLET PACIFIER.
ZZZ...
WHAT KIND OF KID DOES THAT?!
THAT'S WHY HE'S NORMALLY HIDING INSIDE HIS GARBAGE CAN, "TANK NUMBER 3."
WHEN HE'S ON A MISSION, HE NEVER LETS GO OF HIS WEAPONS.
SO ... AS LONG AS HE HAS HIS WEAPONS, HE'S FINE.
RSTL
HERE'S SHINZO'S FAVORITE WEAPONS, HIS LUNCH BOX, AND SOME CANDY.
CAN YOU DELIVER THEM TO HIM IMME-DIATELY?
IS THIS A PICNIC?

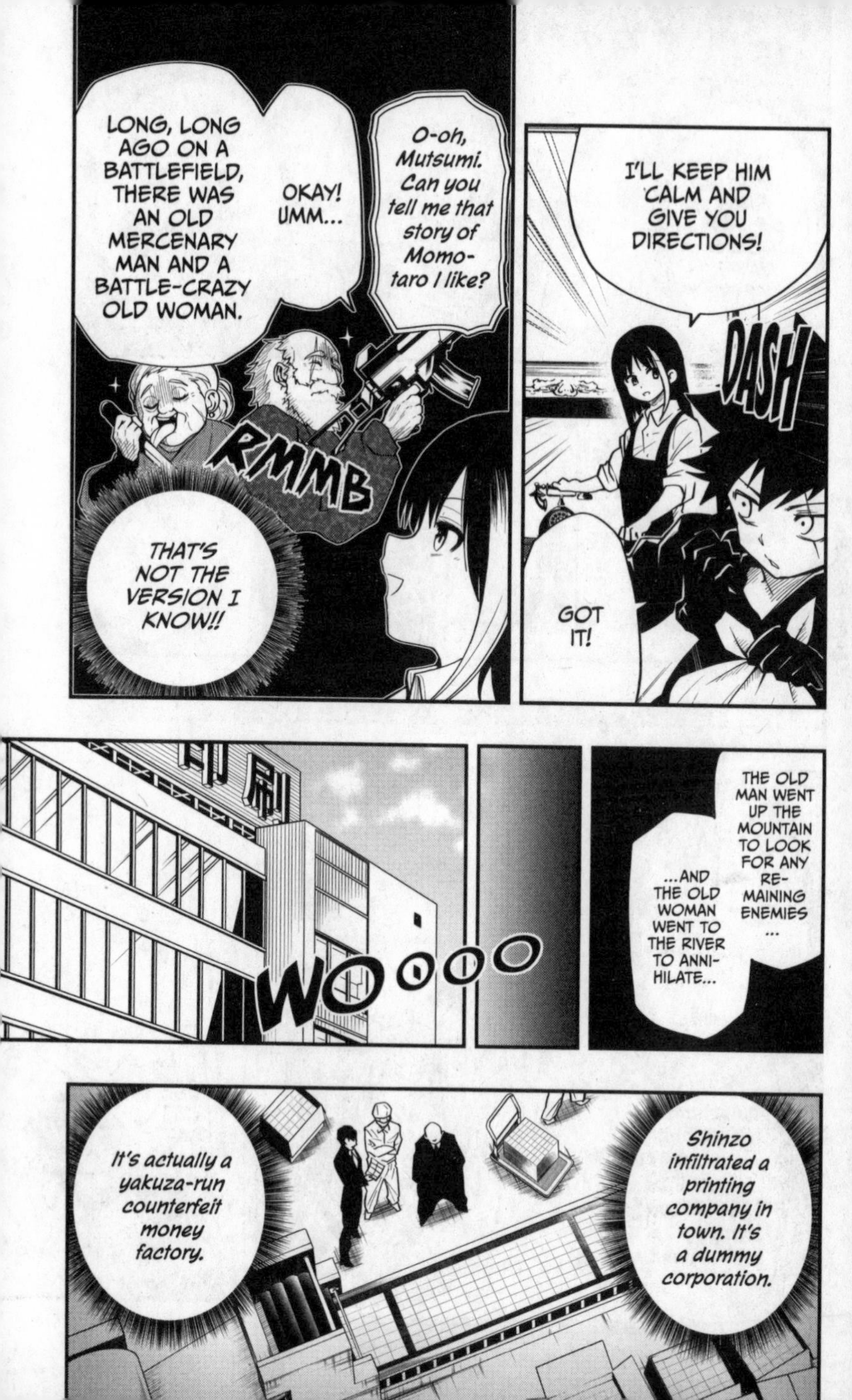
I'LL KEEP HIM CALM AND GIVE YOU DIRECTIONS!
DASH
GOT IT!
O-oh, Mutsumi. Can you tell me that story of Momotaro I like?
OKAY! UMM...
LONG, LONG AGO ON A BATTLEFIELD, THERE WAS AN OLD MERCENARY MAN AND A BATTLE-CRAZY OLD WOMAN.
RMMB
THAT'S NOT THE VERSION I KNOW!!
THE OLD MAN WENT UP THE MOUNTAIN TO LOOK FOR ANY REMAINING ENEMIES...
...AND THE OLD WOMAN WENT TO THE RIVER TO ANNIHILATE...
WOOOO
Shinzo infiltrated a printing company in town. It's a dummy corporation.
It's actually a yakuza-run counterfeit money factory.

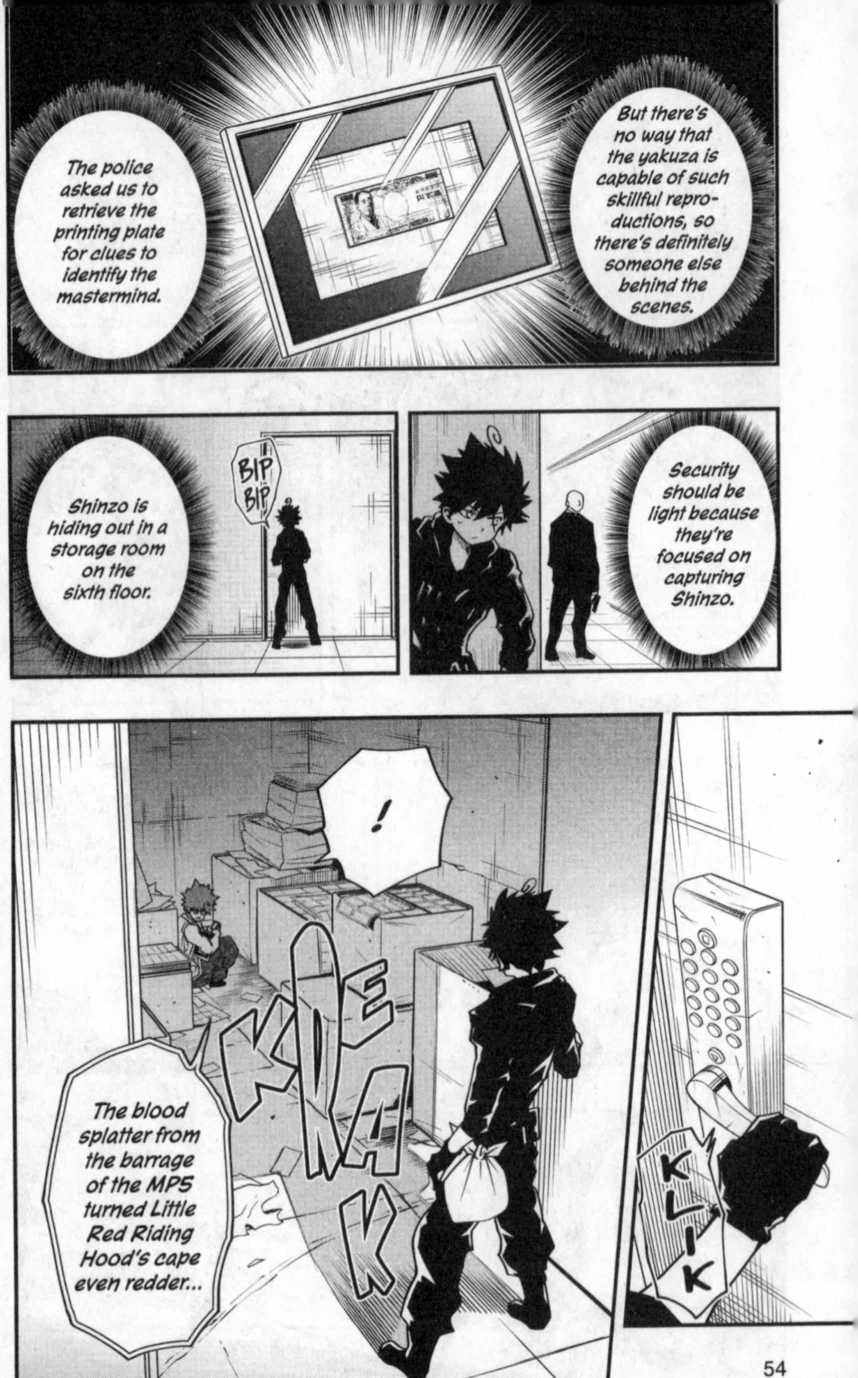
But there's no way that the yakuza is capable of such skillful reproductions, so there's definitely someone else behind the scenes.
The police asked us to retrieve the printing plate for clues to identify the mastermind.
Security should be light because they're focused on capturing Shinzo.
BIP BIP
Shinzo is hiding out in a storage room on the sixth floor.
KLIK
!
KREAK
The blood splatter from the barrage of the MP5 turned Little Red Riding Hood's cape even redder...

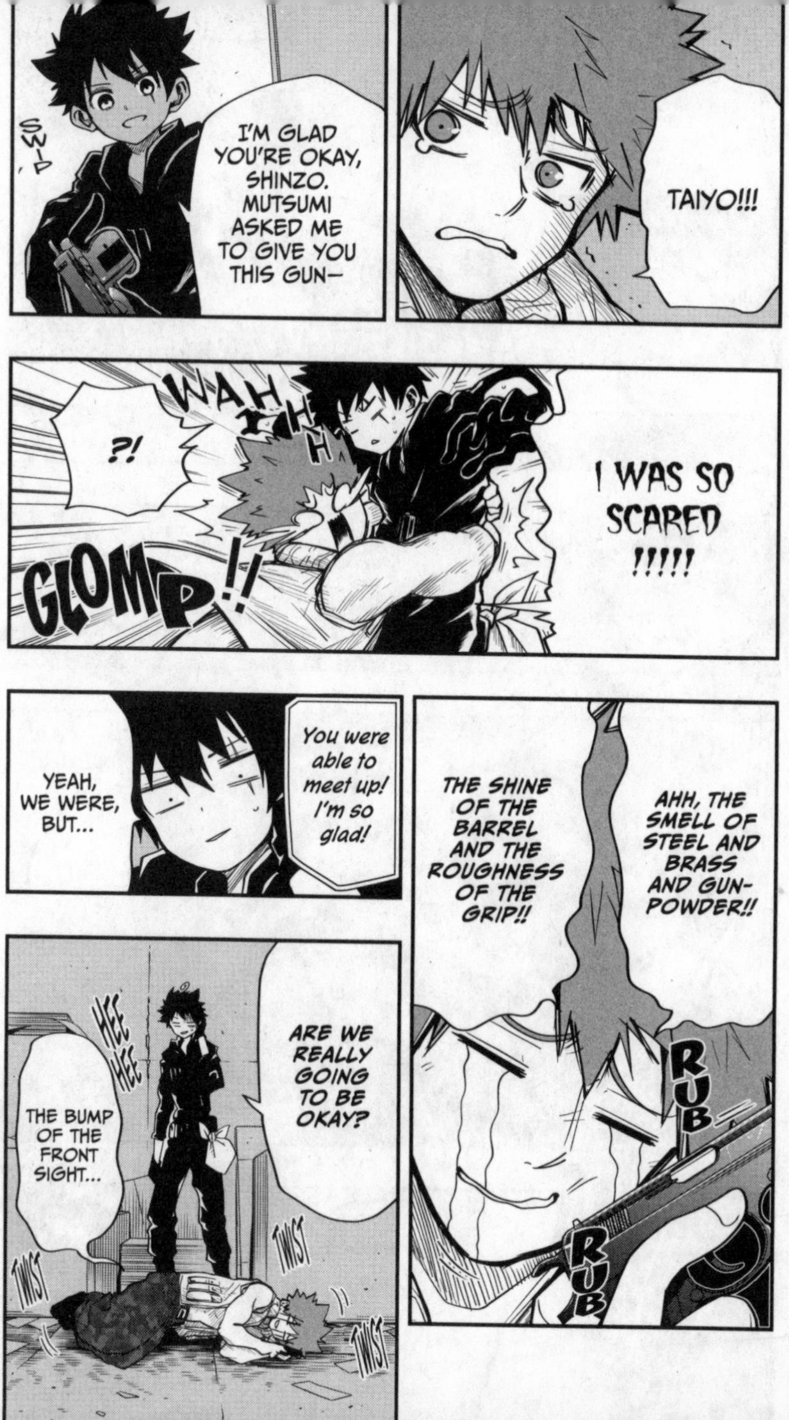
TAIYO!!!
SWIP
I'M GLAD YOU'RE OKAY, SHINZO. MUTSUMI ASKED ME TO GIVE YOU THIS GUN—
I WAS SO SCARED !!!!!
WAHHH
?!
GLOMP!!
AHH, THE SMELL OF STEEL AND BRASS AND GUN-POWDER!!
THE SHINE OF THE BARREL AND THE ROUGHNESS OF THE GRIP!!
RUB
RUB
You were able to meet up! I'm so glad!
YEAH, WE WERE, BUT...
ARE WE REALLY GOING TO BE OKAY?
HEE HEE
THE BUMP OF THE FRONT SIGHT...
TWIST
TWIST
TWIST

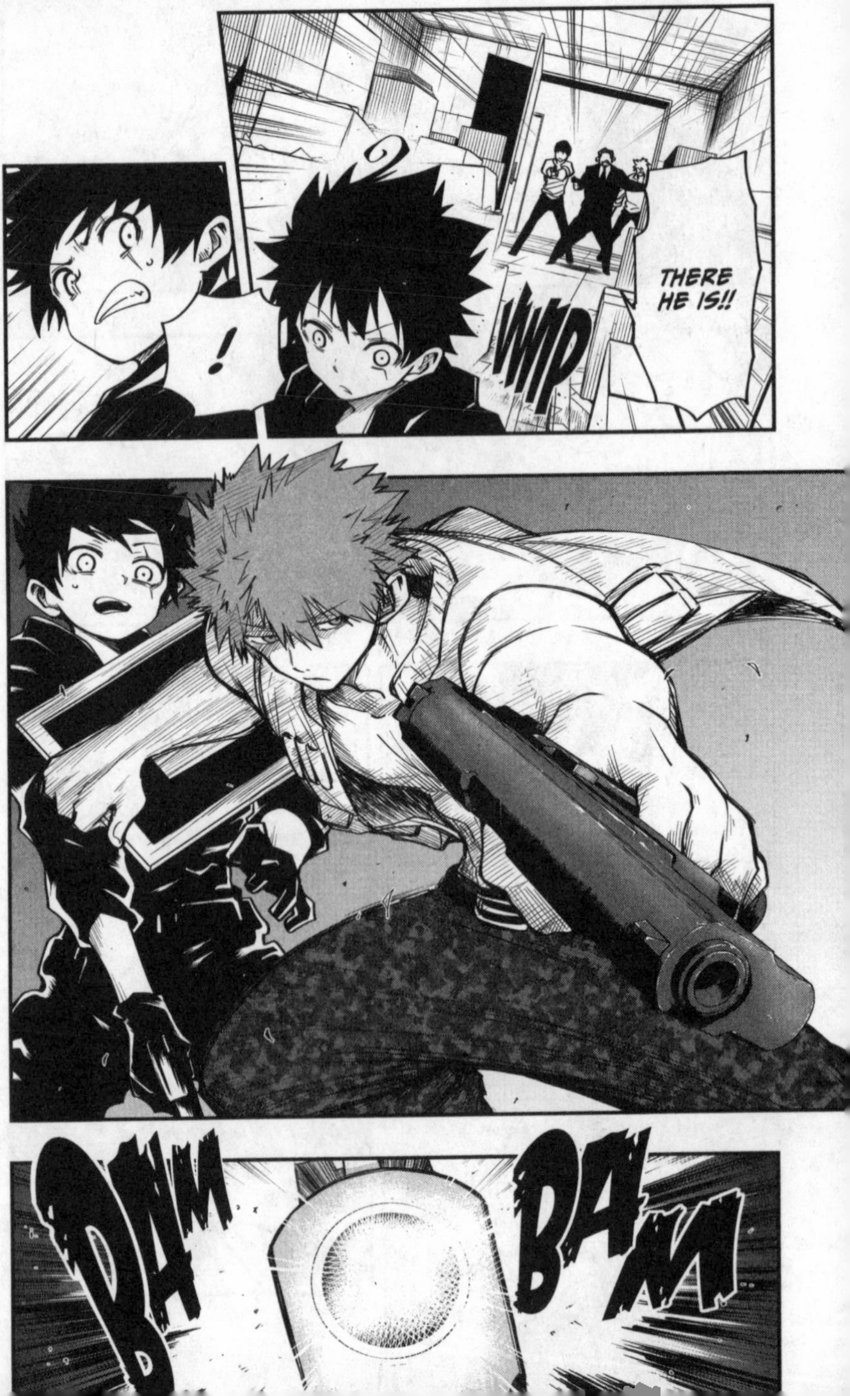
THERE HE IS!!
VWIP
!
BAM
BAM

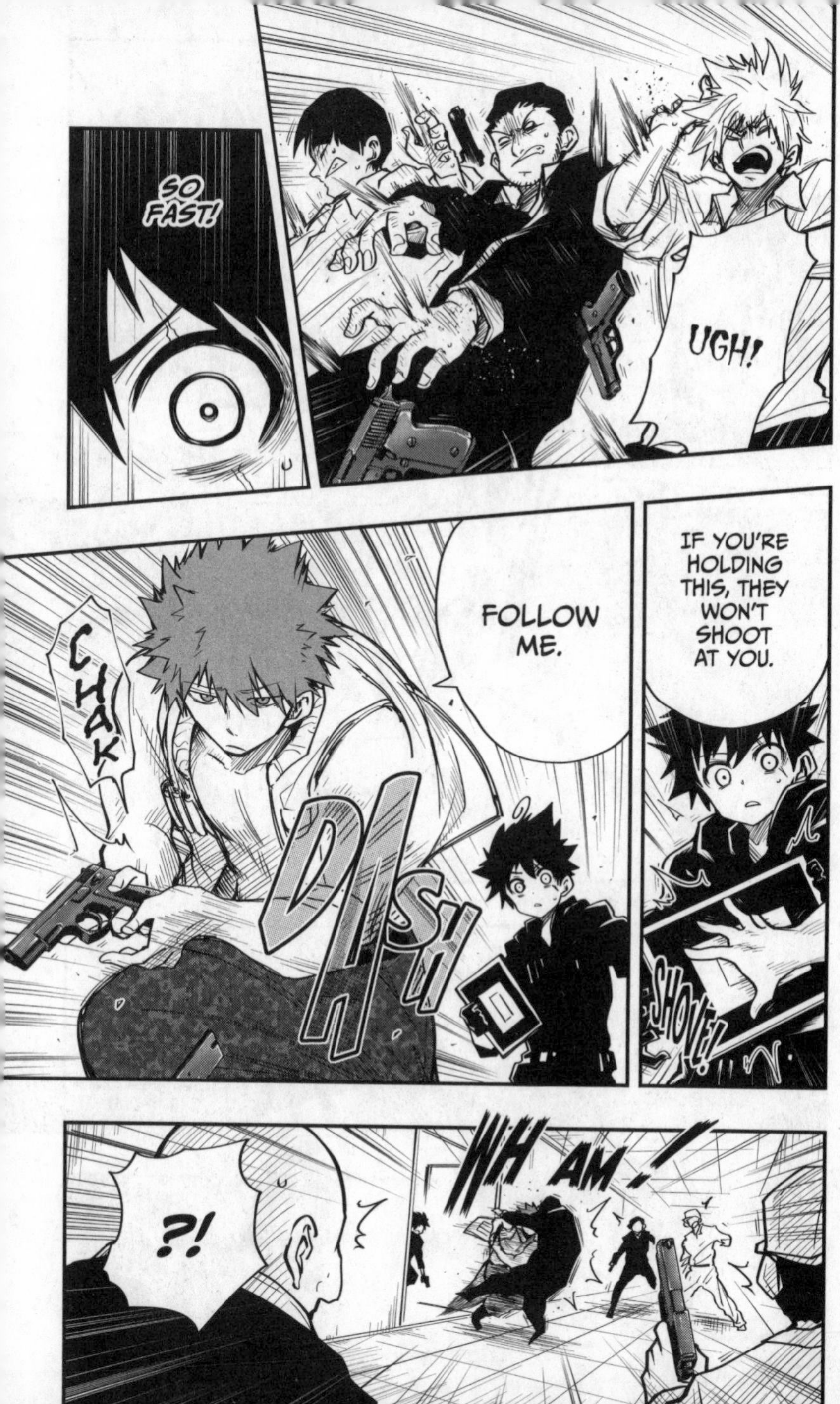

UGH!
SO FAST!
IF YOU'RE HOLDING THIS, THEY WON'T SHOOT AT YOU.
SHOVE!
FOLLOW ME.
CHAK
DASH
WHAM!
?!

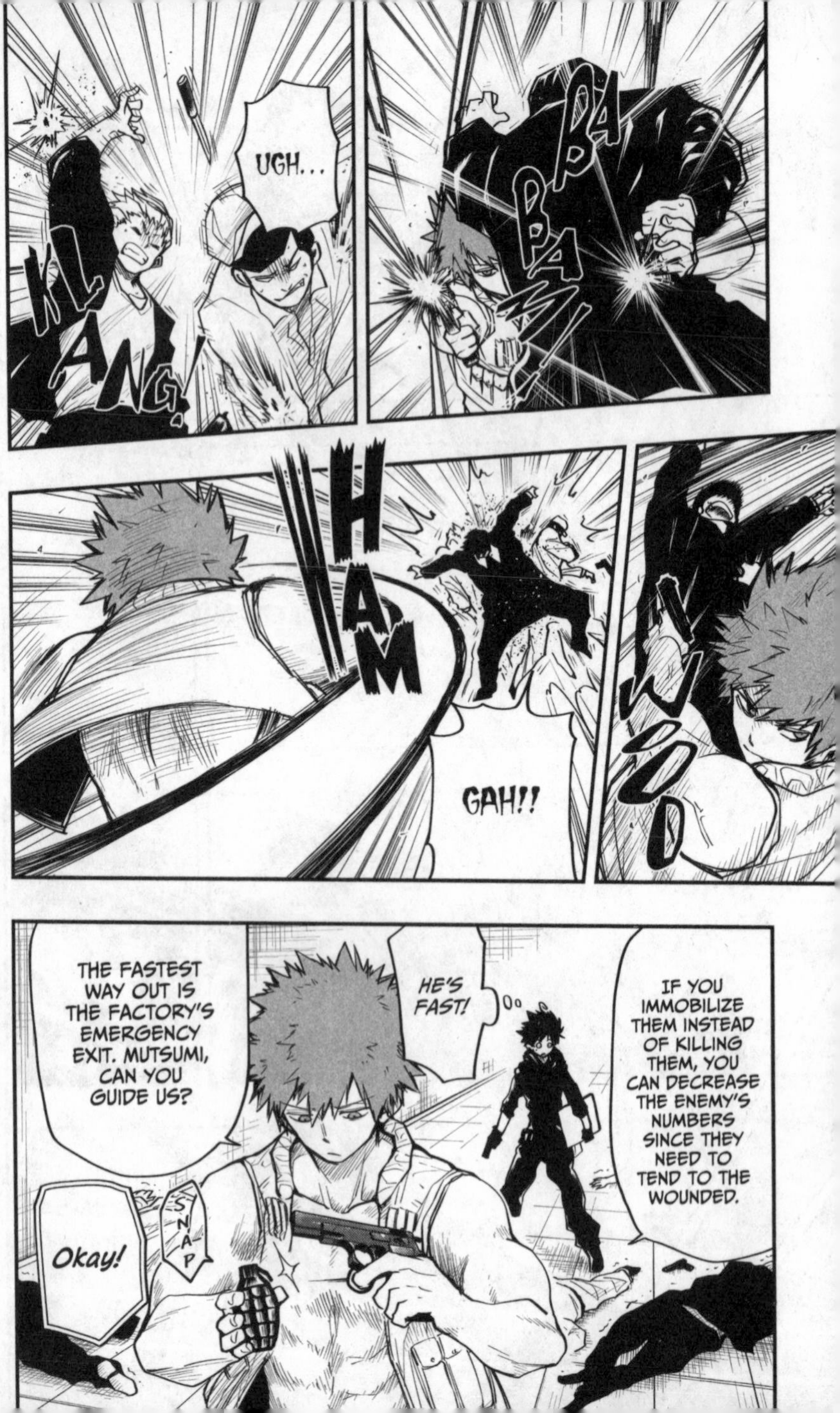
BABABAM!
UGH...
KLANG!
GAH!!
HAM
IF YOU IMMOBILIZE THEM INSTEAD OF KILLING THEM, YOU CAN DECREASE THE ENEMY'S NUMBERS SINCE THEY NEED TO TEND TO THE WOUNDED.
HE'S FAST!
THE FASTEST WAY OUT IS THE FACTORY'S EMERGENCY EXIT. MUTSUMI, CAN YOU GUIDE US?
SNAP
Okay!

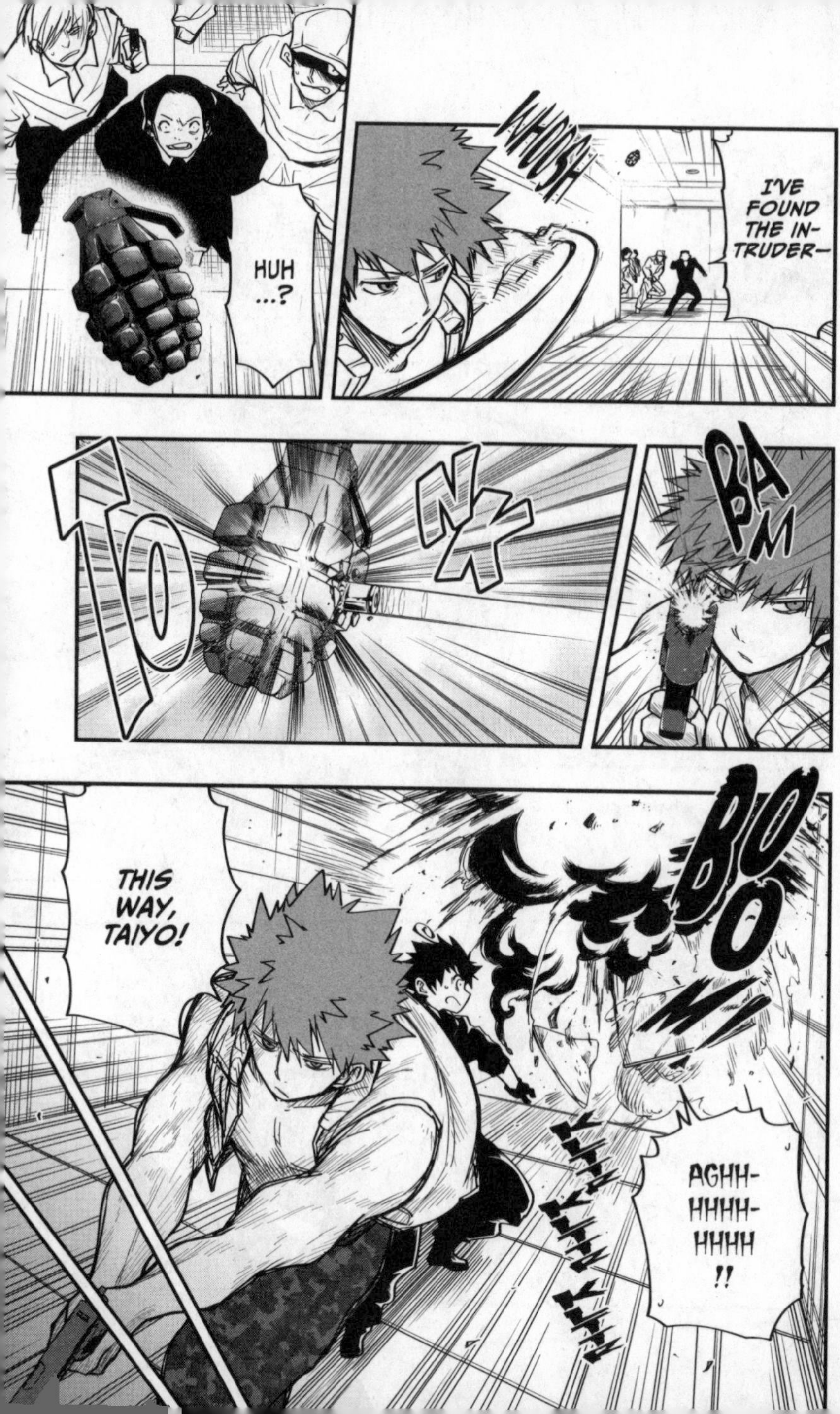
WHOOSH
I'VE FOUND THE IN-TRUDER—
HUH ...?
BAM
TONK
BOOM!
THIS WAY, TAIYO!
AGHH-HHHH-HHHH!!

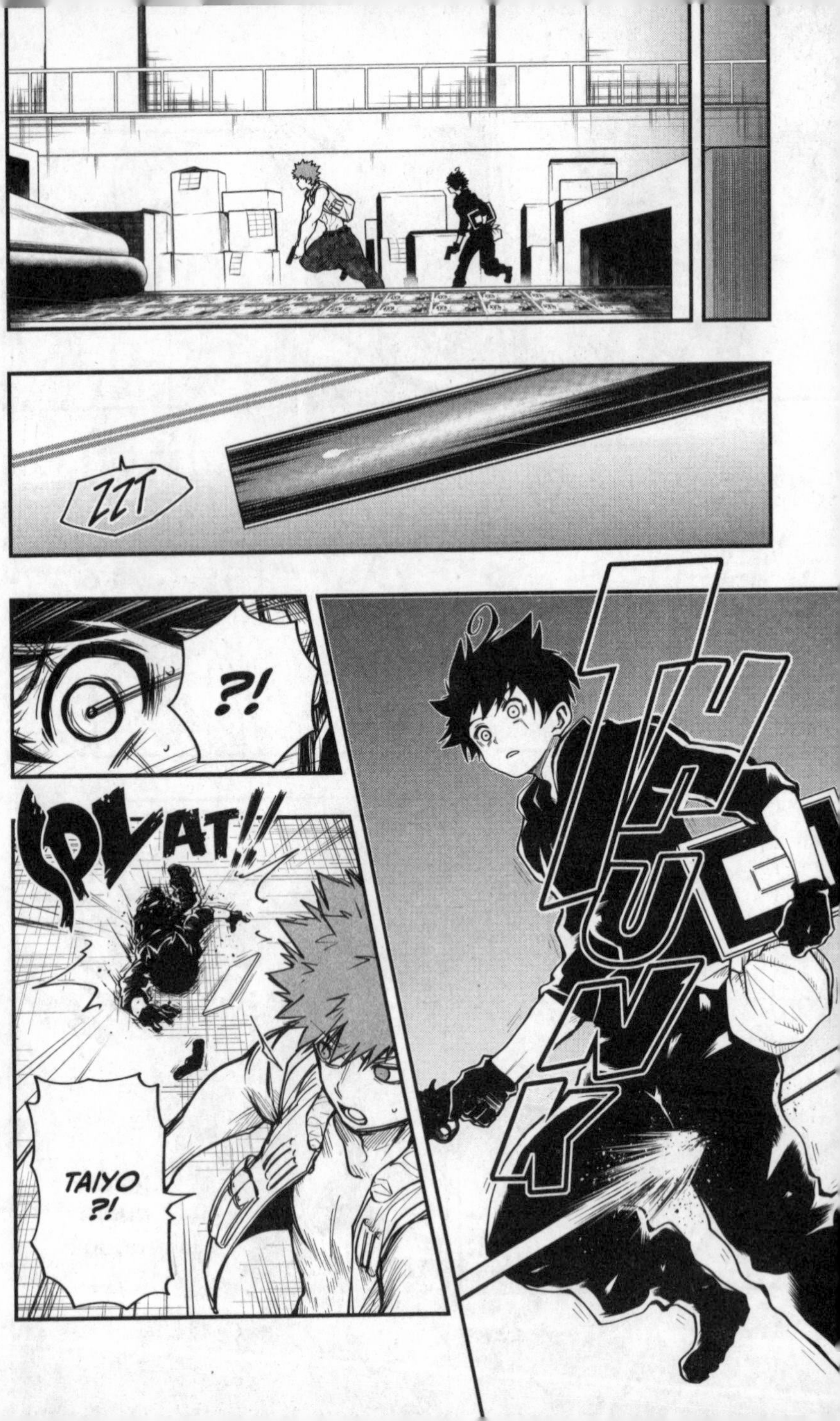
ZZT
THUNK
?!
SPLAT!!
TAIYO ?!

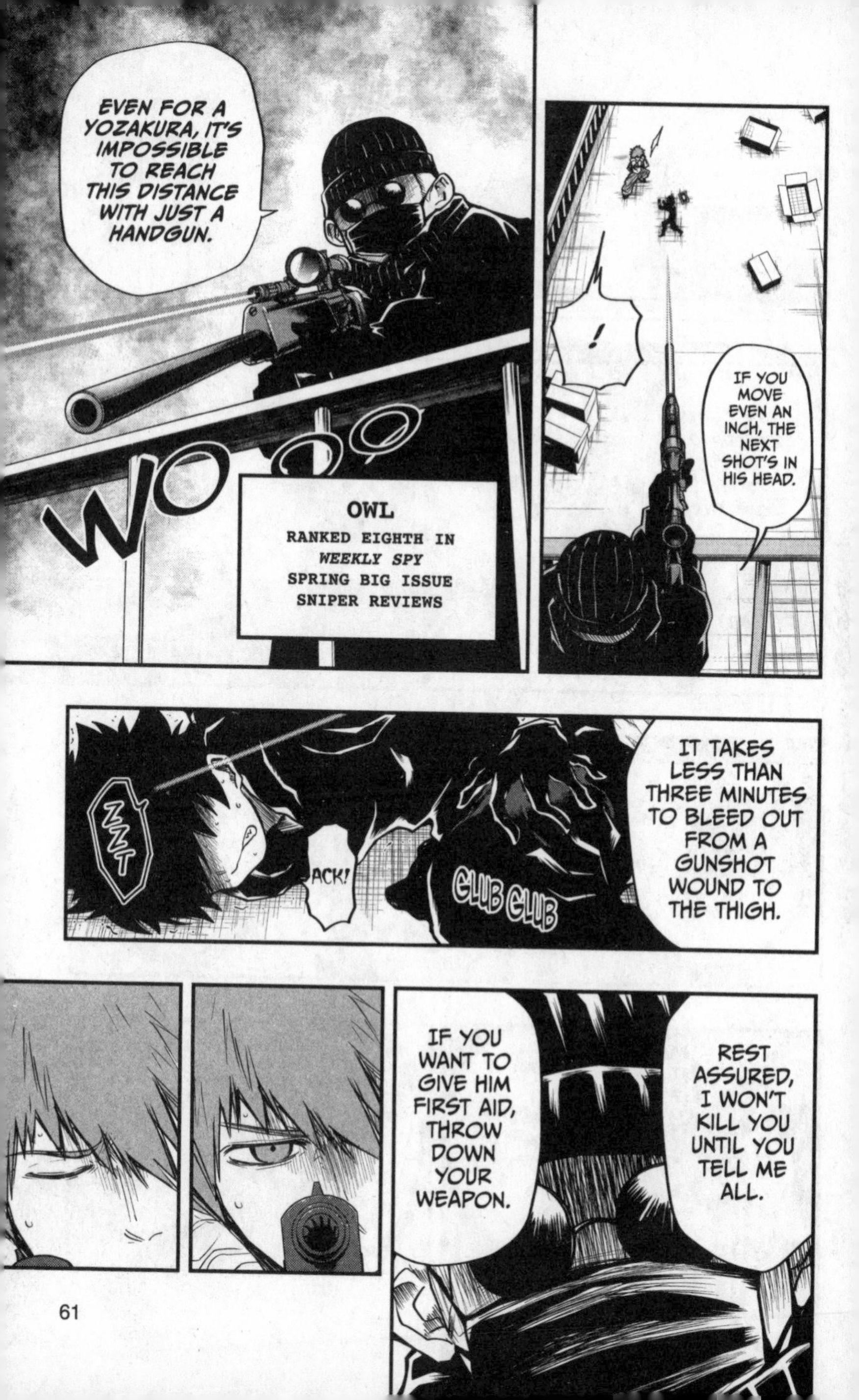
!
IF YOU MOVE EVEN AN INCH, THE NEXT SHOT'S IN HIS HEAD.
EVEN FOR A YOZAKURA, IT'S IMPOSSIBLE TO REACH THIS DISTANCE WITH JUST A HANDGUN.
WOOO
OWL
RANKED EIGHTH IN *WEEKLY SPY* SPRING BIG ISSUE SNIPER REVIEWS
IT TAKES LESS THAN THREE MINUTES TO BLEED OUT FROM A GUNSHOT WOUND TO THE THIGH.
ZZZT
ACK!
CLUB CLUB
REST ASSURED, I WON'T KILL YOU UNTIL YOU TELL ME ALL.
IF YOU WANT TO GIVE HIM FIRST AID, THROW DOWN YOUR WEAPON.

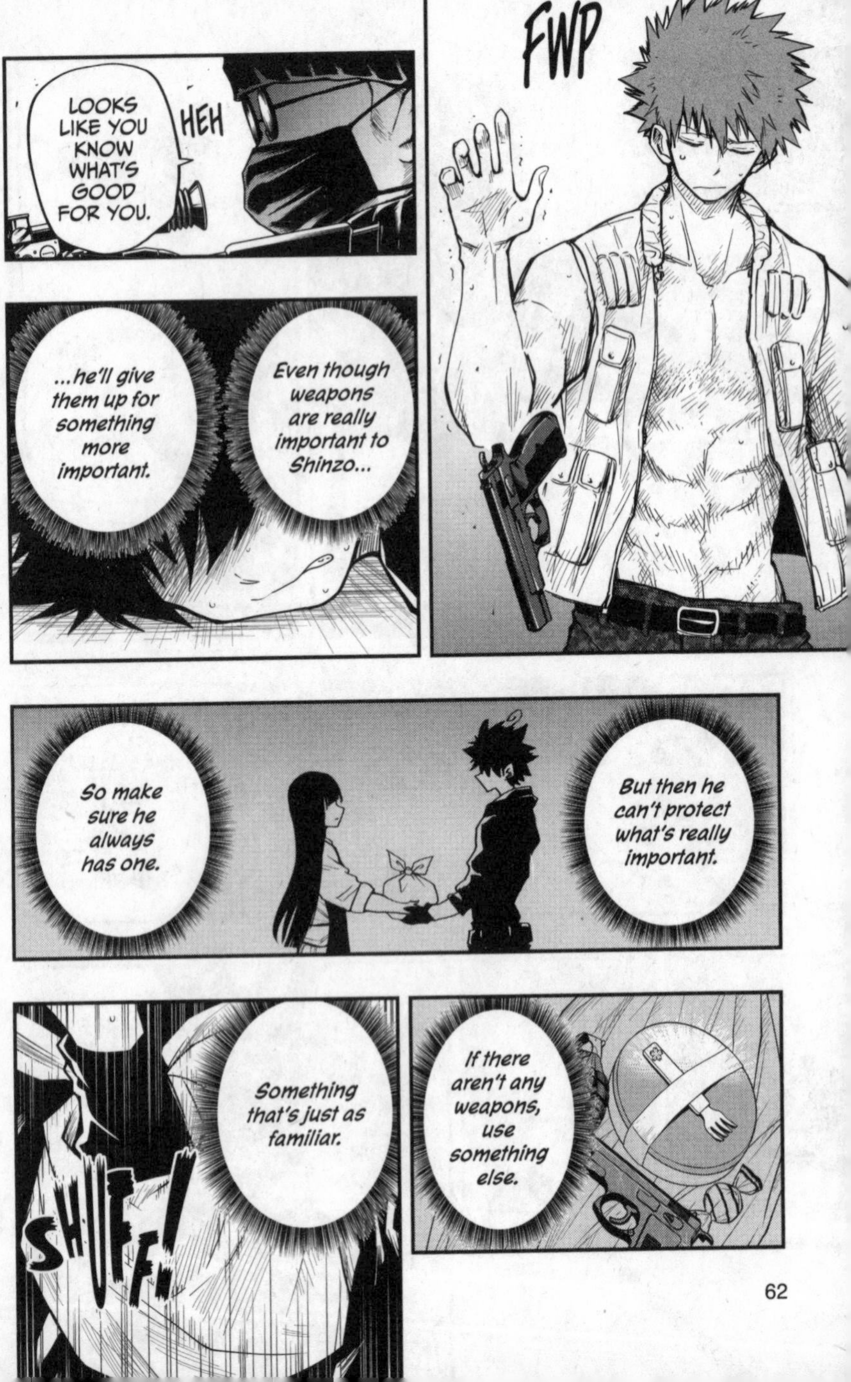
FWP
LOOKS LIKE YOU KNOW WHAT'S GOOD FOR YOU.
HEH
Even though weapons are really important to Shinzo...
...he'll give them up for something more important.
But then he can't protect what's really important.
So make sure he always has one.
If there aren't any weapons, use something else.
Something that's just as familiar.
SHUF!

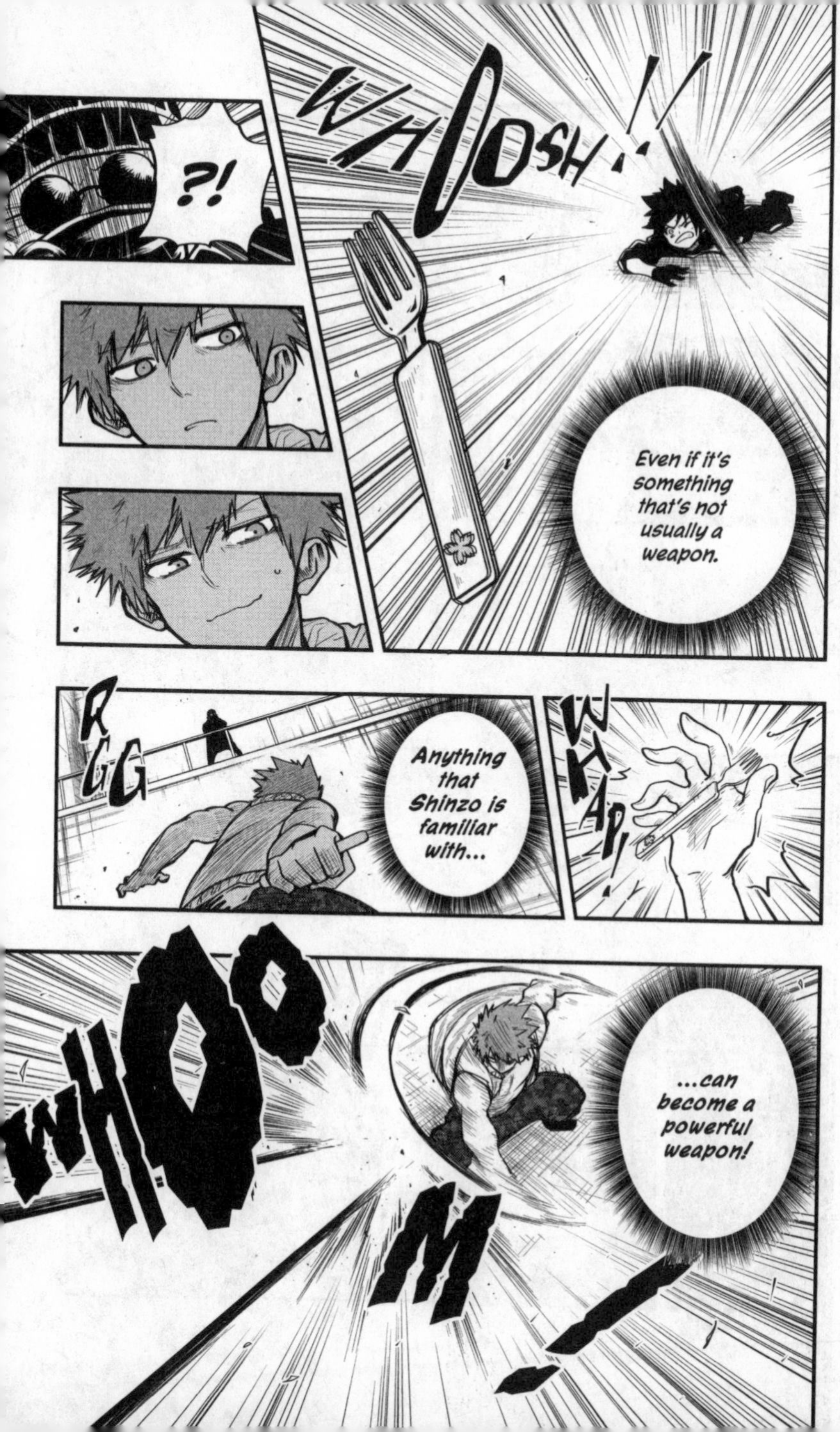
WHOOSH!!
Even if it's something that's not usually a weapon.
?!
WHAP!
Anything that Shinzo is familiar with...
RGG
...can become a powerful weapon!
WHOOM!

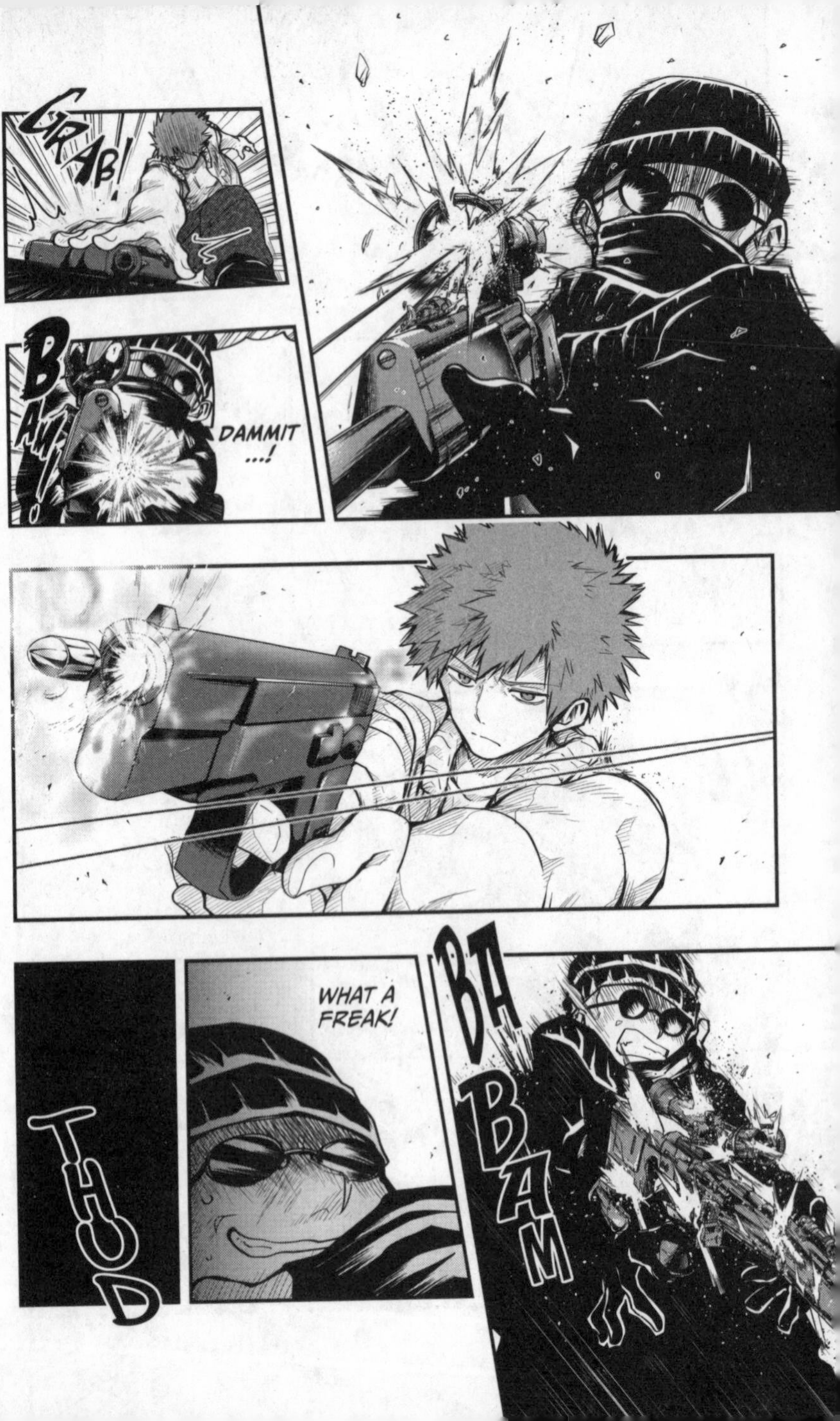
GRAB!
BAM!
DAMMIT ...!
BA BAM
WHAT A FREAK!
THUD

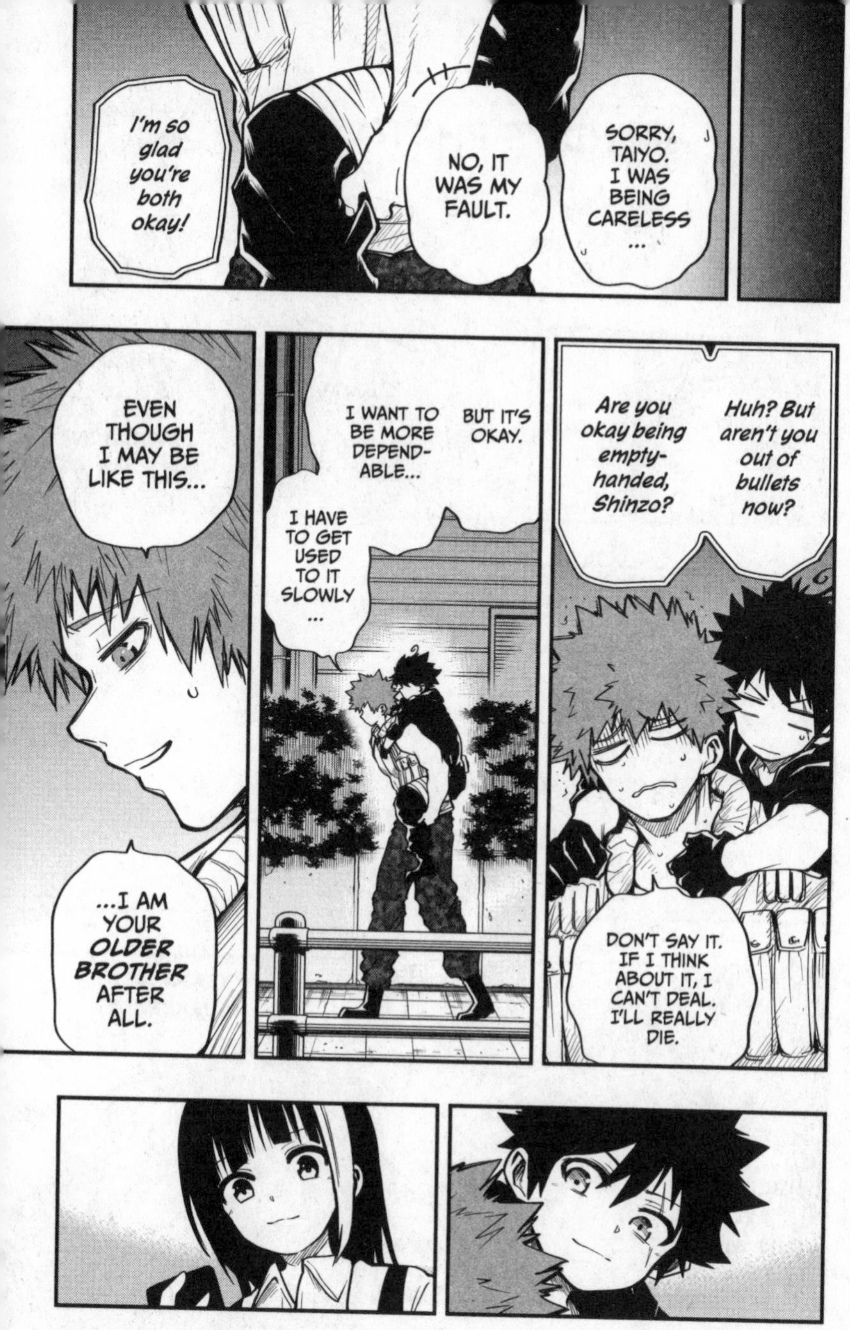
SORRY, TAIYO. I WAS BEING CARELESS ...
NO, IT WAS MY FAULT.
I'm so glad you're both okay!
Huh? But aren't you out of bullets now?
Are you okay being empty-handed, Shinzo?
DON'T SAY IT. IF I THINK ABOUT IT, I CAN'T DEAL. I'LL REALLY DIE.
BUT IT'S OKAY.
I WANT TO BE MORE DEPENDABLE...
I HAVE TO GET USED TO IT SLOWLY ...
EVEN THOUGH I MAY BE LIKE THIS...
...I AM YOUR OLDER BROTHER AFTER ALL.

SHINZO'S PHOTO ALBUM

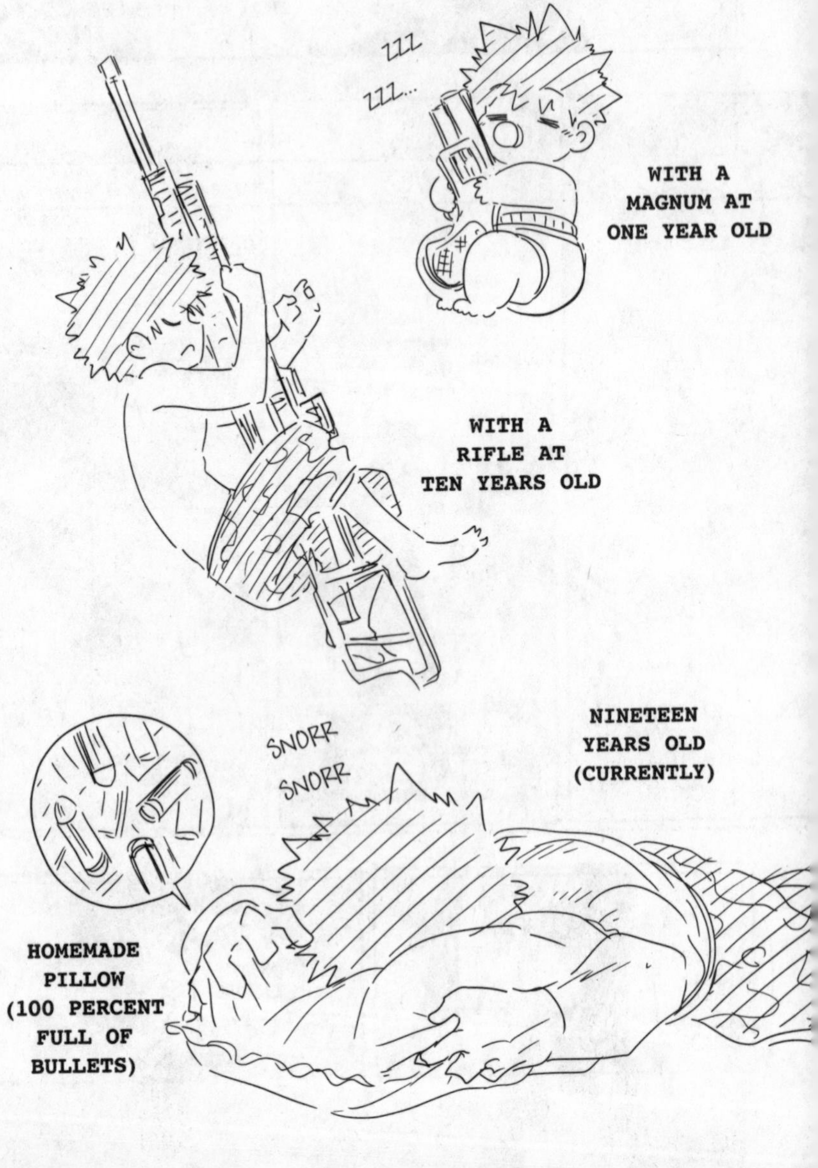
ZZZ
ZZZ...
WITH A MAGNUM AT ONE YEAR OLD
WITH A RIFLE AT TEN YEARS OLD
NINETEEN YEARS OLD (CURRENTLY)
SNORR
SNORR
HOMEMADE PILLOW (100 PERCENT FULL OF BULLETS)

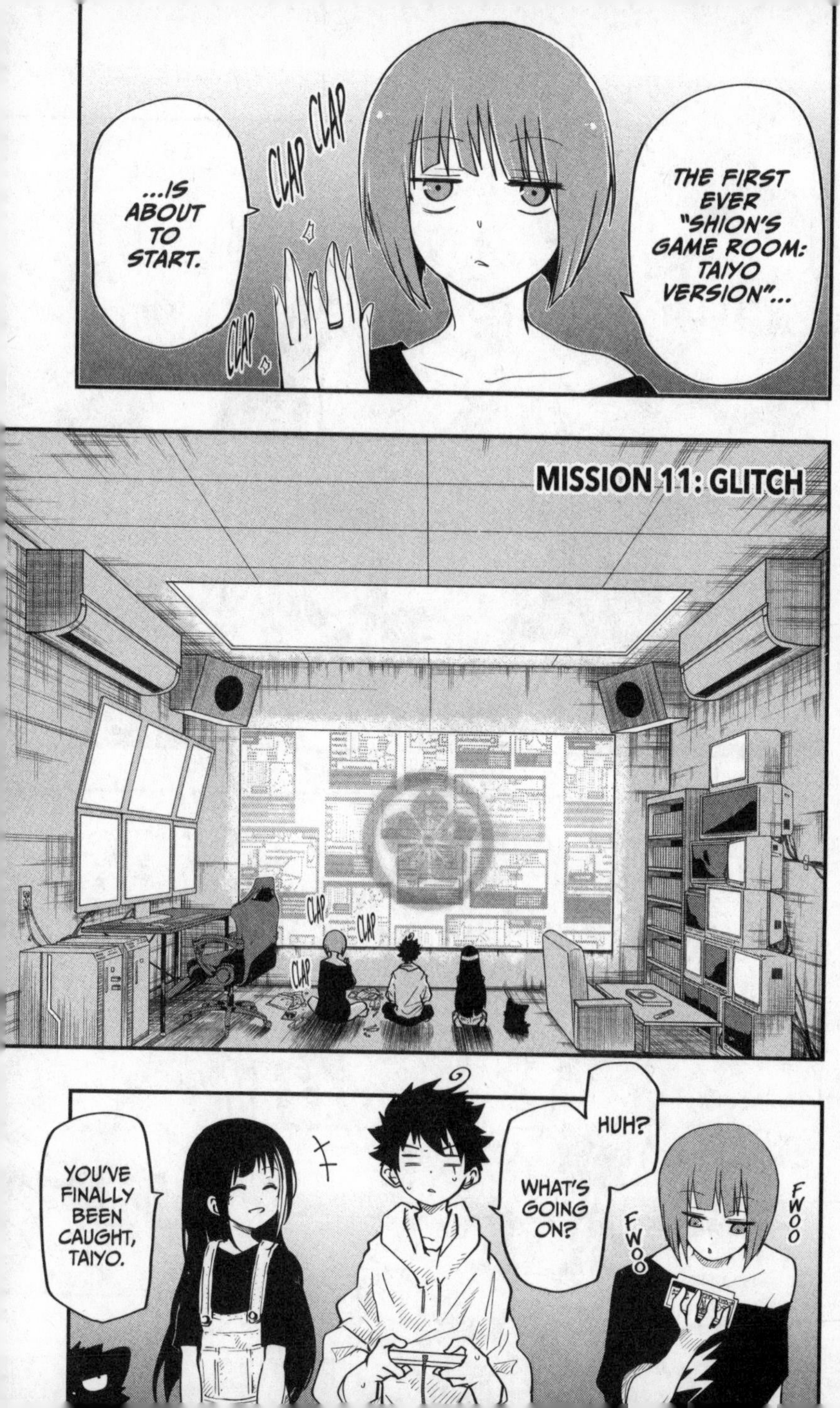
THE FIRST EVER "SHION'S GAME ROOM: TAIYO VERSION"...
CLAP CLAP
CLAP
...IS ABOUT TO START.
MISSION 11: GLITCH
CLAP
CLAP
CLAP
FWOO
FWOO
HUH?
WHAT'S GOING ON?
YOU'VE FINALLY BEEN CAUGHT, TAIYO.

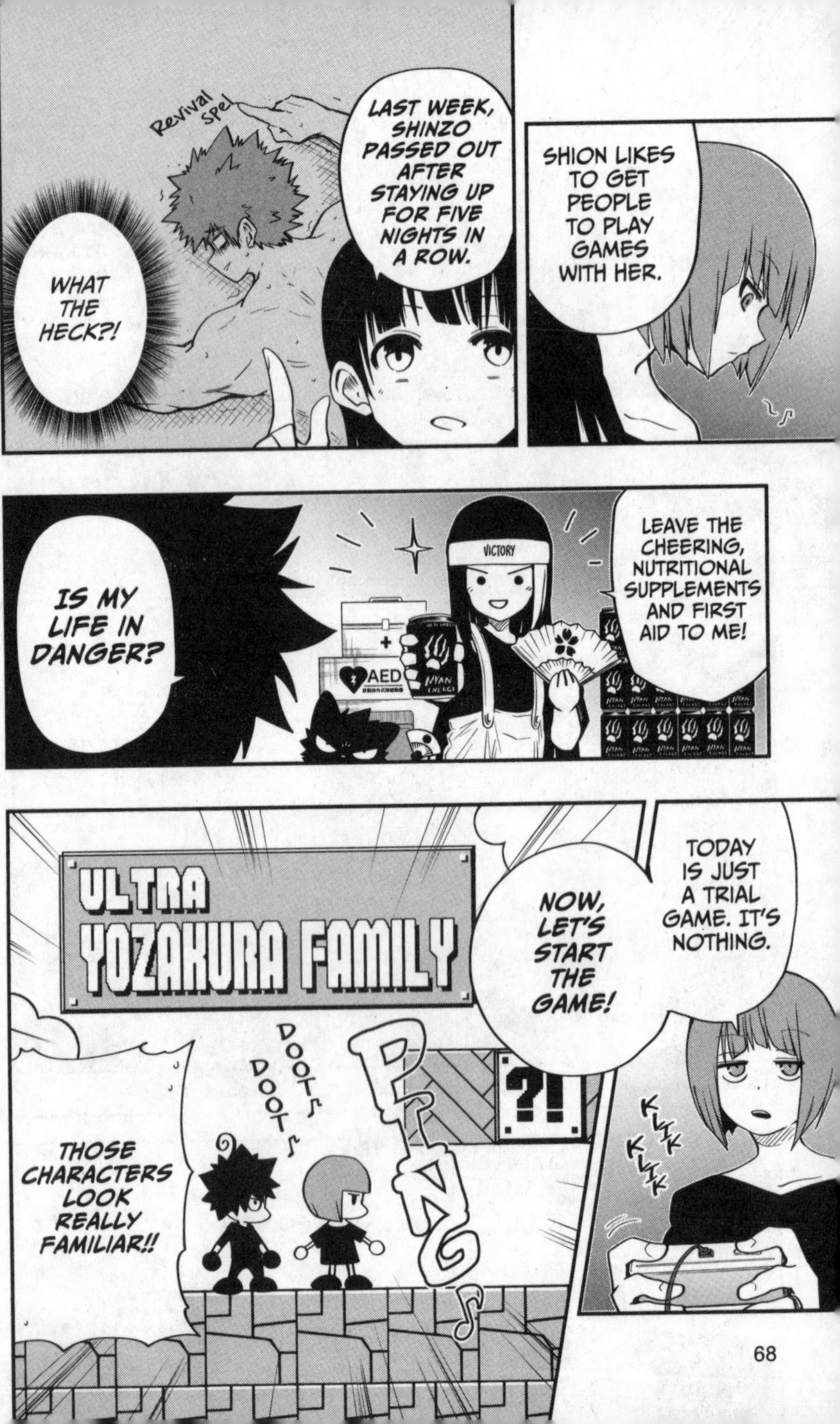
SHION LIKES TO GET PEOPLE TO PLAY GAMES WITH HER.
LAST WEEK, SHINZO PASSED OUT AFTER STAYING UP FOR FIVE NIGHTS IN A ROW.
Revival Spel
WHAT THE HECK?!
LEAVE THE CHEERING, NUTRITIONAL SUPPLEMENTS AND FIRST AID TO ME!
VICTORY
AED
NYAN ENERGY
IS MY LIFE IN DANGER?
TODAY IS JUST A TRIAL GAME. IT'S NOTHING.
KLIK KLIK
NOW, LET'S START THE GAME!
ULTRA YOZAKURA FAMILY
?!
DOOT DOOT
PLING
THOSE CHARACTERS LOOK REALLY FAMILIAR!!

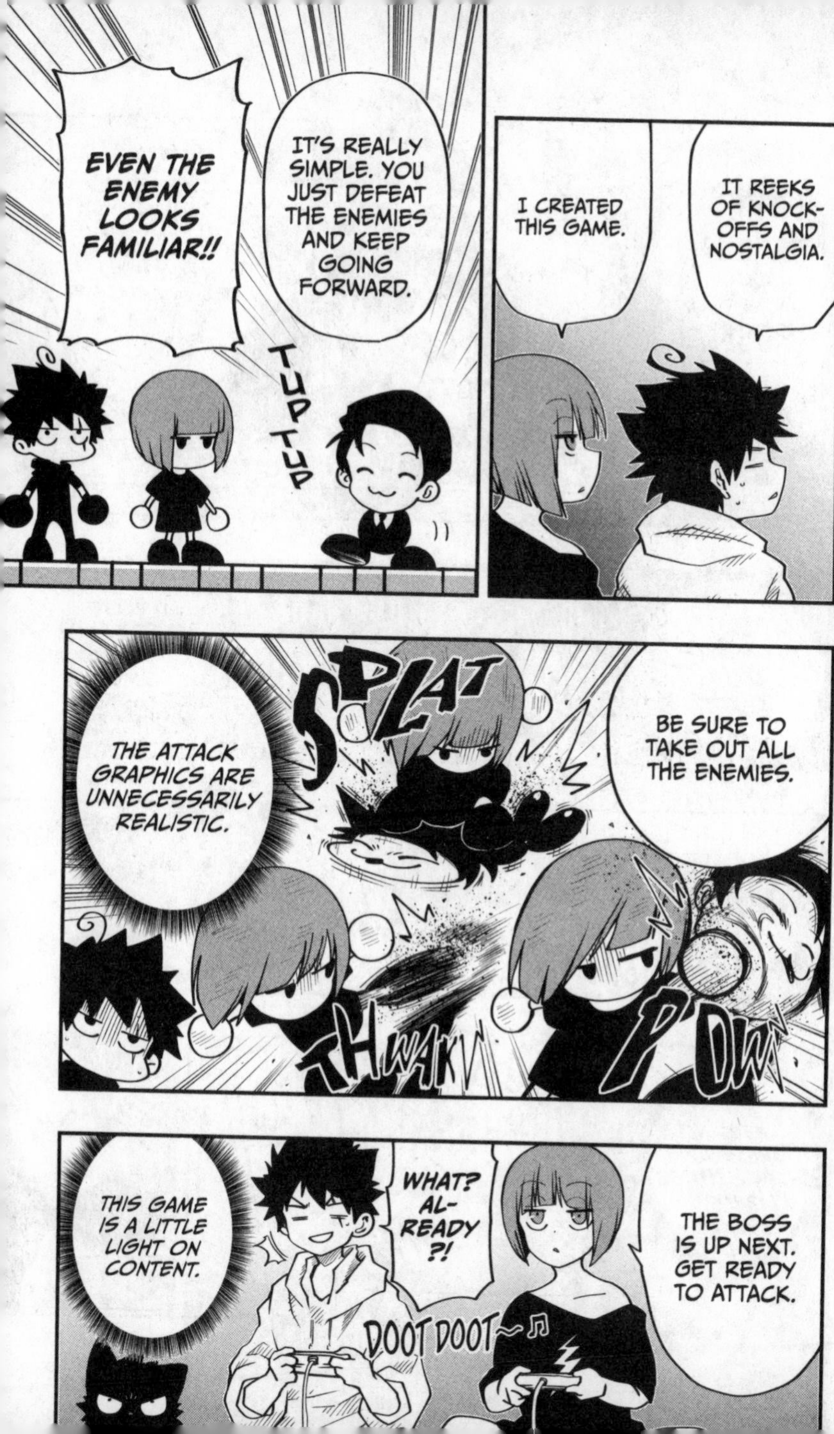
IT REEKS OF KNOCK-OFFS AND NOSTALGIA.
I CREATED THIS GAME.
IT'S REALLY SIMPLE. YOU JUST DEFEAT THE ENEMIES AND KEEP GOING FORWARD.
TUP TUP
EVEN THE ENEMY LOOKS FAMILIAR!!
BE SURE TO TAKE OUT ALL THE ENEMIES.
SPLAT
POW
THWAK
THE ATTACK GRAPHICS ARE UNNECESSARILY REALISTIC.
THE BOSS IS UP NEXT. GET READY TO ATTACK.
DOOT DOOT~♫
WHAT? AL-READY?!
THIS GAME IS A LITTLE LIGHT ON CONTENT.

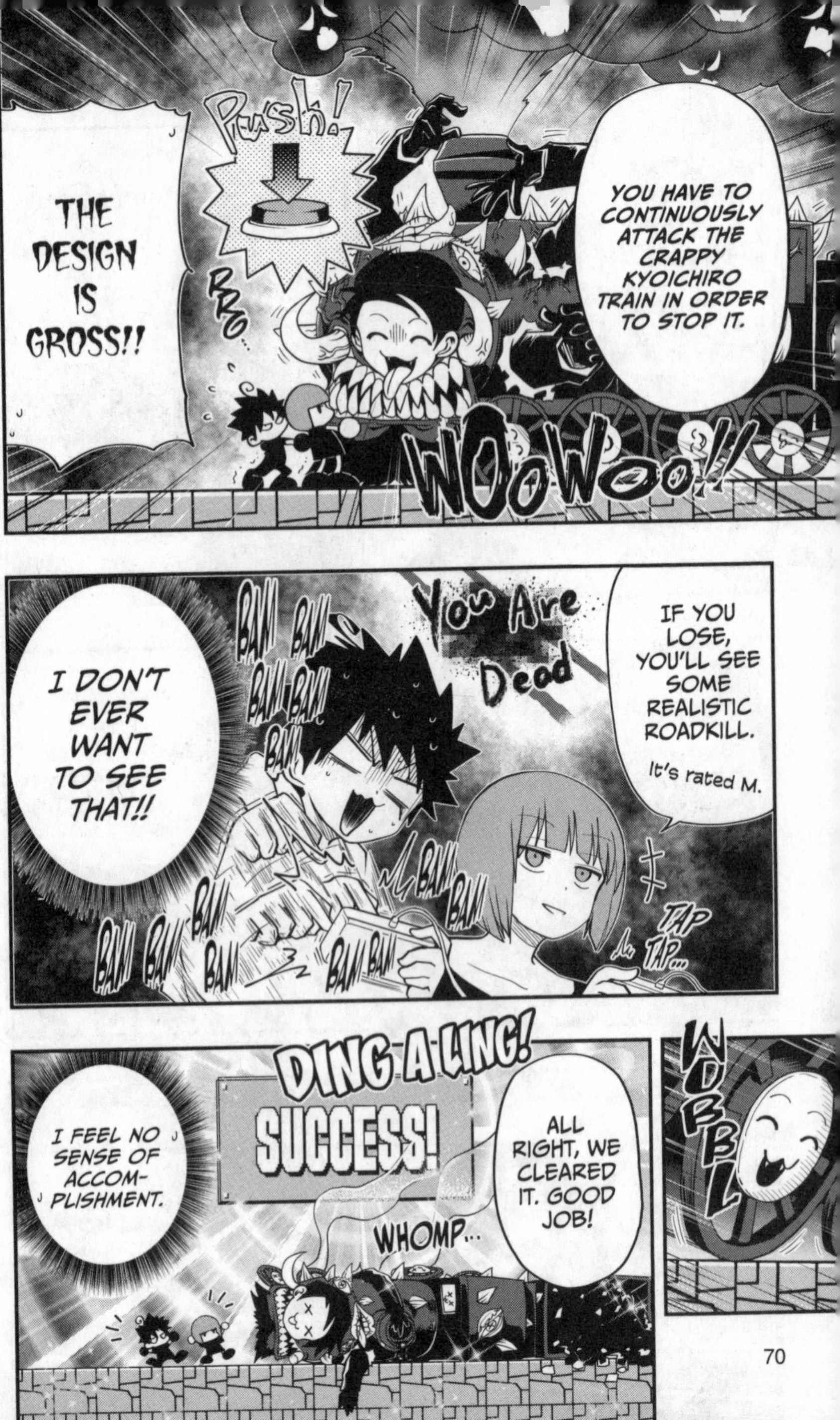

YOU HAVE TO CONTINUOUSLY ATTACK THE CRAPPY KYOICHIRO TRAIN IN ORDER TO STOP IT.
Push!
RRG...
THE DESIGN IS GROSS!!
WOOWOO!!
IF YOU LOSE, YOU'LL SEE SOME REALISTIC ROADKILL.
It's rated M.
You Are Dead
BAM BAM BAM BAM BAM
I DON'T EVER WANT TO SEE THAT!!
BAM BAM BAM BAM BAM BAM BAM BAM BAM
TAP TAP...
WOBBL
DING A LING!
ALL RIGHT, WE CLEARED IT. GOOD JOB!
SUCCESS!
I FEEL NO SENSE OF ACCOM-PLISHMENT.
WHOMP...

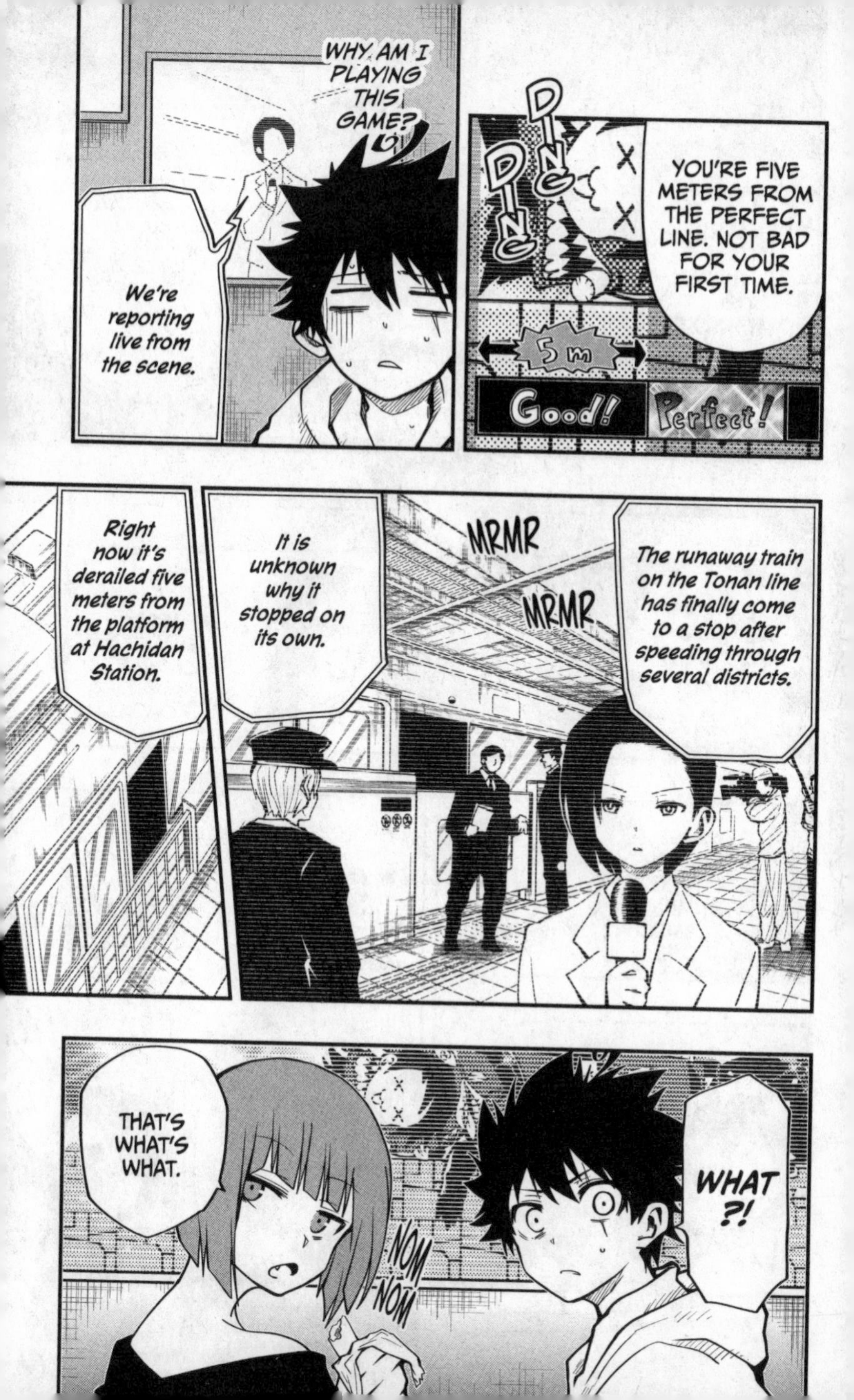
DING
DING
YOU'RE FIVE METERS FROM THE PERFECT LINE. NOT BAD FOR YOUR FIRST TIME.
5 m
Good!
Perfect!
WHY AM I PLAYING THIS GAME?
We're reporting live from the scene.
The runaway train on the Tonan line has finally come to a stop after speeding through several districts.
MRMR
MRMR
It is unknown why it stopped on its own.
Right now it's derailed five meters from the platform at Hachidan Station.
WHAT?!
NOM
NOM
THAT'S WHAT'S WHAT.

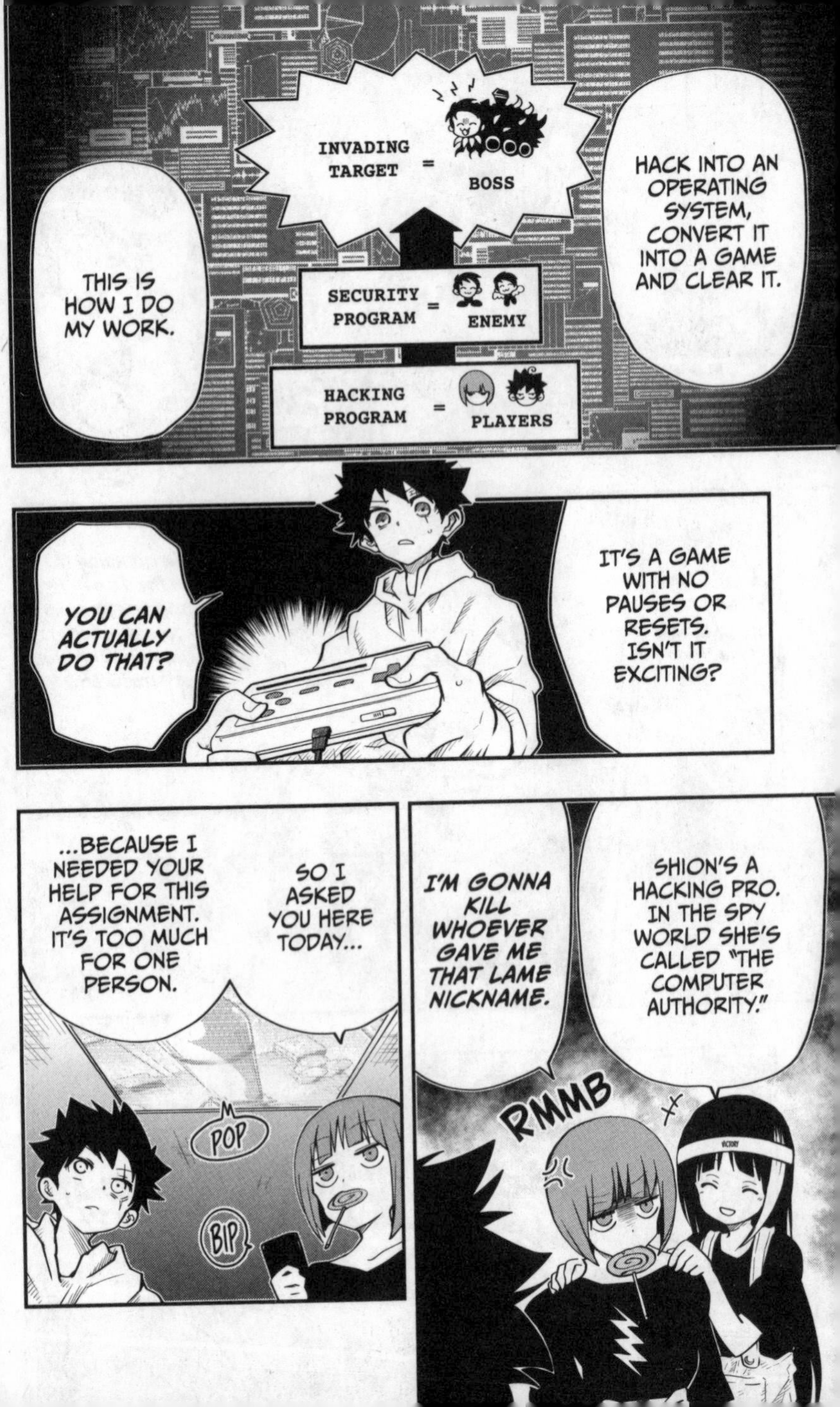
HACK INTO AN OPERATING SYSTEM, CONVERT IT INTO A GAME AND CLEAR IT.
INVADING TARGET = BOSS
SECURITY PROGRAM = ENEMY
HACKING PROGRAM = PLAYERS
THIS IS HOW I DO MY WORK.
IT'S A GAME WITH NO PAUSES OR RESETS. ISN'T IT EXCITING?
YOU CAN ACTUALLY DO THAT?
SHION'S A HACKING PRO. IN THE SPY WORLD SHE'S CALLED "THE COMPUTER AUTHORITY."
I'M GONNA KILL WHOEVER GAVE ME THAT LAME NICKNAME.
RMMB
SO I ASKED YOU HERE TODAY...
...BECAUSE I NEEDED YOUR HELP FOR THIS ASSIGNMENT. IT'S TOO MUCH FOR ONE PERSON.
POP
BIP

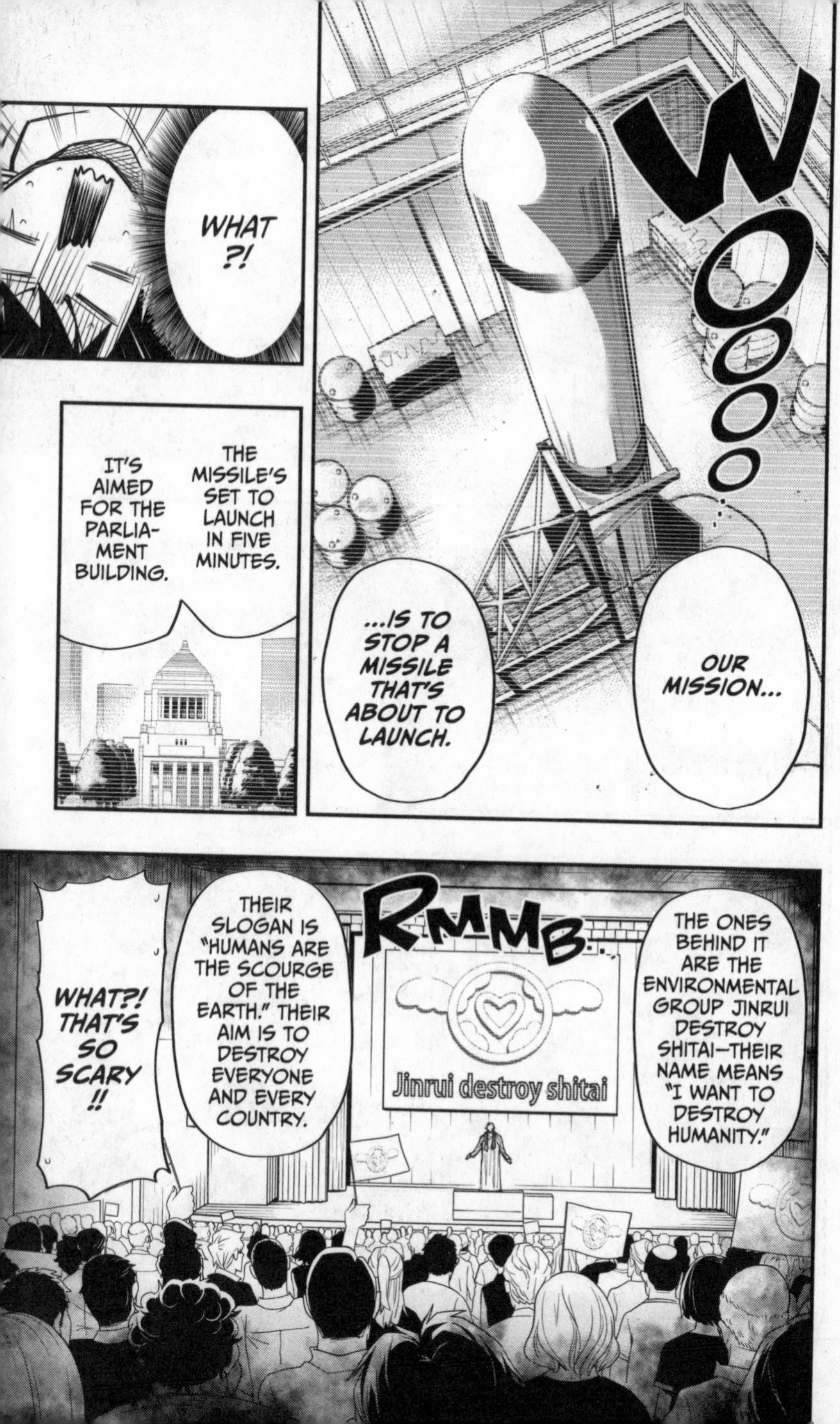
WOOOOO
OUR MISSION...
...IS TO STOP A MISSILE THAT'S ABOUT TO LAUNCH.
WHAT ?!
THE MISSILE'S SET TO LAUNCH IN FIVE MINUTES.
IT'S AIMED FOR THE PARLIAMENT BUILDING.
THE ONES BEHIND IT ARE THE ENVIRONMENTAL GROUP JINRUI DESTROY SHITAI—THEIR NAME MEANS "I WANT TO DESTROY HUMANITY."
RMMB
Jinrui destroy shitai
THEIR SLOGAN IS "HUMANS ARE THE SCOURGE OF THE EARTH." THEIR AIM IS TO DESTROY EVERYONE AND EVERY COUNTRY.
WHAT?! THAT'S SO SCARY!!

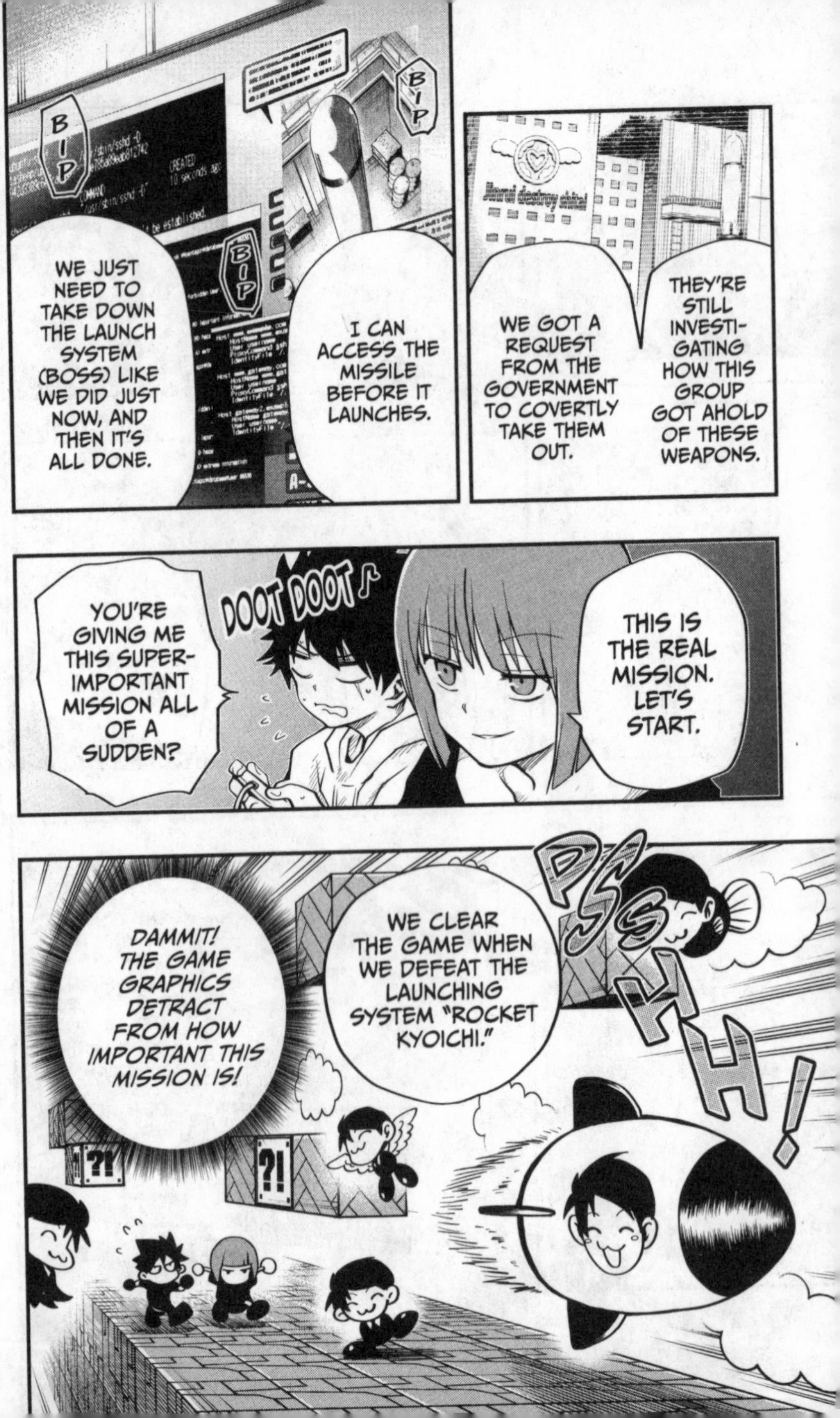
THEY'RE STILL INVESTIGATING HOW THIS GROUP GOT AHOLD OF THESE WEAPONS.
WE GOT A REQUEST FROM THE GOVERNMENT TO COVERTLY TAKE THEM OUT.
BIP
BIP
I CAN ACCESS THE MISSILE BEFORE IT LAUNCHES.
BIP
WE JUST NEED TO TAKE DOWN THE LAUNCH SYSTEM (BOSS) LIKE WE DID JUST NOW, AND THEN IT'S ALL DONE.
THIS IS THE REAL MISSION. LET'S START.
DOOT DOOT ♪
YOU'RE GIVING ME THIS SUPER-IMPORTANT MISSION ALL OF A SUDDEN?
PSSHH!
WE CLEAR THE GAME WHEN WE DEFEAT THE LAUNCHING SYSTEM "ROCKET KYOICHI."
DAMMIT! THE GAME GRAPHICS DETRACT FROM HOW IMPORTANT THIS MISSION IS!
?!
?!

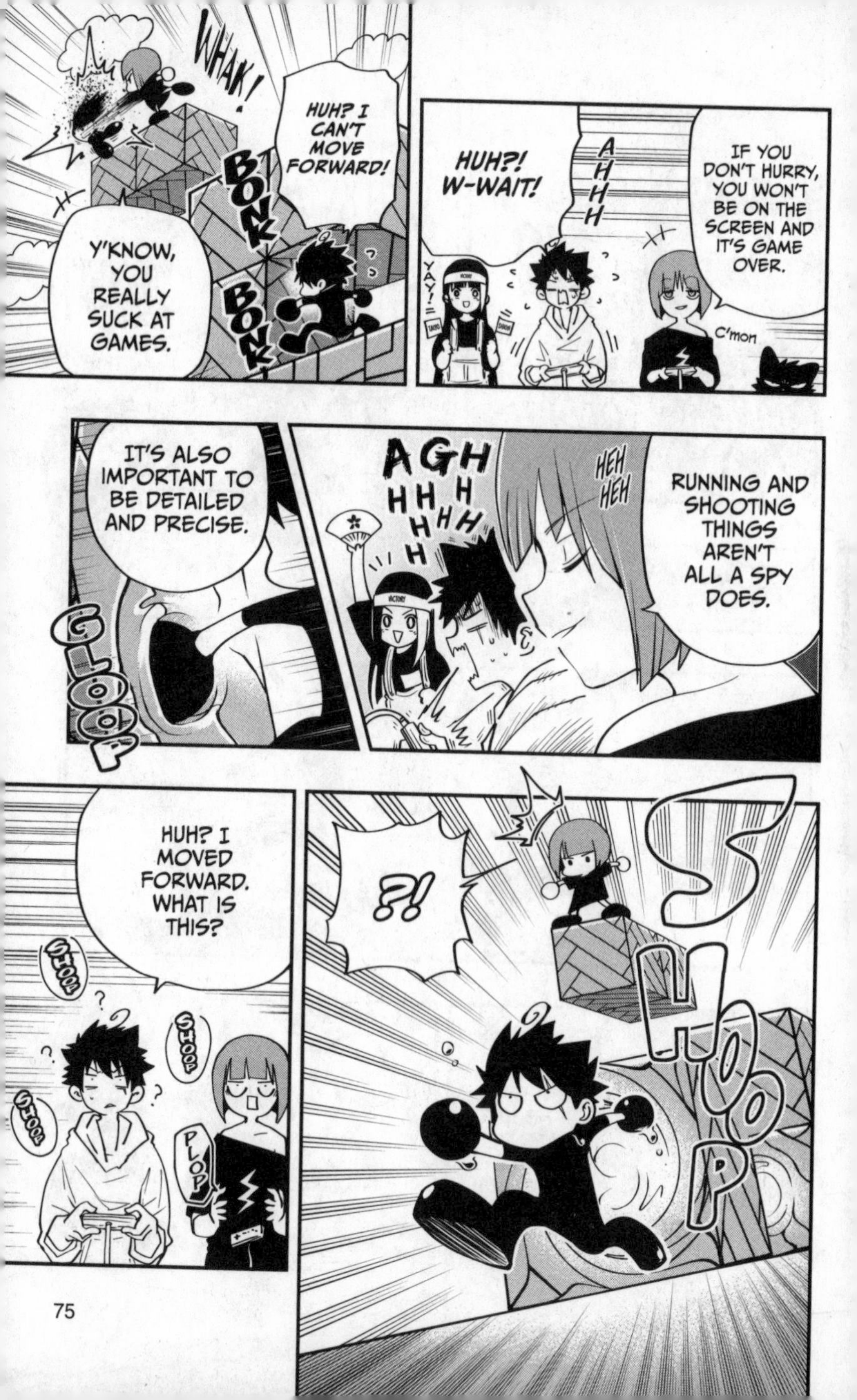

IF YOU DON'T HURRY, YOU WON'T BE ON THE SCREEN AND IT'S GAME OVER.
AHHHH
HUH?! W-WAIT!
YAY!
C'mon
WHAK!
HUH? I CAN'T MOVE FORWARD!
BONK
BONK
Y'KNOW, YOU REALLY SUCK AT GAMES.
RUNNING AND SHOOTING THINGS AREN'T ALL A SPY DOES.
HEH HEH
AGHHHHHHHH
IT'S ALSO IMPORTANT TO BE DETAILED AND PRECISE.
GLOOP
SHOOP
?!
HUH? I MOVED FORWARD. WHAT IS THIS?
SHOOP
SHOOP
SHOOP
PLOP

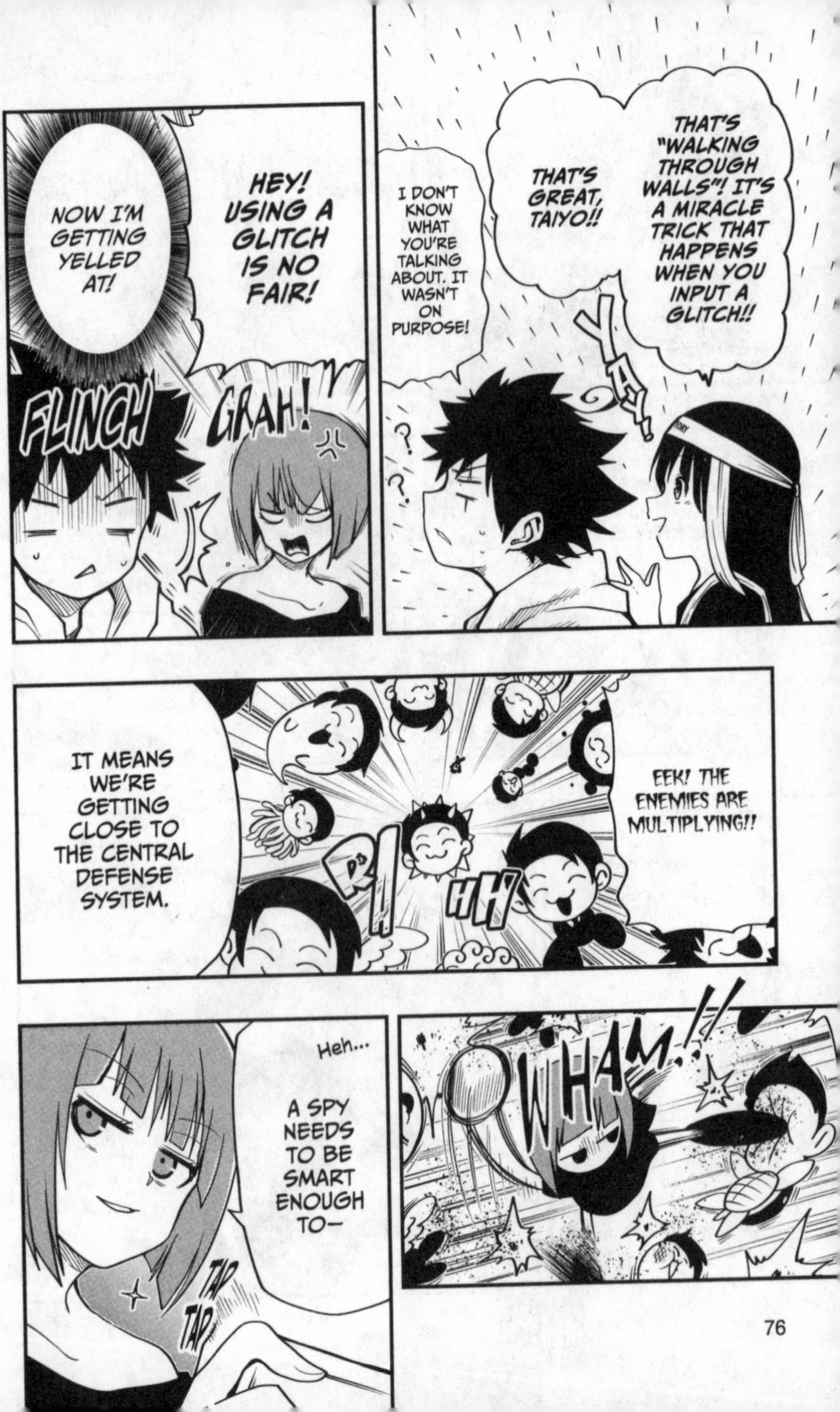
YAY
THAT'S GREAT, TAIYO!!
THAT'S "WALKING THROUGH WALLS"! IT'S A MIRACLE TRICK THAT HAPPENS WHEN YOU INPUT A GLITCH!!
I DON'T KNOW WHAT YOU'RE TALKING ABOUT. IT WASN'T ON PURPOSE!
HEY! USING A GLITCH IS NO FAIR!
GRAH!
NOW I'M GETTING YELLED AT!
FLINCH
EEK! THE ENEMIES ARE MULTIPLYING!!
IT MEANS WE'RE GETTING CLOSE TO THE CENTRAL DEFENSE SYSTEM.
WHAM!!
Heh...
A SPY NEEDS TO BE SMART ENOUGH TO—
TAP TAP

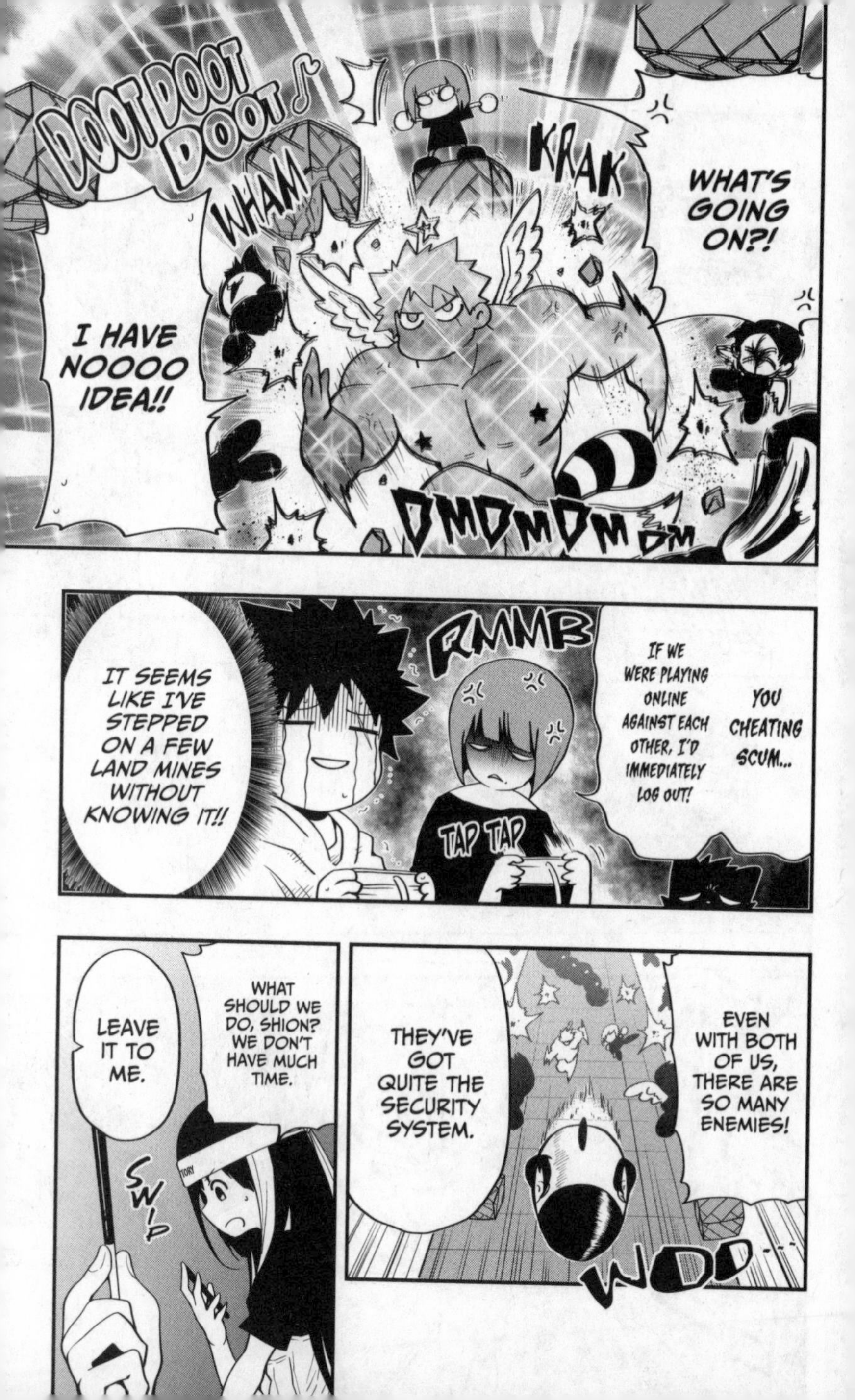
WHAT'S GOING ON?!
KRAK
DOOT DOOT DOOT♪
WHAM
I HAVE NOOOO IDEA!!
DMDMDMDMDM
YOU CHEATING SCUM...
IF WE WERE PLAYING ONLINE AGAINST EACH OTHER, I'D IMMEDIATELY LOG OUT!
RMMB
IT SEEMS LIKE I'VE STEPPED ON A FEW LAND MINES WITHOUT KNOWING IT!!
TAP TAP
EVEN WITH BOTH OF US, THERE ARE SO MANY ENEMIES!
THEY'VE GOT QUITE THE SECURITY SYSTEM.
WOO···
WHAT SHOULD WE DO, SHION? WE DON'T HAVE MUCH TIME.
LEAVE IT TO ME.
TORY
SWIP

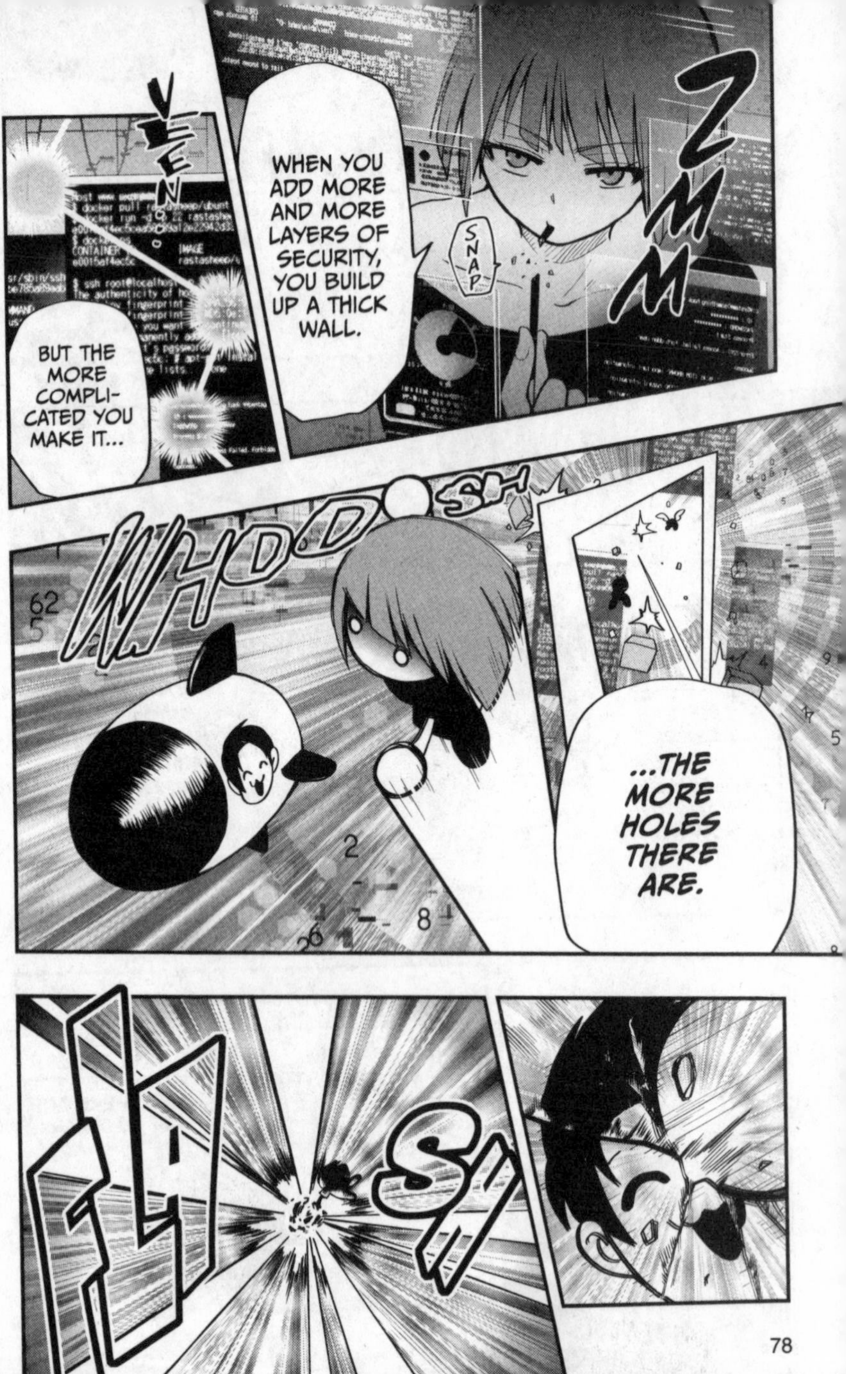
ZMMM
WHEN YOU ADD MORE AND MORE LAYERS OF SECURITY, YOU BUILD UP A THICK WALL.
SNAP
VEEN
BUT THE MORE COMPLI-CATED YOU MAKE IT...
WHOOSH
...THE MORE HOLES THERE ARE.
FLASH

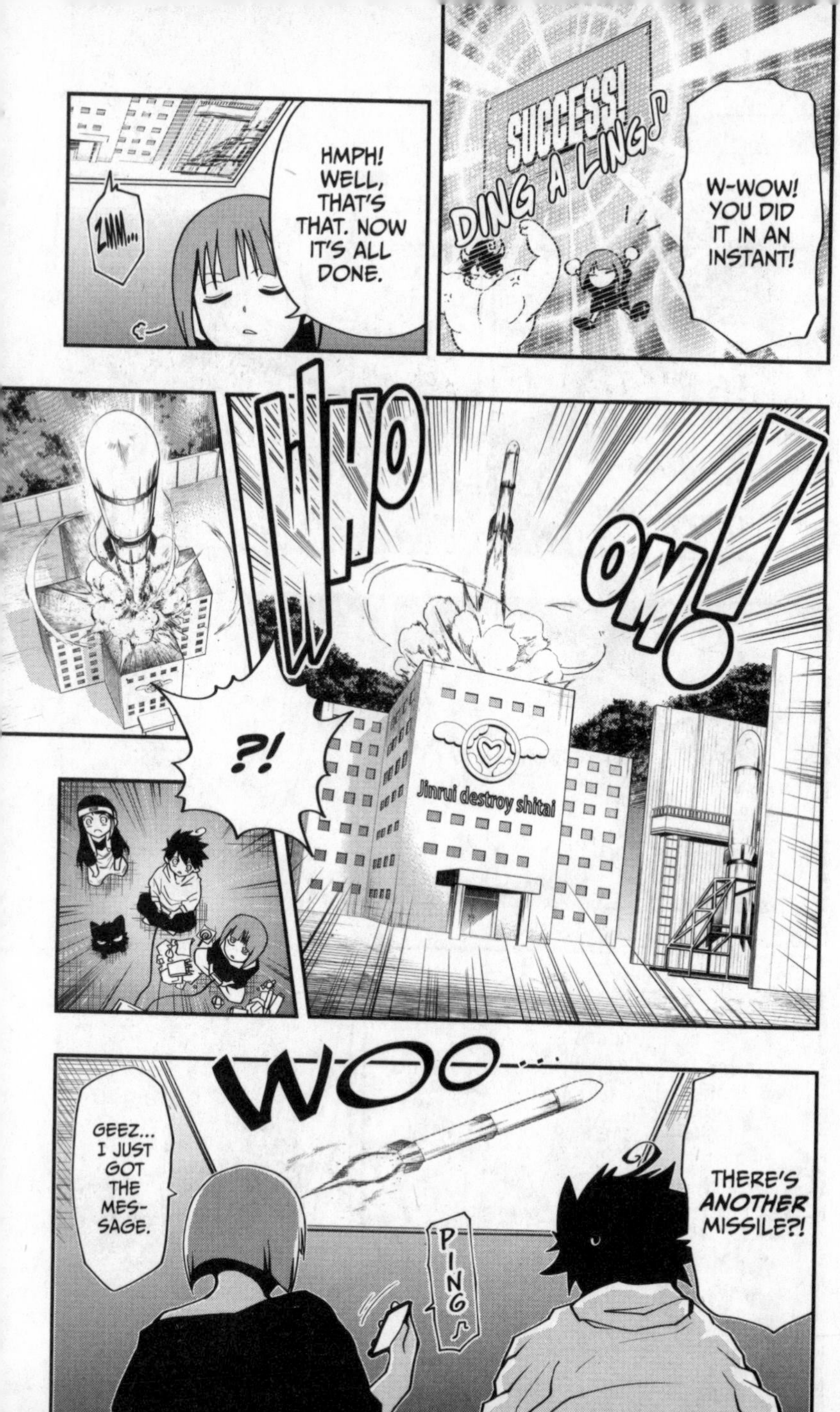
SUCCESS!
DING A LING♪
W-WOW! YOU DID IT IN AN INSTANT!
HMPH! WELL, THAT'S THAT. NOW IT'S ALL DONE.
ZMM...
WHOOM!
?!
Jinrui destroy shitai
WOO---
THERE'S ANOTHER MISSILE?!
GEEZ... I JUST GOT THE MES-SAGE.
PING♪

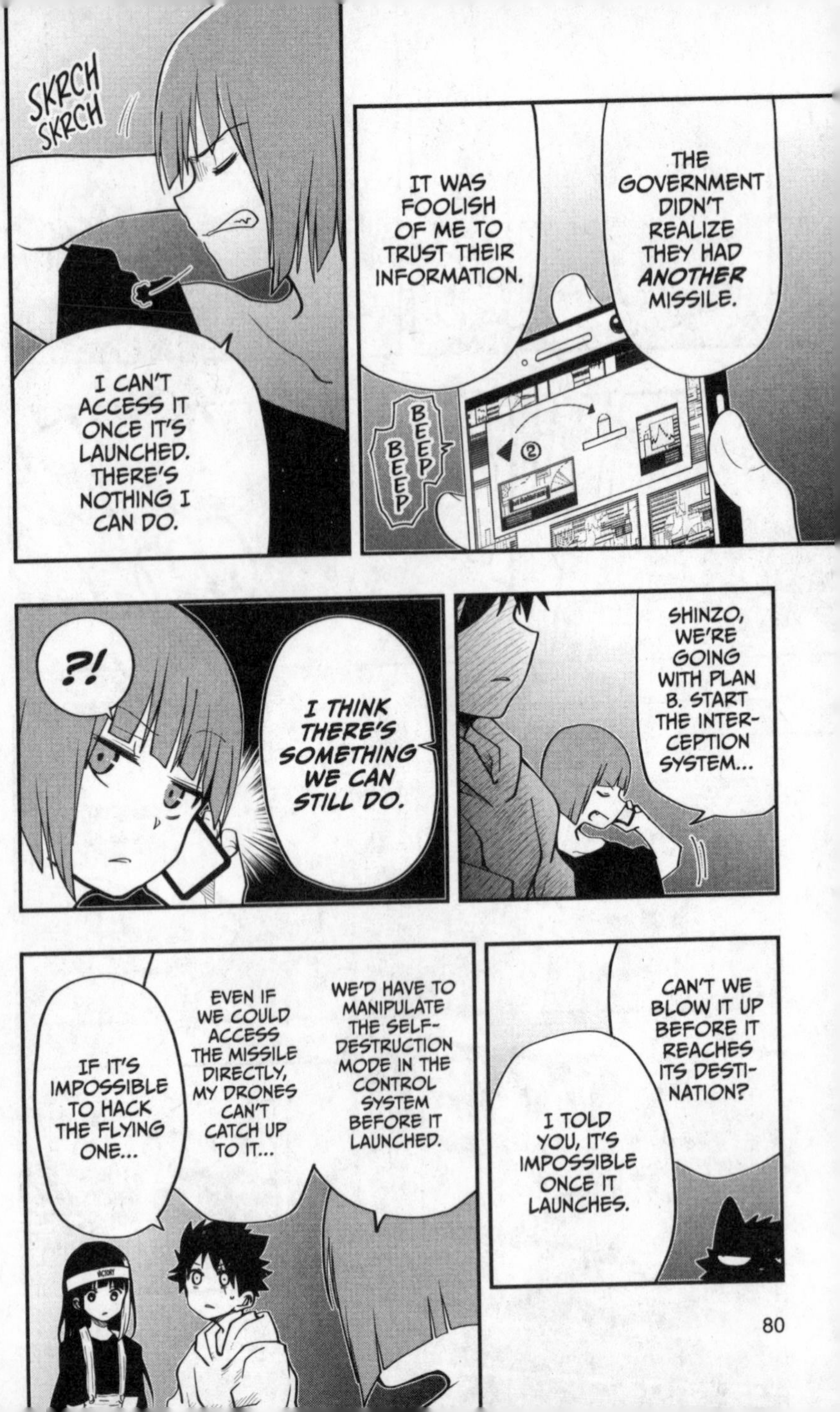
THE GOVERNMENT DIDN'T REALIZE THEY HAD *ANOTHER* MISSILE.
IT WAS FOOLISH OF ME TO TRUST THEIR INFORMATION.
BEEP BEEP
SKRCH SKRCH
I CAN'T ACCESS IT ONCE IT'S LAUNCHED. THERE'S NOTHING I CAN DO.
SHINZO, WE'RE GOING WITH PLAN B. START THE INTER-CEPTION SYSTEM...
I THINK THERE'S SOMETHING WE CAN STILL DO.
?!
CAN'T WE BLOW IT UP BEFORE IT REACHES ITS DESTI-NATION?
I TOLD YOU, IT'S IMPOSSIBLE ONCE IT LAUNCHES.
WE'D HAVE TO MANIPULATE THE SELF-DESTRUCTION MODE IN THE CONTROL SYSTEM BEFORE IT LAUNCHED.
EVEN IF WE COULD ACCESS THE MISSILE DIRECTLY, MY DRONES CAN'T CATCH UP TO IT...
IF IT'S IMPOSSIBLE TO HACK THE FLYING ONE...

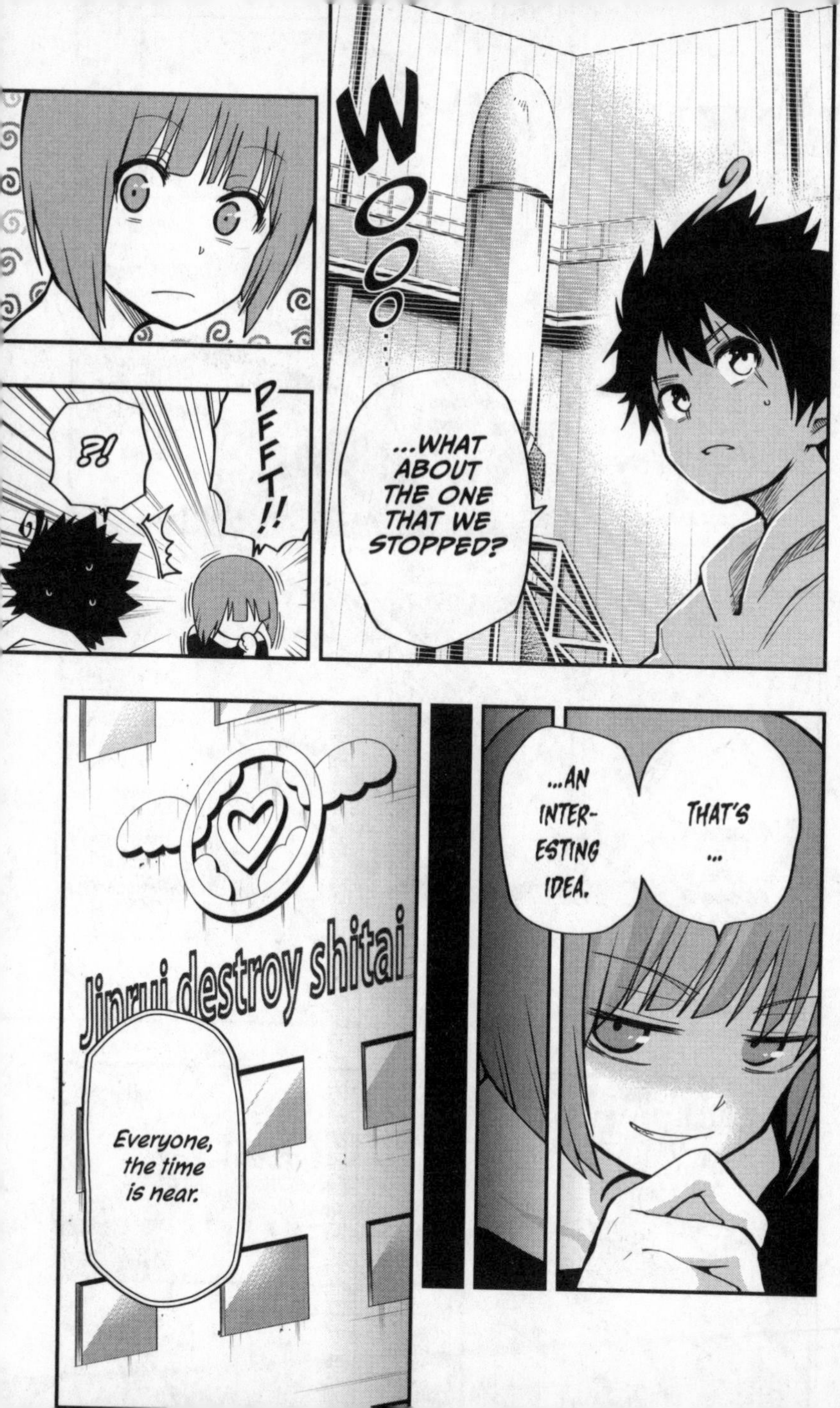
WOOO...
...WHAT ABOUT THE ONE THAT WE STOPPED?
?!
PFFT!!
THAT'S...
...AN INTER-ESTING IDEA.
Jinrui destroy shitai
Everyone, the time is near.

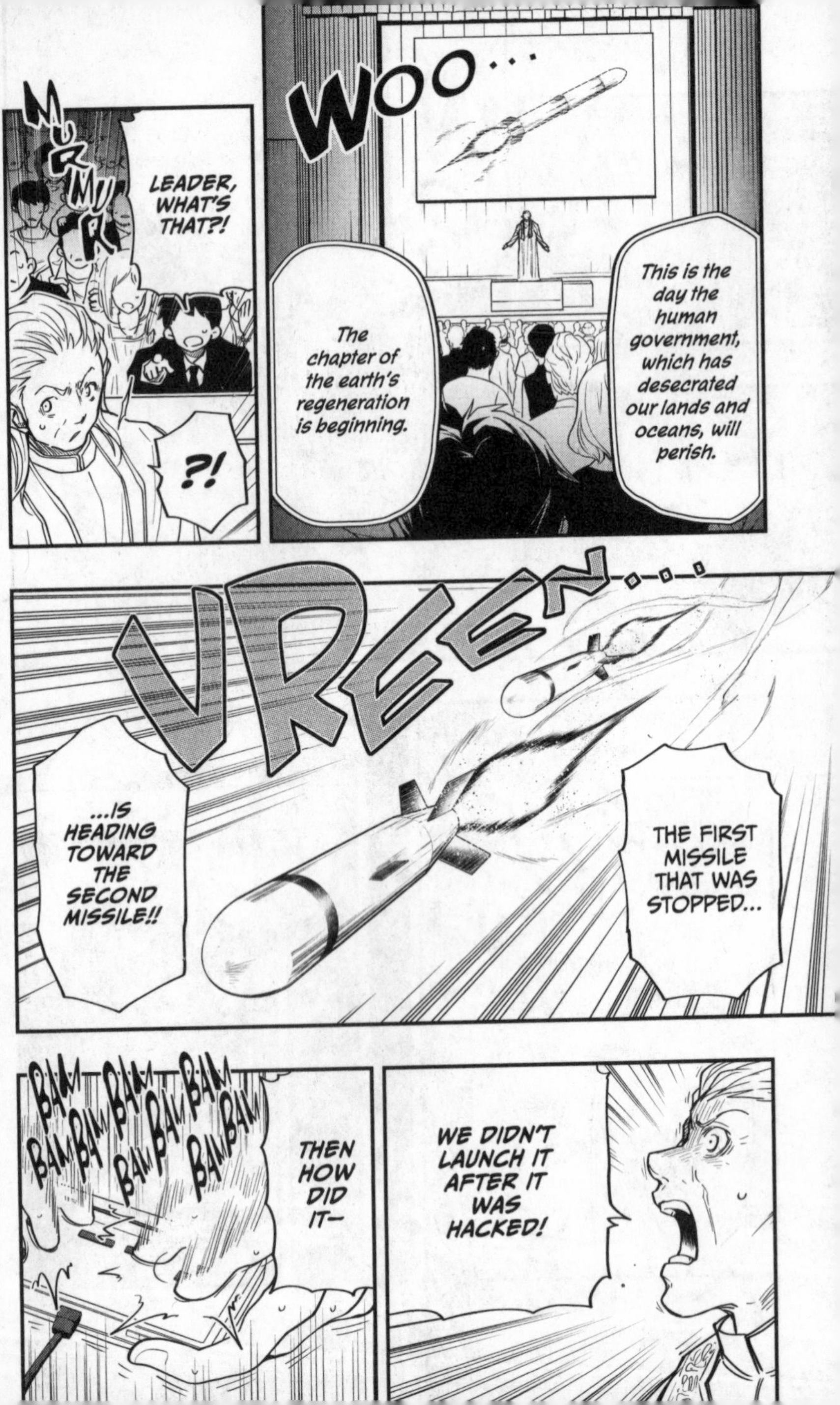
WOO...
This is the day the human government, which has desecrated our lands and oceans, will perish.
The chapter of the earth's regeneration is beginning.
MURMUR
LEADER, WHAT'S THAT?!
?!
VREEN...
THE FIRST MISSILE THAT WAS STOPPED...
...IS HEADING TOWARD THE SECOND MISSILE!!
WE DIDN'T LAUNCH IT AFTER IT WAS HACKED!
THEN HOW DID IT—
BAM BAM BAM BAM BAM BAM BAM BAM

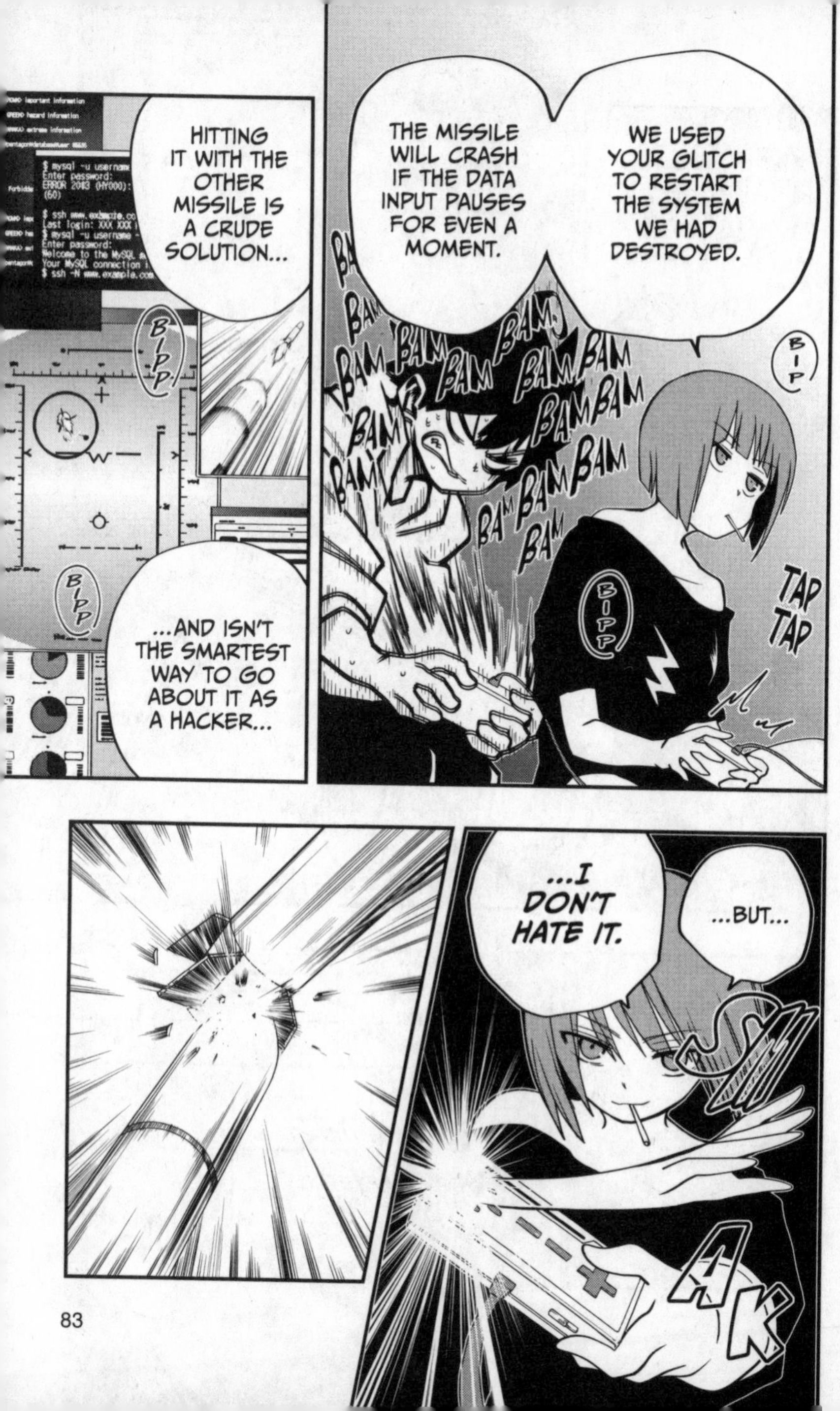
WE USED YOUR GLITCH TO RESTART THE SYSTEM WE HAD DESTROYED.
THE MISSILE WILL CRASH IF THE DATA INPUT PAUSES FOR EVEN A MOMENT.
BIP
BAM BAM BAM BAM BAM BAM BAM BAM BAM BAM BAM BAM BAM BAM BAM BAM BAM
BIPP
TAP TAP
HITTING IT WITH THE OTHER MISSILE IS A CRUDE SOLUTION...
BIPP
BIPP
...AND ISN'T THE SMARTEST WAY TO GO ABOUT IT AS A HACKER...
...BUT...
...I DON'T HATE IT.

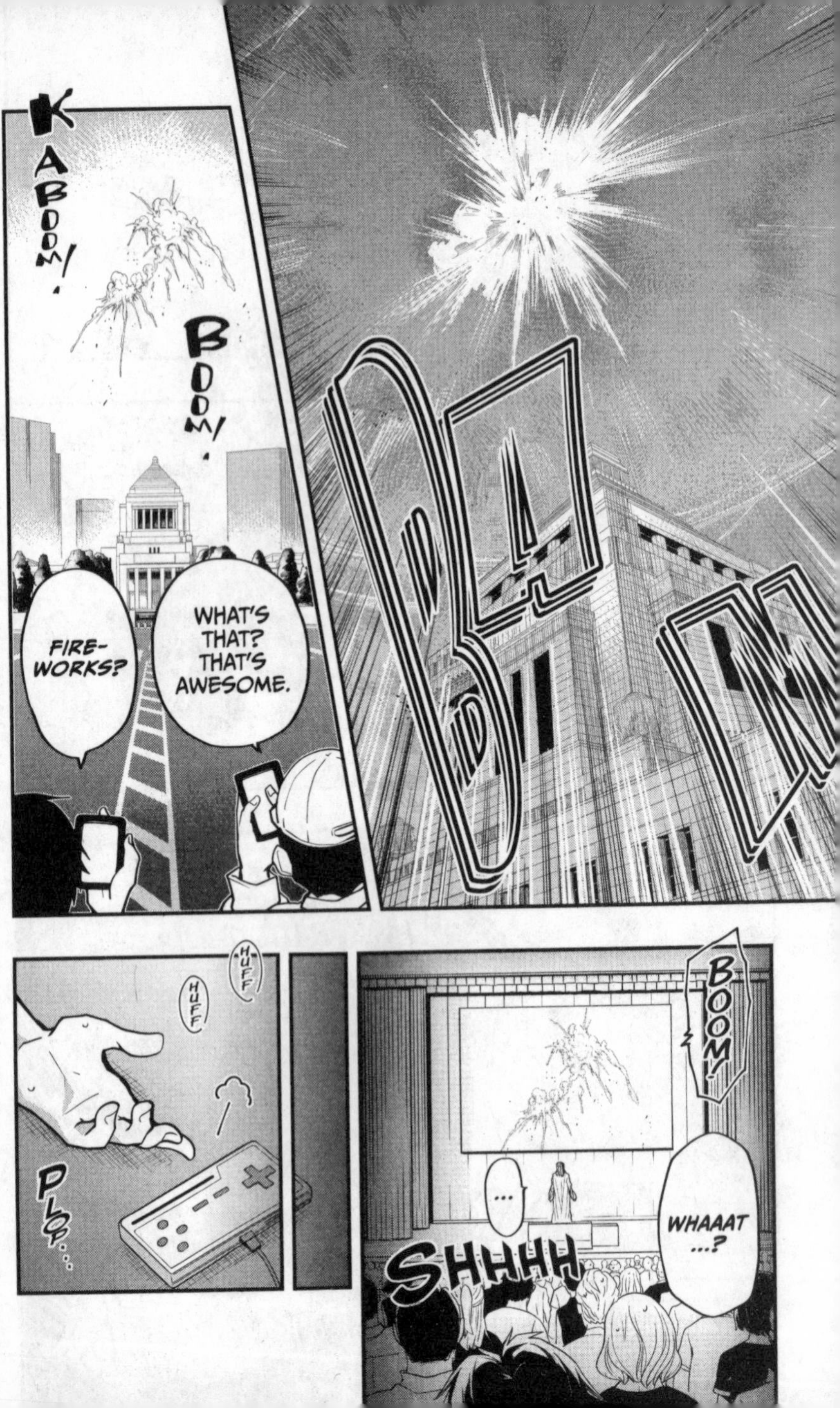
KABOOM!
BOOM!
WHAT'S THAT? THAT'S AWESOME.
FIRE-WORKS?
BOOM!
WHAAAT...?
...
SHHHH
HUFF
HUFF
PLOP...

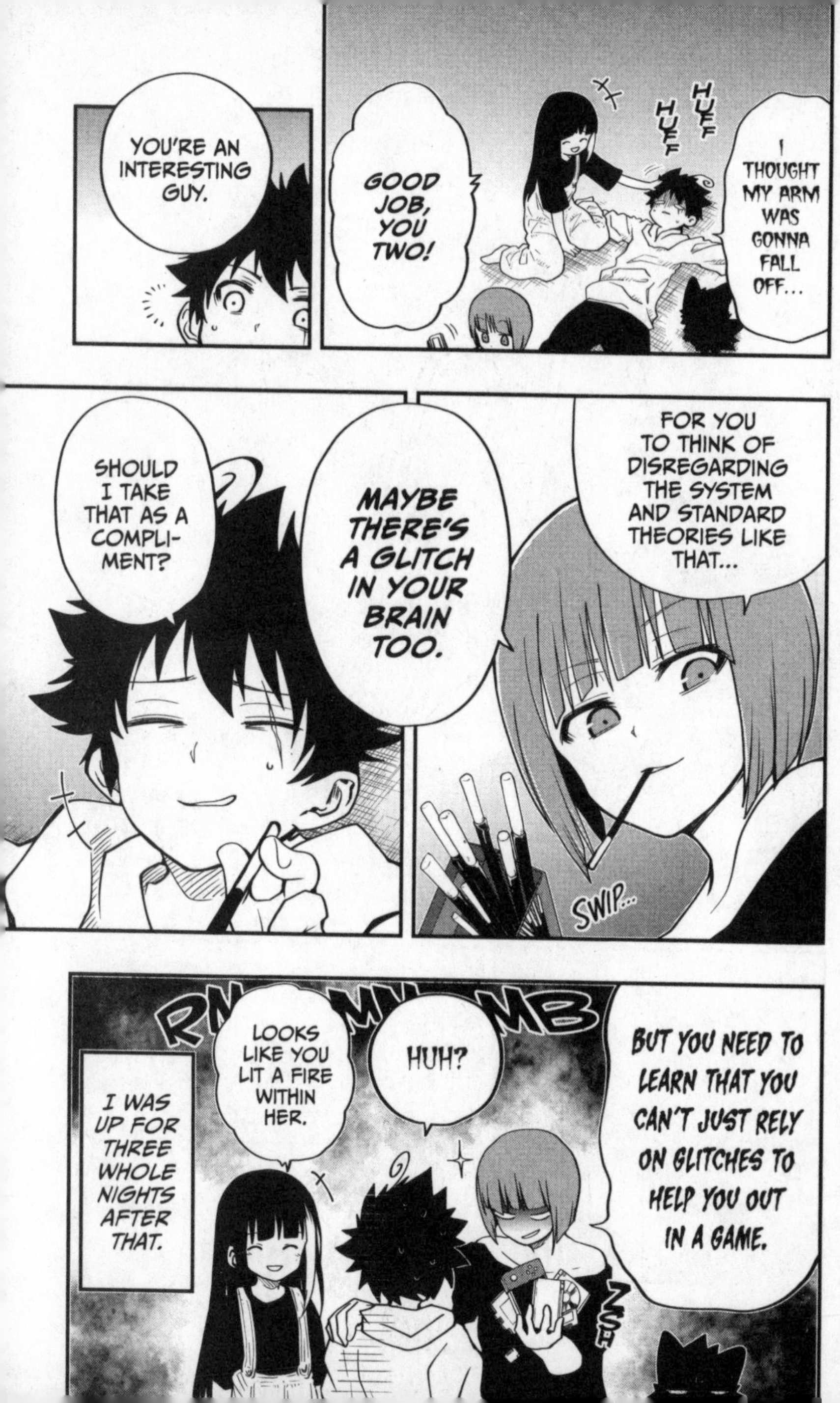
I THOUGHT MY ARM WAS GONNA FALL OFF...
HUFF
HUFF
GOOD JOB, YOU TWO!
YOU'RE AN INTERESTING GUY.
FOR YOU TO THINK OF DISREGARDING THE SYSTEM AND STANDARD THEORIES LIKE THAT...
MAYBE THERE'S A GLITCH IN YOUR BRAIN TOO.
SWIP...
SHOULD I TAKE THAT AS A COMPLI-MENT?
BUT YOU NEED TO LEARN THAT YOU CAN'T JUST RELY ON GLITCHES TO HELP YOU OUT IN A GAME.
HUH?
LOOKS LIKE YOU LIT A FIRE WITHIN HER.
I WAS UP FOR THREE WHOLE NIGHTS AFTER THAT.

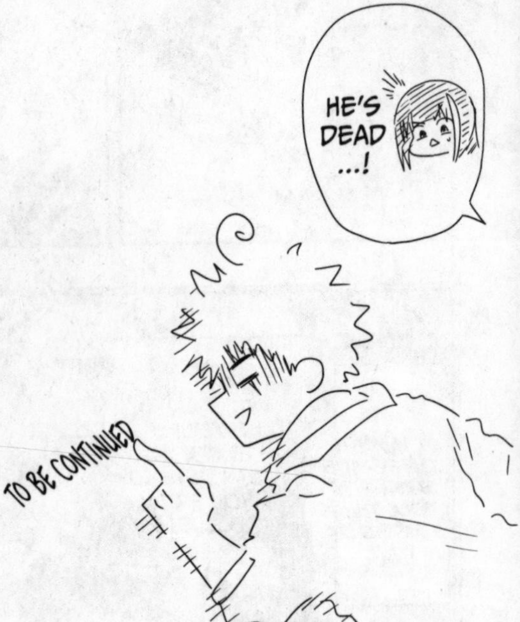
HE'S DEAD ...!
TO BE CONTINUED

MISSION 12: DOZING OFF

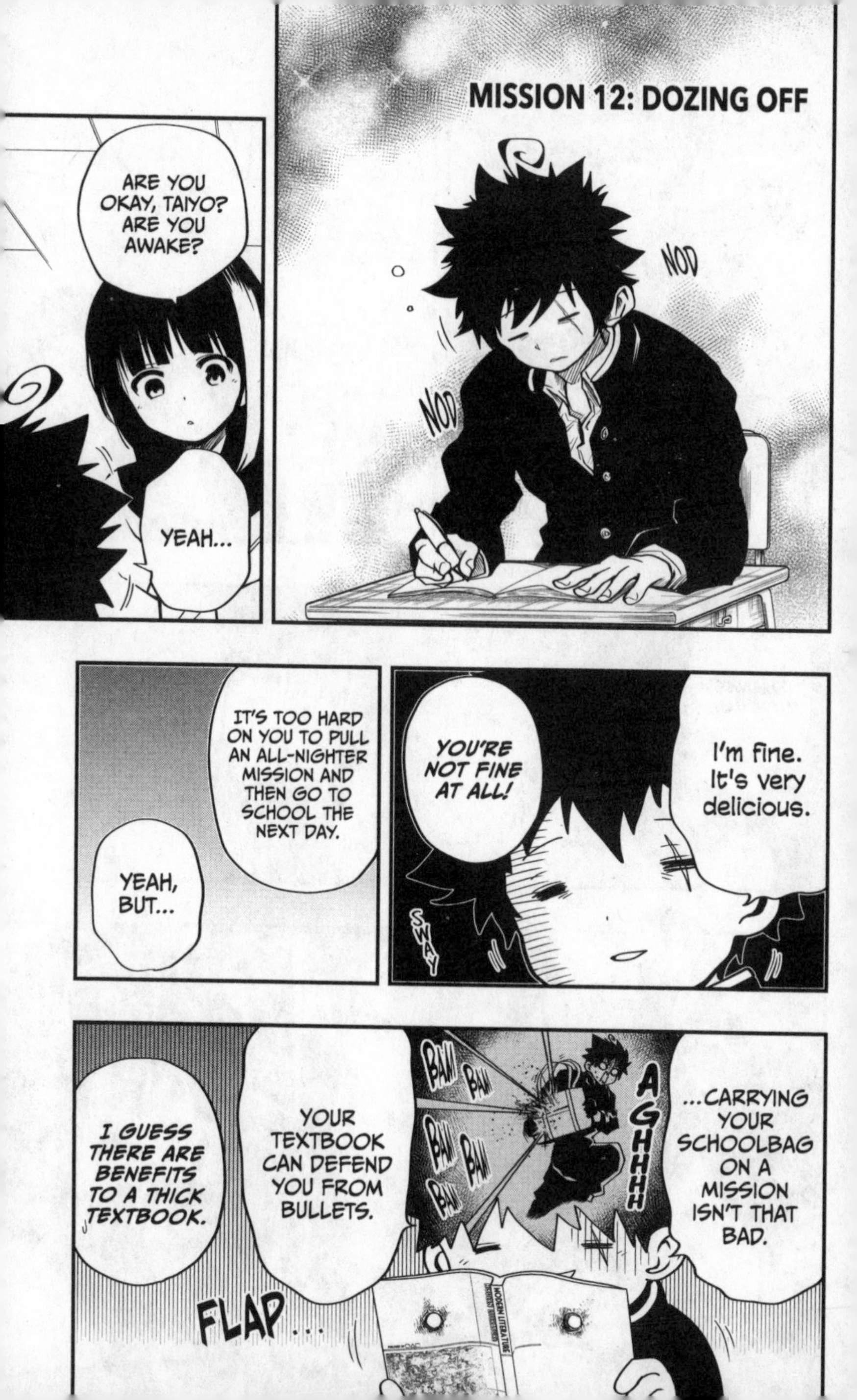
NOD
NOD
ARE YOU OKAY, TAIYO? ARE YOU AWAKE?
YEAH...
I'm fine. It's very delicious.
YOU'RE NOT FINE AT ALL!
SWAY
IT'S TOO HARD ON YOU TO PULL AN ALL-NIGHTER MISSION AND THEN GO TO SCHOOL THE NEXT DAY.
YEAH, BUT...
...CARRYING YOUR SCHOOLBAG ON A MISSION ISN'T THAT BAD.
AGHHHH
BAM
BAM
BAM
BAM
BAM
YOUR TEXTBOOK CAN DEFEND YOU FROM BULLETS.
I GUESS THERE ARE BENEFITS TO A THICK TEXTBOOK.
MODERN LITERATURE
FLAP...

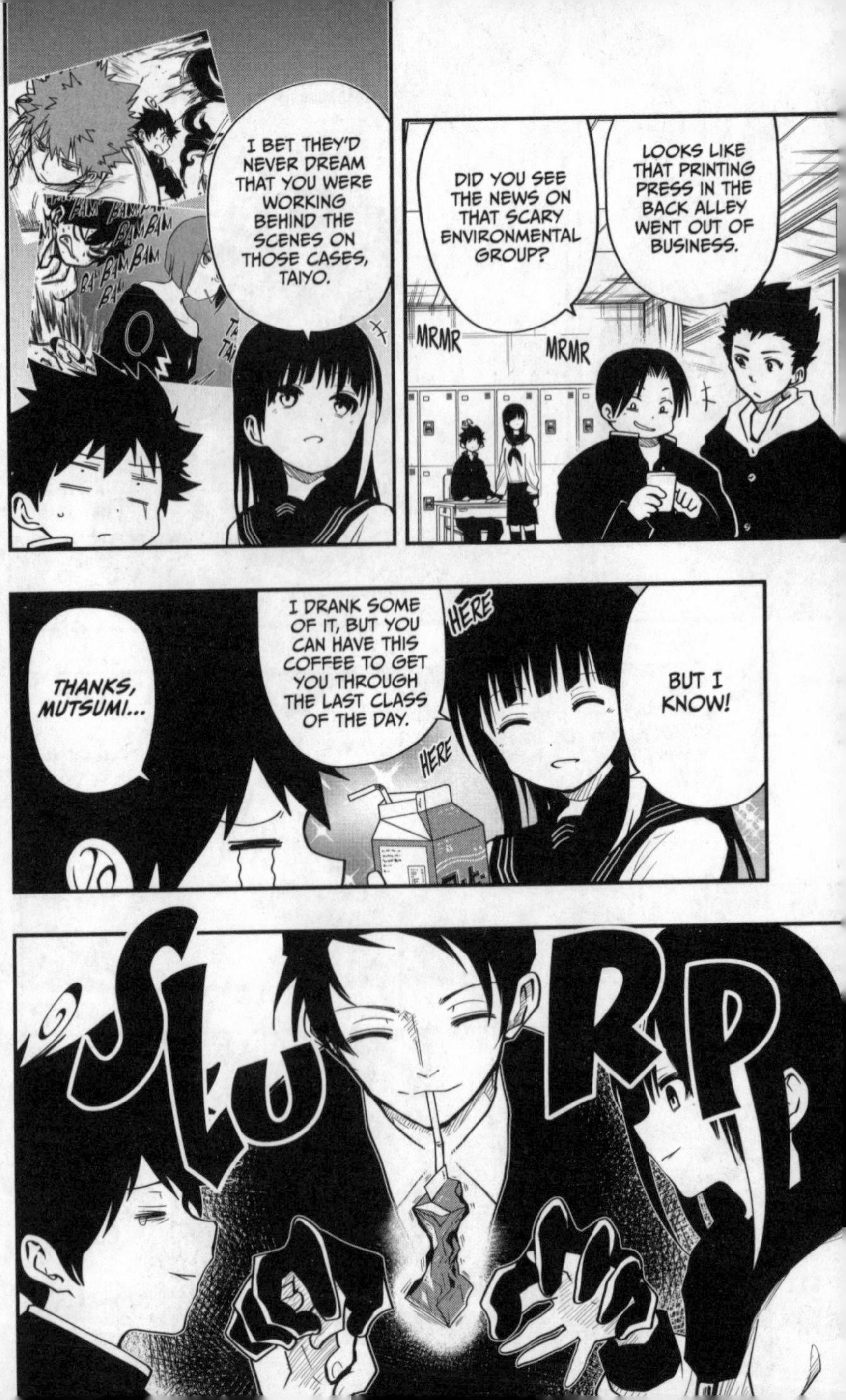
LOOKS LIKE THAT PRINTING PRESS IN THE BACK ALLEY WENT OUT OF BUSINESS.
DID YOU SEE THE NEWS ON THAT SCARY ENVIRONMENTAL GROUP?
MRMR
MRMR
I BET THEY'D NEVER DREAM THAT YOU WERE WORKING BEHIND THE SCENES ON THOSE CASES, TAIYO.
BAM BAM BAM BAM BAM BAM BAM
BUT I KNOW!
HERE
I DRANK SOME OF IT, BUT YOU CAN HAVE THIS COFFEE TO GET YOU THROUGH THE LAST CLASS OF THE DAY.
HERE
THANKS, MUTSUMI...
SLURP

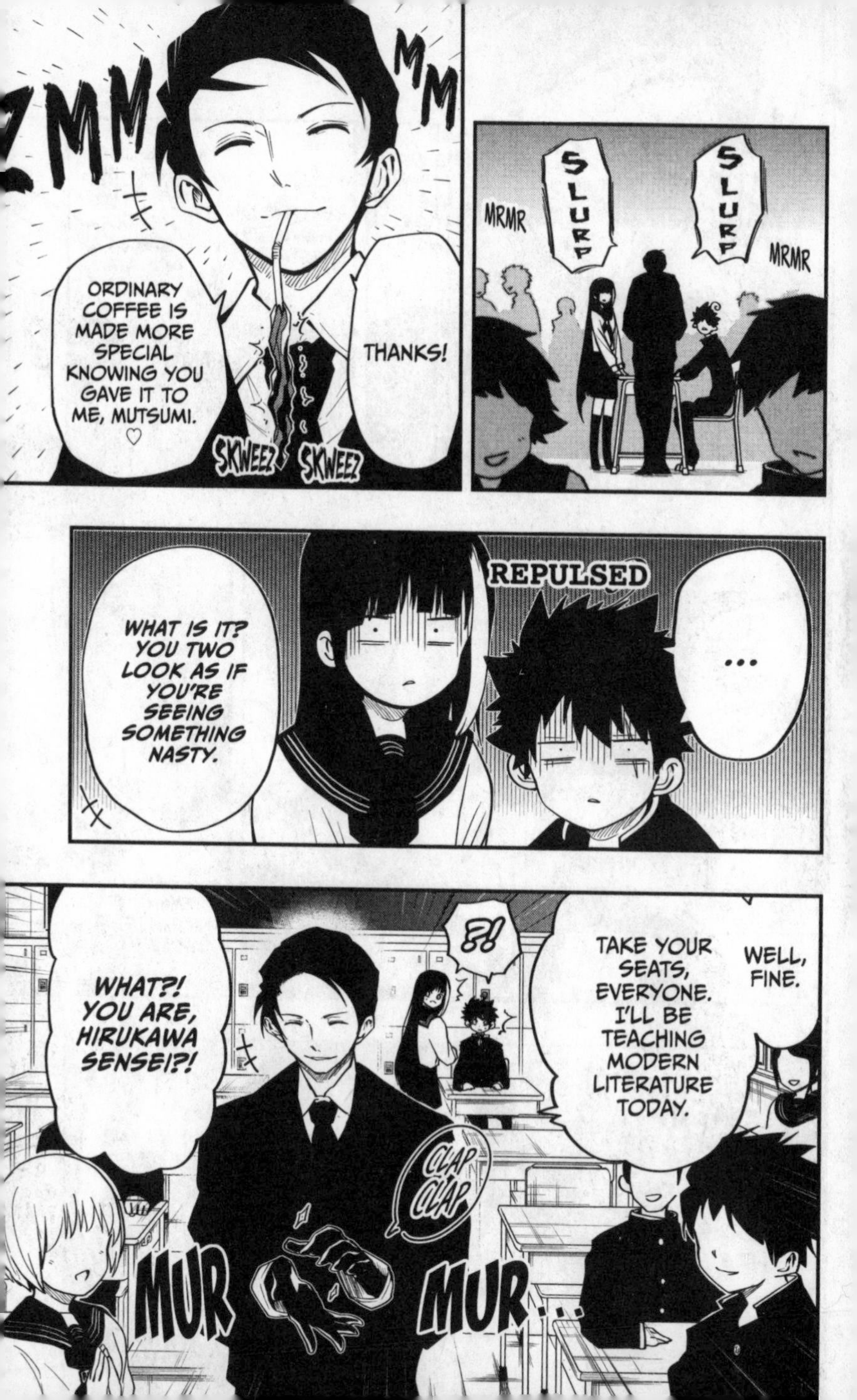
SLURP
SLURP
MRMR
MRMR
ZMMMM
THANKS!
ORDINARY COFFEE IS MADE MORE SPECIAL KNOWING YOU GAVE IT TO ME, MUTSUMI. ♡
SKWEEZ SKWEEZ
...
REPULSED
WHAT IS IT? YOU TWO LOOK AS IF YOU'RE SEEING SOMETHING NASTY.
WELL, FINE.
TAKE YOUR SEATS, EVERYONE. I'LL BE TEACHING MODERN LITERATURE TODAY.
?!
WHAT?! YOU ARE, HIRUKAWA SENSEI?!
CLAP CLAP
MUR MUR...

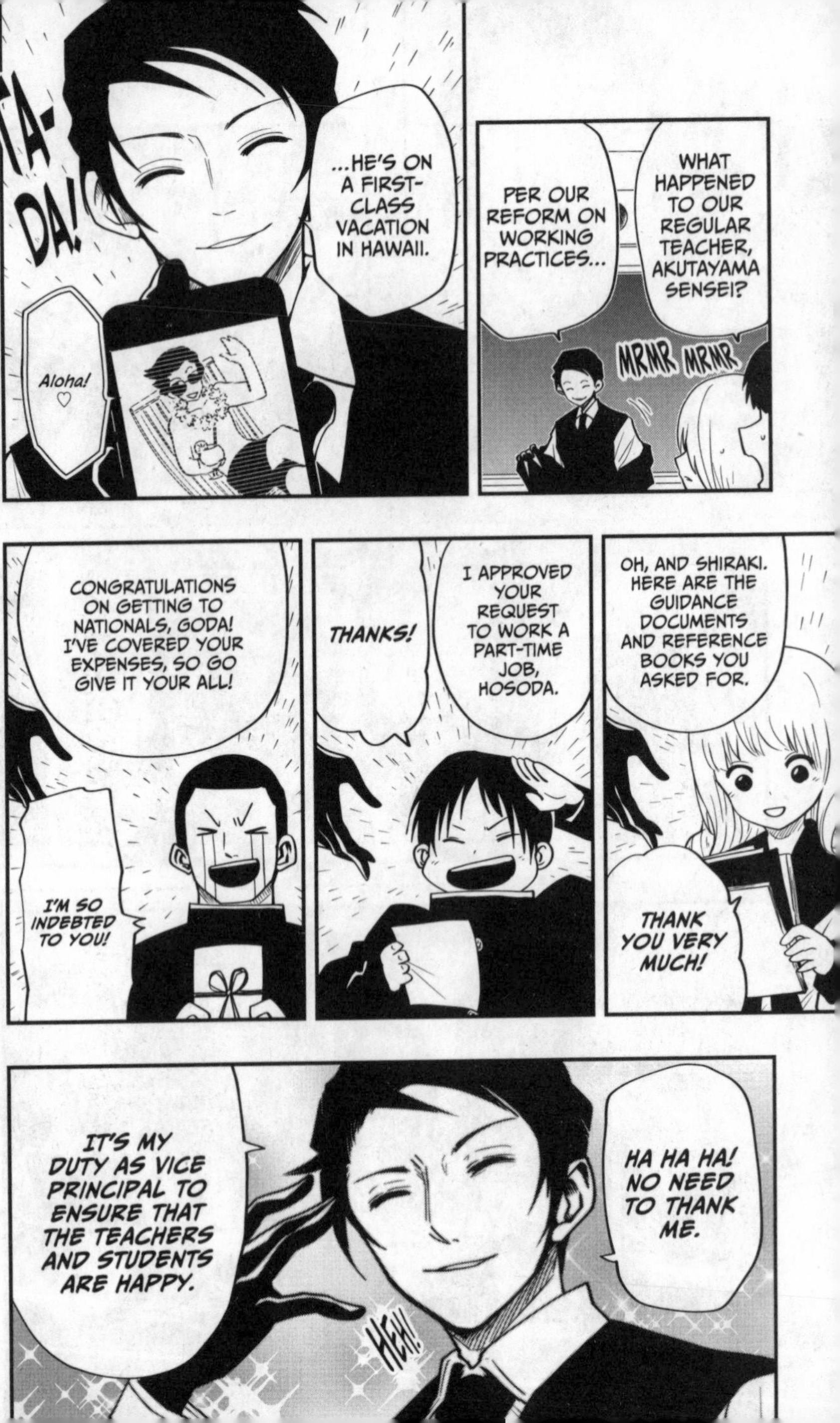
WHAT HAPPENED TO OUR REGULAR TEACHER, AKUTAYAMA SENSEI?
PER OUR REFORM ON WORKING PRACTICES...
MRMR MRMR
...HE'S ON A FIRST-CLASS VACATION IN HAWAII.
TA-DA!
Aloha! ♡
OH, AND SHIRAKI. HERE ARE THE GUIDANCE DOCUMENTS AND REFERENCE BOOKS YOU ASKED FOR.
THANK YOU VERY MUCH!
I APPROVED YOUR REQUEST TO WORK A PART-TIME JOB, HOSODA.
THANKS!
CONGRATULATIONS ON GETTING TO NATIONALS, GODA! I'VE COVERED YOUR EXPENSES, SO GO GIVE IT YOUR ALL!
I'M SO INDEBTED TO YOU!
HA HA HA! NO NEED TO THANK ME.
IT'S MY DUTY AS VICE PRINCIPAL TO ENSURE THAT THE TEACHERS AND STUDENTS ARE HAPPY.
HEH!

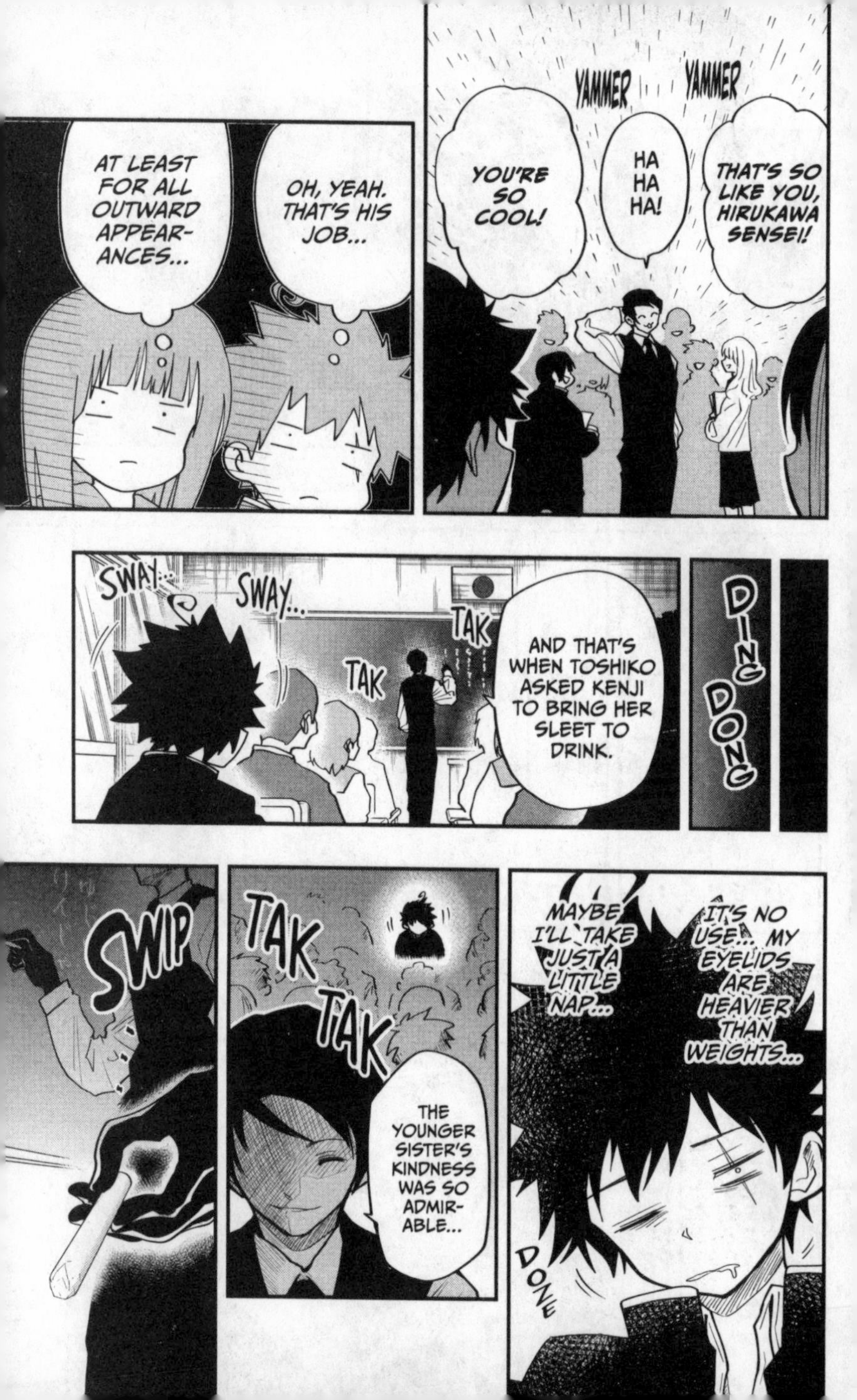
YAMMER
YAMMER
THAT'S SO LIKE YOU, HIRUKAWA SENSEI!
HA HA HA!
YOU'RE SO COOL!
OH, YEAH. THAT'S HIS JOB...
AT LEAST FOR ALL OUTWARD APPEAR-ANCES...
DING DONG
AND THAT'S WHEN TOSHIKO ASKED KENJI TO BRING HER SLEET TO DRINK.
TAK
TAK
SWAY...
SWAY...
IT'S NO USE... MY EYELIDS ARE HEAVIER THAN WEIGHTS...
MAYBE I'LL TAKE JUST A LITTLE NAP...
DOZE
TAK
TAK
THE YOUNGER SISTER'S KINDNESS WAS SO ADMIR-ABLE...
SWIP

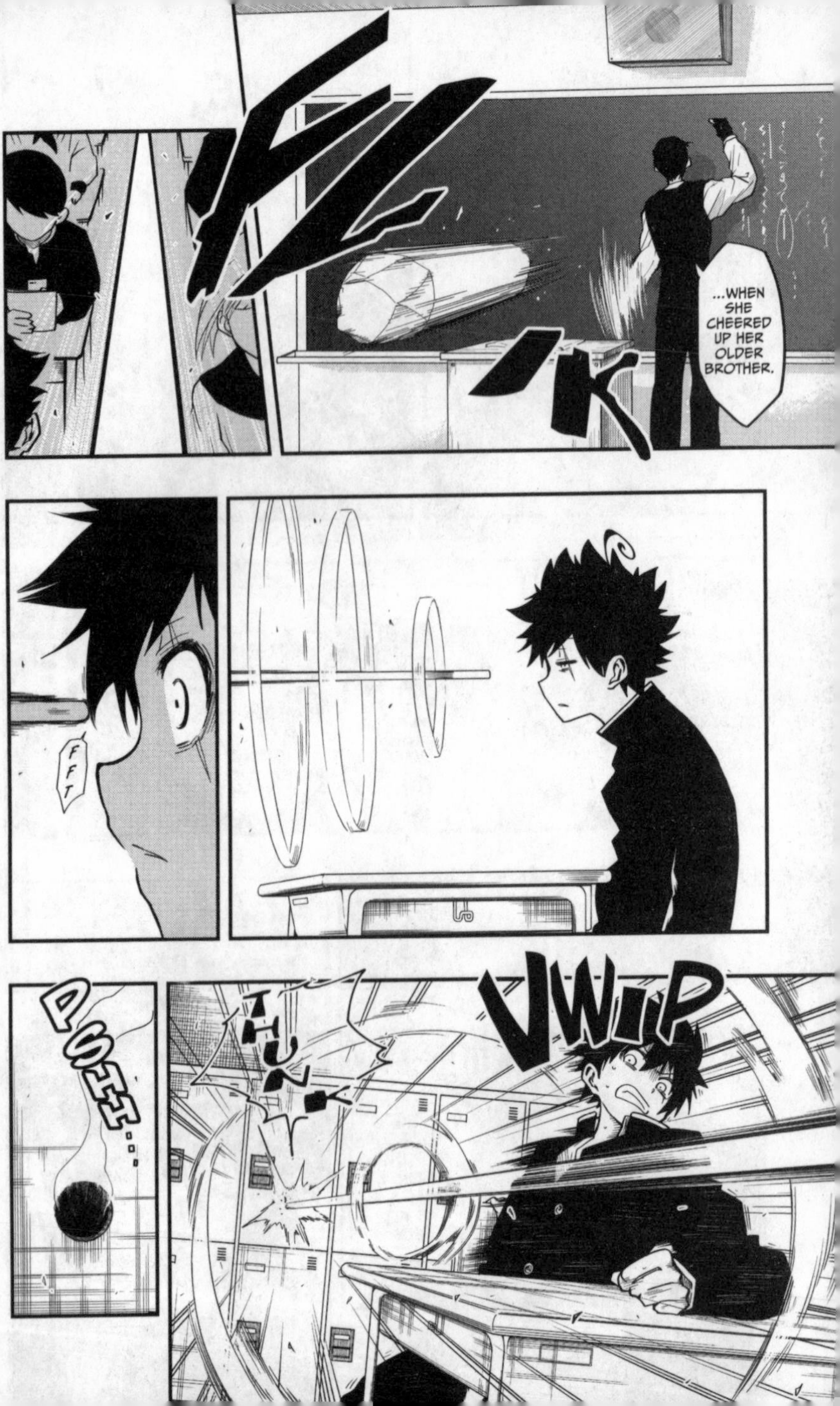
...WHEN SHE CHEERED UP HER OLDER BROTHER.
FLIK
FFT
VWIP
THUNK
PSHH...

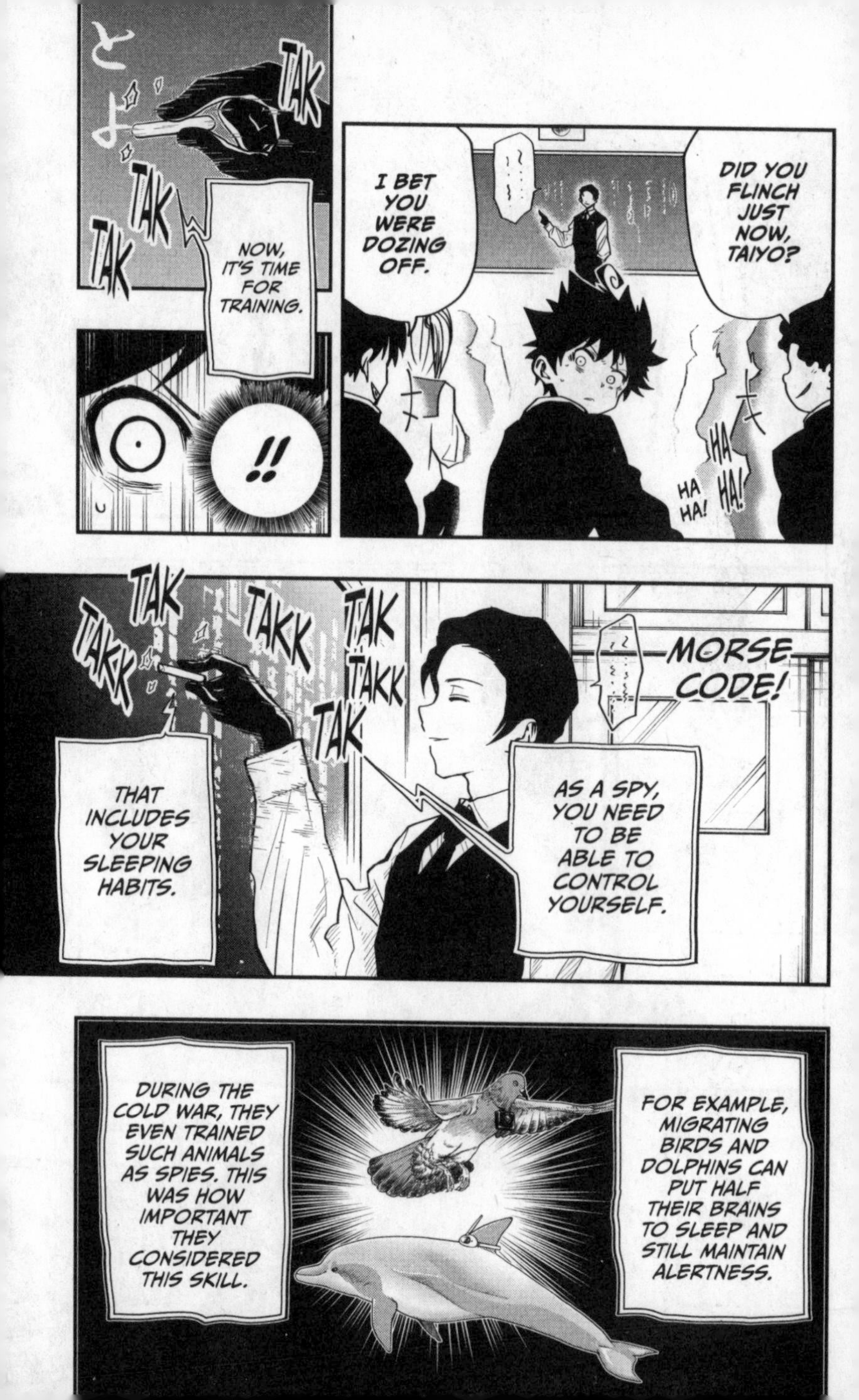
DID YOU FLINCH JUST NOW, TAIYO?
I BET YOU WERE DOZING OFF.
HA HA!
HA HA!
TAK
TAK
TAK
NOW, IT'S TIME FOR TRAINING.
!!
MORSE CODE!
TAK
TAKK
TAK
TAKK
TAK
TAKK
AS A SPY, YOU NEED TO BE ABLE TO CONTROL YOURSELF.
THAT INCLUDES YOUR SLEEPING HABITS.
FOR EXAMPLE, MIGRATING BIRDS AND DOLPHINS CAN PUT HALF THEIR BRAINS TO SLEEP AND STILL MAINTAIN ALERTNESS.
DURING THE COLD WAR, THEY EVEN TRAINED SUCH ANIMALS AS SPIES. THIS WAS HOW IMPORTANT THEY CONSIDERED THIS SKILL.

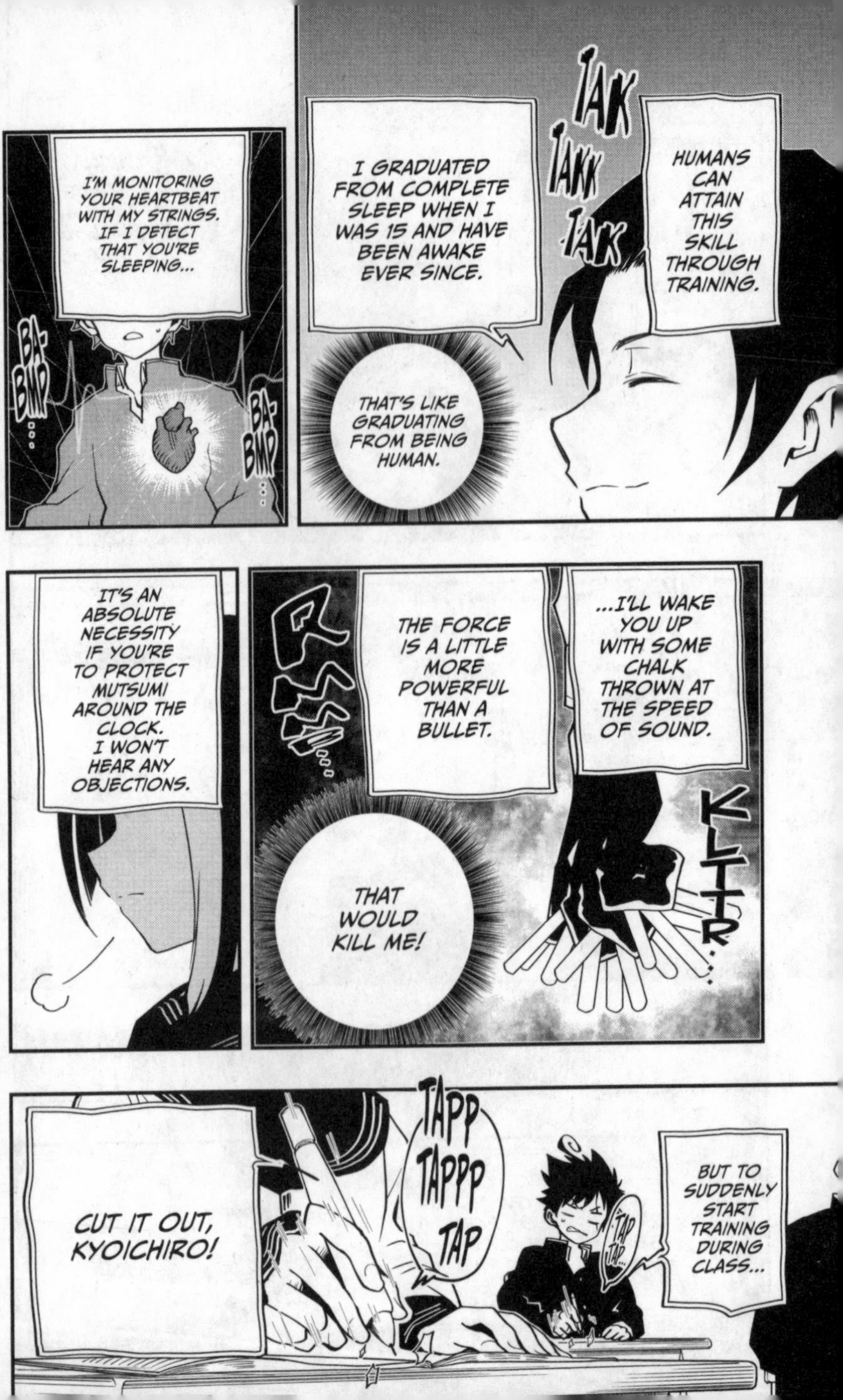
TAK
TAKK
TAK
HUMANS CAN ATTAIN THIS SKILL THROUGH TRAINING.
I GRADUATED FROM COMPLETE SLEEP WHEN I WAS 15 AND HAVE BEEN AWAKE EVER SINCE.
THAT'S LIKE GRADUATING FROM BEING HUMAN.
I'M MONITORING YOUR HEARTBEAT WITH MY STRINGS. IF I DETECT THAT YOU'RE SLEEPING...
BA-BMP...
BA-BMP...
...I'LL WAKE YOU UP WITH SOME CHALK THROWN AT THE SPEED OF SOUND.
THE FORCE IS A LITTLE MORE POWERFUL THAN A BULLET.
KLLTR...
THAT WOULD KILL ME!
IT'S AN ABSOLUTE NECESSITY IF YOU'RE TO PROTECT MUTSUMI AROUND THE CLOCK. I WON'T HEAR ANY OBJECTIONS.
BUT TO SUDDENLY START TRAINING DURING CLASS...
TAP TAP...
TAPP TAPPP TAP
CUT IT OUT, KYOICHIRO!

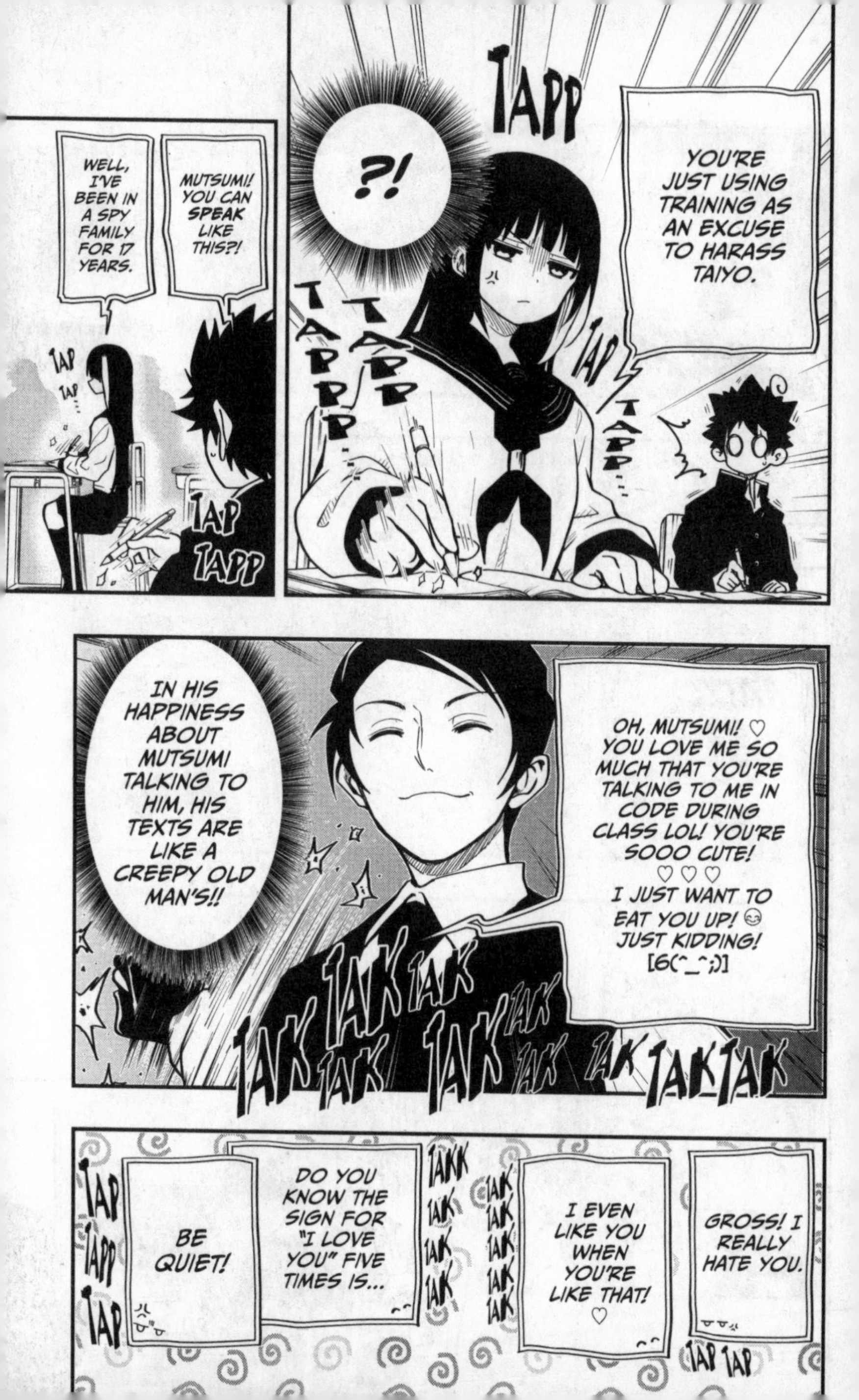
TAPP
YOU'RE JUST USING TRAINING AS AN EXCUSE TO HARASS TAIYO.
?!
TAPP
TAPP
TAP
TAPP
MUTSUMI! YOU CAN SPEAK LIKE THIS?!
WELL, I'VE BEEN IN A SPY FAMILY FOR 17 YEARS.
TAP TAP
TAP TAPP
OH, MUTSUMI! ♡ YOU LOVE ME SO MUCH THAT YOU'RE TALKING TO ME IN CODE DURING CLASS LOL! YOU'RE SOOO CUTE! ♡ ♡ ♡ I JUST WANT TO EAT YOU UP! 😂 JUST KIDDING! [6(^_^;)]
IN HIS HAPPINESS ABOUT MUTSUMI TALKING TO HIM, HIS TEXTS ARE LIKE A CREEPY OLD MAN'S!!
TAK TAK TAK TAK TAK TAK TAK TAK TAK TAK TAK
GROSS! I REALLY HATE YOU.
TAP TAP
I EVEN LIKE YOU WHEN YOU'RE LIKE THAT! ♡
TAK TAK TAK TAK TAK TAK
TAKK TAK TAK TAK TAK
DO YOU KNOW THE SIGN FOR "I LOVE YOU" FIVE TIMES IS...
BE QUIET!
TAP TAPP TAP

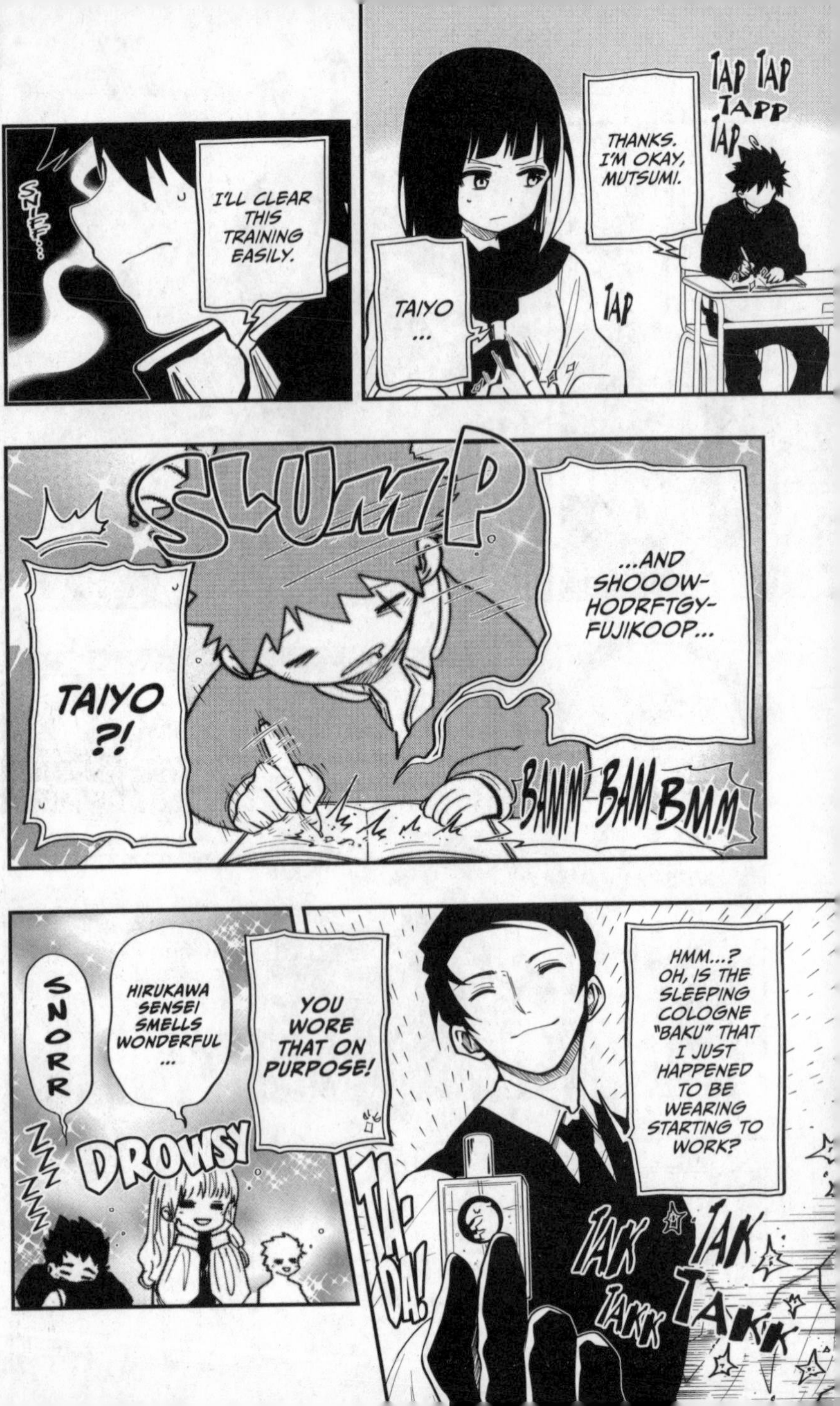
TAP TAP
TAPP
TAP
THANKS. I'M OKAY, MUTSUMI.
TAIYO ...
TAP
I'LL CLEAR THIS TRAINING EASILY.
SNIFF...
SLUMP
...AND SHOOOW-HODRFTGY-FUJIKOOP...
TAIYO ?!
BAMM BAM BMM
HMM...? OH, IS THE SLEEPING COLOGNE "BAKU" THAT I JUST HAPPENED TO BE WEARING STARTING TO WORK?
TA-DA!
TAK TAK
TAKK TAKK
YOU WORE THAT ON PURPOSE!
HIRUKAWA SENSEI SMELLS WONDERFUL ...
SNORR
DROWSY
ZZZ

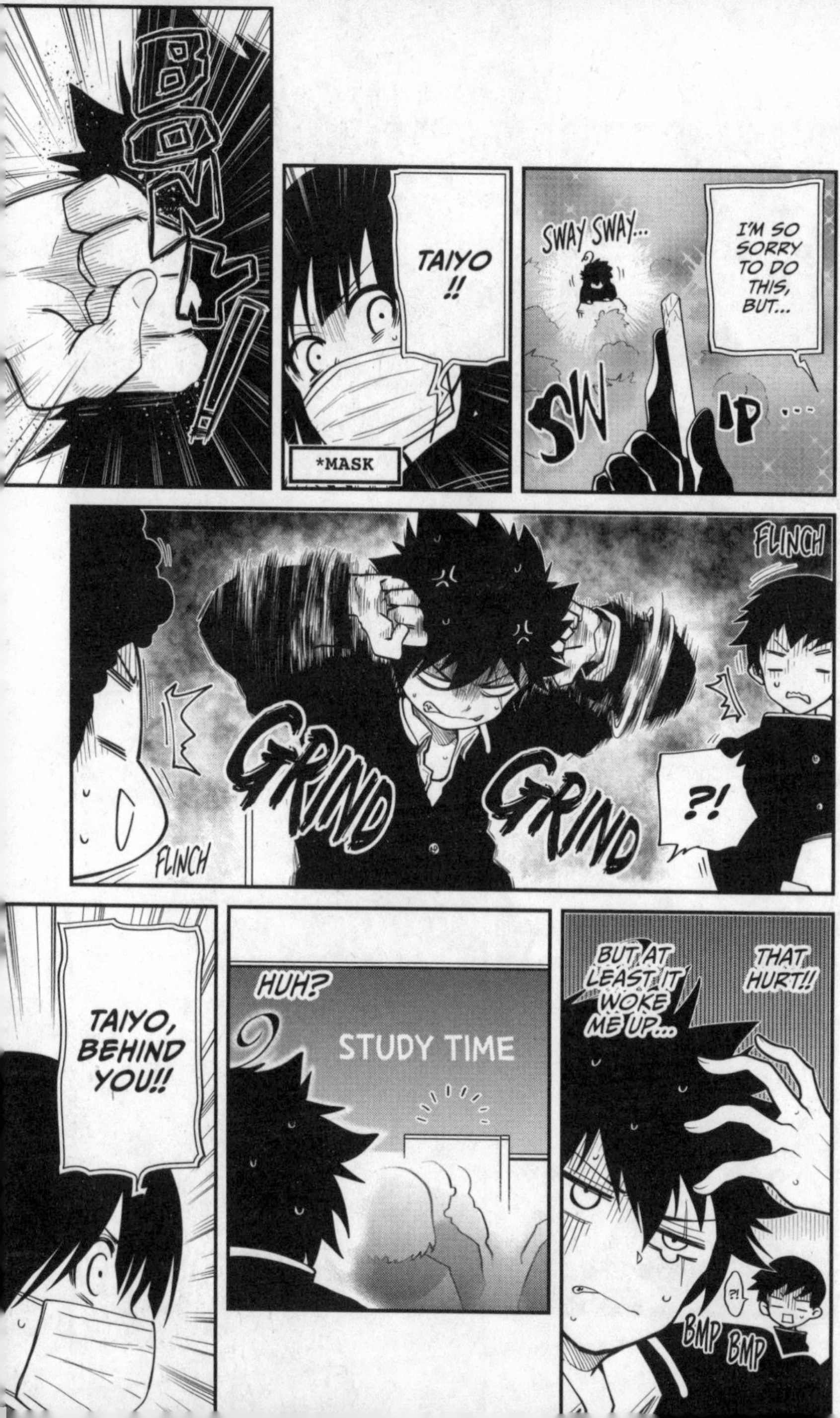
I'M SO SORRY TO DO THIS, BUT...
SWAY SWAY...
SW IP ...
TAIYO !!
*MASK
BONK!
FLINCH
?!
GRIND
GRIND
FLINCH
THAT HURT!!
BUT AT LEAST IT WOKE ME UP...
?!
BMP BMP
HUH?
STUDY TIME
TAIYO, BEHIND YOU!!

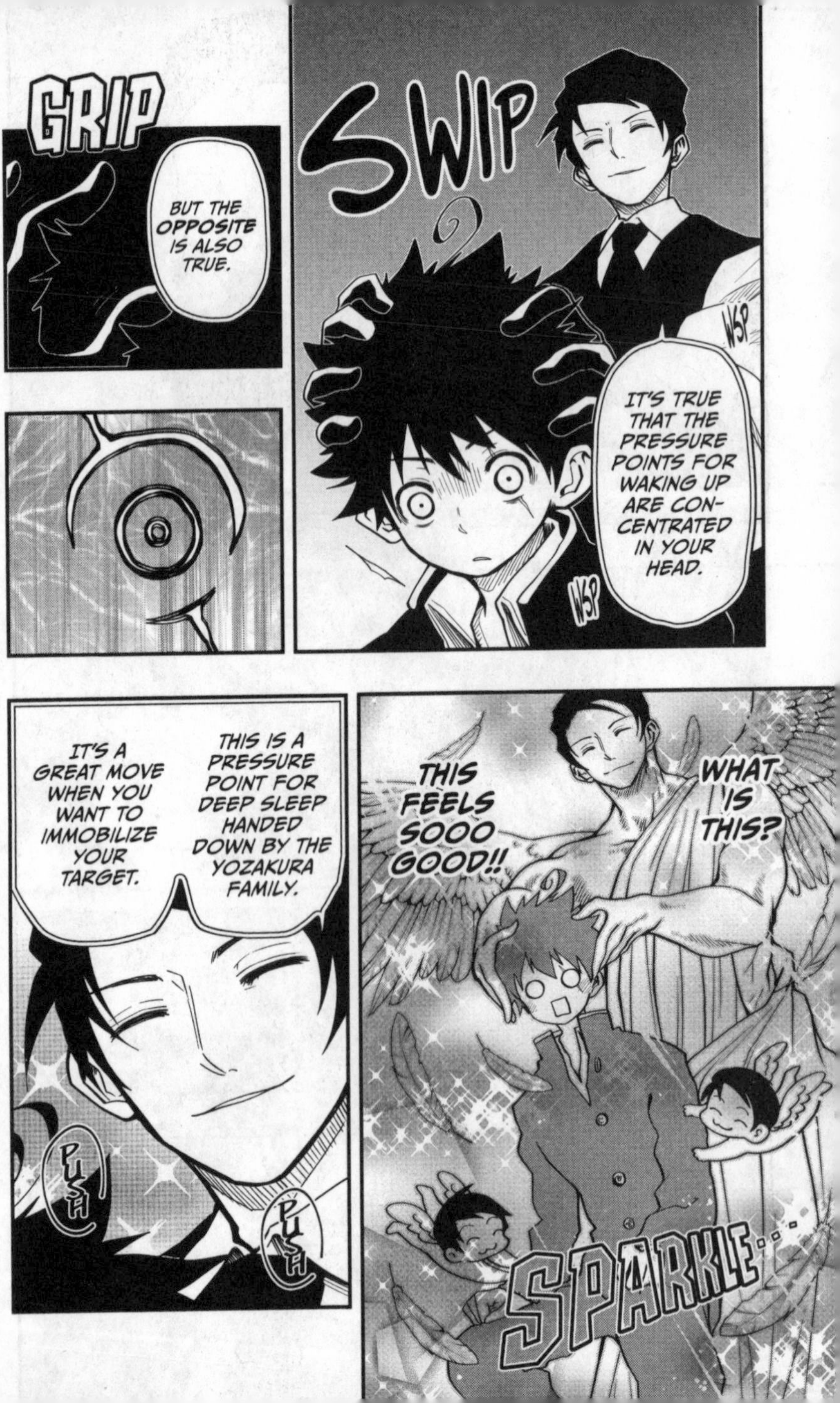
SWIP
WSP
IT'S TRUE THAT THE PRESSURE POINTS FOR WAKING UP ARE CONCENTRATED IN YOUR HEAD.
WSP
GRIP
BUT THE OPPOSITE IS ALSO TRUE.
WHAT IS THIS?
THIS FEELS SOOO GOOD!!
SPARKLE...
THIS IS A PRESSURE POINT FOR DEEP SLEEP HANDED DOWN BY THE YOZAKURA FAMILY.
IT'S A GREAT MOVE WHEN YOU WANT TO IMMOBILIZE YOUR TARGET.
PUSH
PUSH

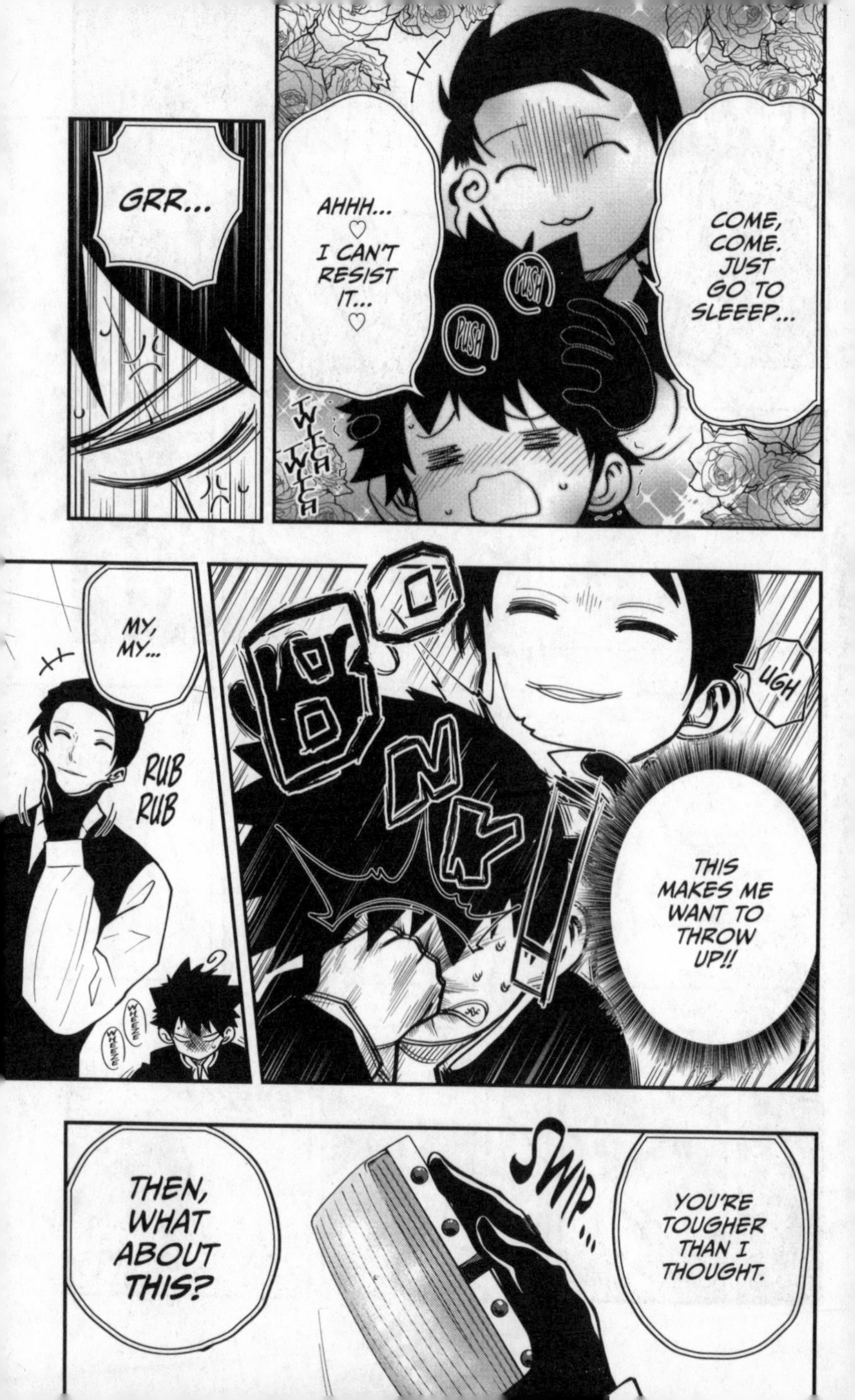
COME, COME. JUST GO TO SLEEEP...
PUSH
PUSH
AHHH... ♡ I CAN'T RESIST IT... ♡
TWITCH TWITCH
GRR...
UGH
BONK!
THIS MAKES ME WANT TO THROW UP!!
MY, MY...
RUB RUB
WHEEZE WHEEZE
YOU'RE TOUGHER THAN I THOUGHT.
SWIP...
THEN, WHAT ABOUT THIS?

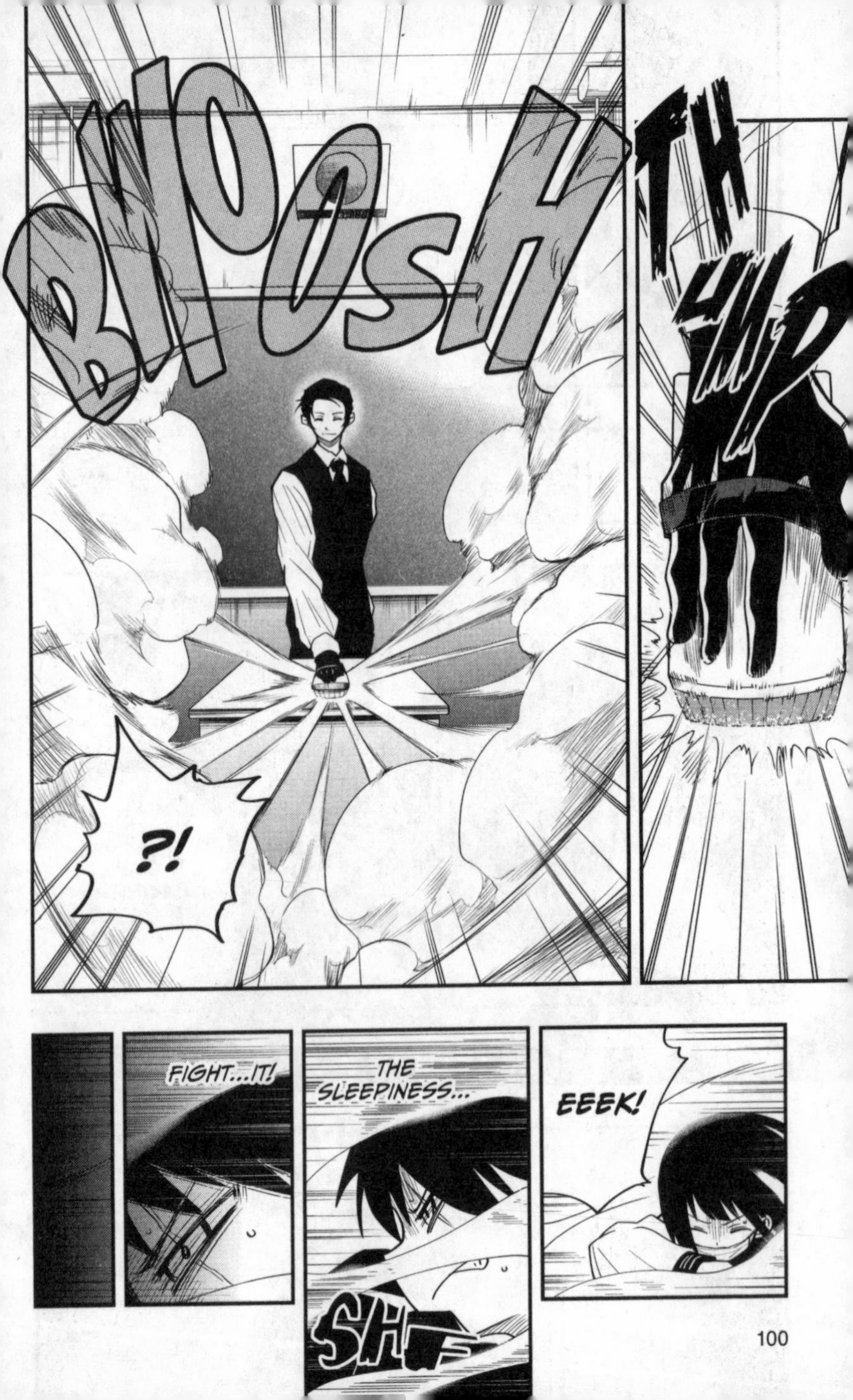
BWOOSH
?!
EEEK!
THE SLEEPINESS...
FIGHT...IT!

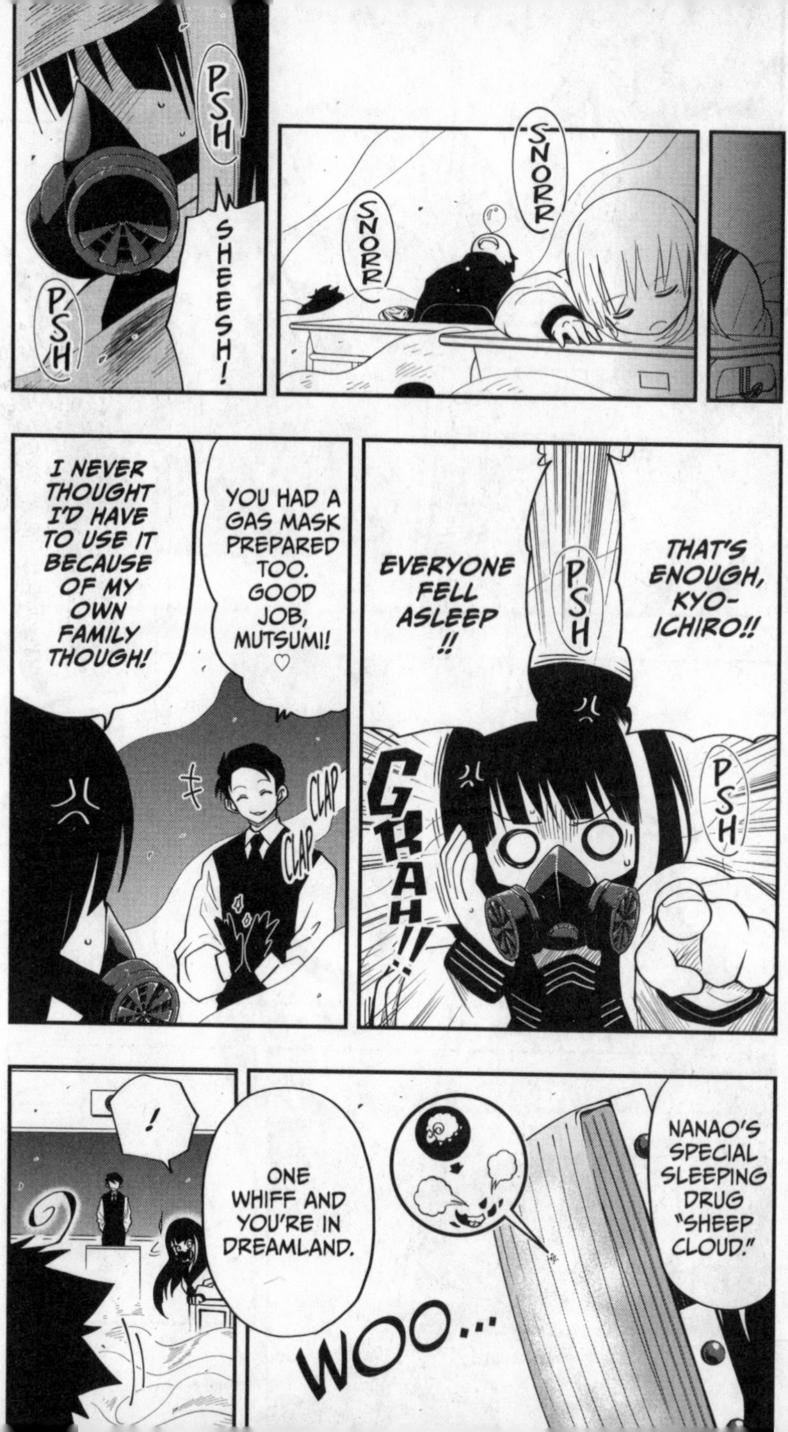
SNORR
SNORR
PSH
SHEESH!
PSH
THAT'S ENOUGH, KYO-ICHIRO!!
PSH
EVERYONE FELL ASLEEP!!
PSH
GRAH!!
YOU HAD A GAS MASK PREPARED TOO. GOOD JOB, MUTSUMI! ♡
I NEVER THOUGHT I'D HAVE TO USE IT BECAUSE OF MY OWN FAMILY THOUGH!
CLAP
CLAP
NANAO'S SPECIAL SLEEPING DRUG "SHEEP CLOUD."
ONE WHIFF AND YOU'RE IN DREAMLAND.
WOO...
!

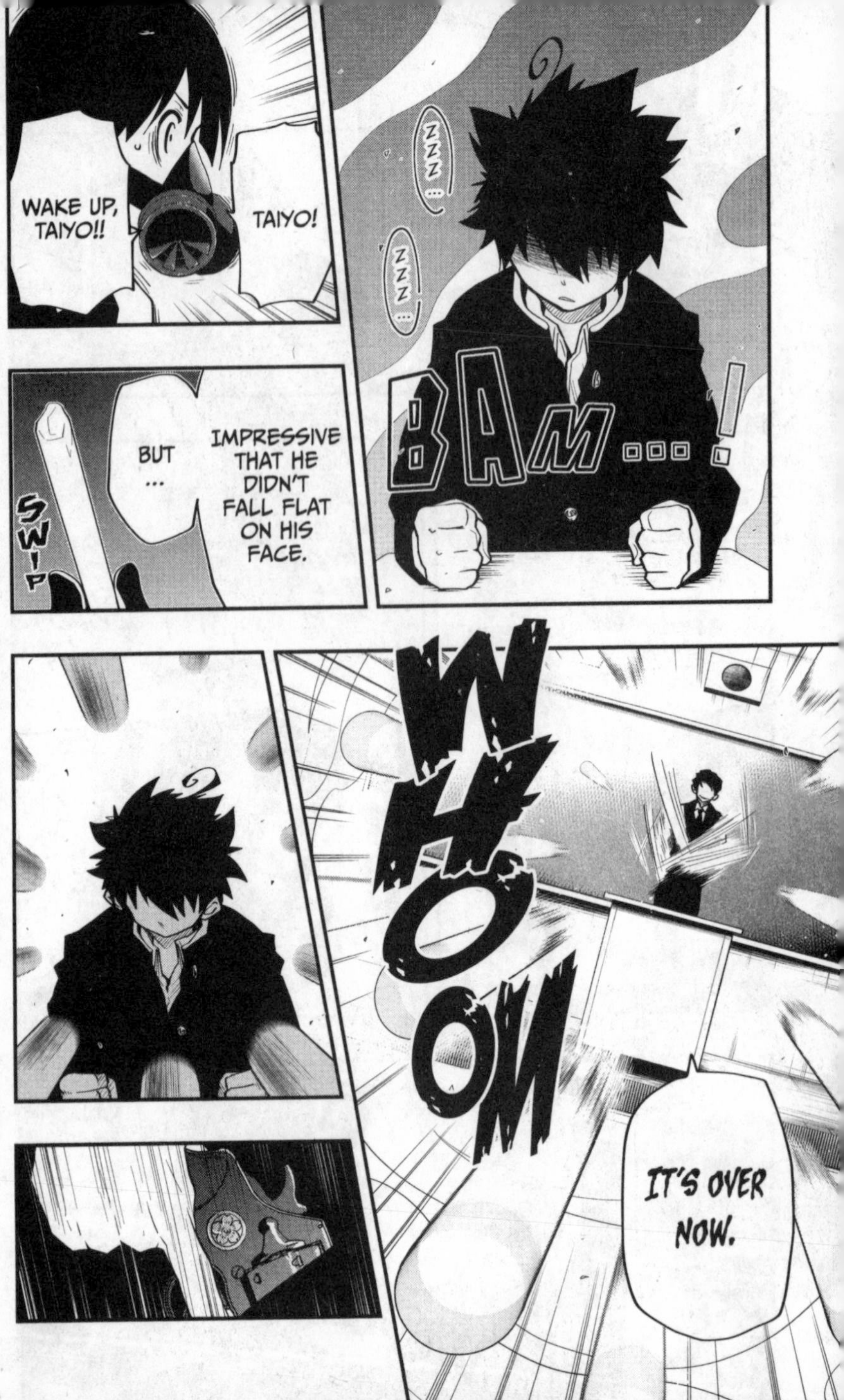
ZZZ...
ZZZ...
BAM...!
TAIYO!
WAKE UP, TAIYO!!
IMPRESSIVE THAT HE DIDN'T FALL FLAT ON HIS FACE.
BUT ...
SWIP
WHOOM
IT'S OVER NOW.

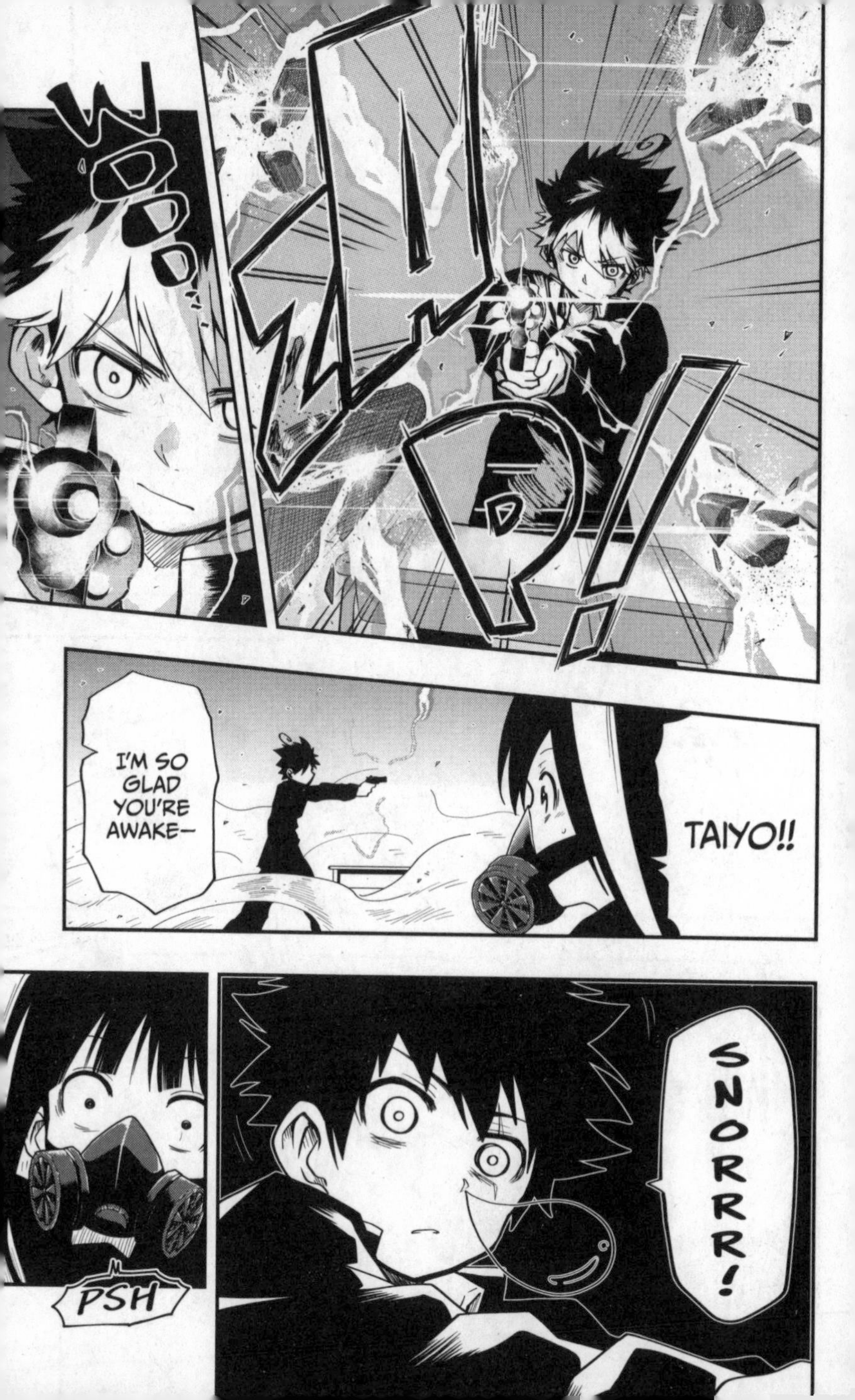
TAIYO!!
I'M SO GLAD YOU'RE AWAKE—
SNORRR!
PSH

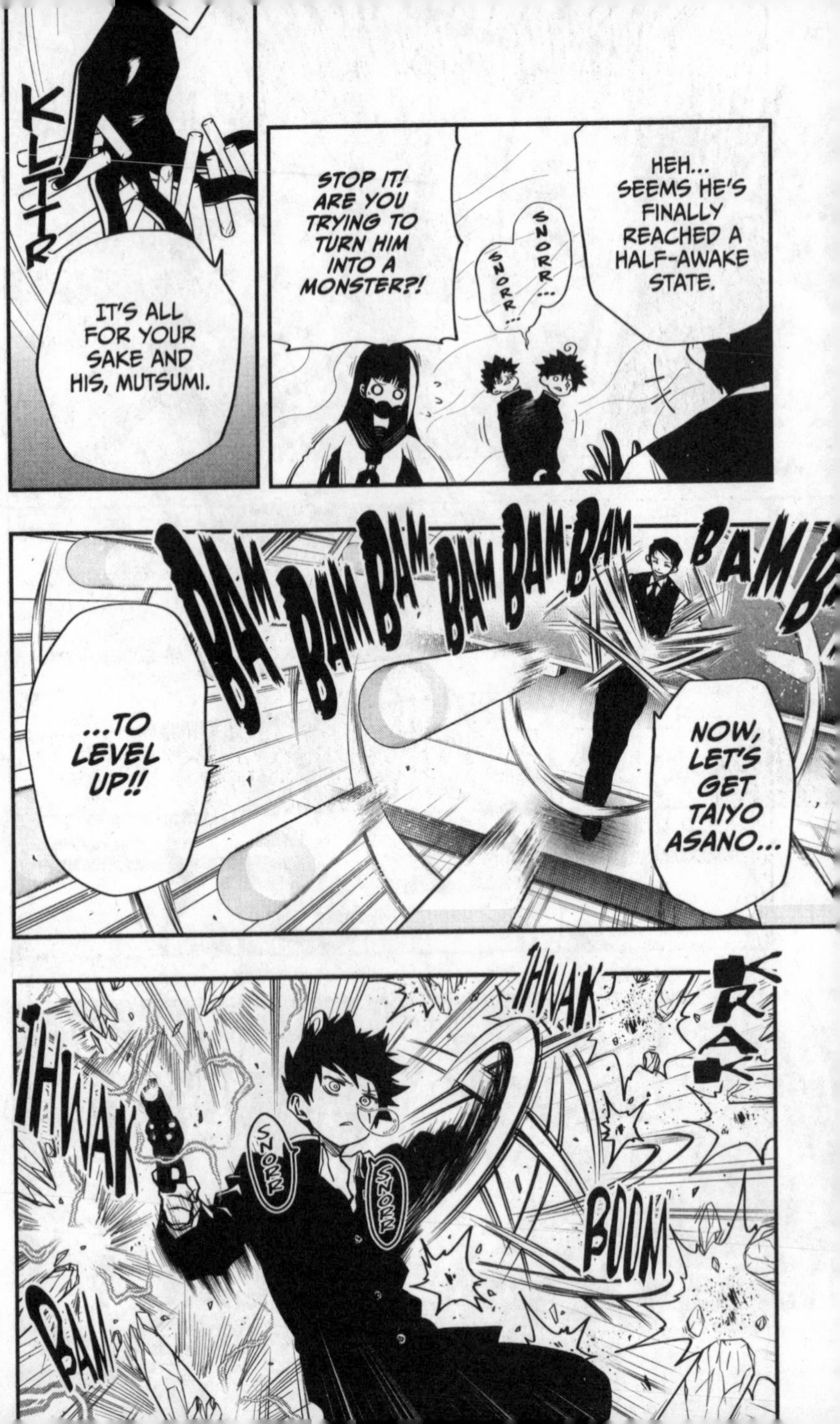
HEH... SEEMS HE'S FINALLY REACHED A HALF-AWAKE STATE.
SNORR...
SNORR...
STOP IT! ARE YOU TRYING TO TURN HIM INTO A MONSTER?!
KLTTR
IT'S ALL FOR YOUR SAKE AND HIS, MUTSUMI.
BAM
NOW, LET'S GET TAIYO ASANO...
BAM BAM BAM
BAM BAM BAM BAM
...TO LEVEL UP!!
KRAK
THWAK
BOOM
SNORR
SNORR
THWAK
BAM

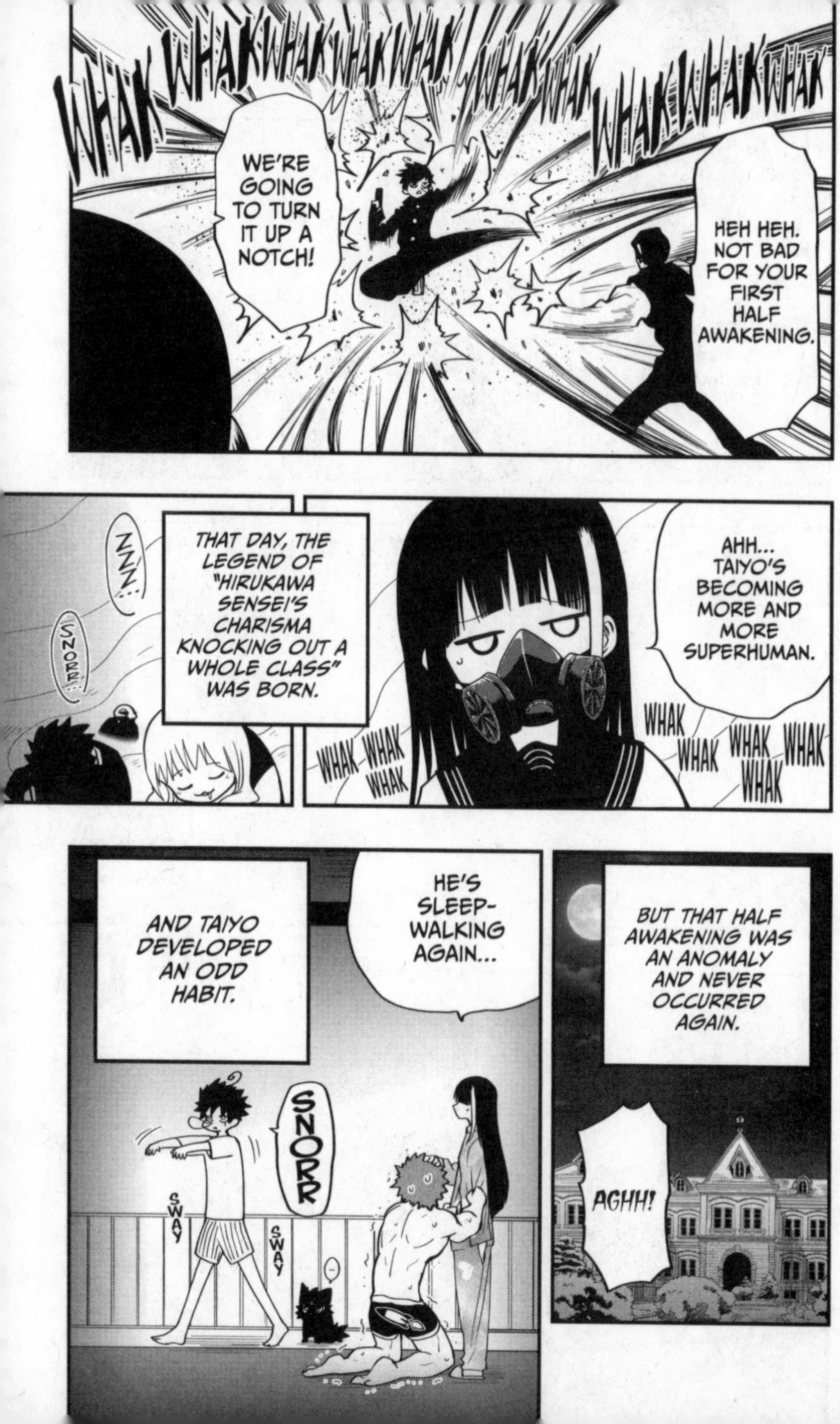
WHAK WHAK WHAK WHAK WHAK WHAK WHAK WHAK WHAK WHAK WHAK
HEH HEH. NOT BAD FOR YOUR FIRST HALF AWAKENING.
WE'RE GOING TO TURN IT UP A NOTCH!
AHH... TAIYO'S BECOMING MORE AND MORE SUPERHUMAN.
WHAK WHAK WHAK WHAK WHAK
WHAK WHAK WHAK
THAT DAY, THE LEGEND OF "HIRUKAWA SENSEI'S CHARISMA KNOCKING OUT A WHOLE CLASS" WAS BORN.
ZZZ...
SNORR...
BUT THAT HALF AWAKENING WAS AN ANOMALY AND NEVER OCCURRED AGAIN.
AGHH!
AND TAIYO DEVELOPED AN ODD HABIT.
HE'S SLEEP-WALKING AGAIN...
SNORR
SWAY
SWAY
...

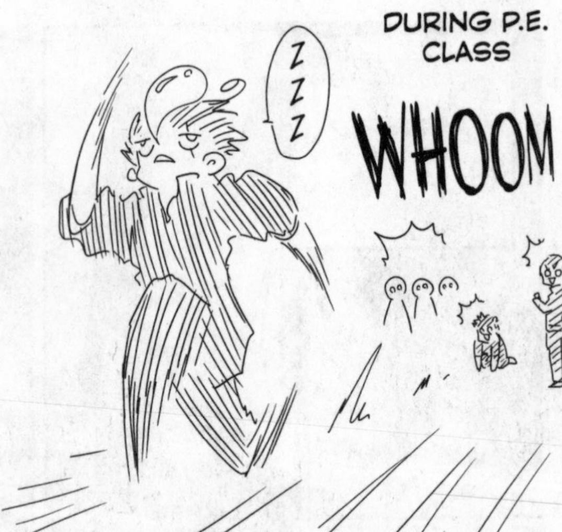
DURING P.E. CLASS
Z Z Z
WHOOM

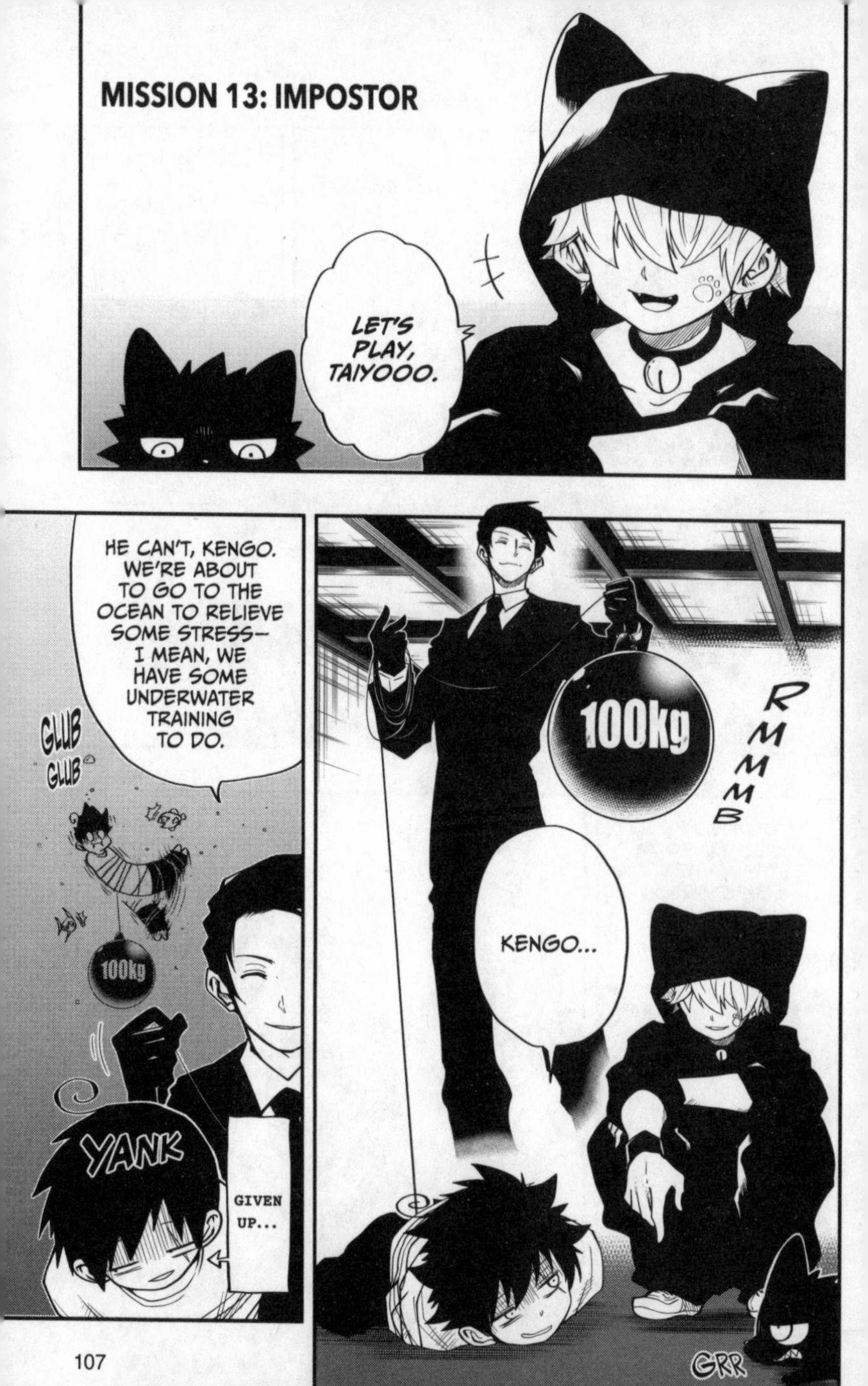
MISSION 13: IMPOSTOR
LET'S PLAY, TAIYOOO.
100kg
RMMMB
KENGO...
GRR
HE CAN'T, KENGO. WE'RE ABOUT TO GO TO THE OCEAN TO RELIEVE SOME STRESS— I MEAN, WE HAVE SOME UNDERWATER TRAINING TO DO.
GLUB GLUB
100kg
YANK
GIVEN UP...

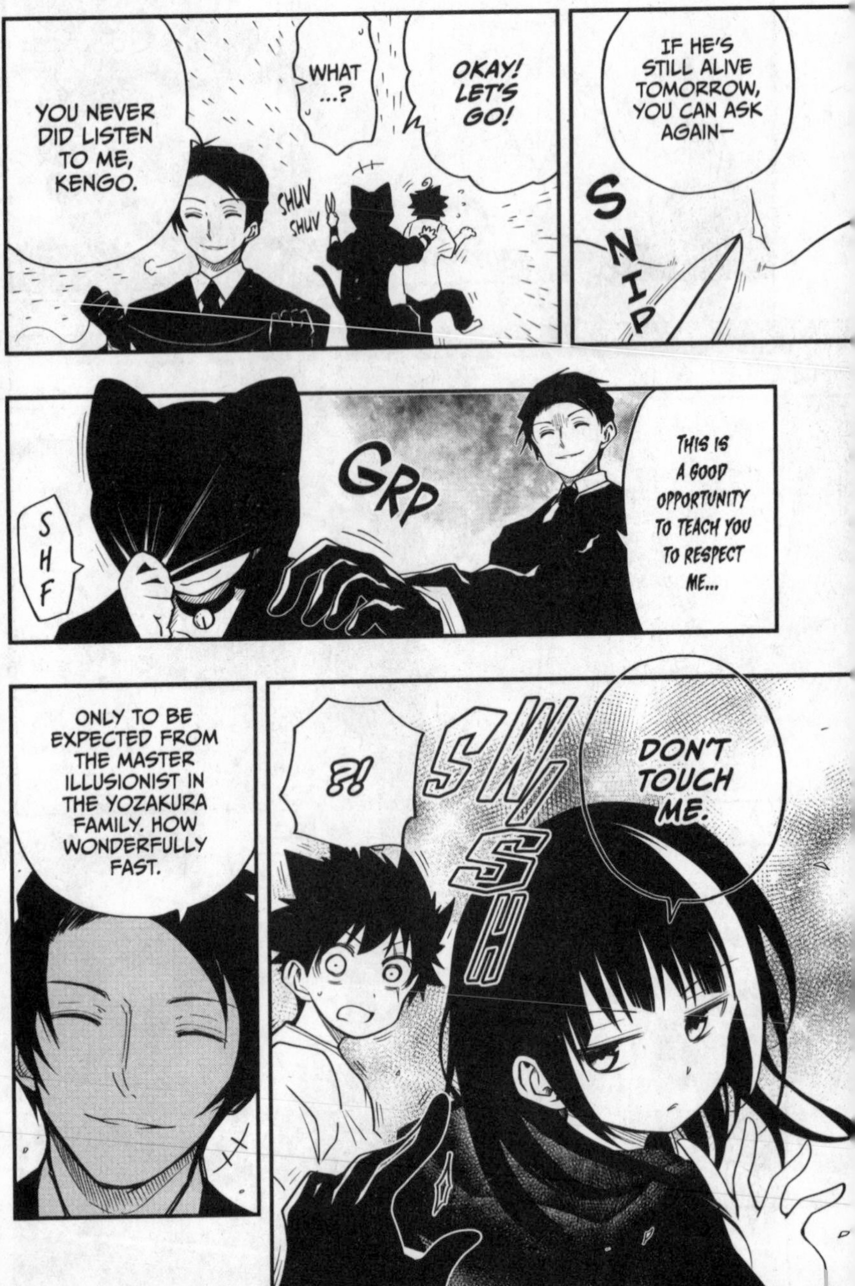
IF HE'S STILL ALIVE TOMORROW, YOU CAN ASK AGAIN—
SNIP
OKAY! LET'S GO!
WHAT ...?
SHUV SHUV
YOU NEVER DID LISTEN TO ME, KENGO.
THIS IS A GOOD OPPORTUNITY TO TEACH YOU TO RESPECT ME...
GRP
SHF
DON'T TOUCH ME.
SWSH
?!
ONLY TO BE EXPECTED FROM THE MASTER ILLUSIONIST IN THE YOZAKURA FAMILY. HOW WONDERFULLY FAST.

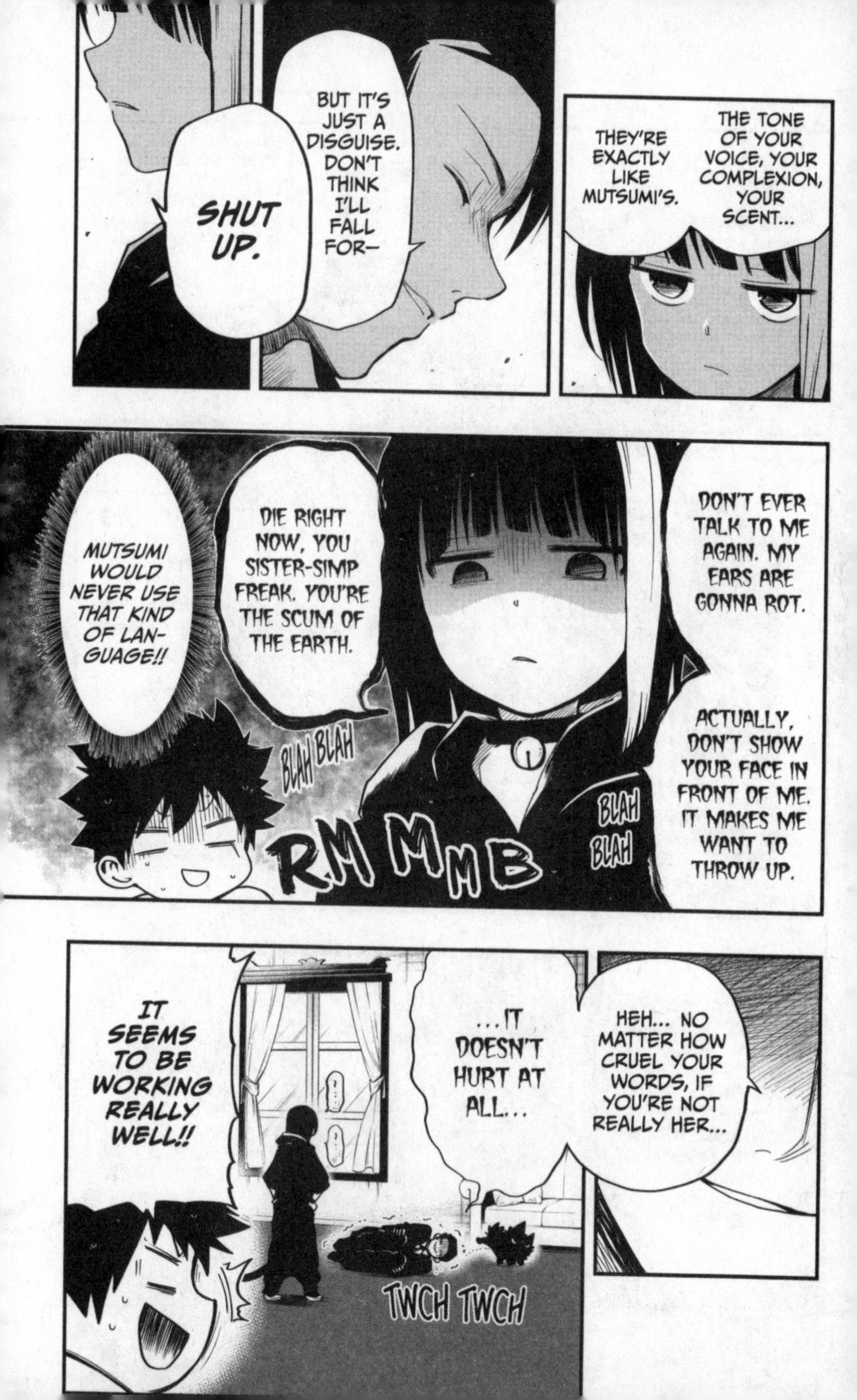
THE TONE OF YOUR VOICE, YOUR COMPLEXION, YOUR SCENT...
THEY'RE EXACTLY LIKE MUTSUMI'S.
BUT IT'S JUST A DISGUISE. DON'T THINK I'LL FALL FOR—
SHUT UP.
DON'T EVER TALK TO ME AGAIN. MY EARS ARE GONNA ROT.
ACTUALLY, DON'T SHOW YOUR FACE IN FRONT OF ME. IT MAKES ME WANT TO THROW UP.
BLAH BLAH
DIE RIGHT NOW, YOU SISTER-SIMP FREAK. YOU'RE THE SCUM OF THE EARTH.
BLAH BLAH
RMMMB
MUTSUMI WOULD NEVER USE THAT KIND OF LAN-GUAGE!!
HEH... NO MATTER HOW CRUEL YOUR WORDS, IF YOU'RE NOT REALLY HER...
...IT DOESN'T HURT AT ALL...
TWCH TWCH
IT SEEMS TO BE WORKING REALLY WELL!!

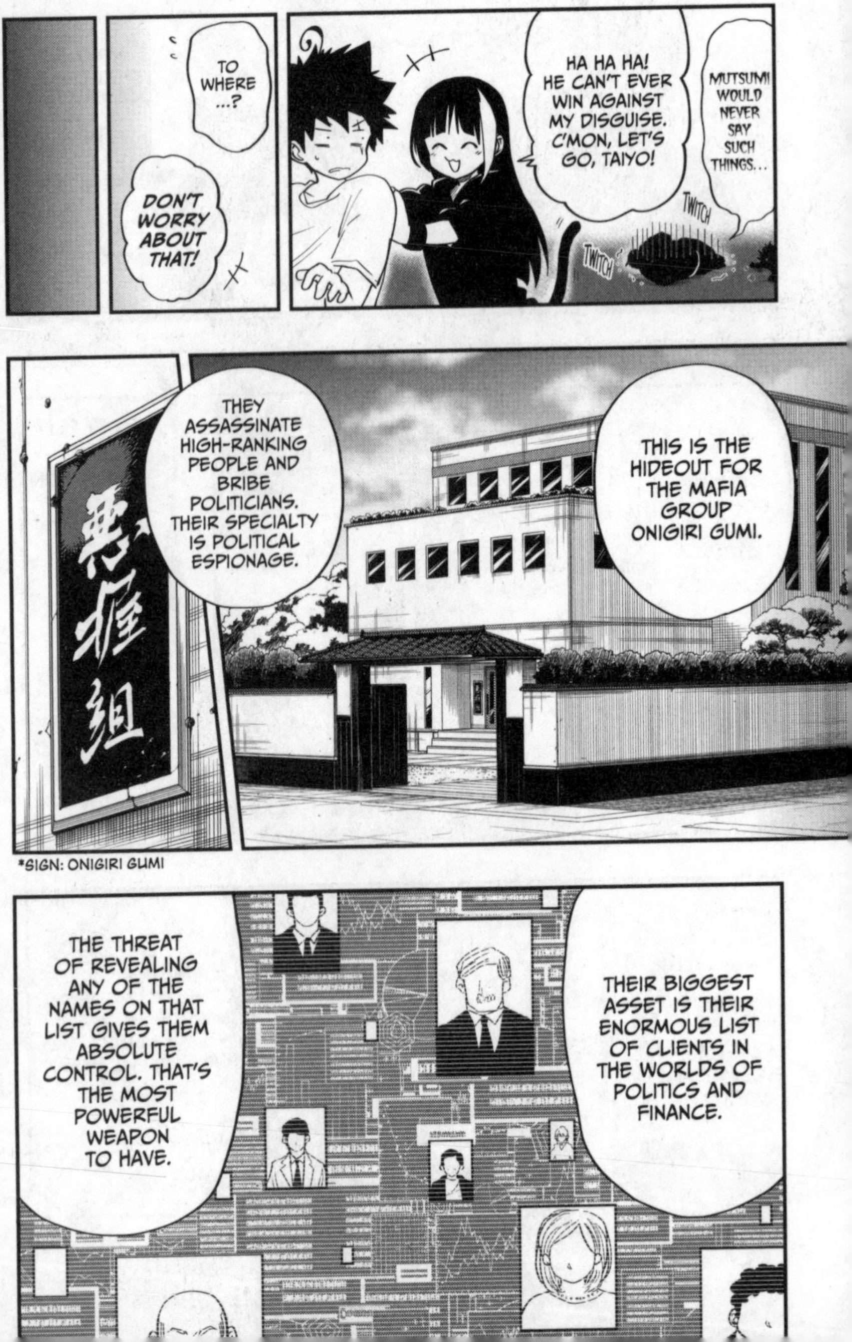
MUTSUMI WOULD NEVER SAY SUCH THINGS...
HA HA HA! HE CAN'T EVER WIN AGAINST MY DISGUISE. C'MON, LET'S GO, TAIYO!
TWITCH
TWITCH
TO WHERE ...?
DON'T WORRY ABOUT THAT!
THIS IS THE HIDEOUT FOR THE MAFIA GROUP ONIGIRI GUMI.
THEY ASSASSINATE HIGH-RANKING PEOPLE AND BRIBE POLITICIANS. THEIR SPECIALTY IS POLITICAL ESPIONAGE.
THEIR BIGGEST ASSET IS THEIR ENORMOUS LIST OF CLIENTS IN THE WORLDS OF POLITICS AND FINANCE.
THE THREAT OF REVEALING ANY OF THE NAMES ON THAT LIST GIVES THEM ABSOLUTE CONTROL. THAT'S THE MOST POWERFUL WEAPON TO HAVE.

*SIGN: ONIGIRI GUMI

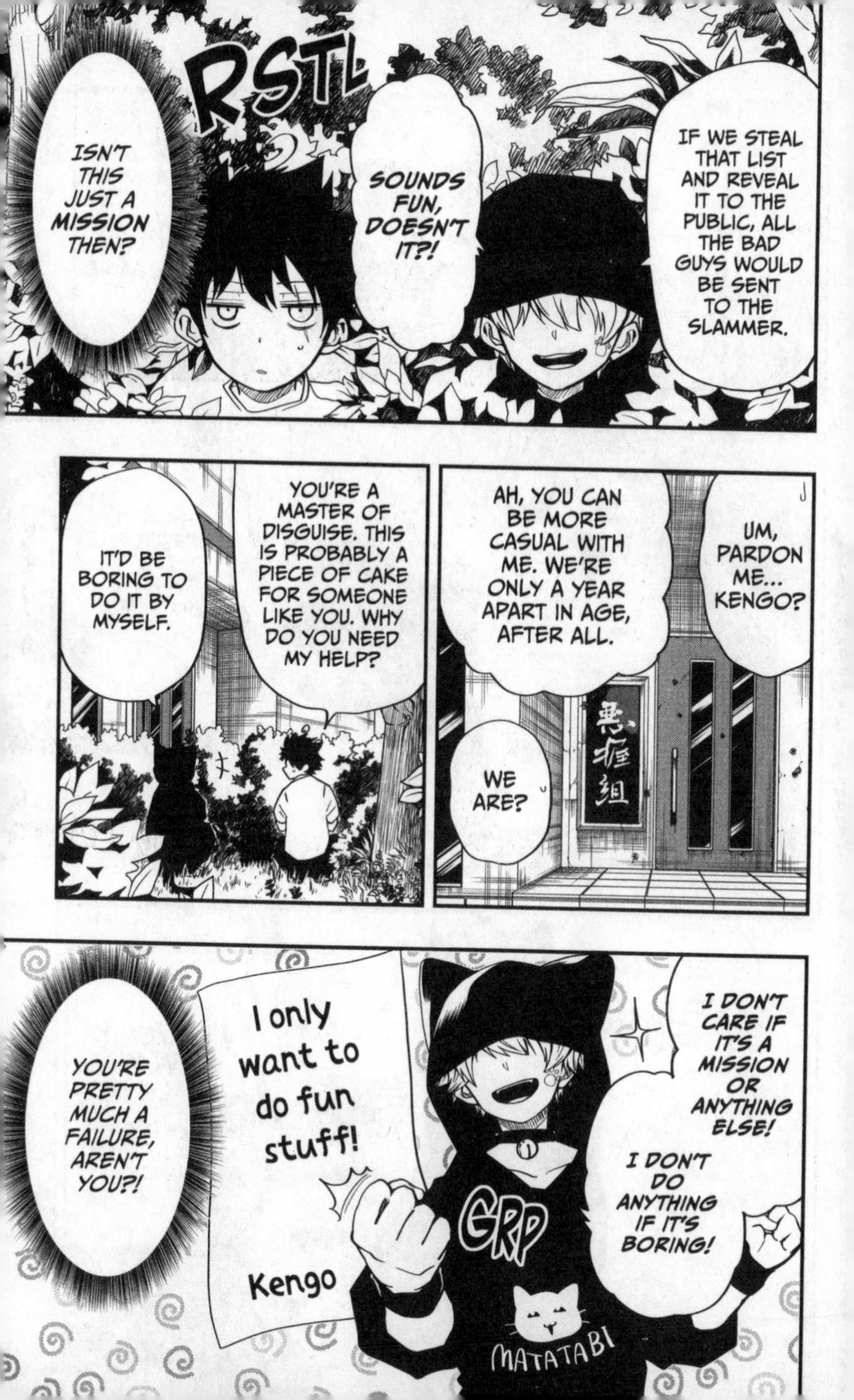
IF WE STEAL THAT LIST AND REVEAL IT TO THE PUBLIC, ALL THE BAD GUYS WOULD BE SENT TO THE SLAMMER.
SOUNDS FUN, DOESN'T IT?!
RSTL
ISN'T THIS JUST A MISSION THEN?
UM, PARDON ME... KENGO?
AH, YOU CAN BE MORE CASUAL WITH ME. WE'RE ONLY A YEAR APART IN AGE, AFTER ALL.
WE ARE?
YOU'RE A MASTER OF DISGUISE. THIS IS PROBABLY A PIECE OF CAKE FOR SOMEONE LIKE YOU. WHY DO YOU NEED MY HELP?
IT'D BE BORING TO DO IT BY MYSELF.
I DON'T CARE IF IT'S A MISSION OR ANYTHING ELSE!
I DON'T DO ANYTHING IF IT'S BORING!
GRP
MATATABI
I only want to do fun stuff!
Kengo
YOU'RE PRETTY MUCH A FAILURE, AREN'T YOU?!

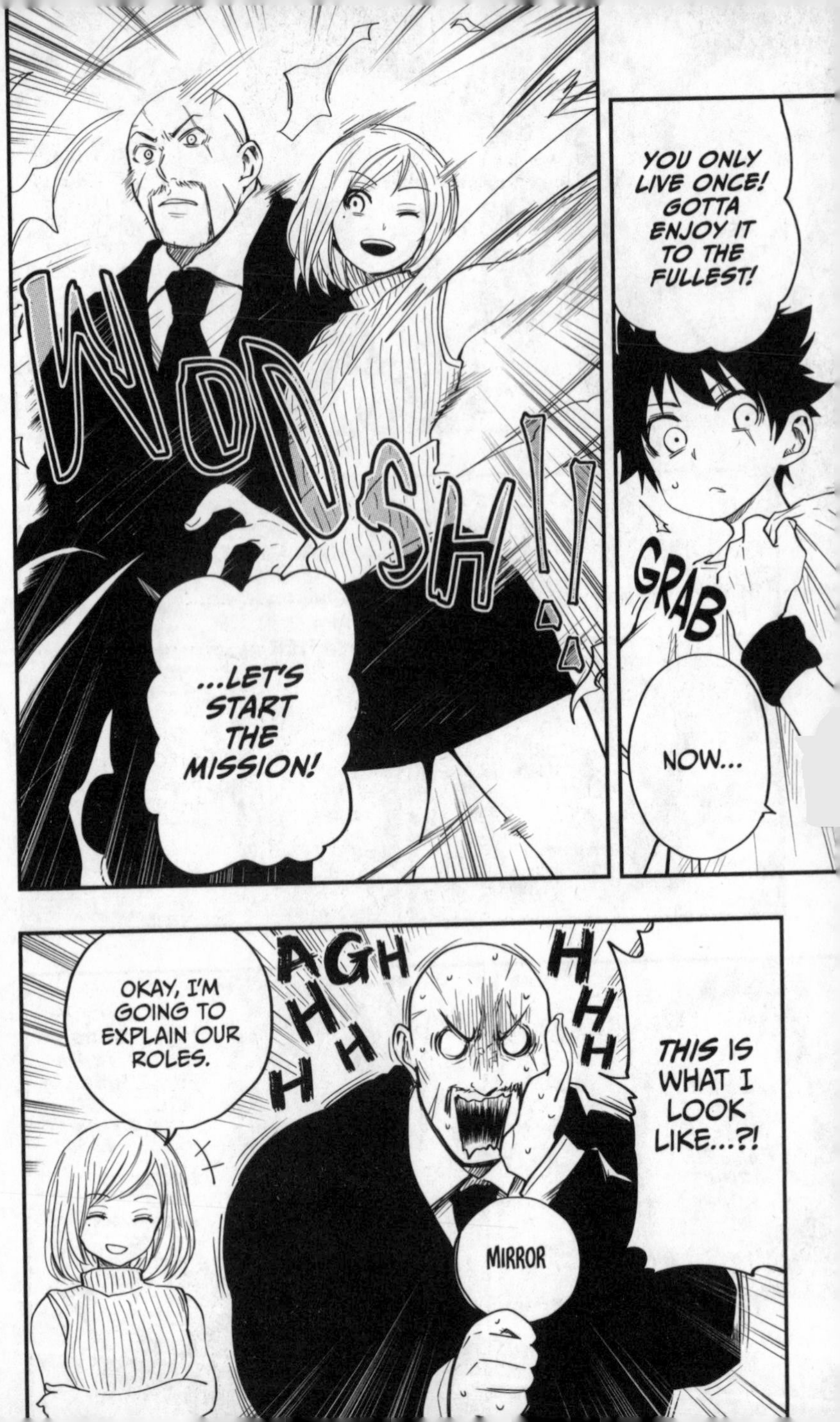
YOU ONLY LIVE ONCE! GOTTA ENJOY IT TO THE FULLEST!
GRAB
NOW...
WOOSH!!
...LET'S START THE MISSION!
THIS IS WHAT I LOOK LIKE...?!
AGHHHHHHHHH
OKAY, I'M GOING TO EXPLAIN OUR ROLES.
MIRROR

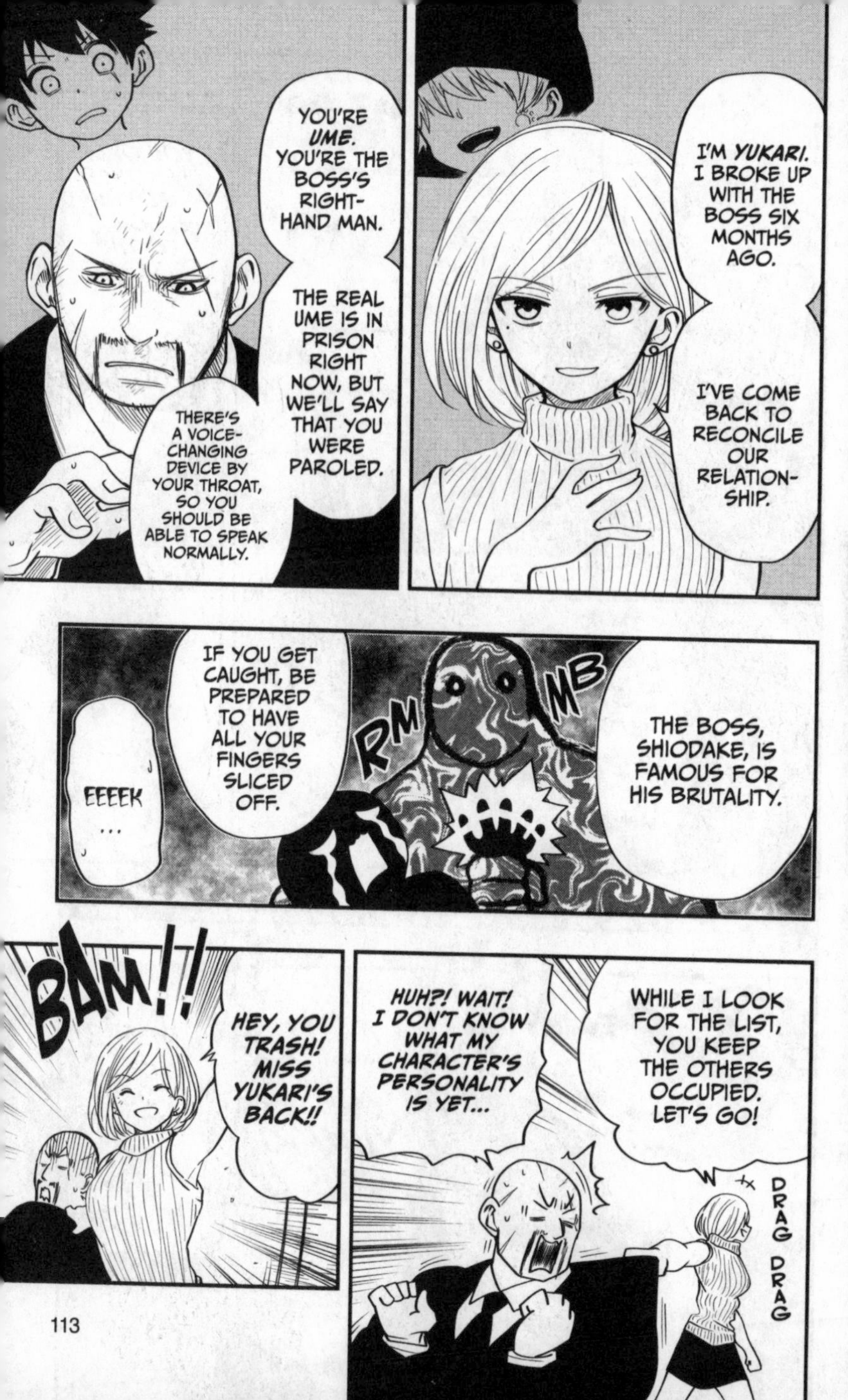
I'M YUKARI. I BROKE UP WITH THE BOSS SIX MONTHS AGO.
I'VE COME BACK TO RECONCILE OUR RELATIONSHIP.
YOU'RE UME. YOU'RE THE BOSS'S RIGHT-HAND MAN.
THE REAL UME IS IN PRISON RIGHT NOW, BUT WE'LL SAY THAT YOU WERE PAROLED.
THERE'S A VOICE-CHANGING DEVICE BY YOUR THROAT, SO YOU SHOULD BE ABLE TO SPEAK NORMALLY.
THE BOSS, SHIODAKE, IS FAMOUS FOR HIS BRUTALITY.
RMMB
IF YOU GET CAUGHT, BE PREPARED TO HAVE ALL YOUR FINGERS SLICED OFF.
EEEEK...
WHILE I LOOK FOR THE LIST, YOU KEEP THE OTHERS OCCUPIED. LET'S GO!
DRAG DRAG
HUH?! WAIT! I DON'T KNOW WHAT MY CHARACTER'S PERSONALITY IS YET...
BAM!!
HEY, YOU TRASH! MISS YUKARI'S BACK!!

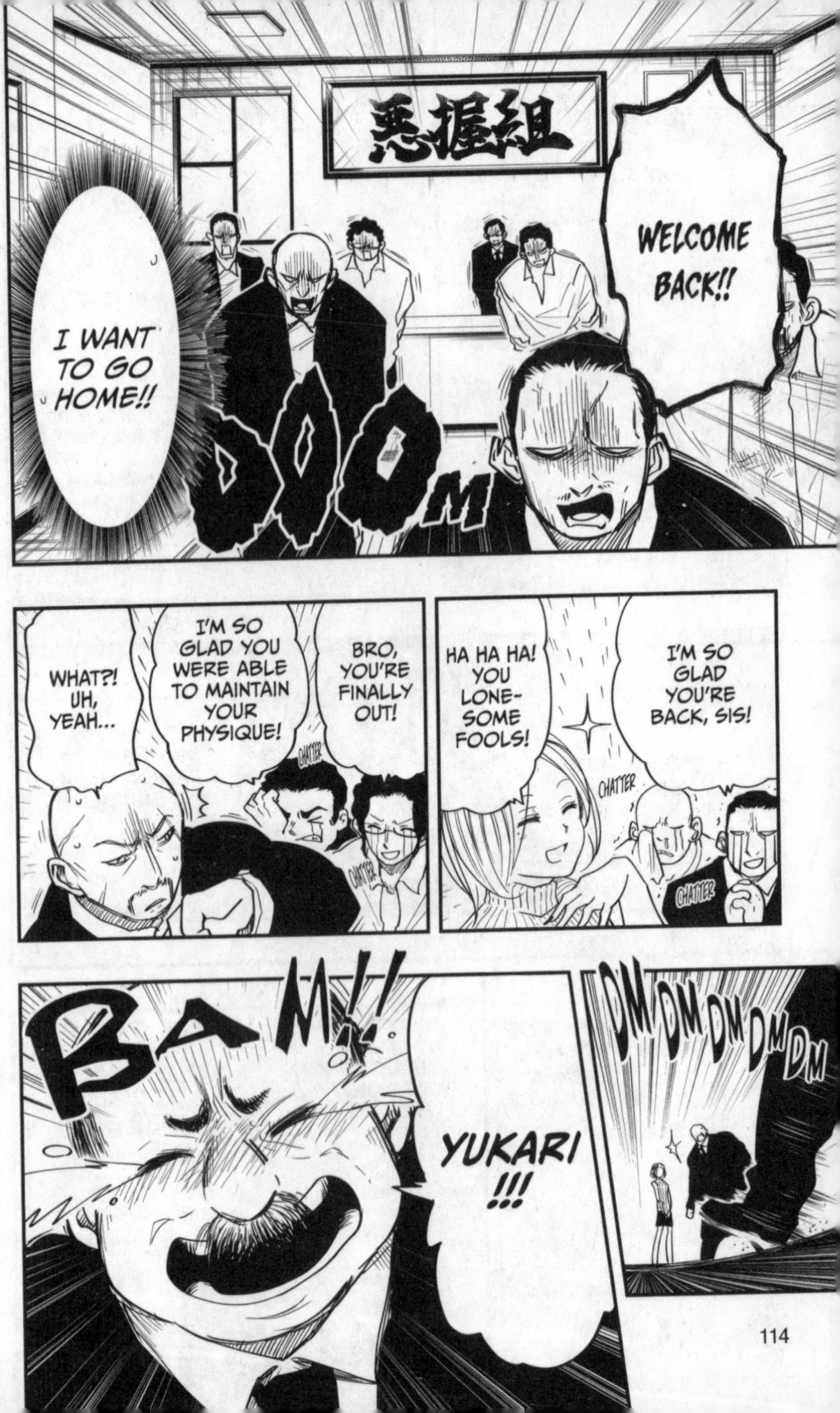
悪握組
WELCOME BACK!!
DOOM
I WANT TO GO HOME!!
I'M SO GLAD YOU'RE BACK, SIS!
CHATTER
CHATTER
HA HA HA! YOU LONE-SOME FOOLS!
BRO, YOU'RE FINALLY OUT!
CHATTER
I'M SO GLAD YOU WERE ABLE TO MAINTAIN YOUR PHYSIQUE!
CHATTER
WHAT?! UH, YEAH...
DM DM DM DM DM
YUKARI!!!
BAM!!

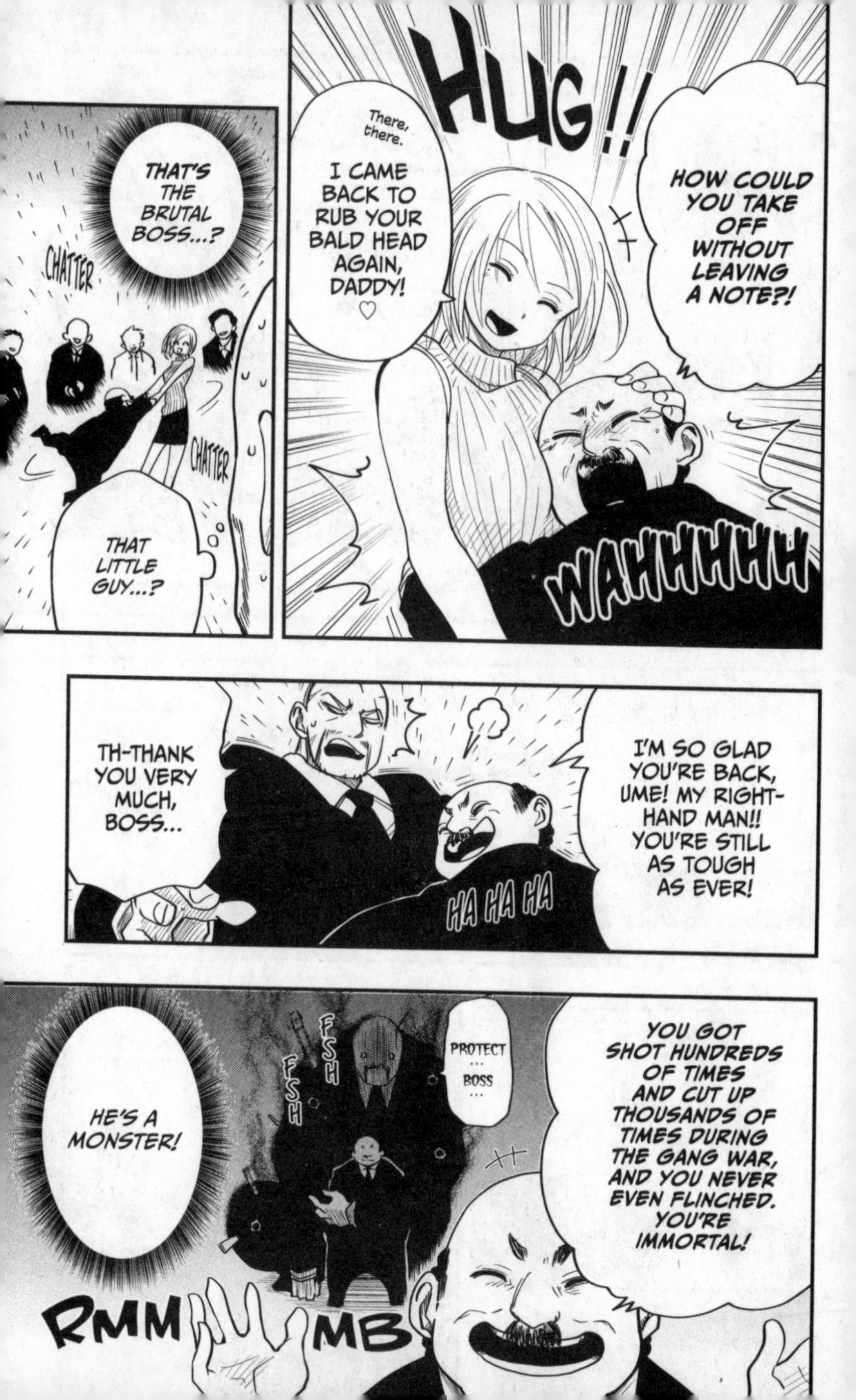
HUG!!
HOW COULD YOU TAKE OFF WITHOUT LEAVING A NOTE?!
There, there.
I CAME BACK TO RUB YOUR BALD HEAD AGAIN, DADDY! ♡
WAHHHHHH
THAT'S THE BRUTAL BOSS...?
CHATTER
CHATTER
THAT LITTLE GUY...?
I'M SO GLAD YOU'RE BACK, UME! MY RIGHT-HAND MAN!! YOU'RE STILL AS TOUGH AS EVER!
HA HA HA
TH-THANK YOU VERY MUCH, BOSS...
YOU GOT SHOT HUNDREDS OF TIMES AND CUT UP THOUSANDS OF TIMES DURING THE GANG WAR, AND YOU NEVER EVEN FLINCHED. YOU'RE IMMORTAL!
PROTECT ... BOSS ...
FSH
FSH
HE'S A MONSTER!
RMMMB

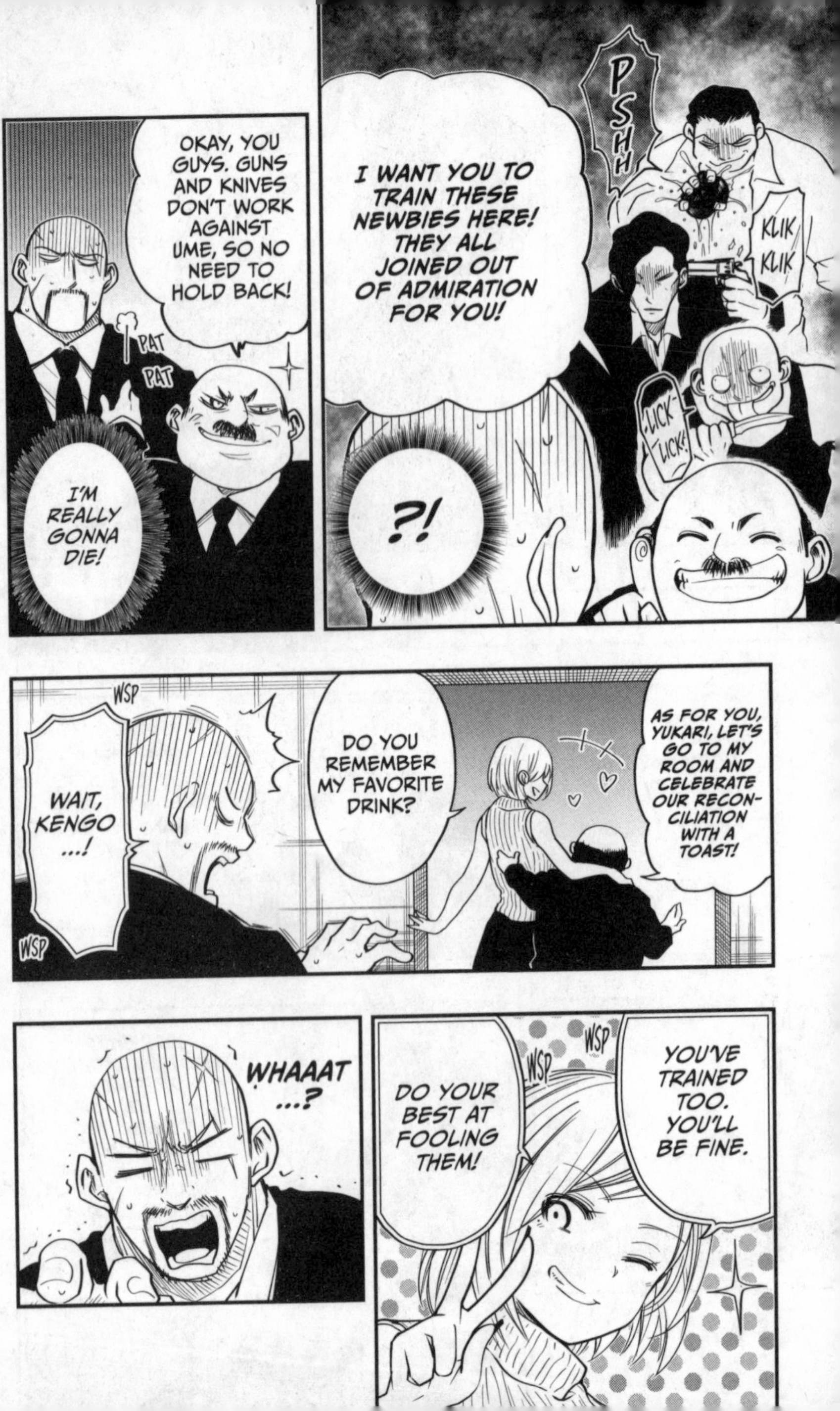
PSHH
I WANT YOU TO TRAIN THESE NEWBIES HERE! THEY ALL JOINED OUT OF ADMIRATION FOR YOU!
KLIK KLIK
LICK LICK
?!
OKAY, YOU GUYS. GUNS AND KNIVES DON'T WORK AGAINST UME, SO NO NEED TO HOLD BACK!
PAT PAT
I'M REALLY GONNA DIE!
AS FOR YOU, YUKARI, LET'S GO TO MY ROOM AND CELEBRATE OUR RECONCILIATION WITH A TOAST!
DO YOU REMEMBER MY FAVORITE DRINK?
WSP
WAIT, KENGO ...!
WSP
YOU'VE TRAINED TOO. YOU'LL BE FINE.
WSP
DO YOUR BEST AT FOOLING THEM!
WSP
WHAAAT ...?

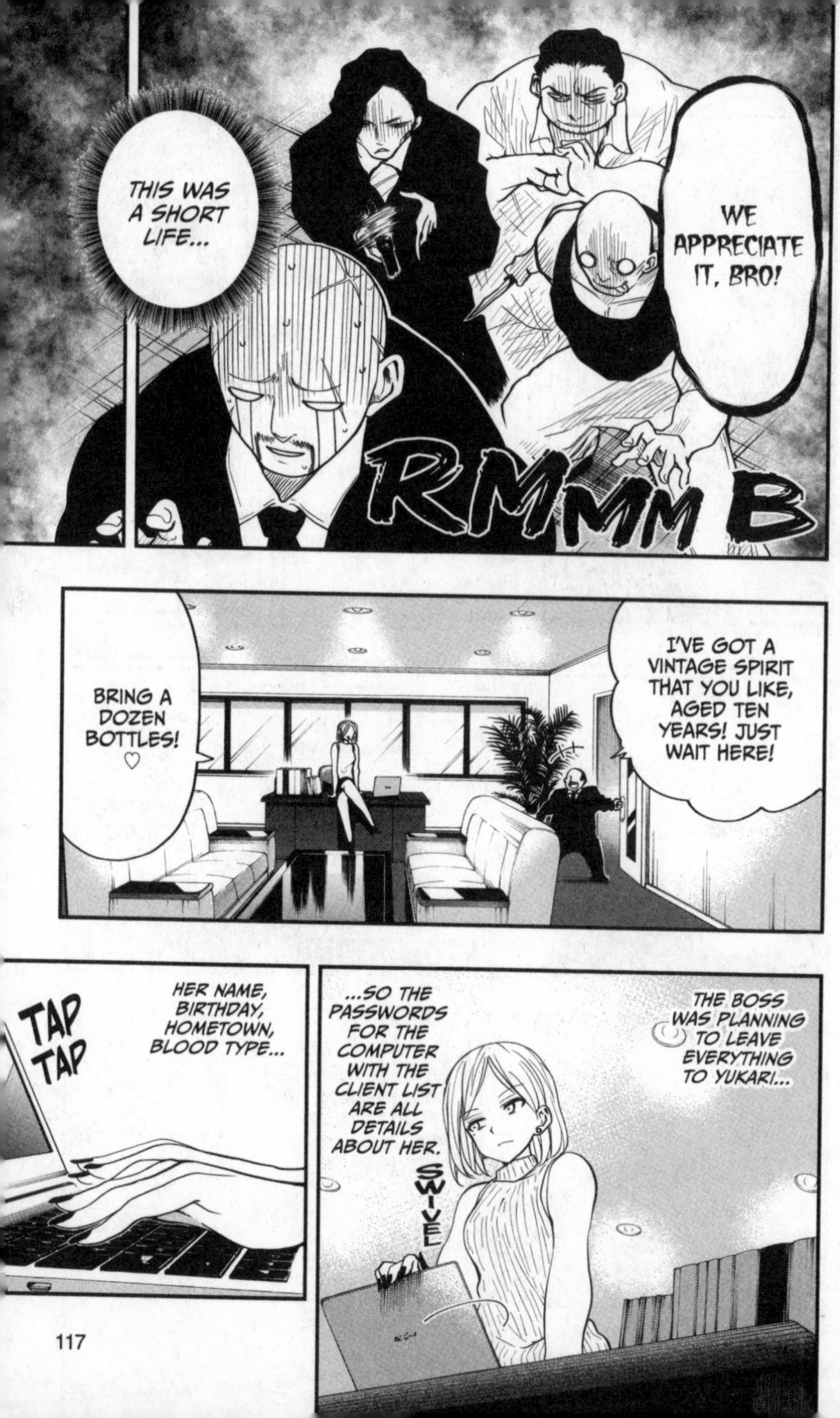
WE APPRECIATE IT, BRO!
THIS WAS A SHORT LIFE...
RMMMB
I'VE GOT A VINTAGE SPIRIT THAT YOU LIKE, AGED TEN YEARS! JUST WAIT HERE!
BRING A DOZEN BOTTLES! ♡
THE BOSS WAS PLANNING TO LEAVE EVERYTHING TO YUKARI...
...SO THE PASSWORDS FOR THE COMPUTER WITH THE CLIENT LIST ARE ALL DETAILS ABOUT HER.
SWIVEL
HER NAME, BIRTHDAY, HOMETOWN, BLOOD TYPE...
TAP TAP

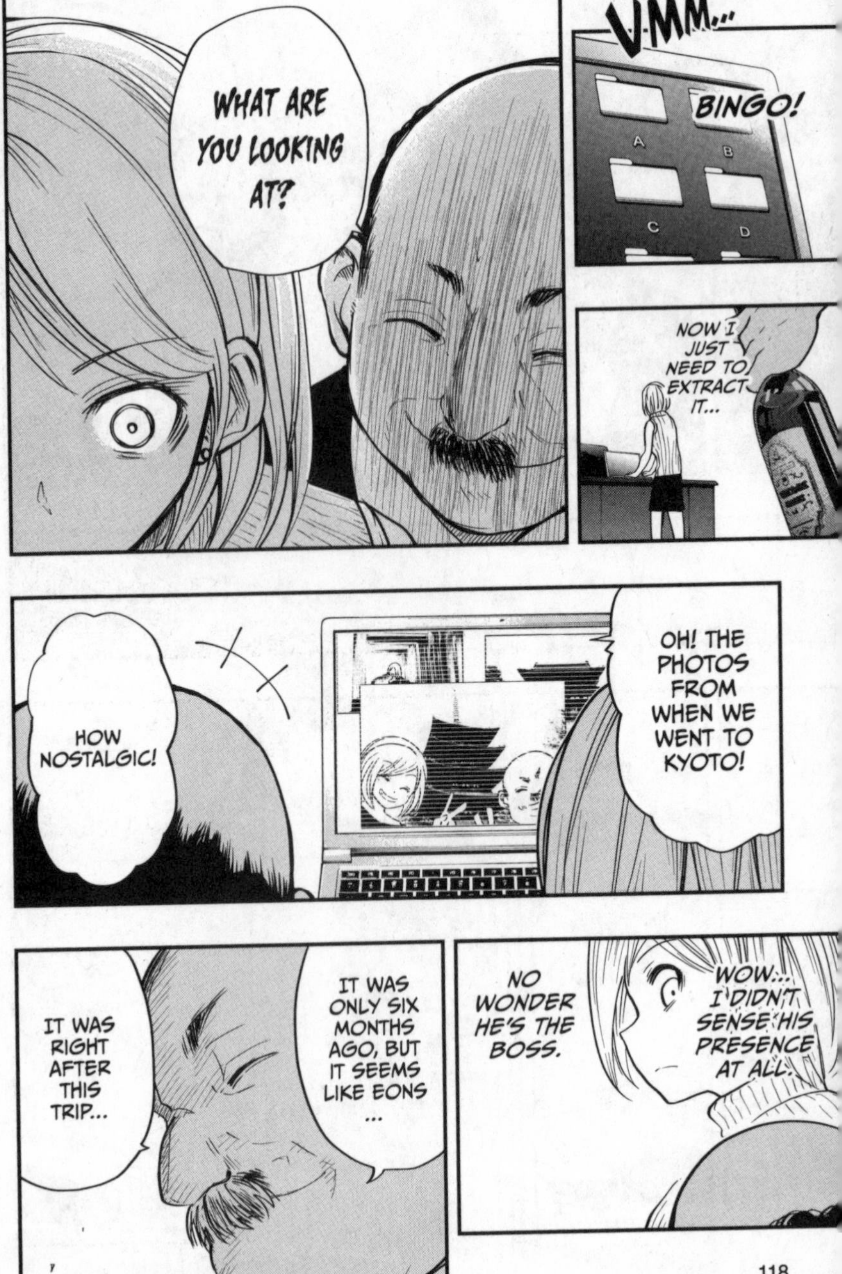
VMM...
BINGO!
NOW I JUST NEED TO EXTRACT IT...
WHAT ARE YOU LOOKING AT?
OH! THE PHOTOS FROM WHEN WE WENT TO KYOTO!
HOW NOSTALGIC!
WOW... I DIDN'T SENSE HIS PRESENCE AT ALL.
NO WONDER HE'S THE BOSS.
IT WAS ONLY SIX MONTHS AGO, BUT IT SEEMS LIKE EONS ...
IT WAS RIGHT AFTER THIS TRIP...

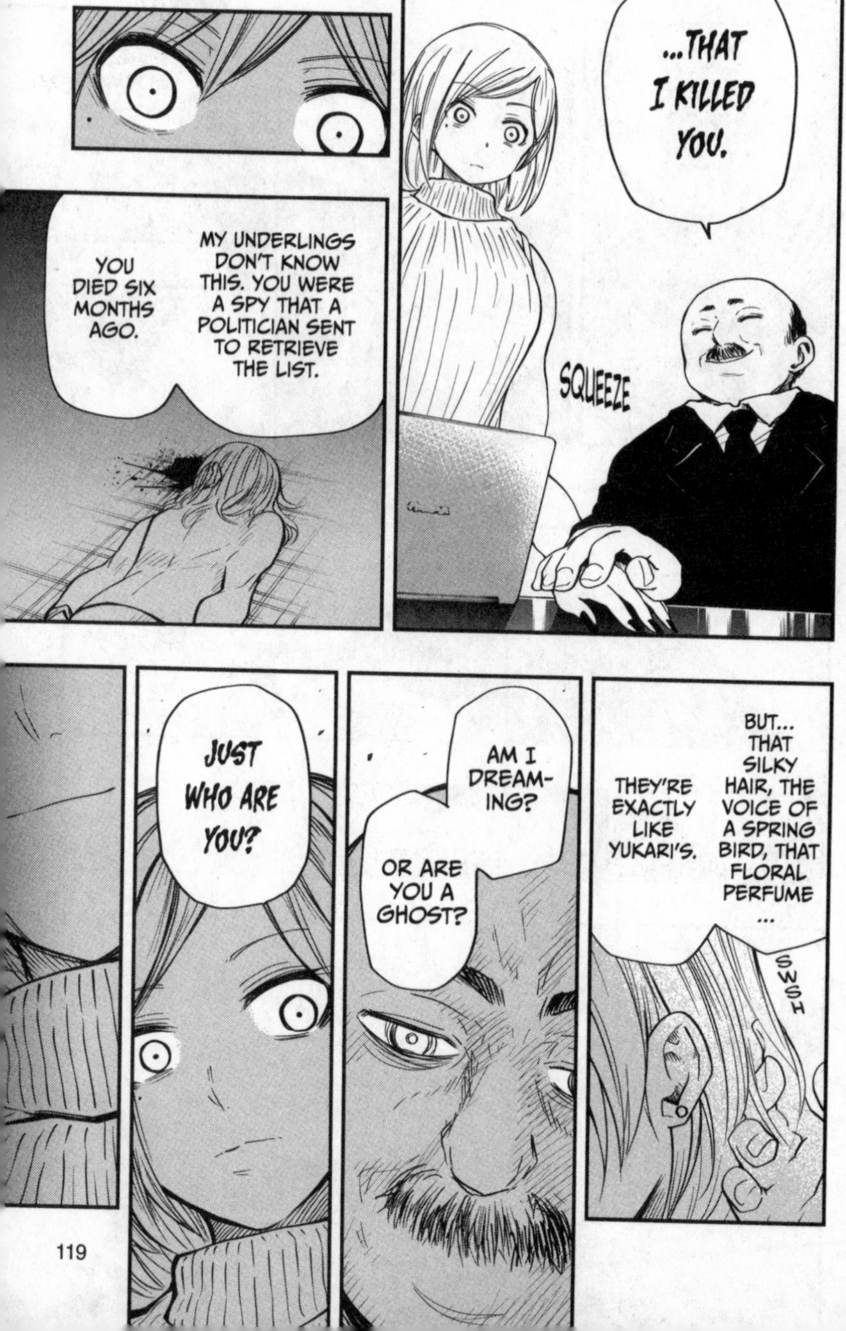
...THAT I KILLED YOU.
SQUEEZE
MY UNDERLINGS DON'T KNOW THIS. YOU WERE A SPY THAT A POLITICIAN SENT TO RETRIEVE THE LIST.
YOU DIED SIX MONTHS AGO.
BUT... THAT SILKY HAIR, THE VOICE OF A SPRING BIRD, THAT FLORAL PERFUME...
THEY'RE EXACTLY LIKE YUKARI'S.
SWSH
AM I DREAMING?
OR ARE YOU A GHOST?
JUST WHO ARE YOU?

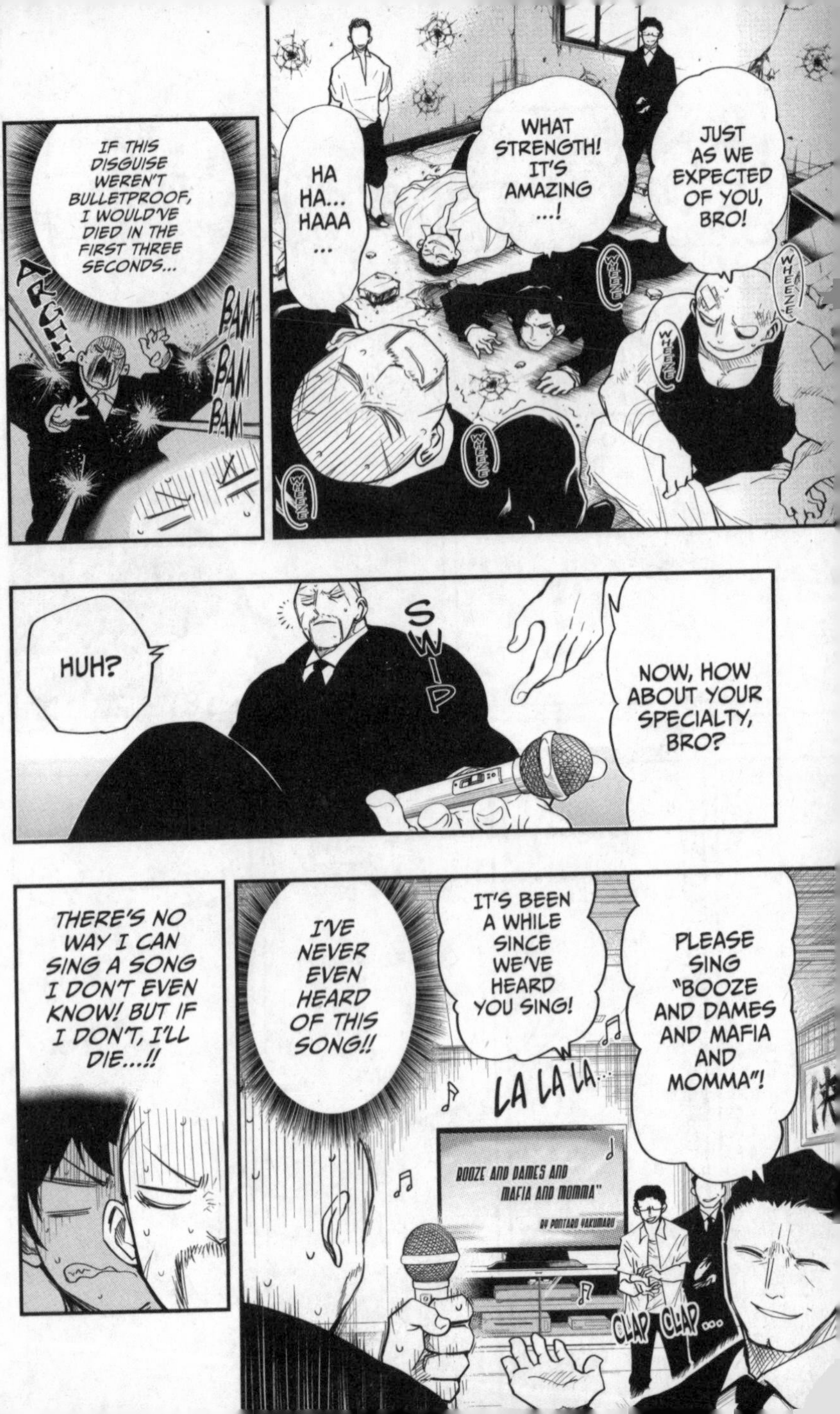
JUST AS WE EXPECTED OF YOU, BRO!
WHAT STRENGTH! IT'S AMAZING ...!
HA HA... HAAA ...
WHEEZE
WHEEZE
WHEEZE
WHEEZE
WHEEZE
IF THIS DISGUISE WEREN'T BULLETPROOF, I WOULD'VE DIED IN THE FIRST THREE SECONDS...
BAM BAM BAM BAM
ARGHH
NOW, HOW ABOUT YOUR SPECIALTY, BRO?
SWIP
HUH?
PLEASE SING "BOOZE AND DAMES AND MAFIA AND MOMMA"!
IT'S BEEN A WHILE SINCE WE'VE HEARD YOU SING!
LA LA LA...
I'VE NEVER EVEN HEARD OF THIS SONG!!
BOOZE AND DAMES AND MAFIA AND MOMMA"
BY PONTARO YAKUMARU
CLAP CLAP...
THERE'S NO WAY I CAN SING A SONG I DON'T EVEN KNOW! BUT IF I DON'T, I'LL DIE...!!

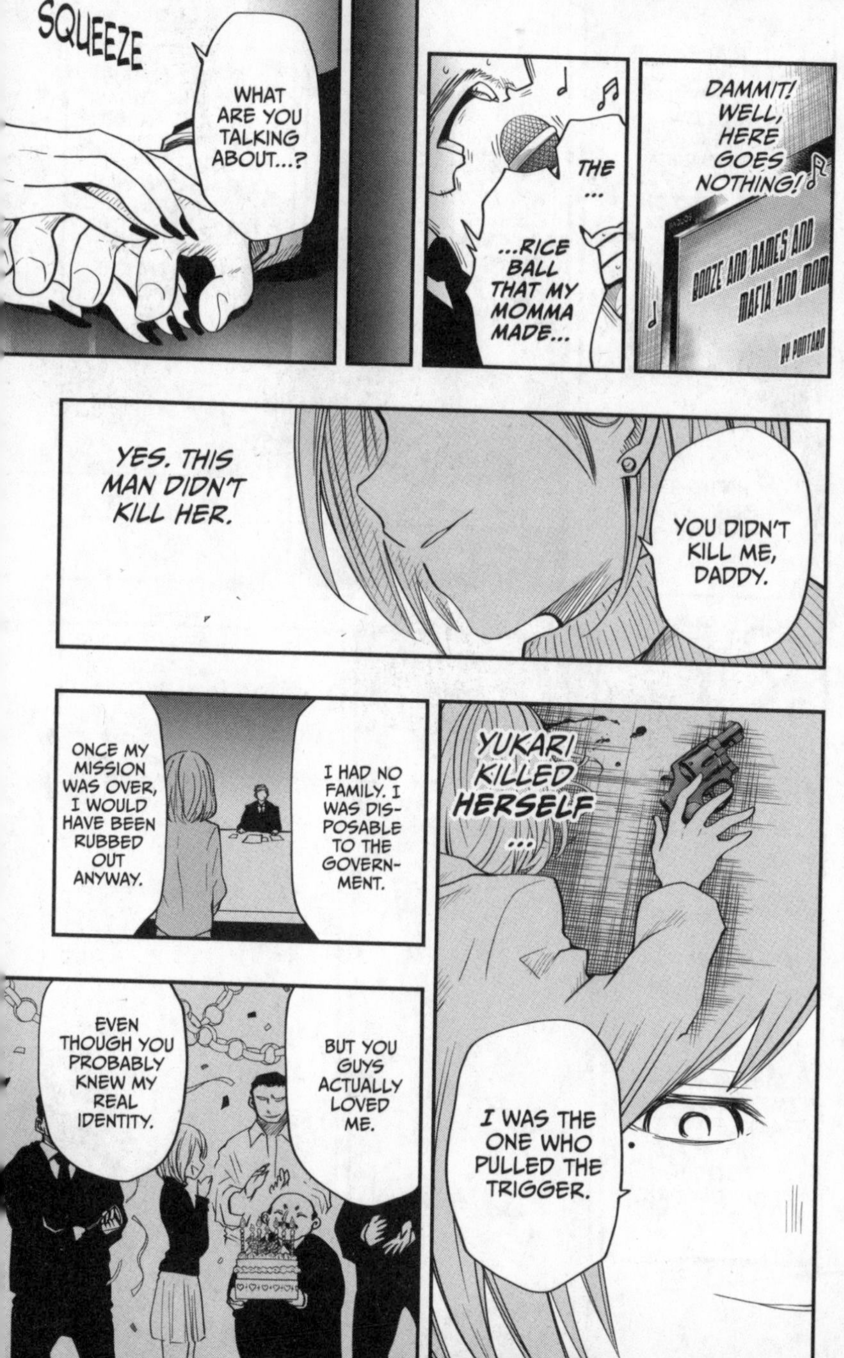
DAMMIT! WELL, HERE GOES NOTHING!
BOOZE AND DAMES AND
MAFIA AND MOM
BY PONTARO
THE ...
...RICE BALL THAT MY MOMMA MADE...
SQUEEZE
WHAT ARE YOU TALKING ABOUT...?
YOU DIDN'T KILL ME, DADDY.
YES. THIS MAN DIDN'T KILL HER.
YUKARI KILLED HERSELF ...
I WAS THE ONE WHO PULLED THE TRIGGER.
I HAD NO FAMILY. I WAS DISPOSABLE TO THE GOVERNMENT.
ONCE MY MISSION WAS OVER, I WOULD HAVE BEEN RUBBED OUT ANYWAY.
BUT YOU GUYS ACTUALLY LOVED ME.
EVEN THOUGH YOU PROBABLY KNEW MY REAL IDENTITY.

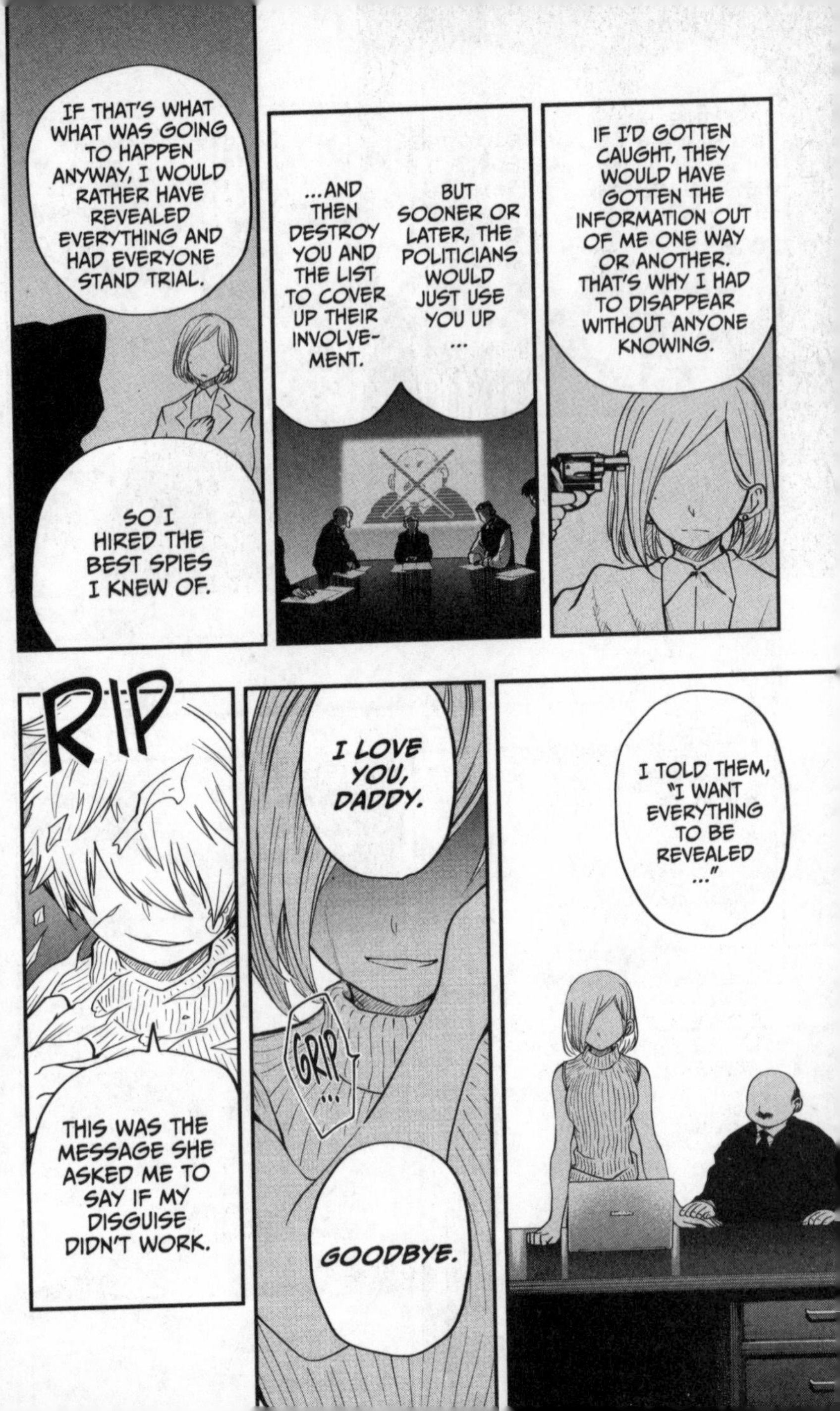
IF I'D GOTTEN CAUGHT, THEY WOULD HAVE GOTTEN THE INFORMATION OUT OF ME ONE WAY OR ANOTHER. THAT'S WHY I HAD TO DISAPPEAR WITHOUT ANYONE KNOWING.
BUT SOONER OR LATER, THE POLITICIANS WOULD JUST USE YOU UP ...
...AND THEN DESTROY YOU AND THE LIST TO COVER UP THEIR INVOLVE-MENT.
IF THAT'S WHAT WHAT WAS GOING TO HAPPEN ANYWAY, I WOULD RATHER HAVE REVEALED EVERYTHING AND HAD EVERYONE STAND TRIAL.
SO I HIRED THE BEST SPIES I KNEW OF.
I TOLD THEM, "I WANT EVERYTHING TO BE REVEALED ..."
I LOVE YOU, DADDY.
GRIP ...
GOODBYE.
RIP
THIS WAS THE MESSAGE SHE ASKED ME TO SAY IF MY DISGUISE DIDN'T WORK.

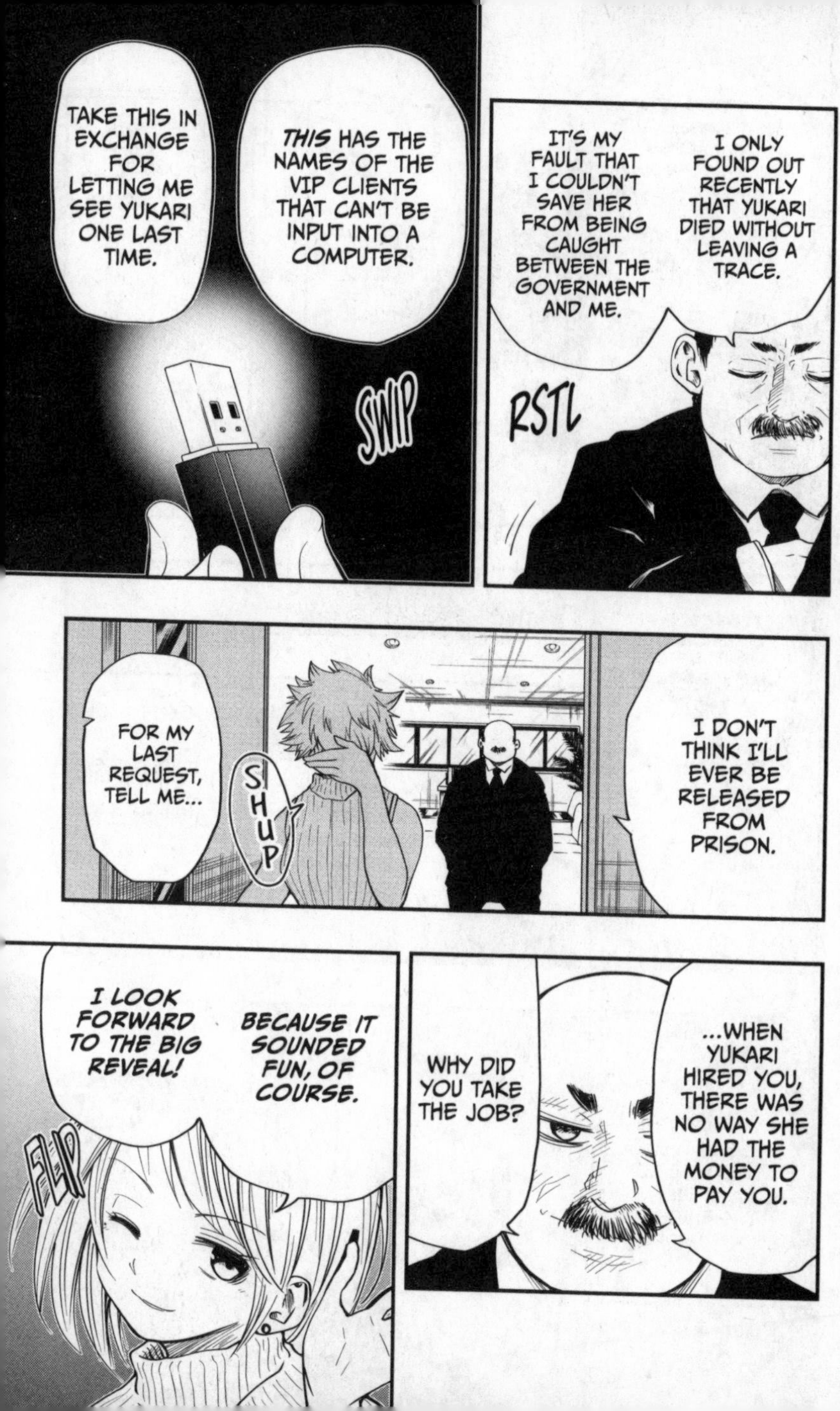
I ONLY FOUND OUT RECENTLY THAT YUKARI DIED WITHOUT LEAVING A TRACE.
IT'S MY FAULT THAT I COULDN'T SAVE HER FROM BEING CAUGHT BETWEEN THE GOVERNMENT AND ME.
RSTL
THIS HAS THE NAMES OF THE VIP CLIENTS THAT CAN'T BE INPUT INTO A COMPUTER.
TAKE THIS IN EXCHANGE FOR LETTING ME SEE YUKARI ONE LAST TIME.
SWIP
I DON'T THINK I'LL EVER BE RELEASED FROM PRISON.
SHUP
FOR MY LAST REQUEST, TELL ME...
...WHEN YUKARI HIRED YOU, THERE WAS NO WAY SHE HAD THE MONEY TO PAY YOU.
WHY DID YOU TAKE THE JOB?
BECAUSE IT SOUNDED FUN, OF COURSE.
I LOOK FORWARD TO THE BIG REVEAL!
FLIP

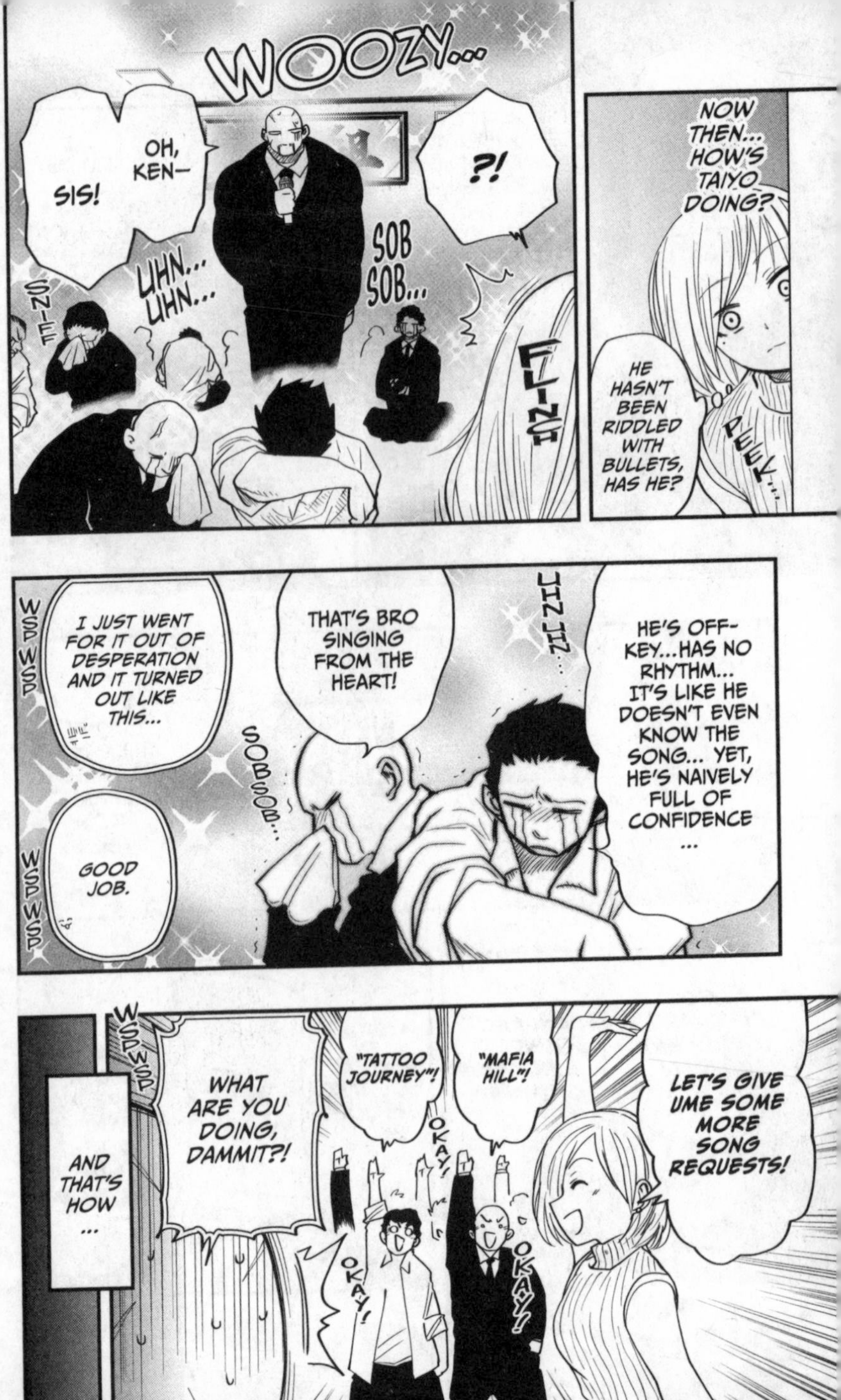
NOW THEN... HOW'S TAIYO DOING?
HE HASN'T BEEN RIDDLED WITH BULLETS, HAS HE?
PEEK...
WOOZY...
?!
FLINCH
SOB SOB...
OH, KEN—
SIS!
UHN... UHN...
SNIFF
HE'S OFF-KEY...HAS NO RHYTHM... IT'S LIKE HE DOESN'T EVEN KNOW THE SONG... YET, HE'S NAIVELY FULL OF CONFIDENCE ...
UHN UHN...
THAT'S BRO SINGING FROM THE HEART!
SOBSOB...
I JUST WENT FOR IT OUT OF DESPERATION AND IT TURNED OUT LIKE THIS...
WSP WSP
GOOD JOB.
WSP WSP
LET'S GIVE UME SOME MORE SONG REQUESTS!
OKAY!
"MAFIA HILL"!
OKAY!
"TATTOO JOURNEY"!
OKAY!
WHAT ARE YOU DOING, DAMMIT?!
WSP WSP
AND THAT'S HOW ...

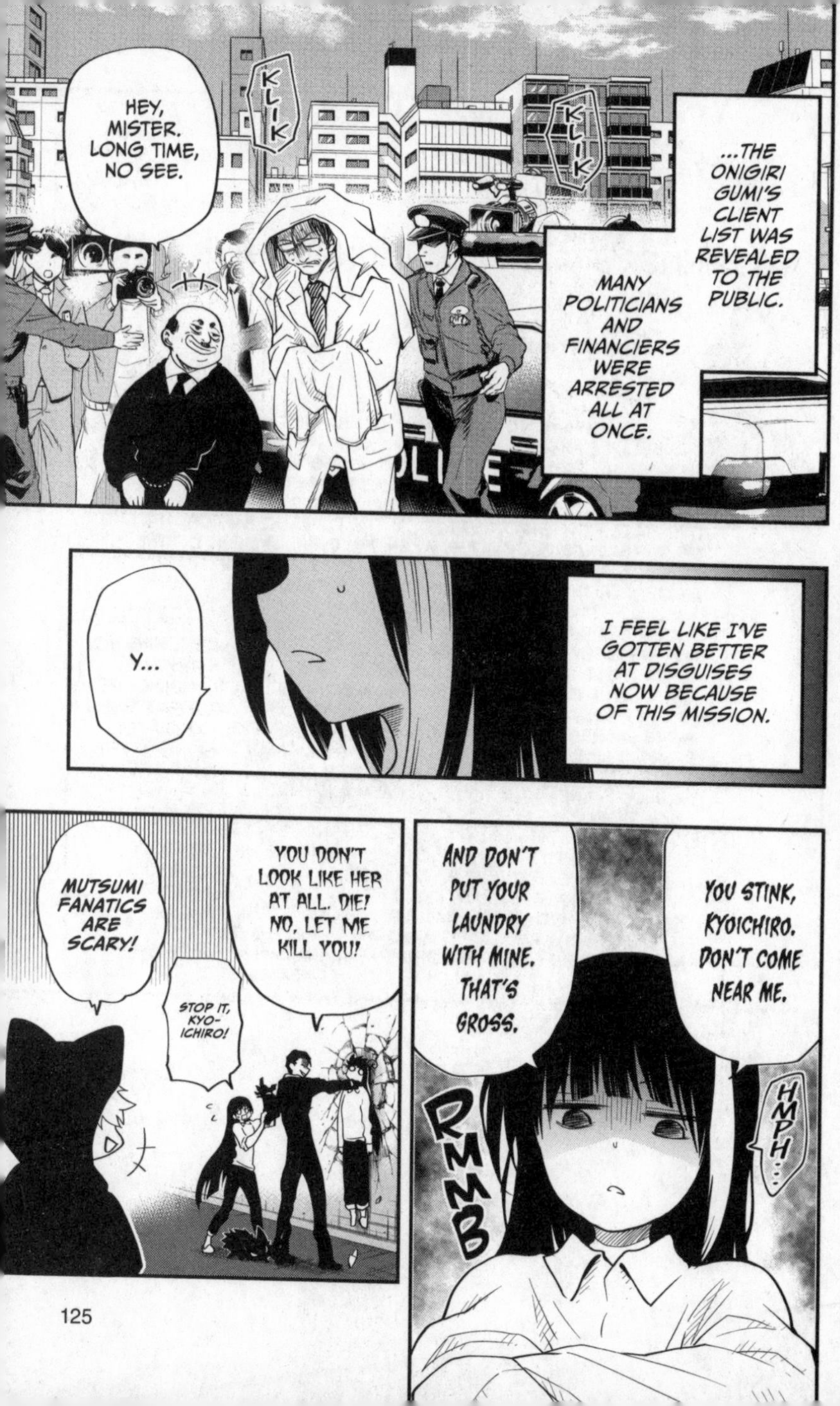
...THE ONIGIRI GUMI'S CLIENT LIST WAS REVEALED TO THE PUBLIC.
MANY POLITICIANS AND FINANCIERS WERE ARRESTED ALL AT ONCE.
KLIK
KLIK
HEY, MISTER. LONG TIME, NO SEE.
I FEEL LIKE I'VE GOTTEN BETTER AT DISGUISES NOW BECAUSE OF THIS MISSION.
Y...
YOU STINK, KYOICHIRO. DON'T COME NEAR ME.
AND DON'T PUT YOUR LAUNDRY WITH MINE. THAT'S GROSS.
HMPH...
RMMB
YOU DON'T LOOK LIKE HER AT ALL. DIE! NO, LET ME KILL YOU!
MUTSUMI FANATICS ARE SCARY!
STOP IT, KYO-ICHIRO!

According to Kyoichiro...

A BEGINNER'S GUIDE TO DISTINGUISHING MUTSUMI

(*You don't have to read this.)

THERE'S NO PRECISE WAY TO TELL HER APART... WELL, IF I ABSOLUTELY HAD TO CHOOSE SOMETHING, IT'D PROBABLY BE HER EYES. MUTSUMI'S EYES ARE A BEAUTIFUL INDIGO BLUE. HER IRIS DILATOR MUSCLE FIBERS ARE VERY FINE AND THERE ARE DOZENS MORE THAN YOUR TYPICAL PERSON. THIS MAKES THE GRADATION FROM THE PUPIL SO SMOOTH THAT ITS DIFFERENCE IS OBVIOUS. WHEN THE EVENING LIGHT OR THE MORNING SUN REFLECTS OFF OF HER EYES, IT'S AS IF THERE'S AN OPAL BURNING IN THEM. MYSTERIOUS, ELUSIVE, BEAUTIFUL—I COULD STARE AT THEM FOR ETERNITY. OF COURSE, IF YOU KEEP STARING AT MUTSUMI, SHE'LL BEGIN TO LOOK AT YOU SUSPICIOUSLY. BUT THAT LOOK WILL CHANGE FROM SUSPICION TO DISTRUST TO DISGUST TO ANGER. IT IS SUPREME BLISS TO SEE SUCH A RANGE OF EMOTIONS. ALSO, IN ADDITION TO HER EYES, HER EYELASHES ARE THIN, AND SHE HAS 18 TO 20 PERCENT MORE LASHES THAN AN ORDINARY PERSON. AND THE CUTICLES SPARKLE LIKE A CROW'S GLOSSY FEATHER. THEIR DARK, DARK BLACK SEDUCES THE VIEWER'S SOUL WITH A BLINK. THIS BEAUTY EXTENDS TO HER HAIR TOO. THE CALM AND STATELY JET-BLACK COLOR EXUDES FORMALNESS THAT TAKES ON A MATERNAL NATURE. HOWEVER, ONCE IT GETS CAUGHT UP IN THE WIND, IT FLUTTERS AS IF IT WEIGHED NOTHING FROM THE BEGINNING. IT HAS A FRESH SCENT LIKE A YOUNG CHILD RUNNING AROUND IN THE SPRING BREEZE. SUCH EXQUISITE HAIR BRUSHES AGAINST SKIN THAT IS FIRM AND GRACEFUL. HER SKIN IS 30 PERCENT PLUMPER THAN A REGULAR PERSON'S, ITS GLOSS SURPASSING THAT OF WOVEN SILK. HER VOICE HAS A CHARMING TIMBRE OF AROUND 1,200 HERTZ, WHICH IS RICH IN OVERTONES. IT'S AS LIGHT AS A FLUTE AND AS SMOOTH AS A VIOLA...

BLAH BLAH

BLAH BLAH

BLAH BLAH

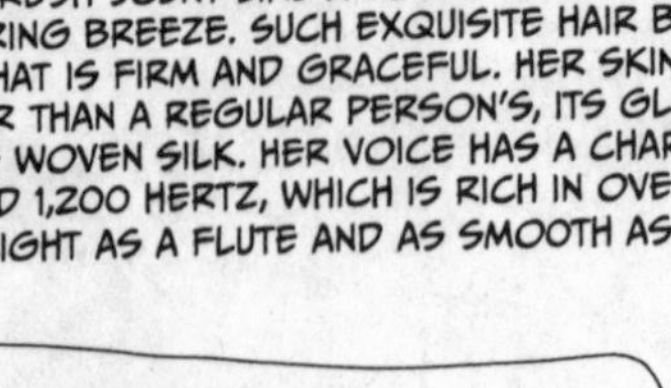

GO AWAY.

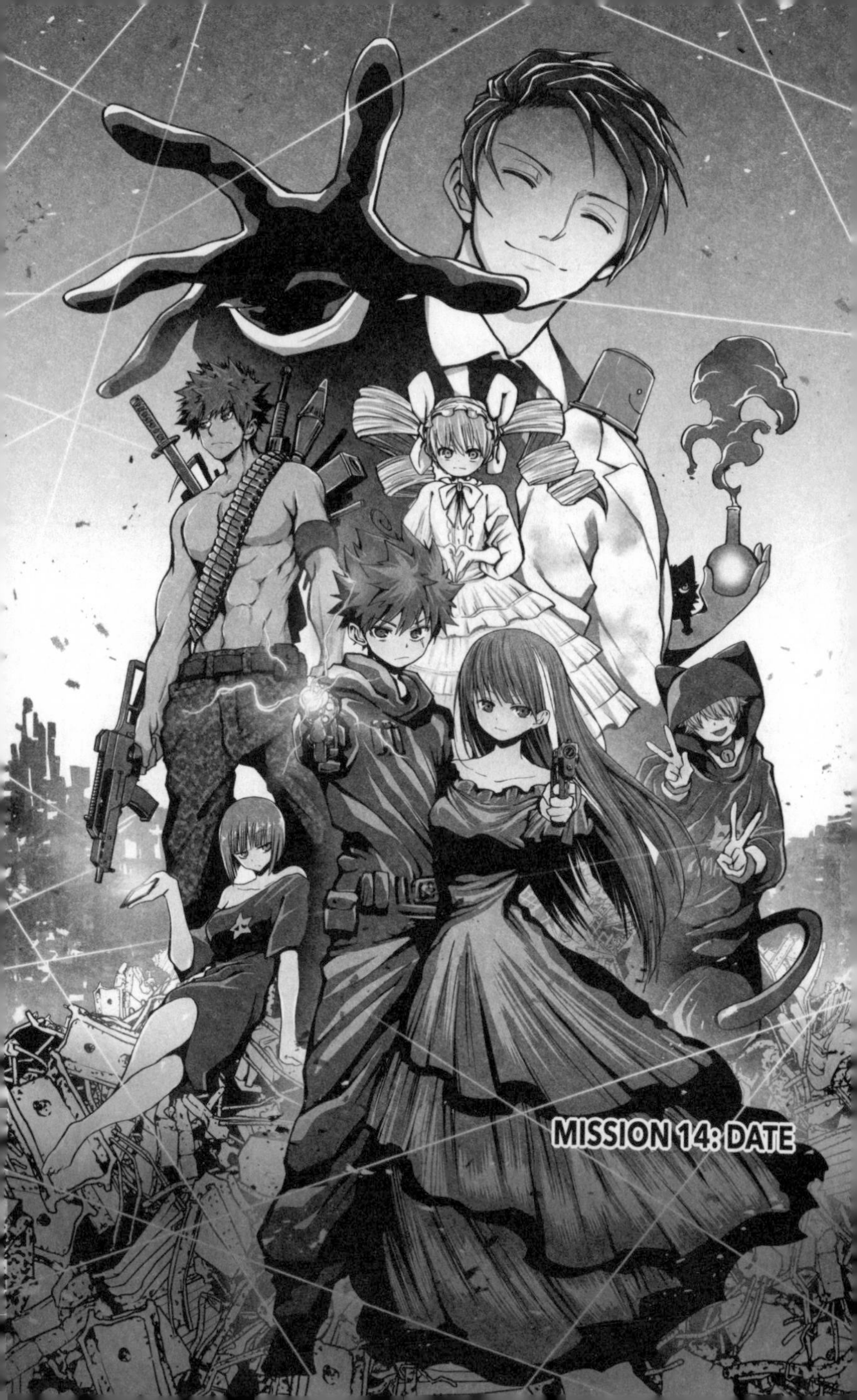
MISSION 14: DATE

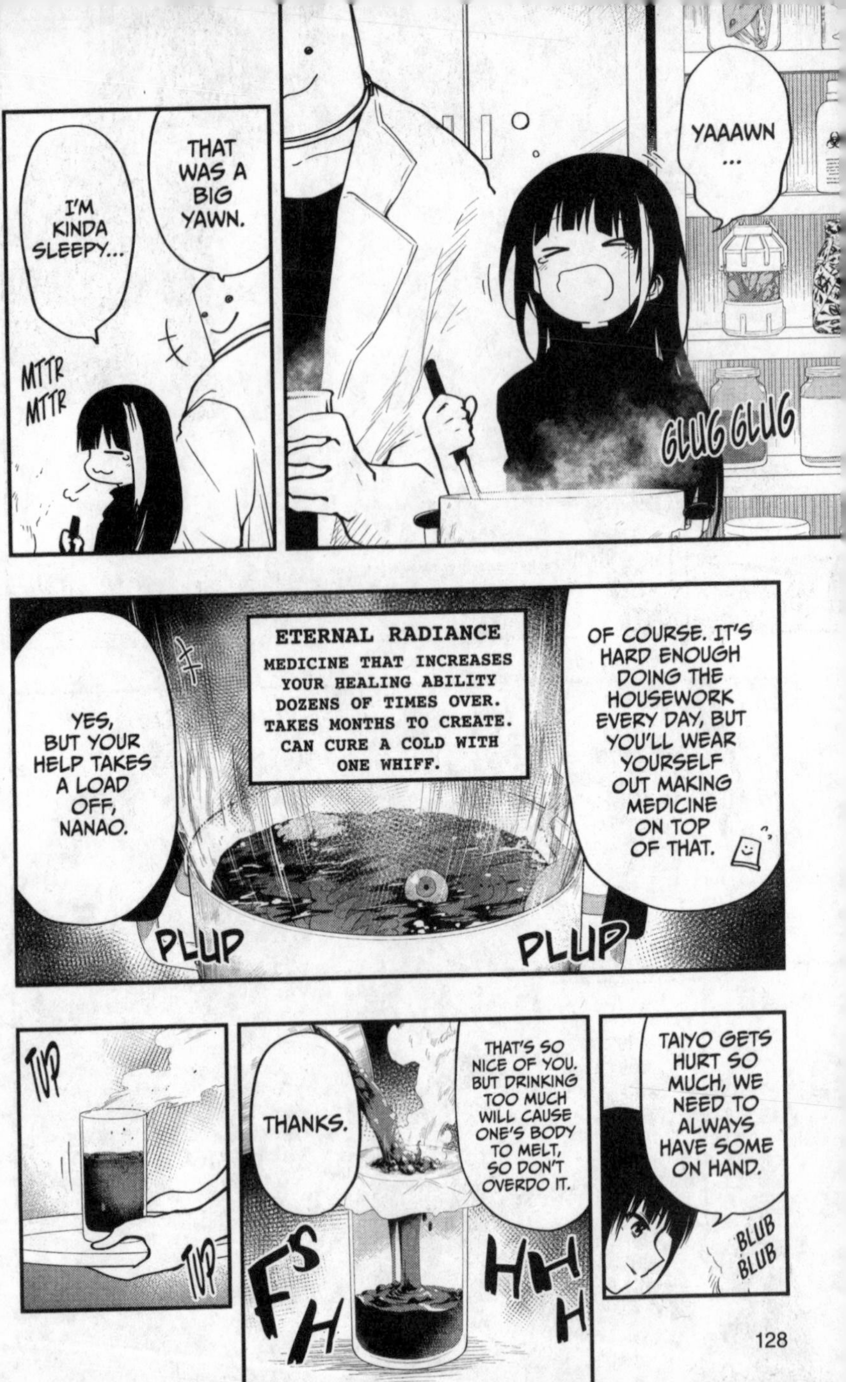
YAAAWN...
GLUG GLUG
THAT WAS A BIG YAWN.
I'M KINDA SLEEPY...
MTTR MTTR
OF COURSE. IT'S HARD ENOUGH DOING THE HOUSEWORK EVERY DAY, BUT YOU'LL WEAR YOURSELF OUT MAKING MEDICINE ON TOP OF THAT.
ETERNAL RADIANCE
MEDICINE THAT INCREASES YOUR HEALING ABILITY DOZENS OF TIMES OVER. TAKES MONTHS TO CREATE. CAN CURE A COLD WITH ONE WHIFF.
YES, BUT YOUR HELP TAKES A LOAD OFF, NANAO.
PLUP
PLUP
TAIYO GETS HURT SO MUCH, WE NEED TO ALWAYS HAVE SOME ON HAND.
BLUB BLUB
THAT'S SO NICE OF YOU. BUT DRINKING TOO MUCH WILL CAUSE ONE'S BODY TO MELT, SO DON'T OVERDO IT.
THANKS.
FSHHHH
TUP
TUP

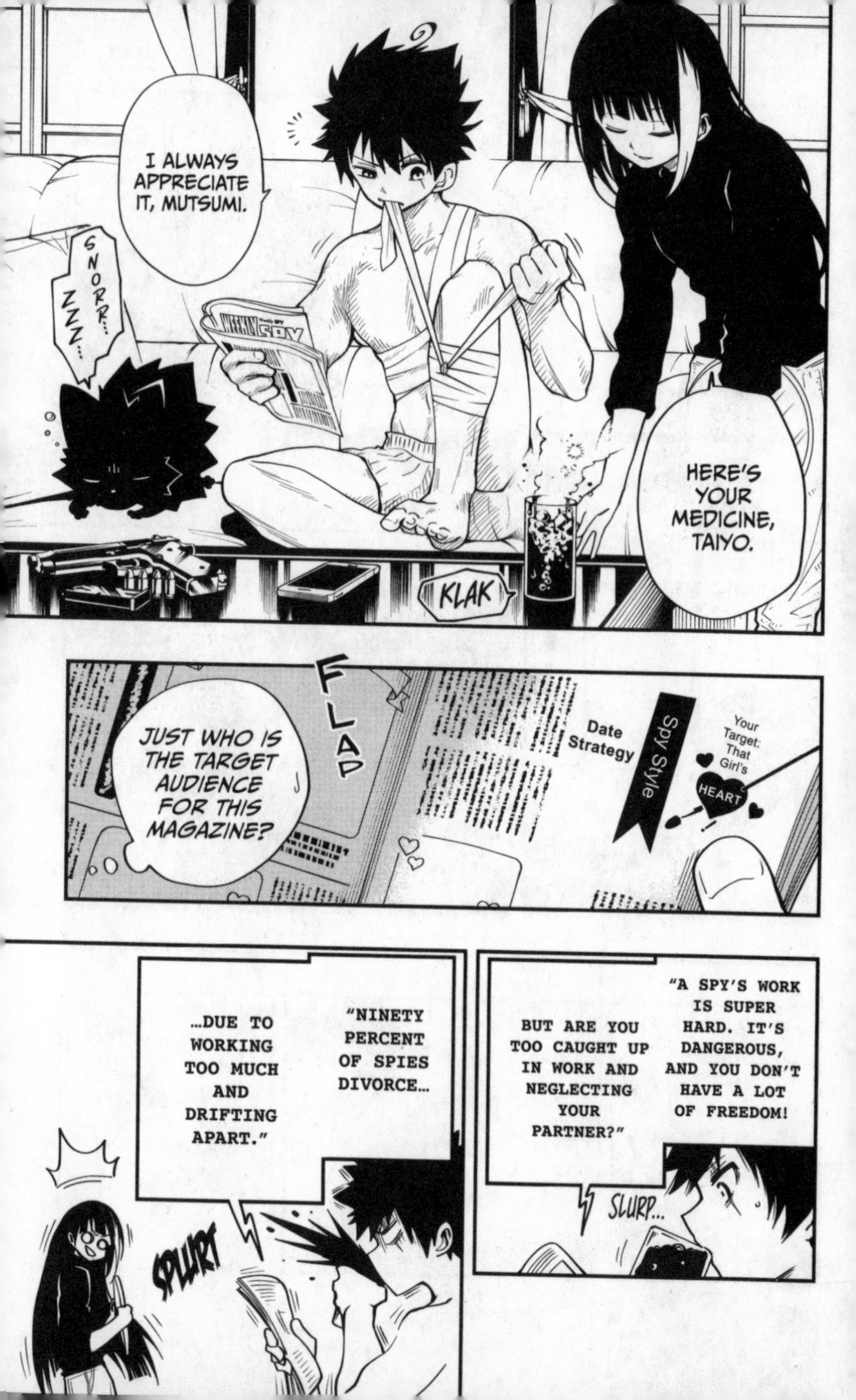
HERE'S YOUR MEDICINE, TAIYO.
KLAK
I ALWAYS APPRECIATE IT, MUTSUMI.
SNORR... ZZZ...
Your Target: That Girl's HEART
Spy Style
Date Strategy
FLAP
JUST WHO IS THE TARGET AUDIENCE FOR THIS MAGAZINE?
"A SPY'S WORK IS SUPER HARD. IT'S DANGEROUS, AND YOU DON'T HAVE A LOT OF FREEDOM!
BUT ARE YOU TOO CAUGHT UP IN WORK AND NEGLECTING YOUR PARTNER?"
SLURP...
"NINETY PERCENT OF SPIES DIVORCE...
...DUE TO WORKING TOO MUCH AND DRIFTING APART."
SPLURT

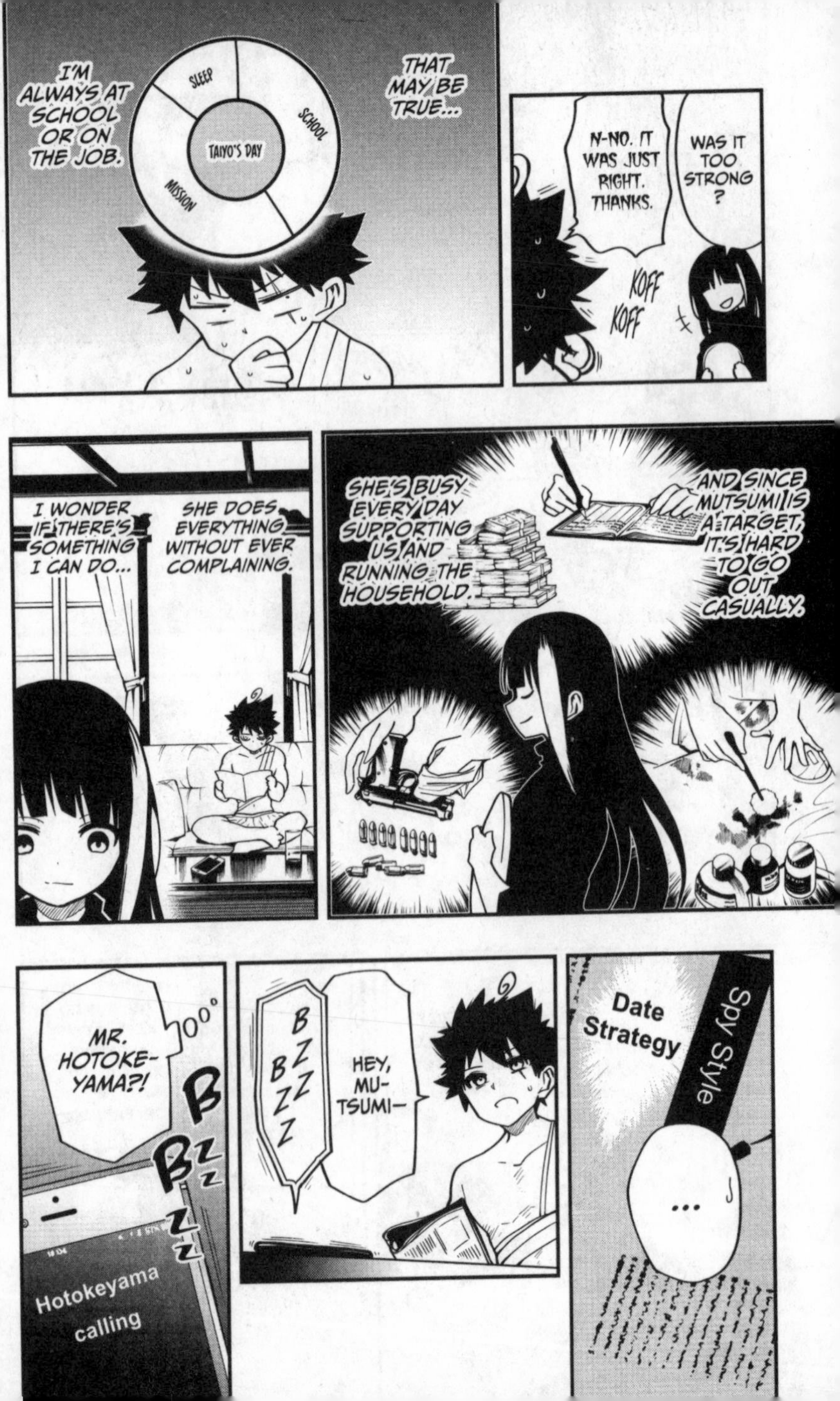
WAS IT TOO STRONG?
N-NO. IT WAS JUST RIGHT. THANKS.
KOFF KOFF
THAT MAY BE TRUE...
I'M ALWAYS AT SCHOOL OR ON THE JOB.
SLEEP
SCHOOL
MISSION
TAIYO'S DAY
AND SINCE MUTSUMI IS A TARGET, IT'S HARD TO GO OUT CASUALLY.
SHE'S BUSY EVERY DAY SUPPORTING US AND RUNNING THE HOUSEHOLD.
SHE DOES EVERYTHING WITHOUT EVER COMPLAINING.
I WONDER IF THERE'S SOMETHING I CAN DO...
Spy Style
Date Strategy
...
HEY, MU-TSUMI—
BZZZ BZZZ
MR. HOTOKE-YAMA?!
BZZZ
Hotokeyama calling

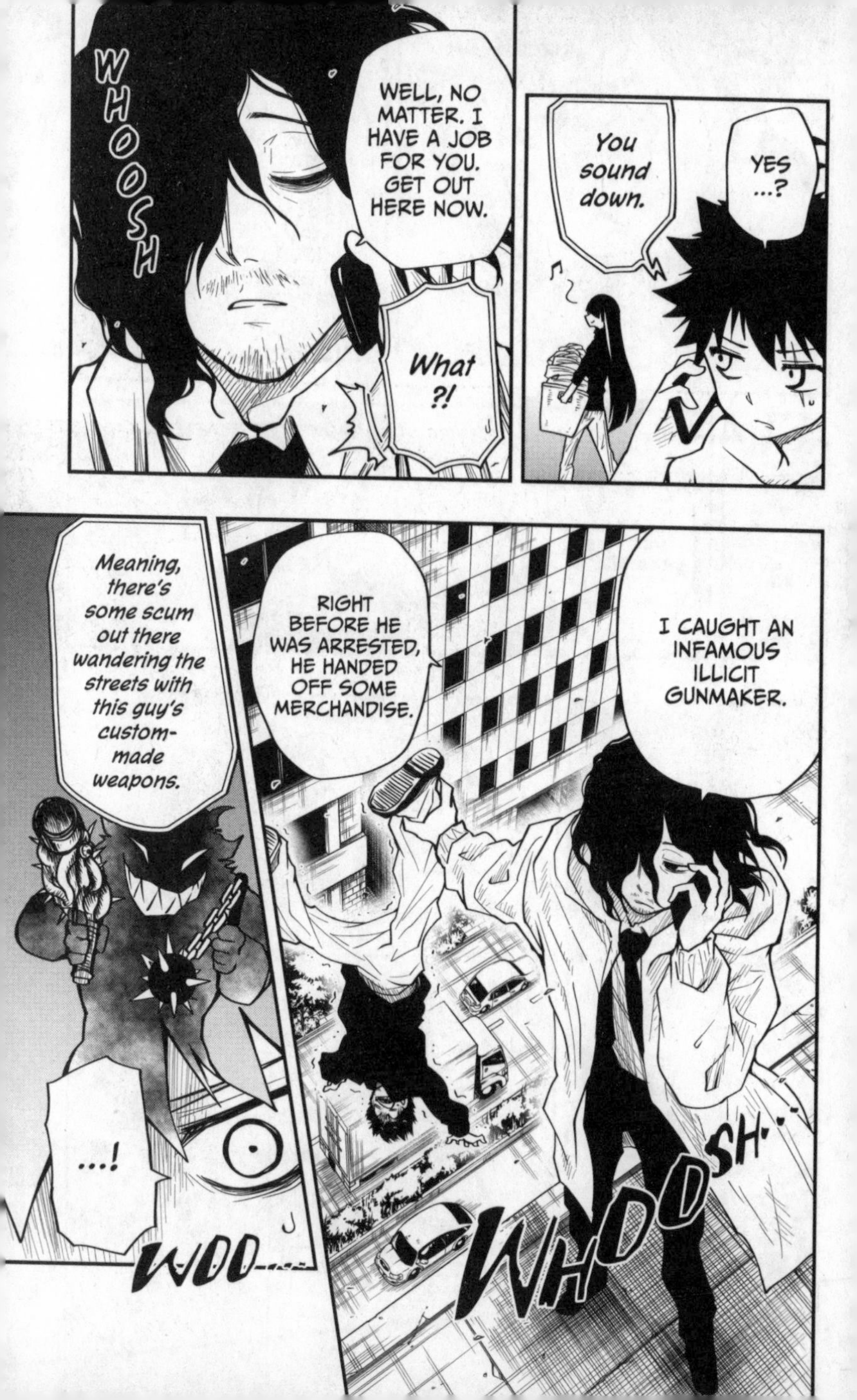
YES ...?
You sound down.
WELL, NO MATTER. I HAVE A JOB FOR YOU. GET OUT HERE NOW.
WHOOSH
What ?!
I CAUGHT AN INFAMOUS ILLICIT GUNMAKER.
RIGHT BEFORE HE WAS ARRESTED, HE HANDED OFF SOME MERCHANDISE.
WHOOSH
Meaning, there's some scum out there wandering the streets with this guy's custom-made weapons.
...!
WOO---

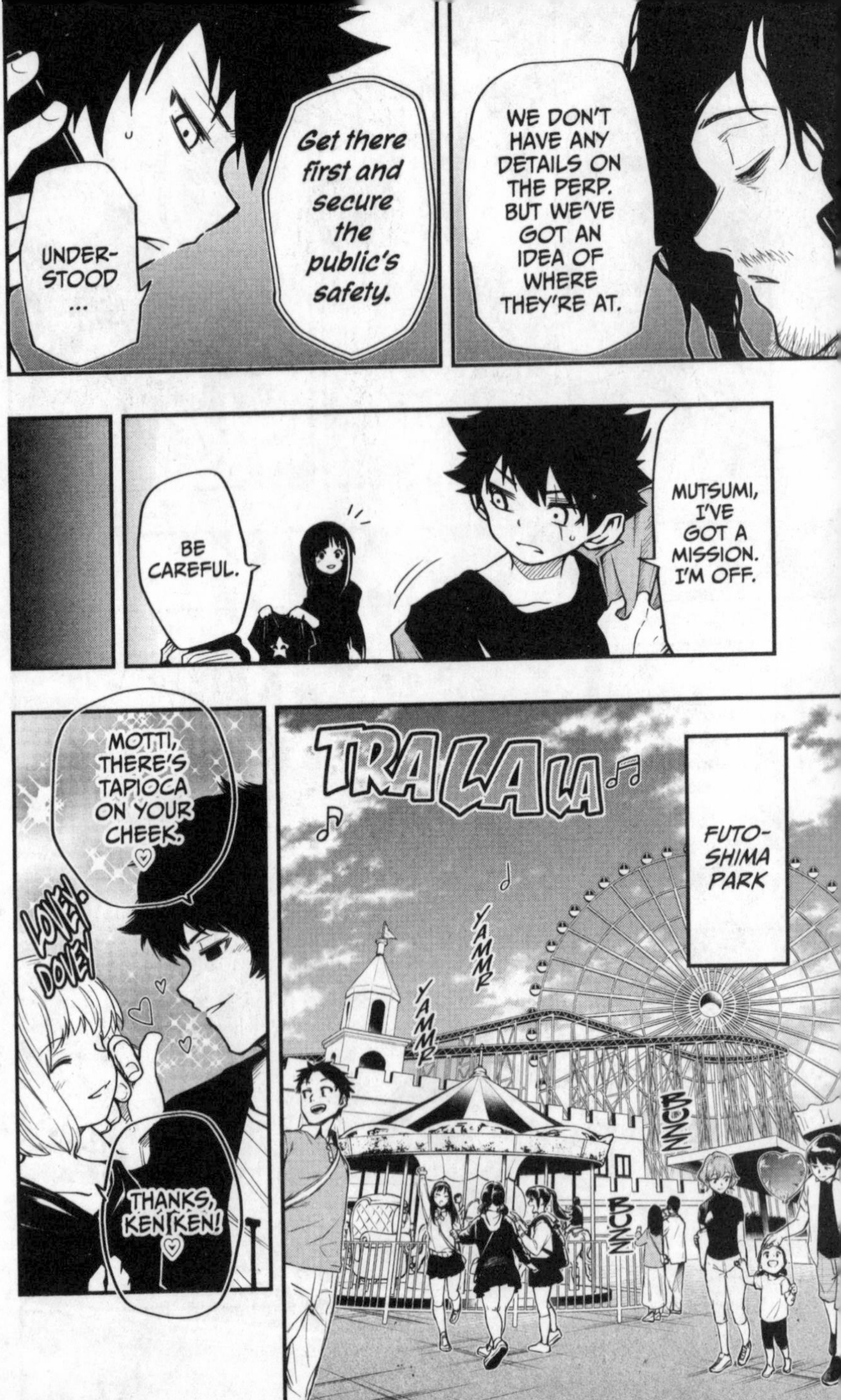
WE DON'T HAVE ANY DETAILS ON THE PERP. BUT WE'VE GOT AN IDEA OF WHERE THEY'RE AT.
Get there first and secure the public's safety.
UNDER-STOOD ...
MUTSUMI, I'VE GOT A MISSION. I'M OFF.
BE CAREFUL.
TRALALA
FUTO-SHIMA PARK
YAMMR
YAMMR
BUZZ
BUZZ
MOTTI, THERE'S TAPIOCA ON YOUR CHEEK.
LOVEY DOVEY
THANKS, KEN KEN!

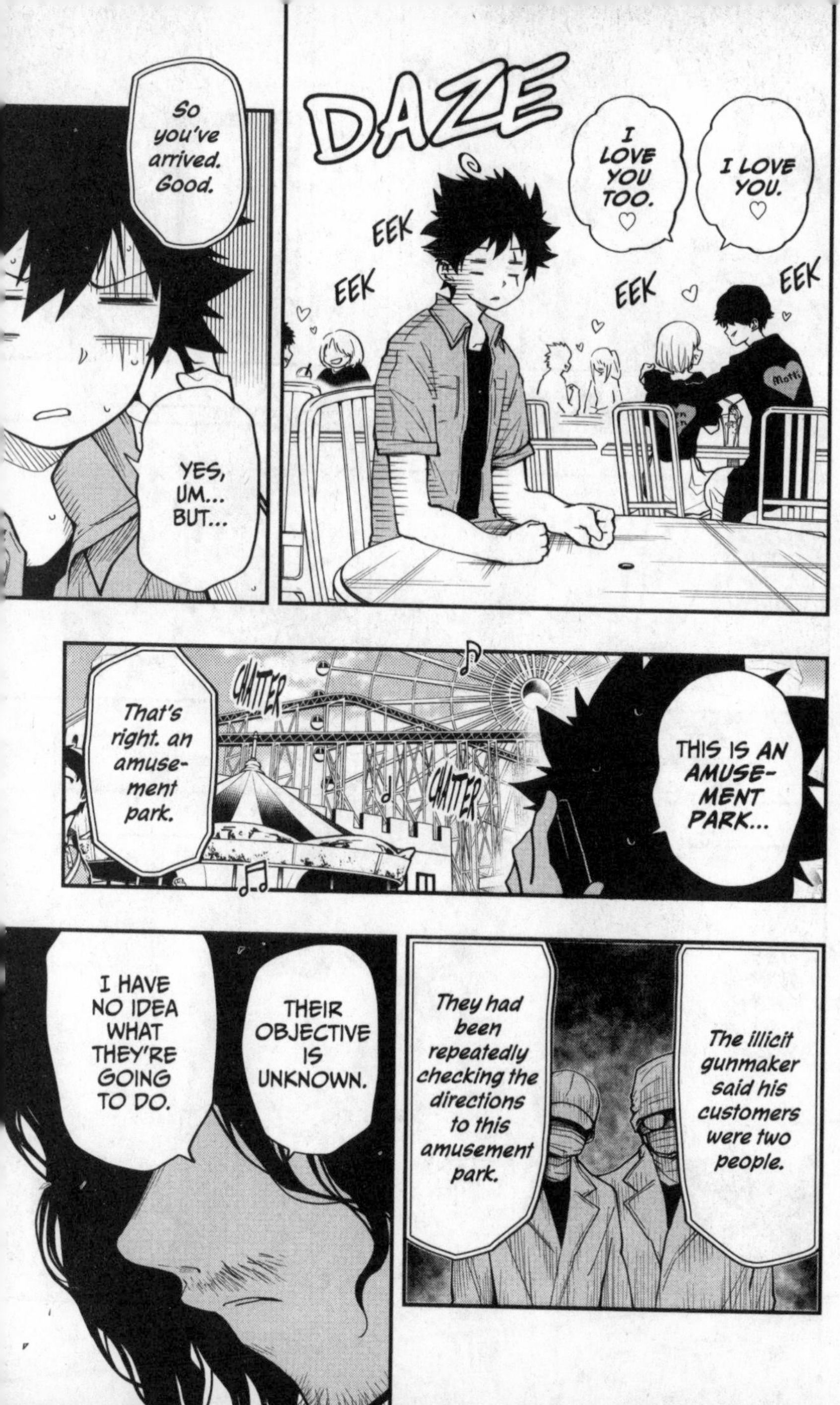
I LOVE YOU. ♡
I LOVE YOU TOO. ♡
DAZE
EEK
EEK
EEK
EEK
So you've arrived. Good.
YES, UM... BUT...
THIS IS AN AMUSEMENT PARK...
CHATTER
CHATTER
That's right. an amusement park.
The illicit gunmaker said his customers were two people.
They had been repeatedly checking the directions to this amusement park.
THEIR OBJECTIVE IS UNKNOWN.
I HAVE NO IDEA WHAT THEY'RE GOING TO DO.

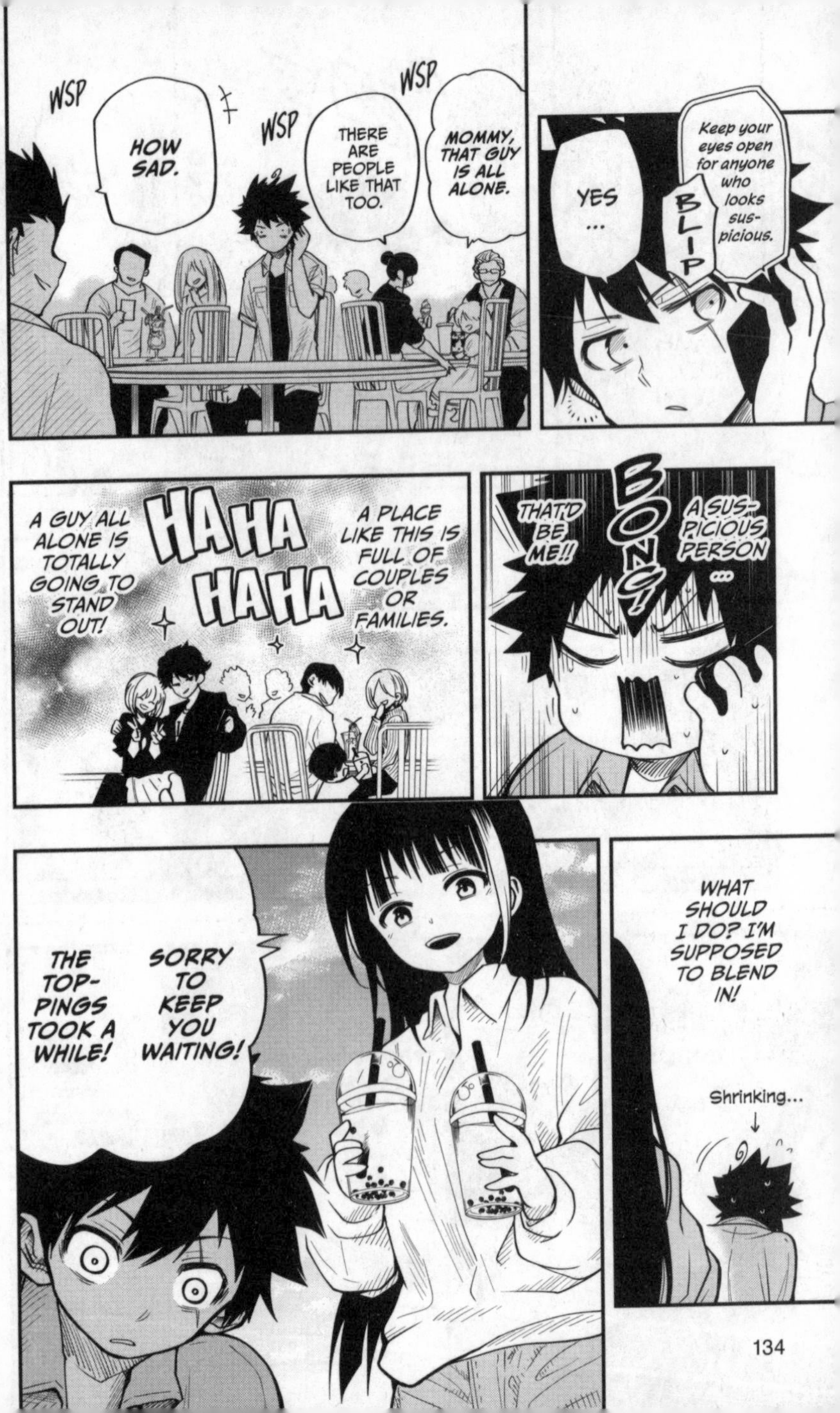
Keep your eyes open for anyone who looks sus- picious.
BLIP
YES ...
WSP
MOMMY, THAT GUY IS ALL ALONE.
WSP
THERE ARE PEOPLE LIKE THAT TOO.
WSP
HOW SAD.
A SUS- PICIOUS PERSON ...
BONG!
THAT'D BE ME!!
A PLACE LIKE THIS IS FULL OF COUPLES OR FAMILIES.
HAHA HAHA
A GUY ALL ALONE IS TOTALLY GOING TO STAND OUT!
WHAT SHOULD I DO? I'M SUPPOSED TO BLEND IN!
Shrinking...
SORRY TO KEEP YOU WAITING!
THE TOP- PINGS TOOK A WHILE!

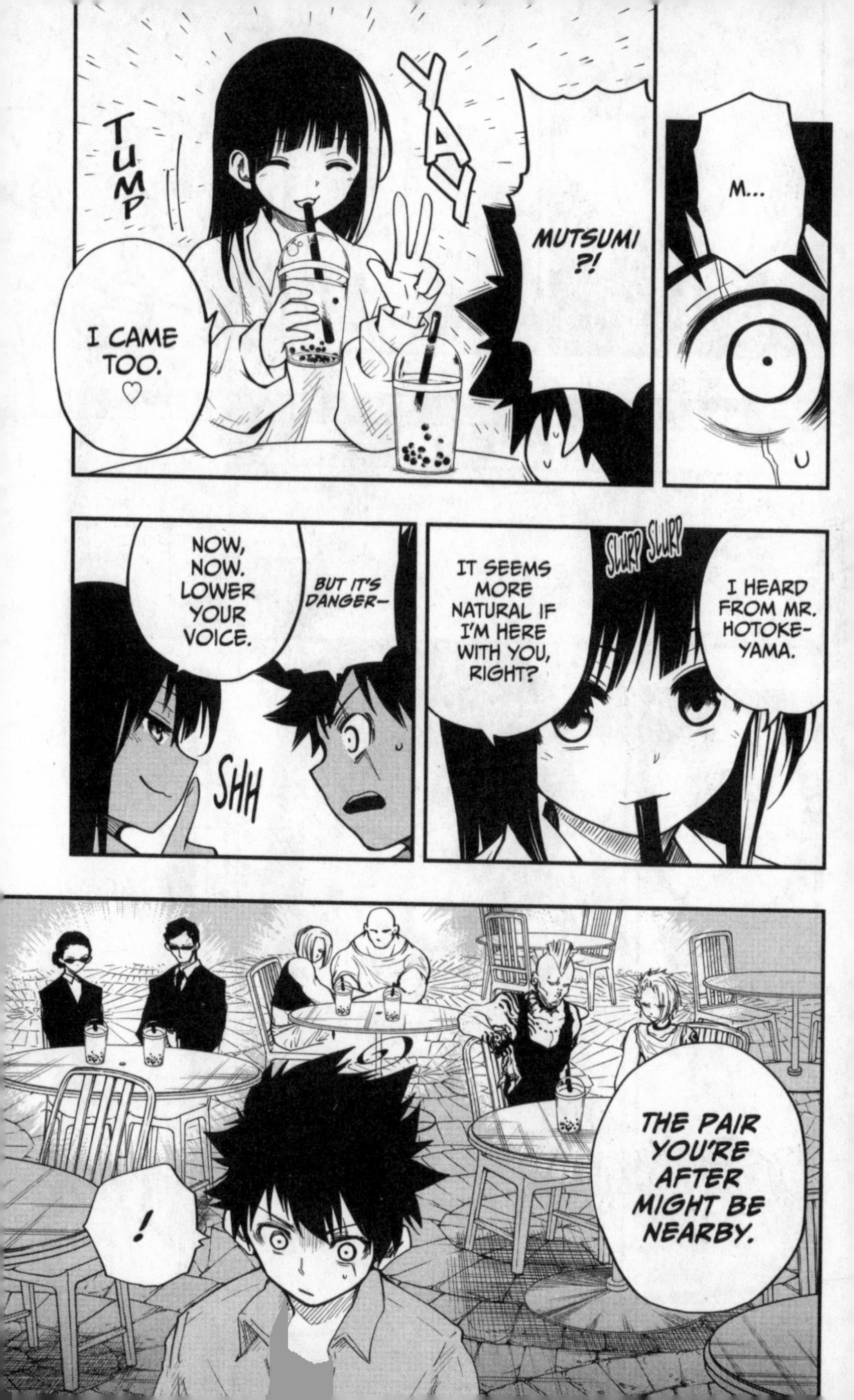
M...
MUTSUMI ?!
YAY
TUMP
I CAME TOO. ♡
SLURP SLURP
I HEARD FROM MR. HOTOKE-YAMA.
IT SEEMS MORE NATURAL IF I'M HERE WITH YOU, RIGHT?
BUT IT'S DANGER—
NOW, NOW. LOWER YOUR VOICE.
SHH
THE PAIR YOU'RE AFTER MIGHT BE NEARBY.
!

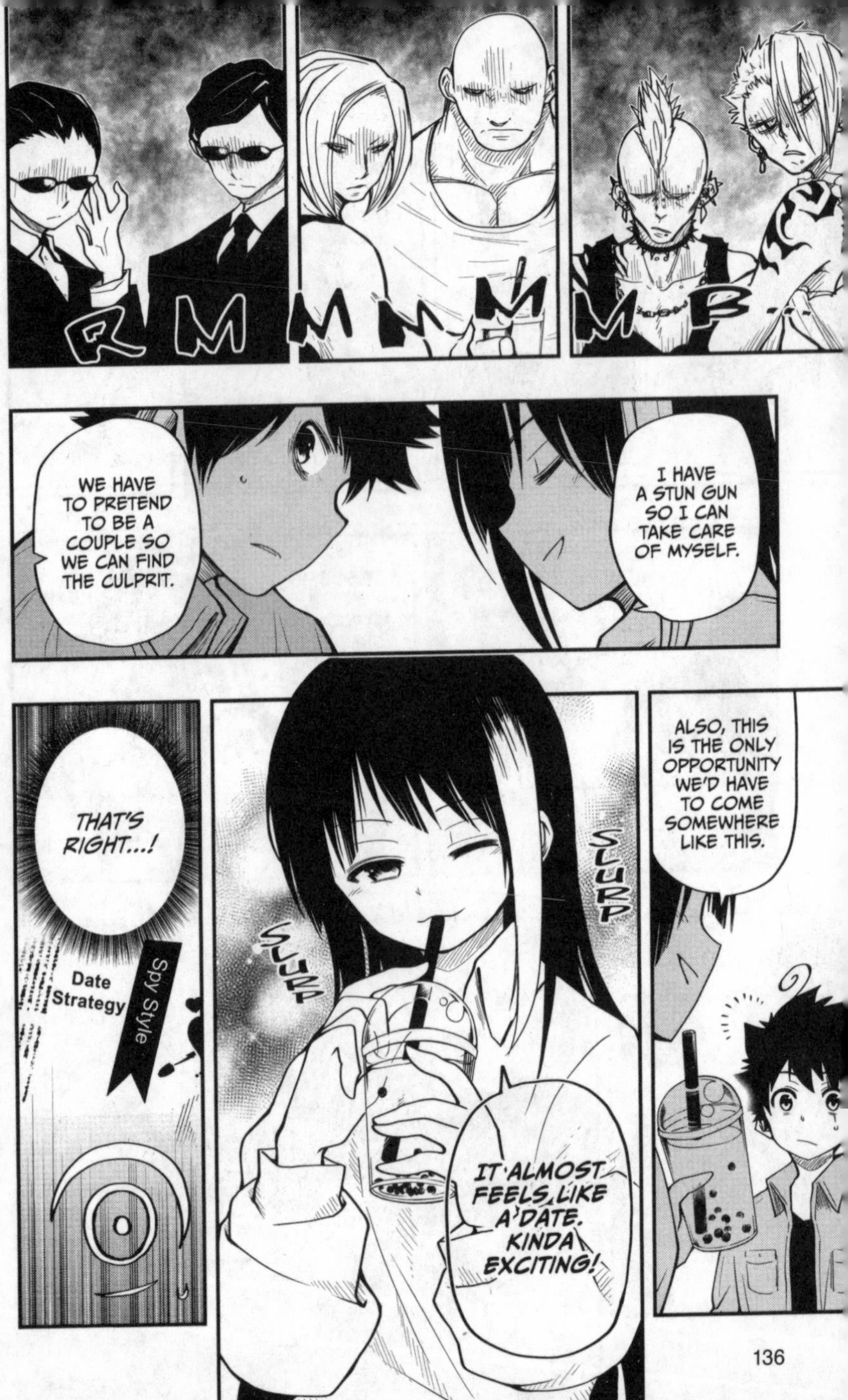
RMMMMMB
I HAVE A STUN GUN SO I CAN TAKE CARE OF MYSELF.
WE HAVE TO PRETEND TO BE A COUPLE SO WE CAN FIND THE CULPRIT.
ALSO, THIS IS THE ONLY OPPORTUNITY WE'D HAVE TO COME SOMEWHERE LIKE THIS.
SLURP
SLURP
IT ALMOST FEELS LIKE A DATE. KINDA EXCITING!
THAT'S RIGHT...!
Spy Style
Date Strategy

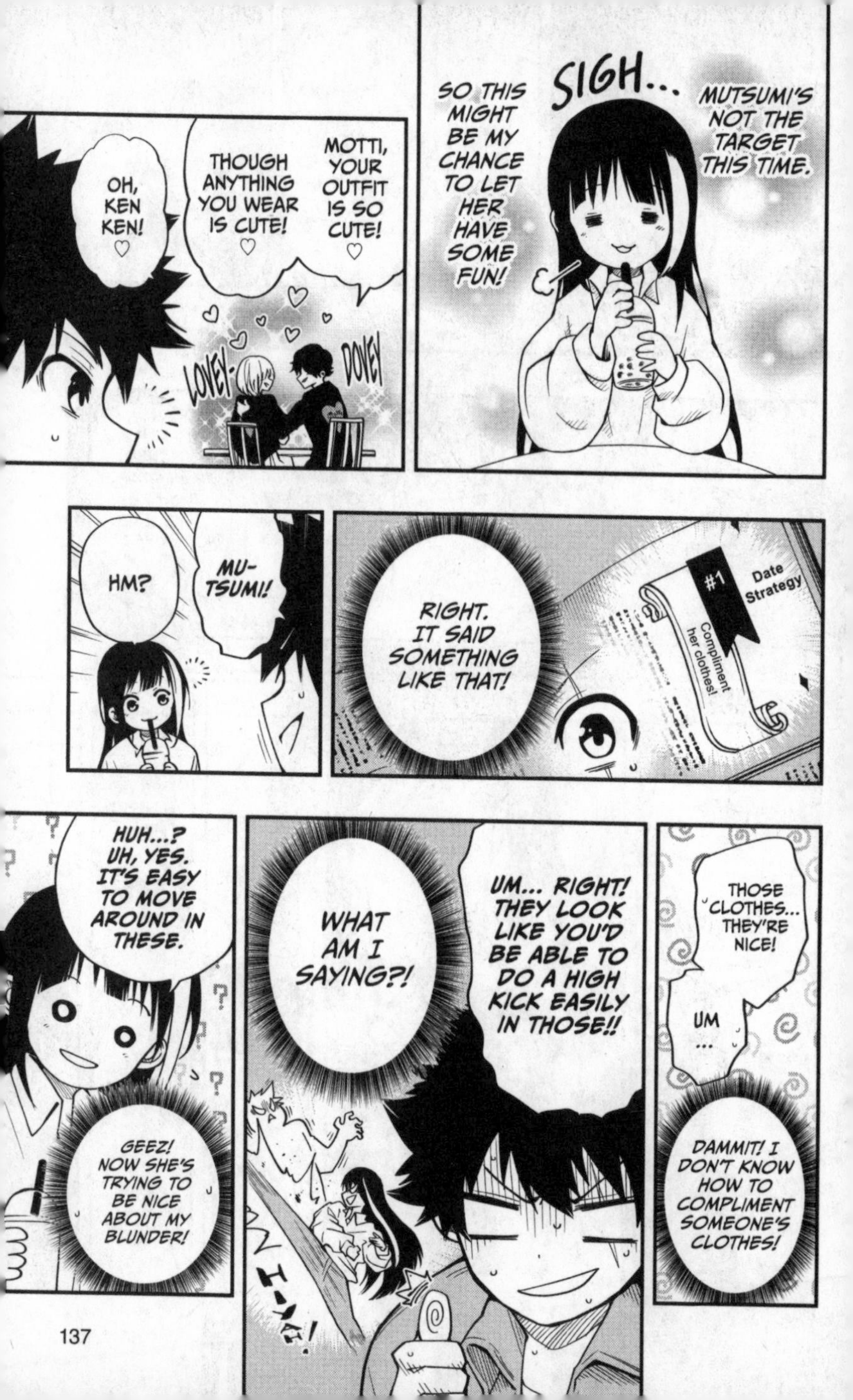
MUTSUMI'S NOT THE TARGET THIS TIME.
SIGH...
SO THIS MIGHT BE MY CHANCE TO LET HER HAVE SOME FUN!
MOTTI, YOUR OUTFIT IS SO CUTE! ♡
THOUGH ANYTHING YOU WEAR IS CUTE! ♡
OH, KEN KEN! ♡
LOVEY-DOVEY
#1 Date Strategy
Compliment her clothes!
RIGHT. IT SAID SOMETHING LIKE THAT!
MU-TSUMI!
HM?
THOSE CLOTHES... THEY'RE NICE!
UM...
DAMMIT! I DON'T KNOW HOW TO COMPLIMENT SOMEONE'S CLOTHES!
UM... RIGHT! THEY LOOK LIKE YOU'D BE ABLE TO DO A HIGH KICK EASILY IN THOSE!!
WHAT AM I SAYING?!
HUH...? UH, YES. IT'S EASY TO MOVE AROUND IN THESE.
GEEZ! NOW SHE'S TRYING TO BE NICE ABOUT MY BLUNDER!

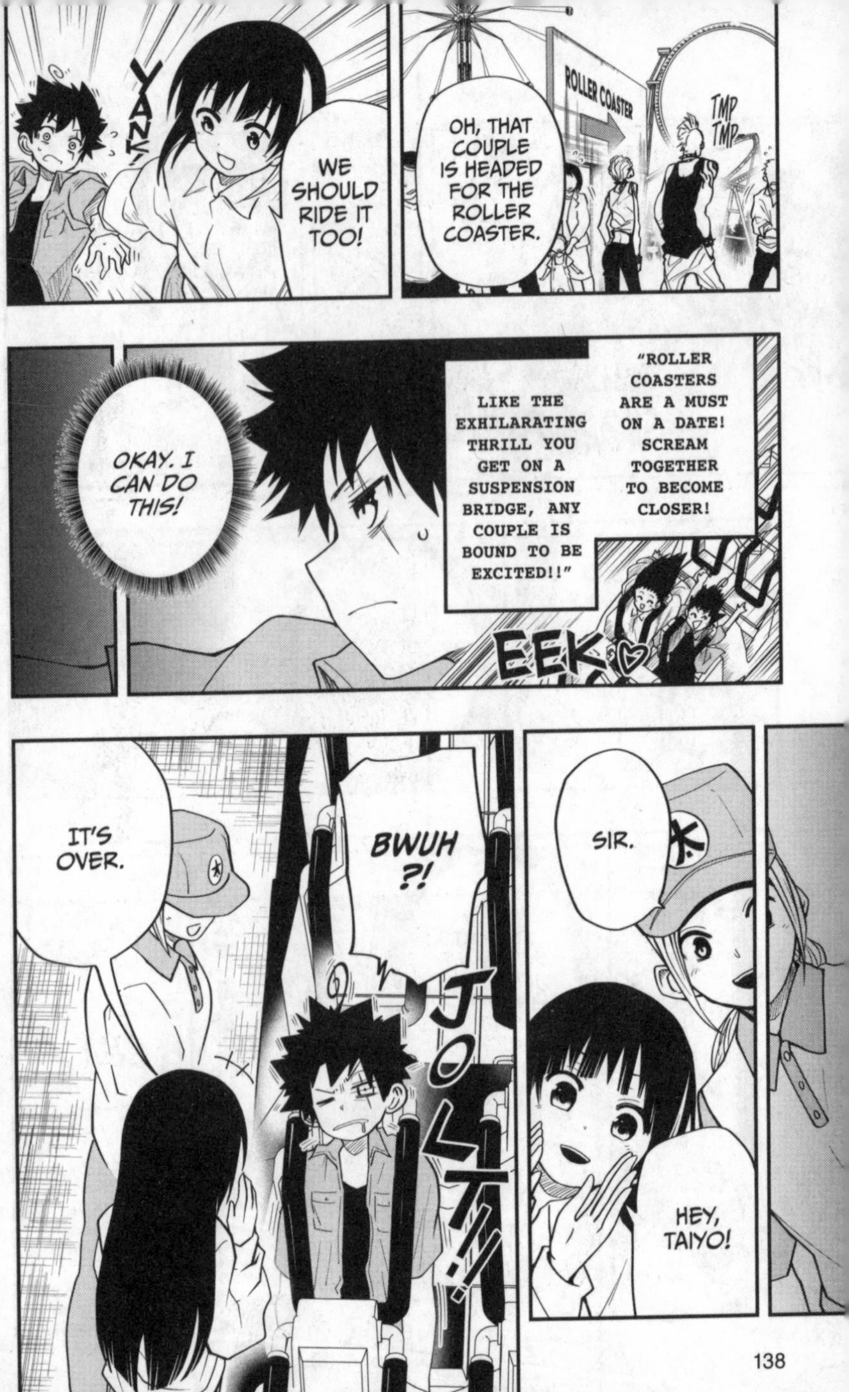
ROLLER COASTER
OH, THAT COUPLE IS HEADED FOR THE ROLLER COASTER.
TMP TMP
YANK!
WE SHOULD RIDE IT TOO!
"ROLLER COASTERS ARE A MUST ON A DATE! SCREAM TOGETHER TO BECOME CLOSER!
LIKE THE EXHILARATING THRILL YOU GET ON A SUSPENSION BRIDGE, ANY COUPLE IS BOUND TO BE EXCITED!!"
EEK
OKAY. I CAN DO THIS!
SIR.
HEY, TAIYO!
BWUH?!
JOLT!!
IT'S OVER.

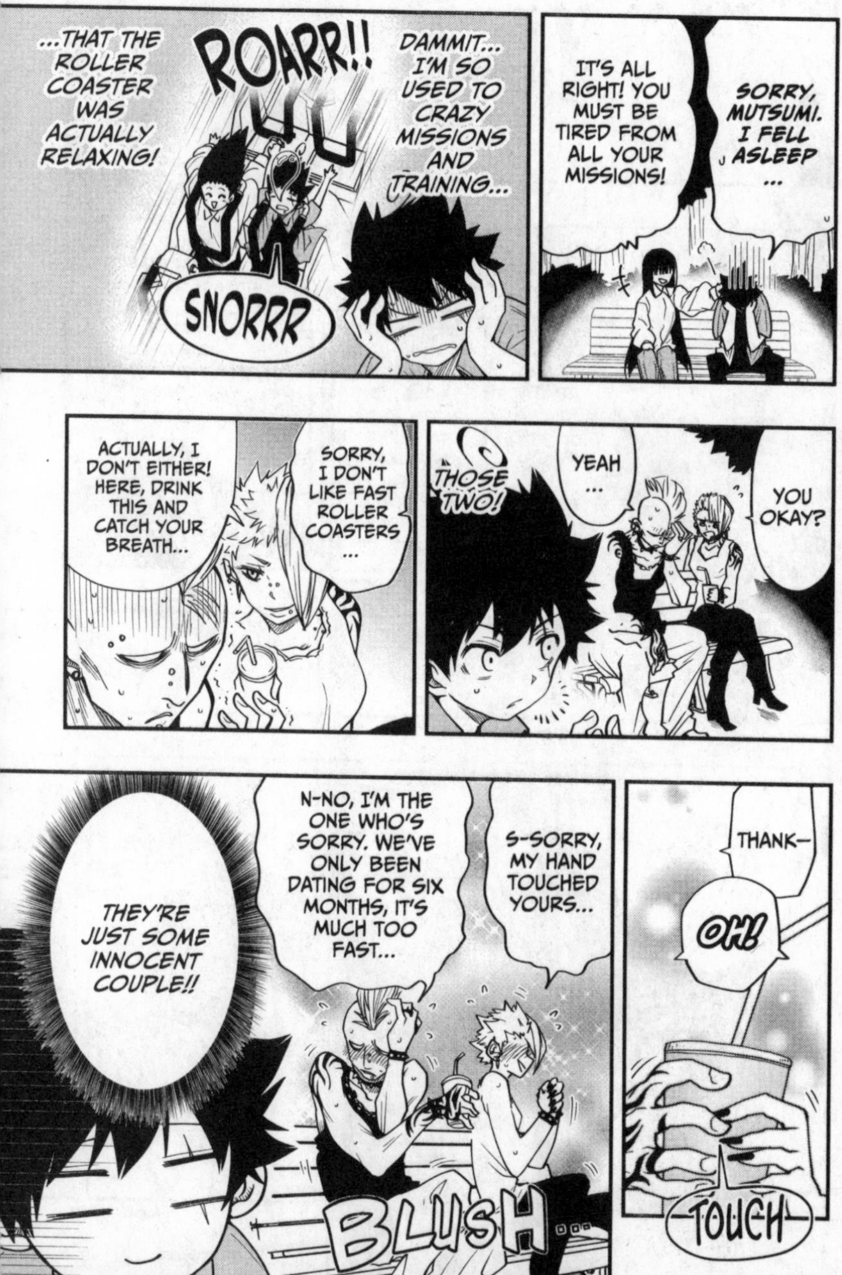
SORRY, MUTSUMI. I FELL ASLEEP ...
IT'S ALL RIGHT! YOU MUST BE TIRED FROM ALL YOUR MISSIONS!
DAMMIT... I'M SO USED TO CRAZY MISSIONS AND TRAINING...
ROARR!!
...THAT THE ROLLER COASTER WAS ACTUALLY RELAXING!
SNORRR
YOU OKAY?
YEAH ...
THOSE TWO!
SORRY, I DON'T LIKE FAST ROLLER COASTERS ...
ACTUALLY, I DON'T EITHER! HERE, DRINK THIS AND CATCH YOUR BREATH...
THANK—
OH!
TOUCH
S-SORRY, MY HAND TOUCHED YOURS...
N-NO, I'M THE ONE WHO'S SORRY. WE'VE ONLY BEEN DATING FOR SIX MONTHS, IT'S MUCH TOO FAST...
BLUSH...
THEY'RE JUST SOME INNOCENT COUPLE!!

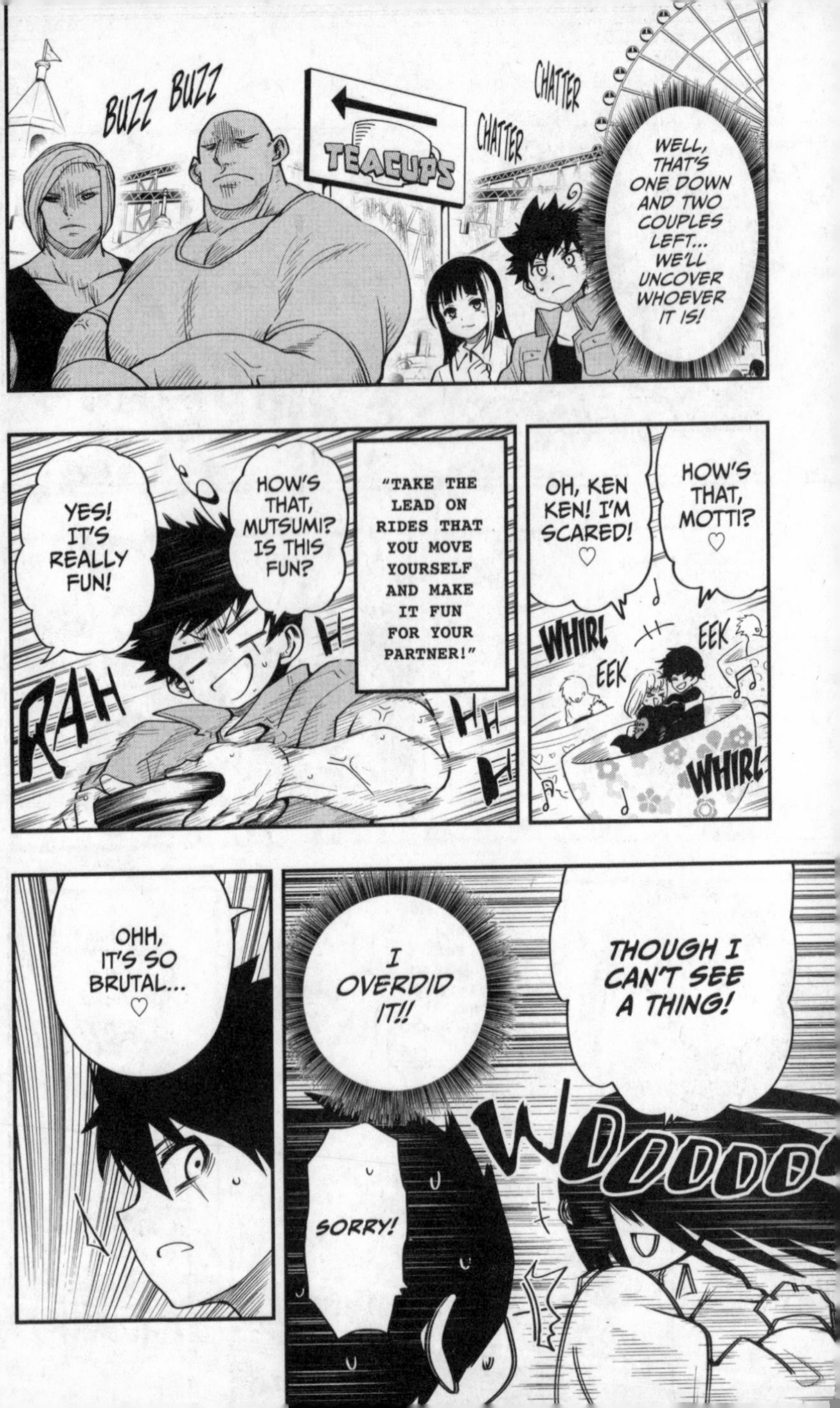
CHATTER
CHATTER
WELL, THAT'S ONE DOWN AND TWO COUPLES LEFT... WE'LL UNCOVER WHOEVER IT IS!
TEACUPS
BUZZ BUZZ
HOW'S THAT, MOTTI? ♡
OH, KEN KEN! I'M SCARED! ♡
WHIRL
EEK
EEK
WHIRL
"TAKE THE LEAD ON RIDES THAT YOU MOVE YOURSELF AND MAKE IT FUN FOR YOUR PARTNER!"
HOW'S THAT, MUTSUMI? IS THIS FUN?
YES! IT'S REALLY FUN!
RAH
THOUGH I CAN'T SEE A THING!
I OVERDID IT!!
SORRY!
OHH, IT'S SO BRUTAL... ♡

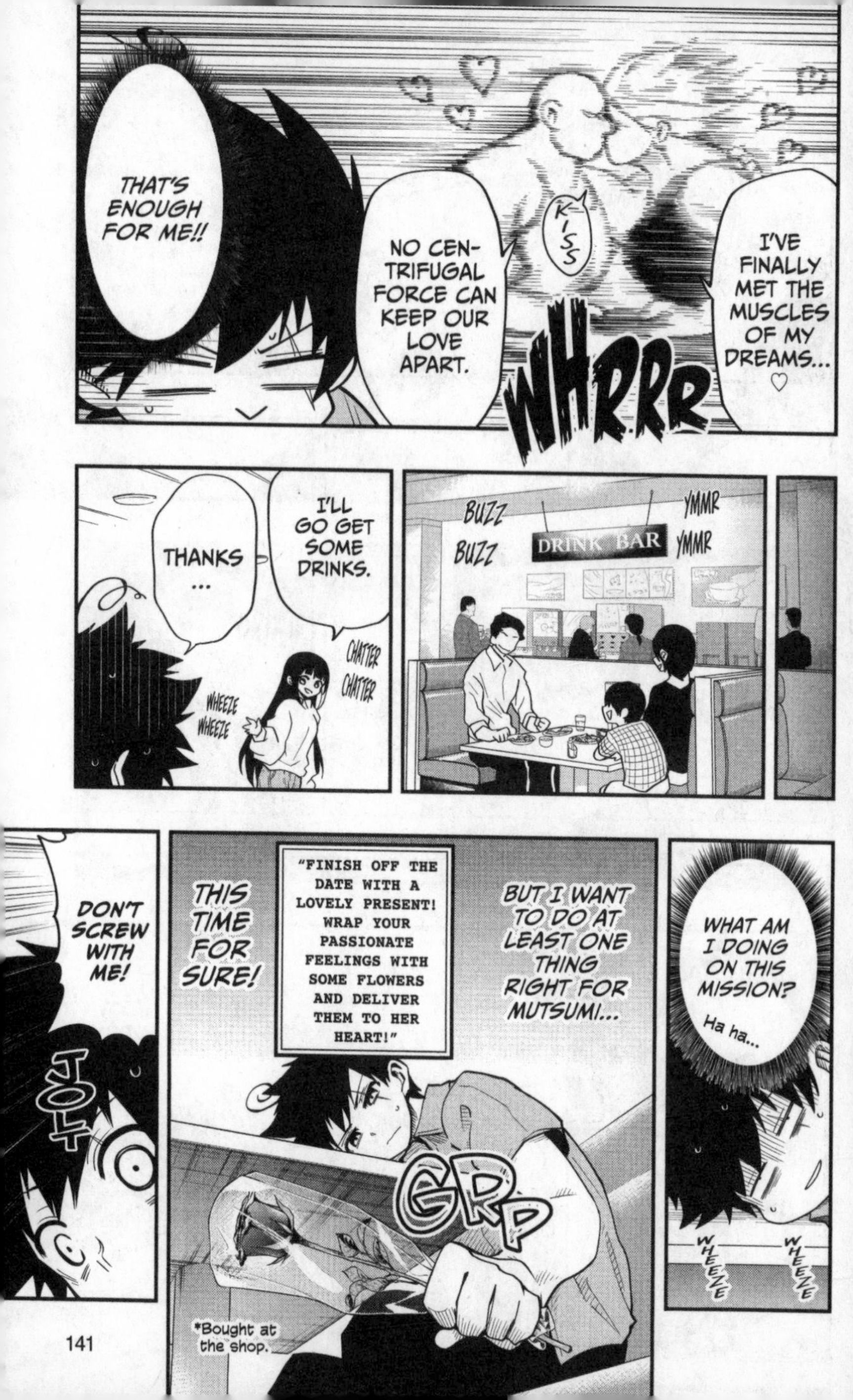
I'VE FINALLY MET THE MUSCLES OF MY DREAMS... ♡
KISS
WHRRR
NO CEN-TRIFUGAL FORCE CAN KEEP OUR LOVE APART.
THAT'S ENOUGH FOR ME!!
YMMR YMMR
BUZZ BUZZ
DRINK BAR
I'LL GO GET SOME DRINKS.
THANKS ...
CHATTER CHATTER
WHEEZE WHEEZE
WHAT AM I DOING ON THIS MISSION?
Ha ha...
WHEEZE WHEEZE
BUT I WANT TO DO AT LEAST ONE THING RIGHT FOR MUTSUMI...
"FINISH OFF THE DATE WITH A LOVELY PRESENT! WRAP YOUR PASSIONATE FEELINGS WITH SOME FLOWERS AND DELIVER THEM TO HER HEART!"
THIS TIME FOR SURE!
GRP
*Bought at the shop.
DON'T SCREW WITH ME!
JOLT

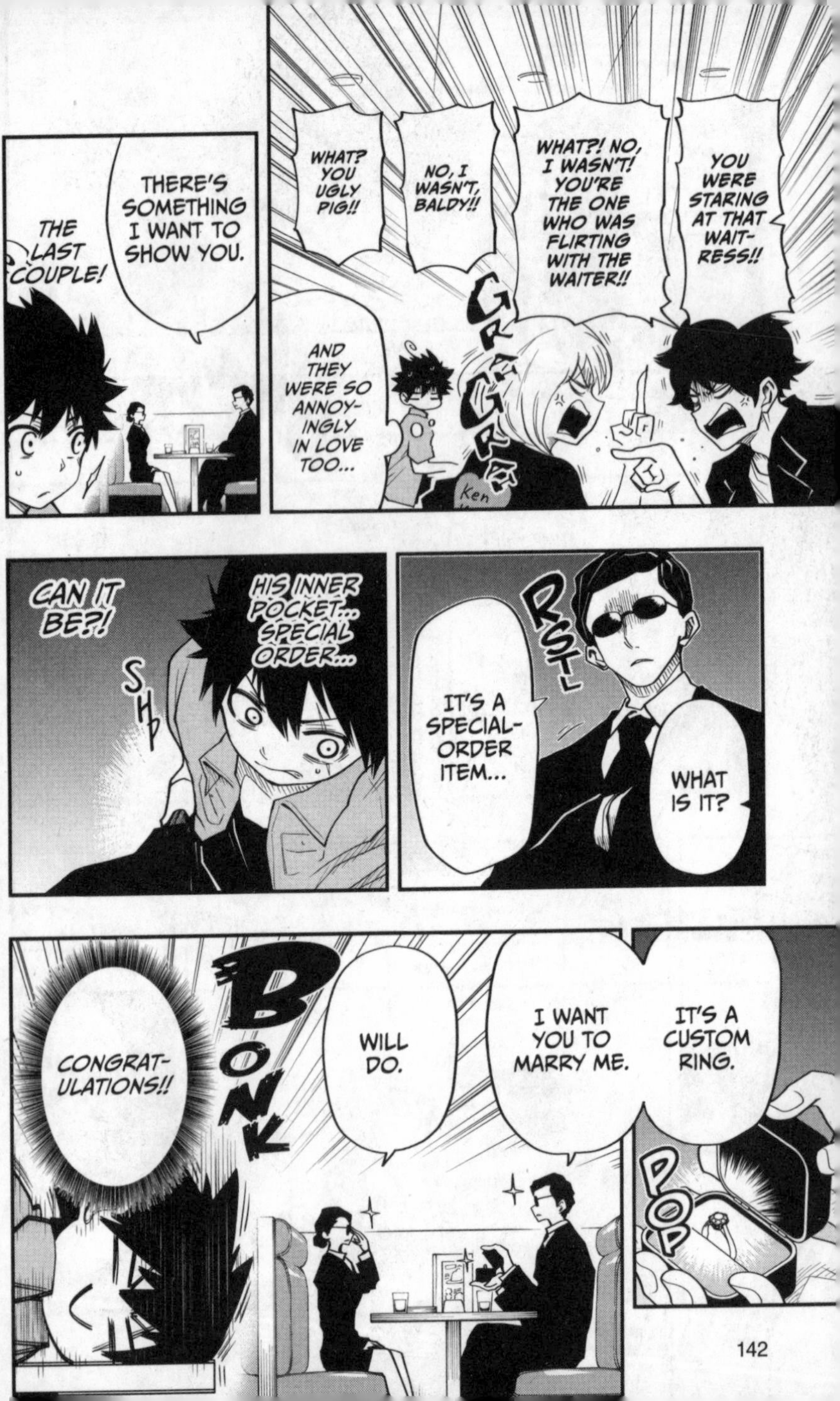
YOU WERE STARING AT THAT WAIT-RESS!!
WHAT?! NO, I WASN'T! YOU'RE THE ONE WHO WAS FLIRTING WITH THE WAITER!!
NO, I WASN'T, BALDY!!
WHAT? YOU UGLY PIG!!
GRAGRA
AND THEY WERE SO ANNOY-INGLY IN LOVE TOO...
Ken
THERE'S SOMETHING I WANT TO SHOW YOU.
THE LAST COUPLE!
RSTL
WHAT IS IT?
IT'S A SPECIAL-ORDER ITEM...
HIS INNER POCKET... SPECIAL ORDER...
CAN IT BE?!
SHP
IT'S A CUSTOM RING.
POP
I WANT YOU TO MARRY ME.
WILL DO.
BONK
CONGRAT-ULATIONS!!

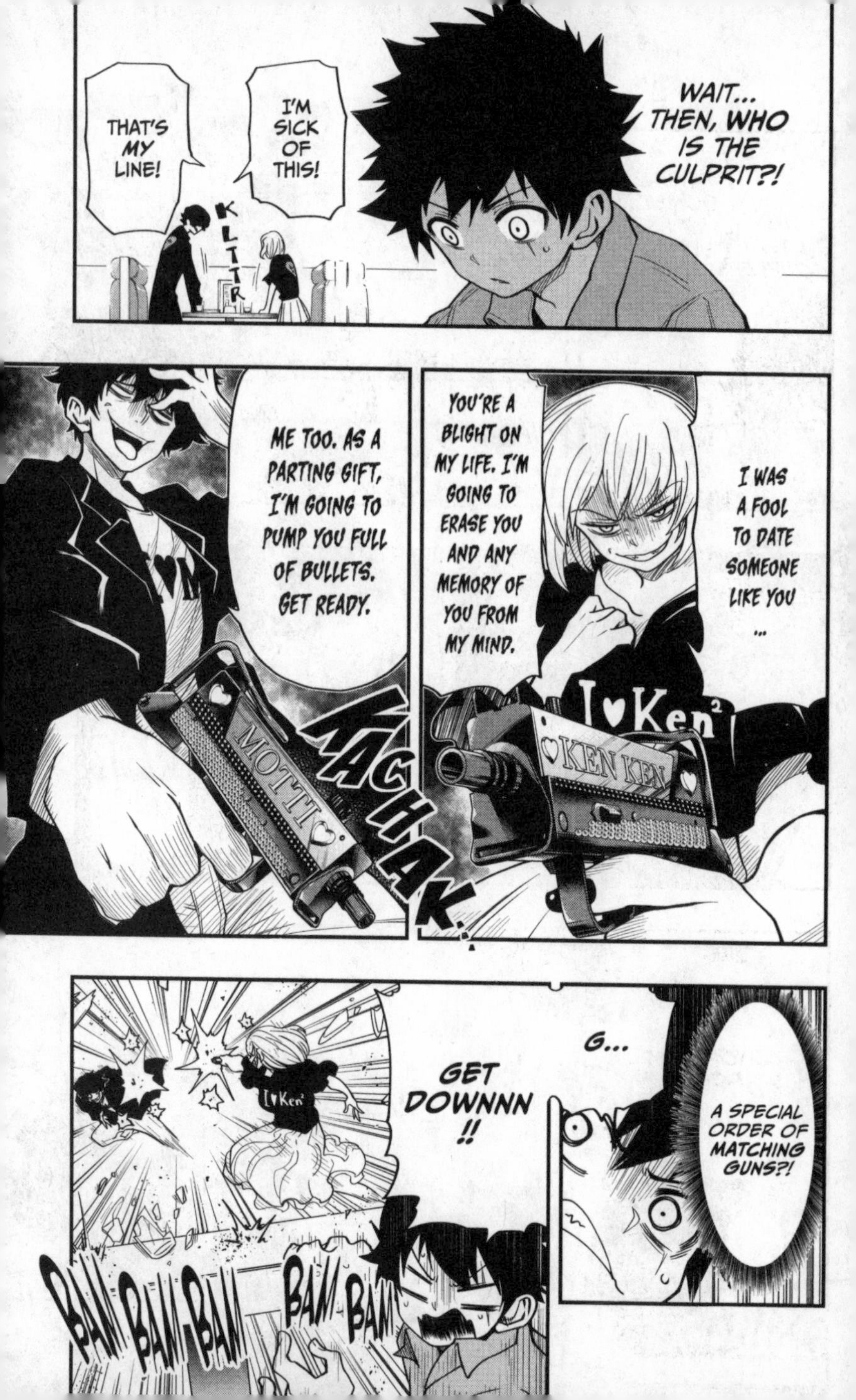
WAIT... THEN, WHO IS THE CULPRIT?!
I'M SICK OF THIS!
KLTTR
THAT'S MY LINE!
I WAS A FOOL TO DATE SOMEONE LIKE YOU ...
YOU'RE A BLIGHT ON MY LIFE. I'M GOING TO ERASE YOU AND ANY MEMORY OF YOU FROM MY MIND.
I♥Ken²
KEN KEN
ME TOO. AS A PARTING GIFT, I'M GOING TO PUMP YOU FULL OF BULLETS. GET READY.
MOTTI
KACHAK
G...
A SPECIAL ORDER OF MATCHING GUNS?!
GET DOWNNN !!
I♥Ken²
BAM BAM
BAM BAM BAM

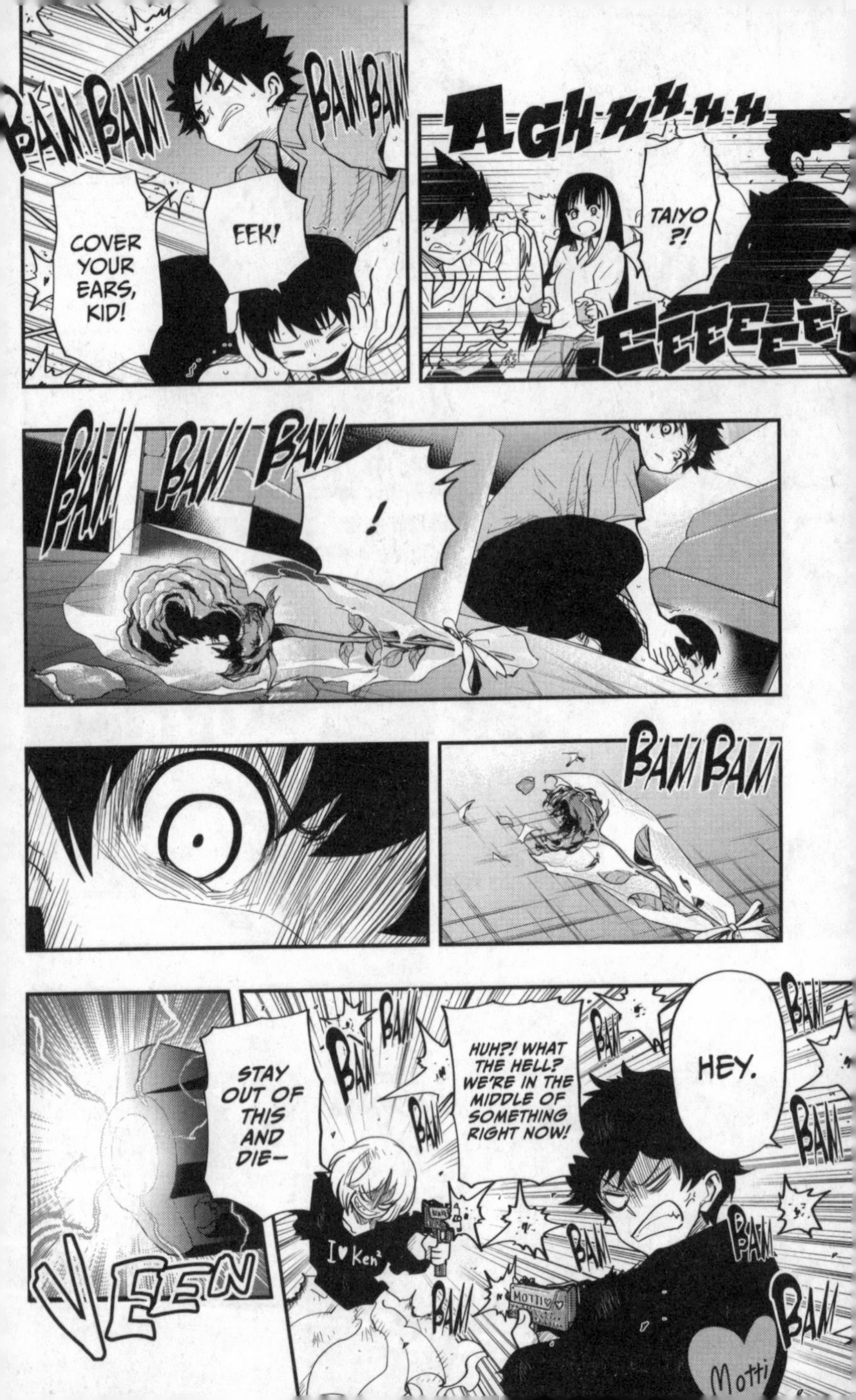
AGHHHHHH
TAIYO ?!
EEEEEE
BAM BAM
EEK!
BAM BAM
COVER YOUR EARS, KID!
BAM BAM BAM
!
BAM BAM
BAM
HEY.
BAM
BAM
BAM
HUH?! WHAT THE HELL? WE'RE IN THE MIDDLE OF SOMETHING RIGHT NOW!
BAM
BAM
BAM
STAY OUT OF THIS AND DIE—
I ♥ Ken²
MOTTI♥
BAM
Motti
VEEEN

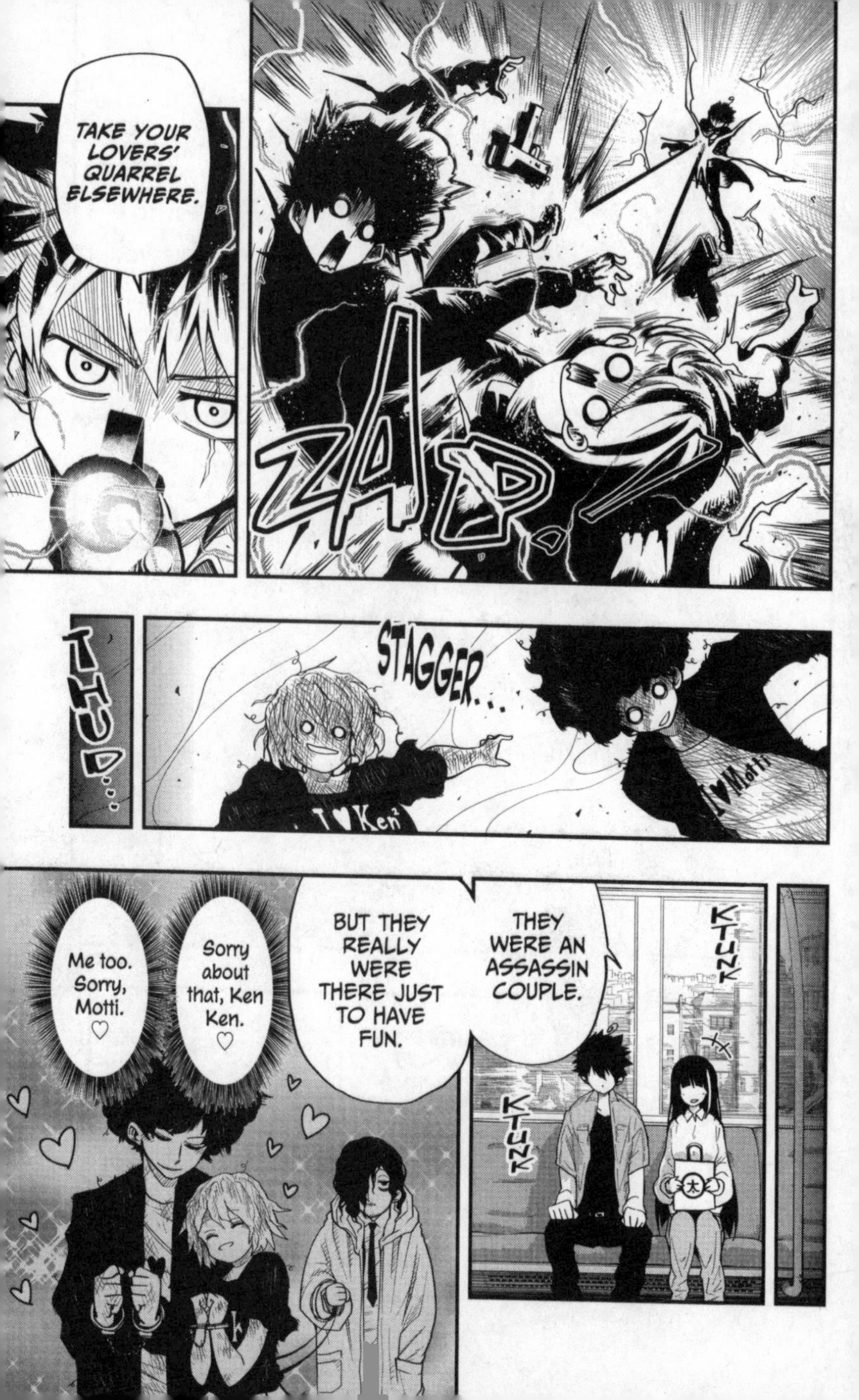
ZZAP.
TAKE YOUR LOVERS' QUARREL ELSEWHERE.
STAGGER...
I ♥ Motti
I ♥ Ken²
THUD...
KTUNK
KTUNK
THEY WERE AN ASSASSIN COUPLE.
BUT THEY REALLY WERE THERE JUST TO HAVE FUN.
Sorry about that, Ken Ken. ♡
Me too. Sorry, Motti. ♡

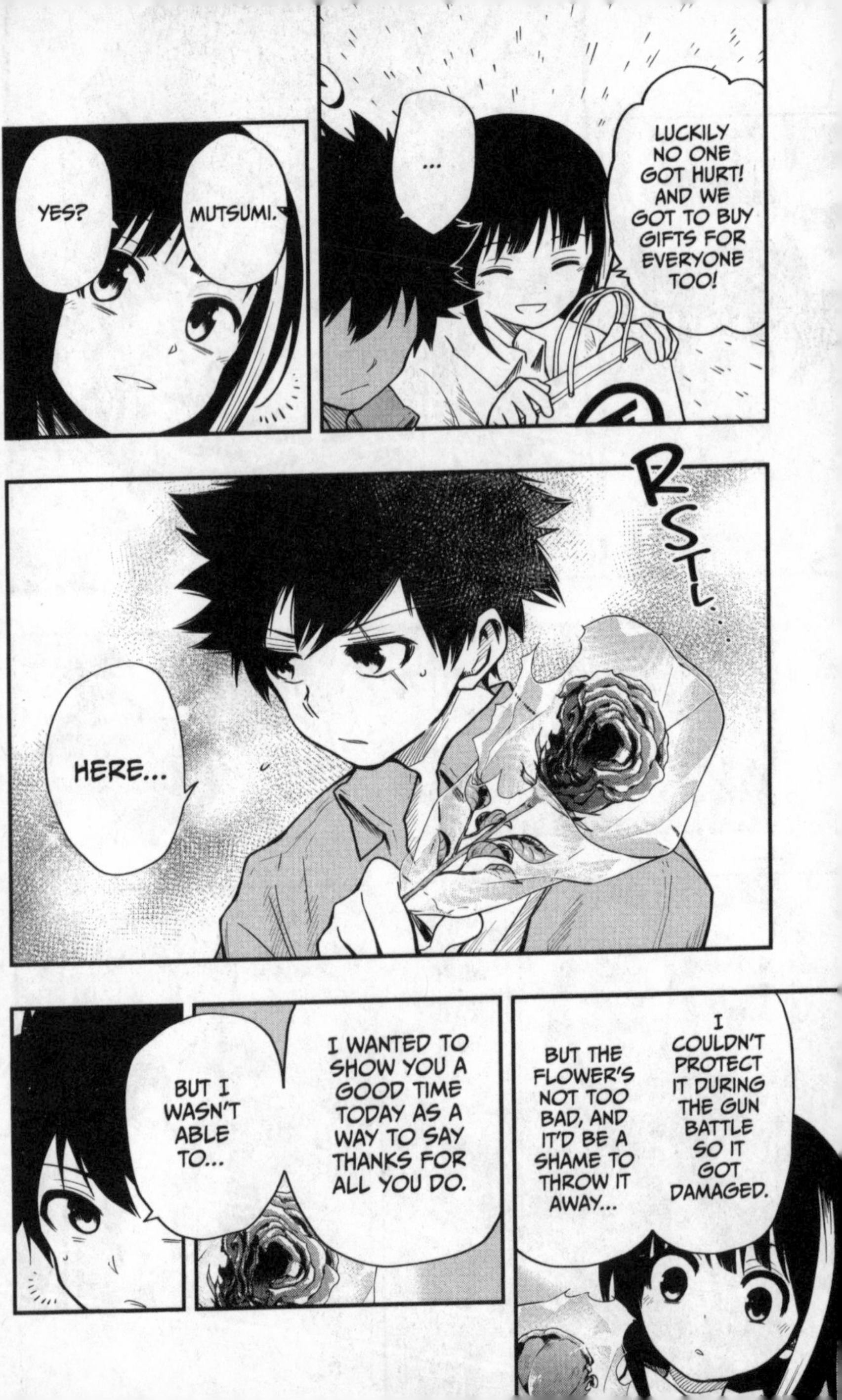
LUCKILY NO ONE GOT HURT! AND WE GOT TO BUY GIFTS FOR EVERYONE TOO!
...
MUTSUMI.
YES?
RSTL
HERE...
I COULDN'T PROTECT IT DURING THE GUN BATTLE SO IT GOT DAMAGED.
BUT THE FLOWER'S NOT TOO BAD, AND IT'D BE A SHAME TO THROW IT AWAY...
I WANTED TO SHOW YOU A GOOD TIME TODAY AS A WAY TO SAY THANKS FOR ALL YOU DO.
BUT I WASN'T ABLE TO...

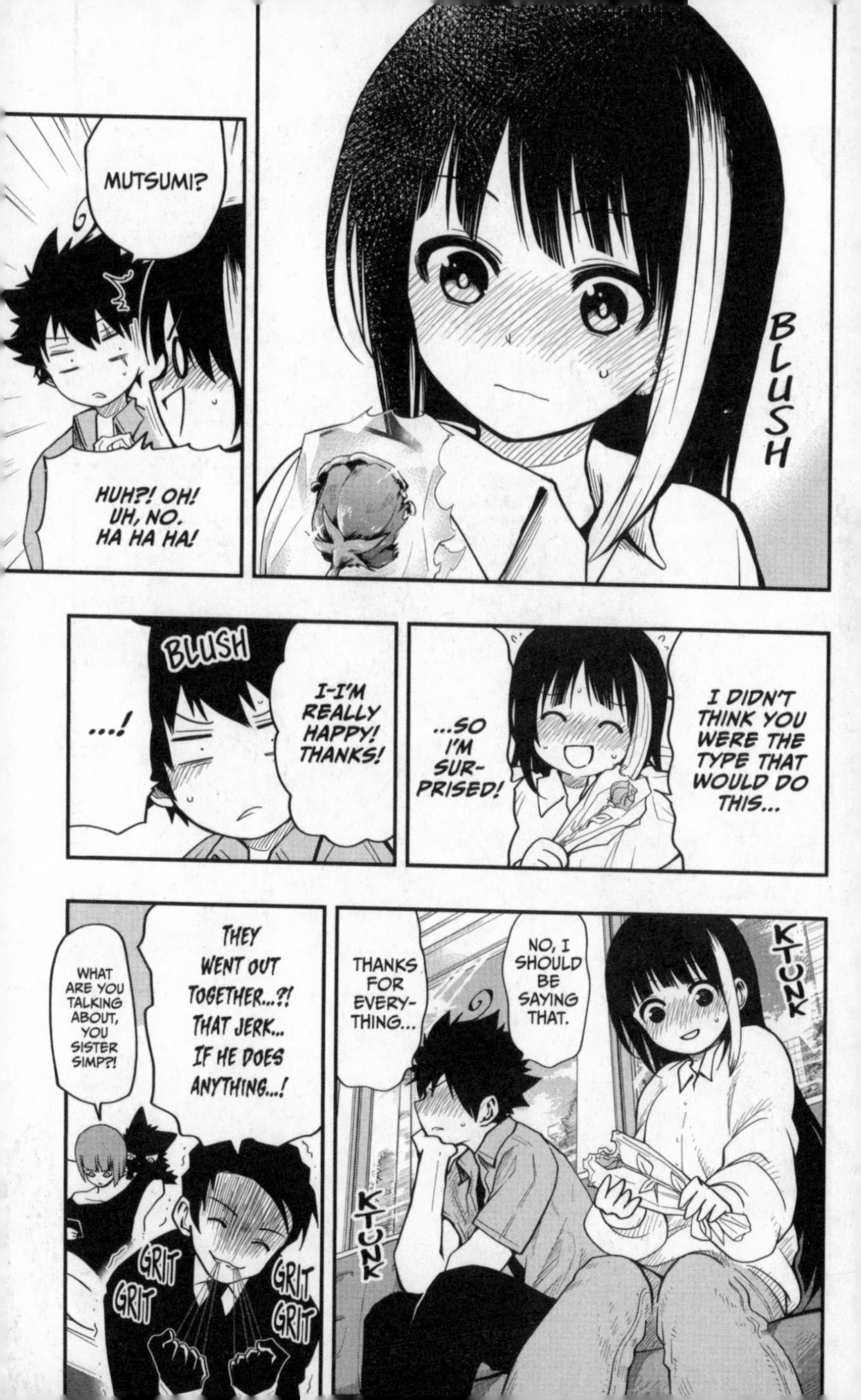
BLUSH
MUTSUMI?
HUH?! OH! UH, NO. HA HA HA!
I DIDN'T THINK YOU WERE THE TYPE THAT WOULD DO THIS...
...SO I'M SURPRISED!
BLUSH
I-I'M REALLY HAPPY! THANKS!
...!
KTUNK
NO, I SHOULD BE SAYING THAT.
THANKS FOR EVERYTHING...
KTUNK
THEY WENT OUT TOGETHER...?! THAT JERK... IF HE DOES ANYTHING...!
WHAT ARE YOU TALKING ABOUT, YOU SISTER SIMP?!
GRIT GRIT
GRIT GRIT

INTERROGATING LOVE

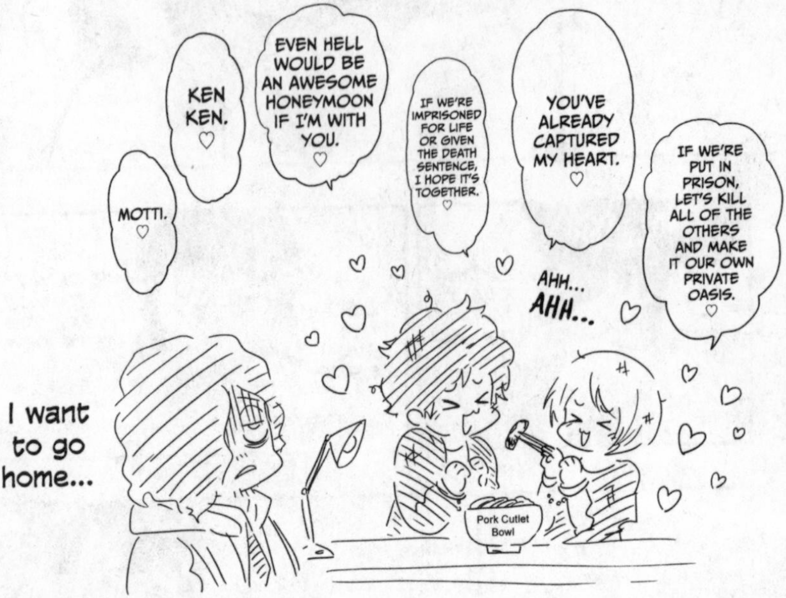
YOU'VE ALREADY CAPTURED MY HEART. ♡
IF WE'RE PUT IN PRISON, LET'S KILL ALL OF THE OTHERS AND MAKE IT OUR OWN PRIVATE OASIS. ♡
AHH... AHH...
IF WE'RE IMPRISONED FOR LIFE OR GIVEN THE DEATH SENTENCE, I HOPE IT'S TOGETHER. ♡
EVEN HELL WOULD BE AN AWESOME HONEYMOON IF I'M WITH YOU. ♡
KEN KEN. ♡
MOTTI. ♡
Pork Cutlet Bowl
I want to go home...

MISSION 15: CUPID'S NEEDLE

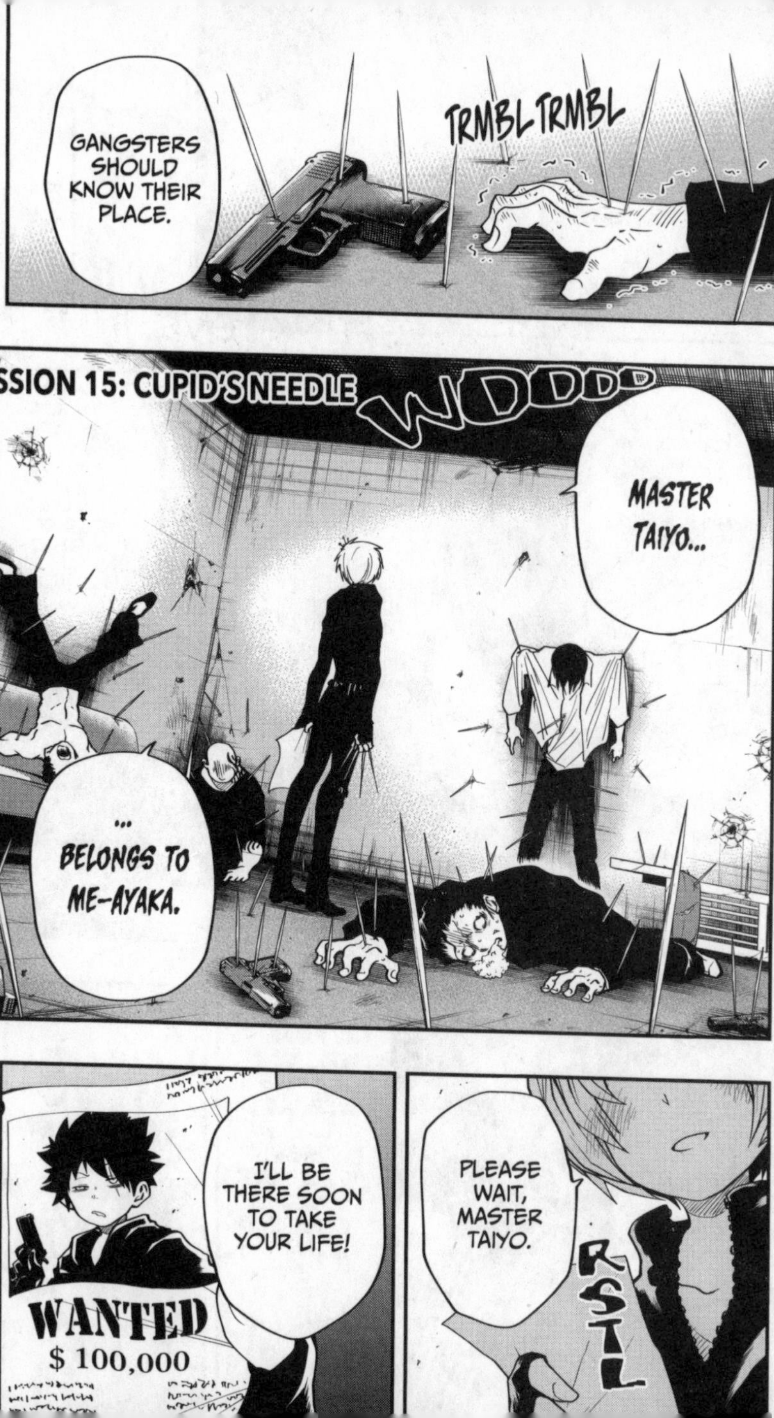
TRMBL TRMBL
GANGSTERS SHOULD KNOW THEIR PLACE.
WDDD
MASTER TAIYO...
... BELONGS TO ME—AYAKA.
PLEASE WAIT, MASTER TAIYO.
RSTL
I'LL BE THERE SOON TO TAKE YOUR LIFE!
WANTED
$ 100,000

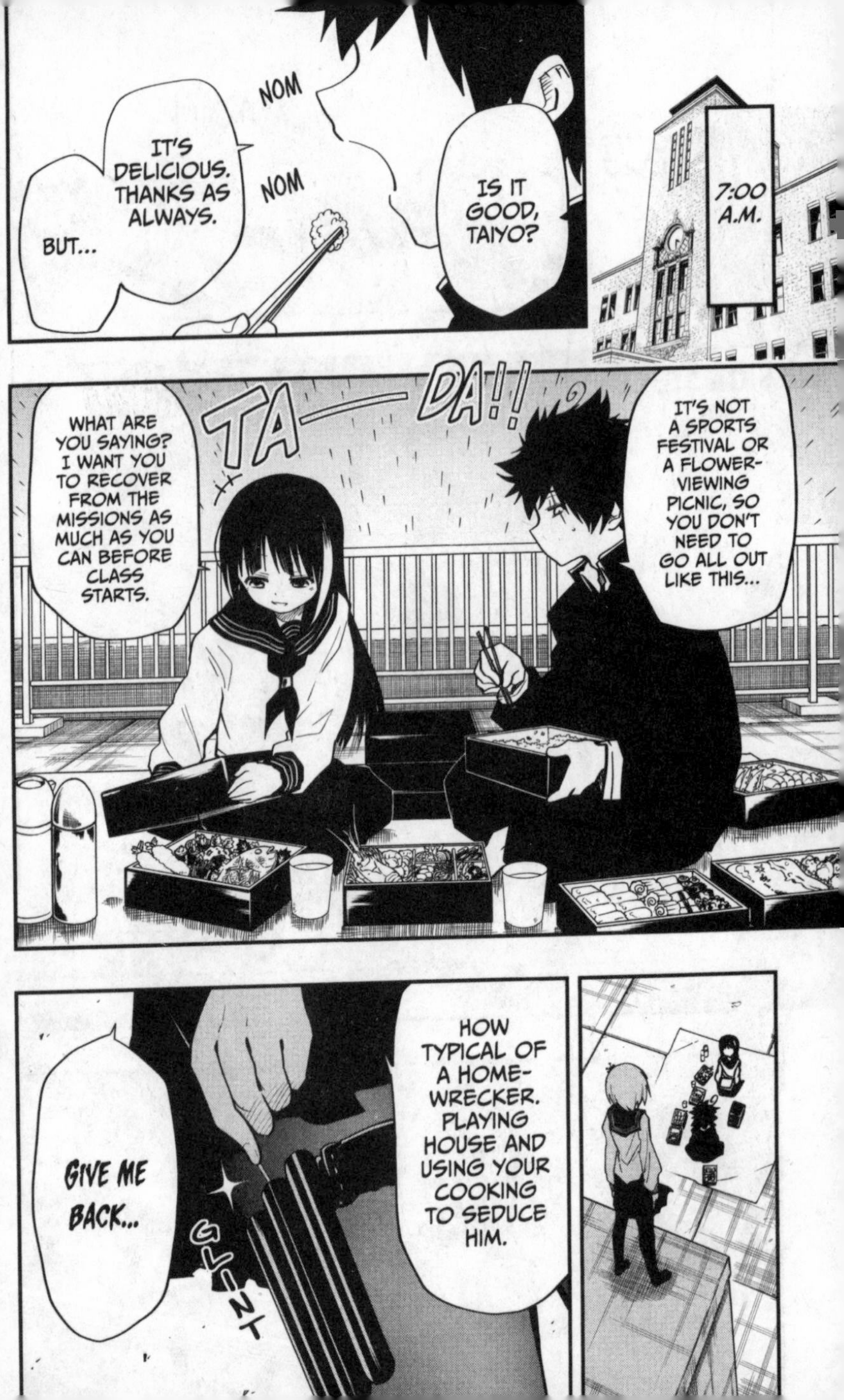
7:00 A.M.
IS IT GOOD, TAIYO?
NOM
NOM
IT'S DELICIOUS. THANKS AS ALWAYS.
BUT...
TA—DA!!
IT'S NOT A SPORTS FESTIVAL OR A FLOWER-VIEWING PICNIC, SO YOU DON'T NEED TO GO ALL OUT LIKE THIS...
WHAT ARE YOU SAYING? I WANT YOU TO RECOVER FROM THE MISSIONS AS MUCH AS YOU CAN BEFORE CLASS STARTS.
HOW TYPICAL OF A HOME-WRECKER. PLAYING HOUSE AND USING YOUR COOKING TO SEDUCE HIM.
GLINT
GIVE ME BACK...

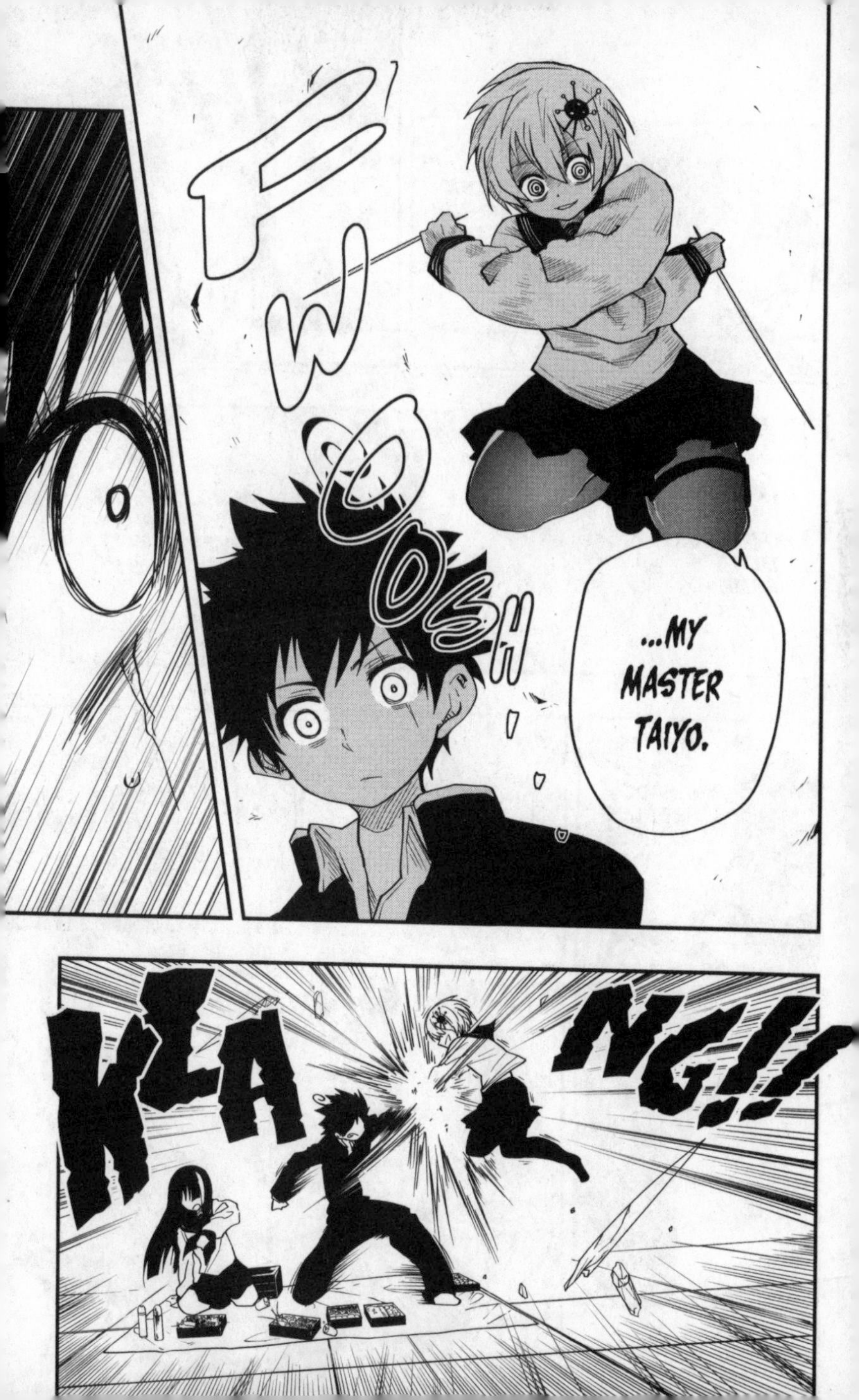
FWOOSH
...MY MASTER TAIYO.
KLANG!!

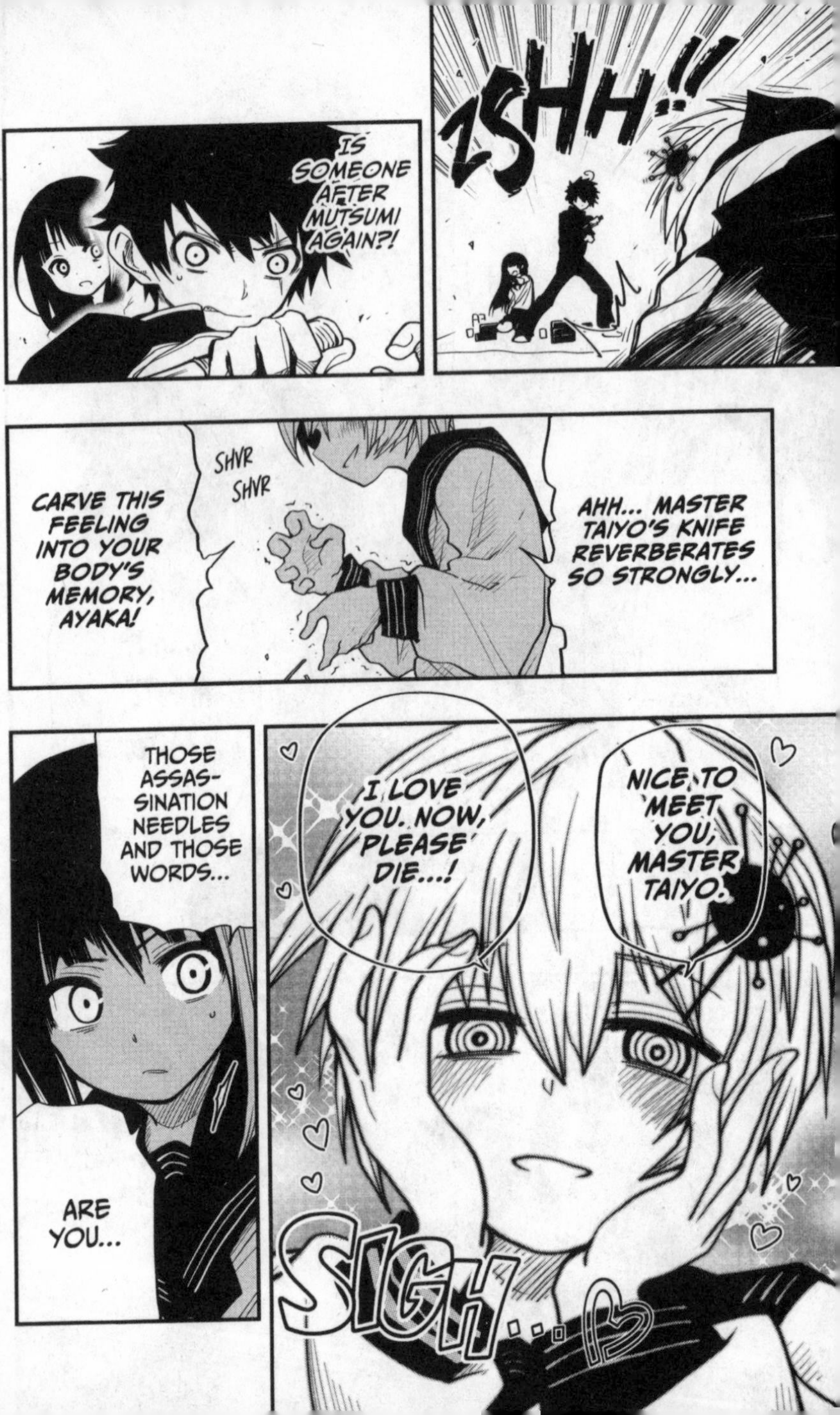
ZSHH!!
IS SOMEONE AFTER MUTSUMI AGAIN?!
AHH... MASTER TAIYO'S KNIFE REVERBERATES SO STRONGLY...
SHVR SHVR
CARVE THIS FEELING INTO YOUR BODY'S MEMORY, AYAKA!
NICE TO MEET YOU, MASTER TAIYO.
I LOVE YOU. NOW, PLEASE DIE...!
SIGH...
THOSE ASSAS-SINATION NEEDLES AND THOSE WORDS...
ARE YOU...

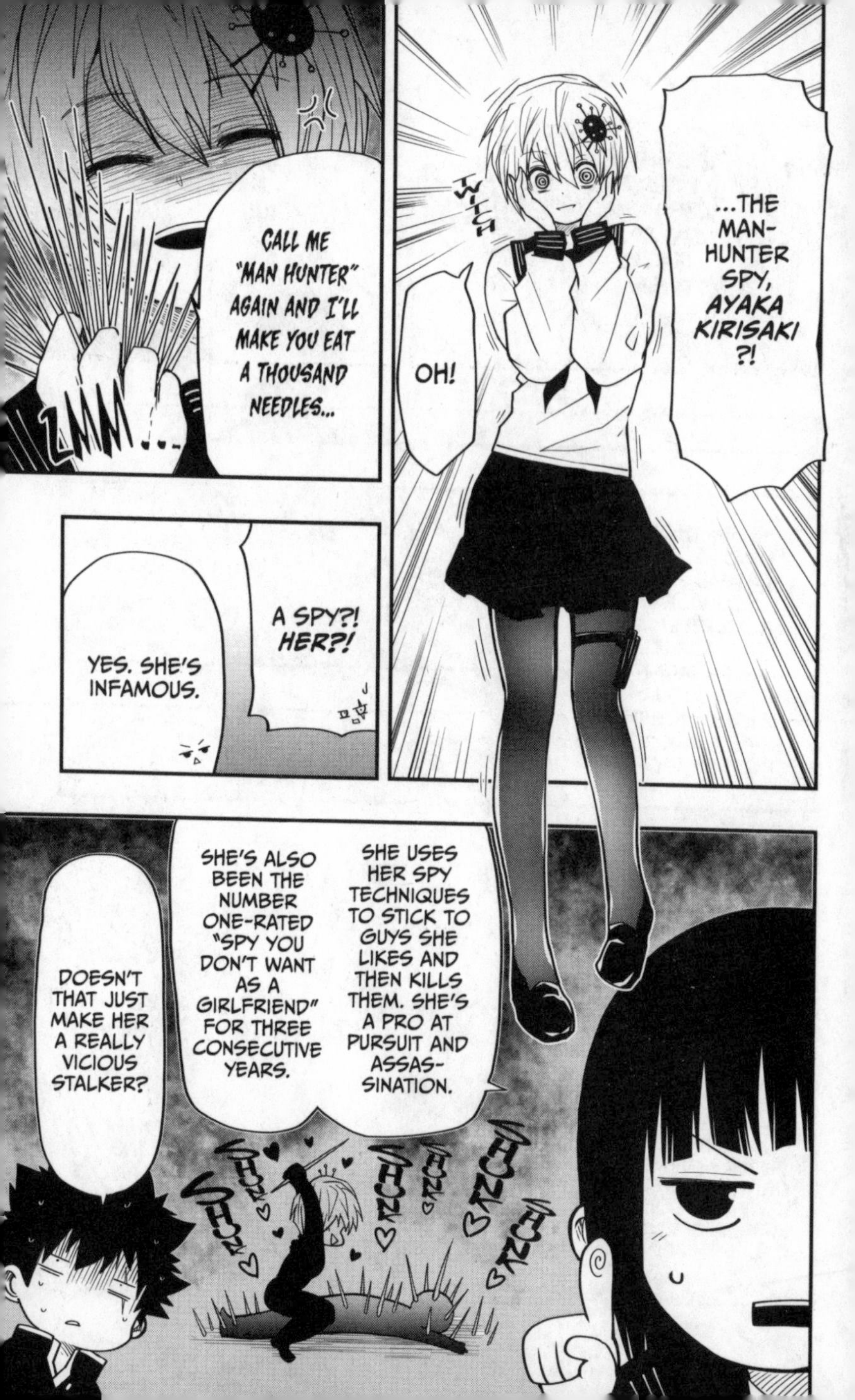
...THE MAN-HUNTER SPY, AYAKA KIRISAKI?!
TWICH
OH!
CALL ME "MAN HUNTER" AGAIN AND I'LL MAKE YOU EAT A THOUSAND NEEDLES...
ZMM...
A SPY?! HER?!
YES. SHE'S INFAMOUS.
SHE USES HER SPY TECHNIQUES TO STICK TO GUYS SHE LIKES AND THEN KILLS THEM. SHE'S A PRO AT PURSUIT AND ASSAS-SINATION.
SHE'S ALSO BEEN THE NUMBER ONE-RATED "SPY YOU DON'T WANT AS A GIRLFRIEND" FOR THREE CONSECUTIVE YEARS.
DOESN'T THAT JUST MAKE HER A REALLY VICIOUS STALKER?
SHUNK
SHUNK
SHUNK
SHUNK
SHUNK
SHUNK

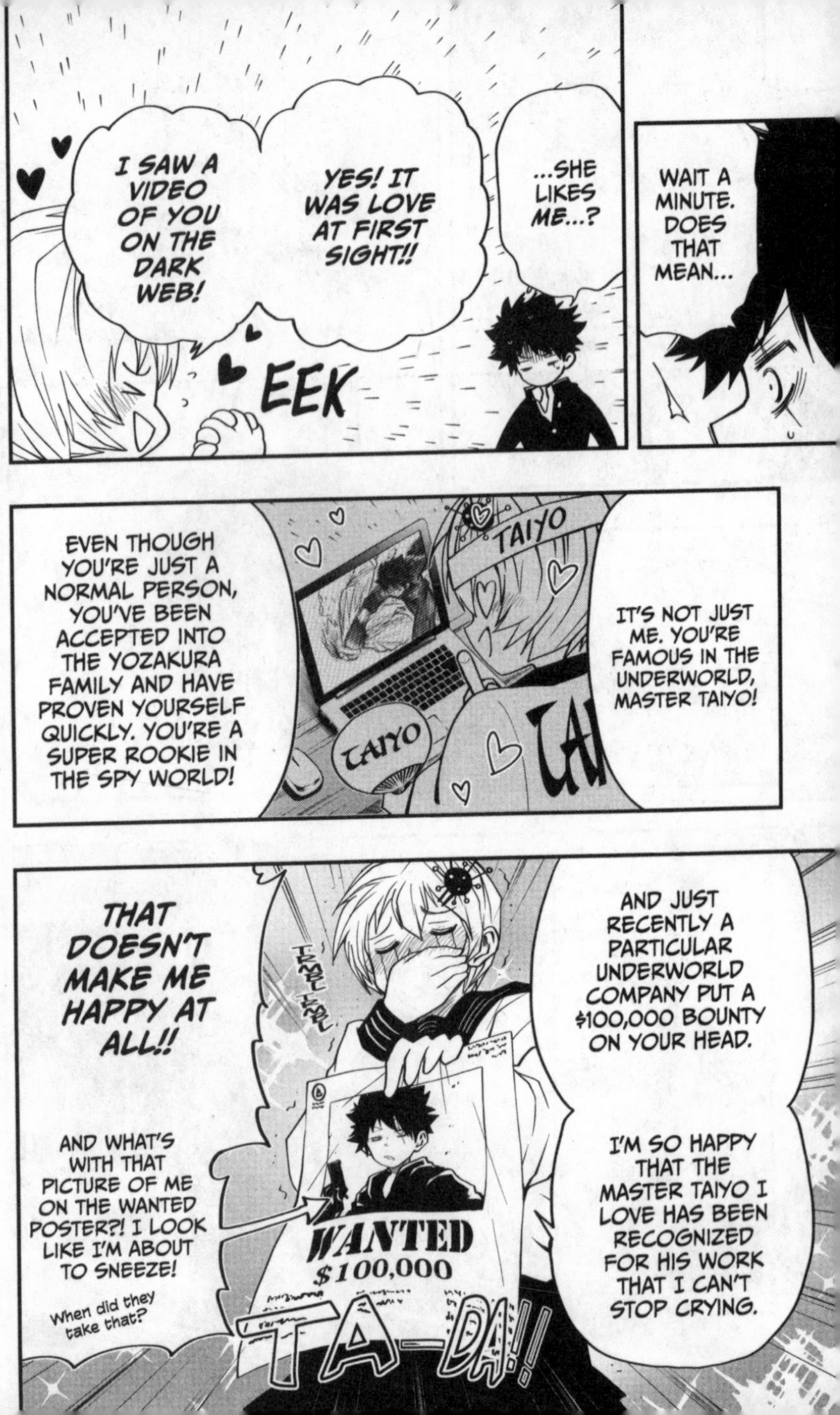
WAIT A MINUTE. DOES THAT MEAN...
...SHE LIKES ME...?
YES! IT WAS LOVE AT FIRST SIGHT!!
I SAW A VIDEO OF YOU ON THE DARK WEB!
EEK
TAIYO
IT'S NOT JUST ME. YOU'RE FAMOUS IN THE UNDERWORLD, MASTER TAIYO!
TAIYO
EVEN THOUGH YOU'RE JUST A NORMAL PERSON, YOU'VE BEEN ACCEPTED INTO THE YOZAKURA FAMILY AND HAVE PROVEN YOURSELF QUICKLY. YOU'RE A SUPER ROOKIE IN THE SPY WORLD!
AND JUST RECENTLY A PARTICULAR UNDERWORLD COMPANY PUT A $100,000 BOUNTY ON YOUR HEAD.
I'M SO HAPPY THAT THE MASTER TAIYO I LOVE HAS BEEN RECOGNIZED FOR HIS WORK THAT I CAN'T STOP CRYING.
TREMBL TREMBL
THAT DOESN'T MAKE ME HAPPY AT ALL!!
AND WHAT'S WITH THAT PICTURE OF ME ON THE WANTED POSTER?! I LOOK LIKE I'M ABOUT TO SNEEZE!
When did they take that?
WANTED
$100,000
TA-DA!!

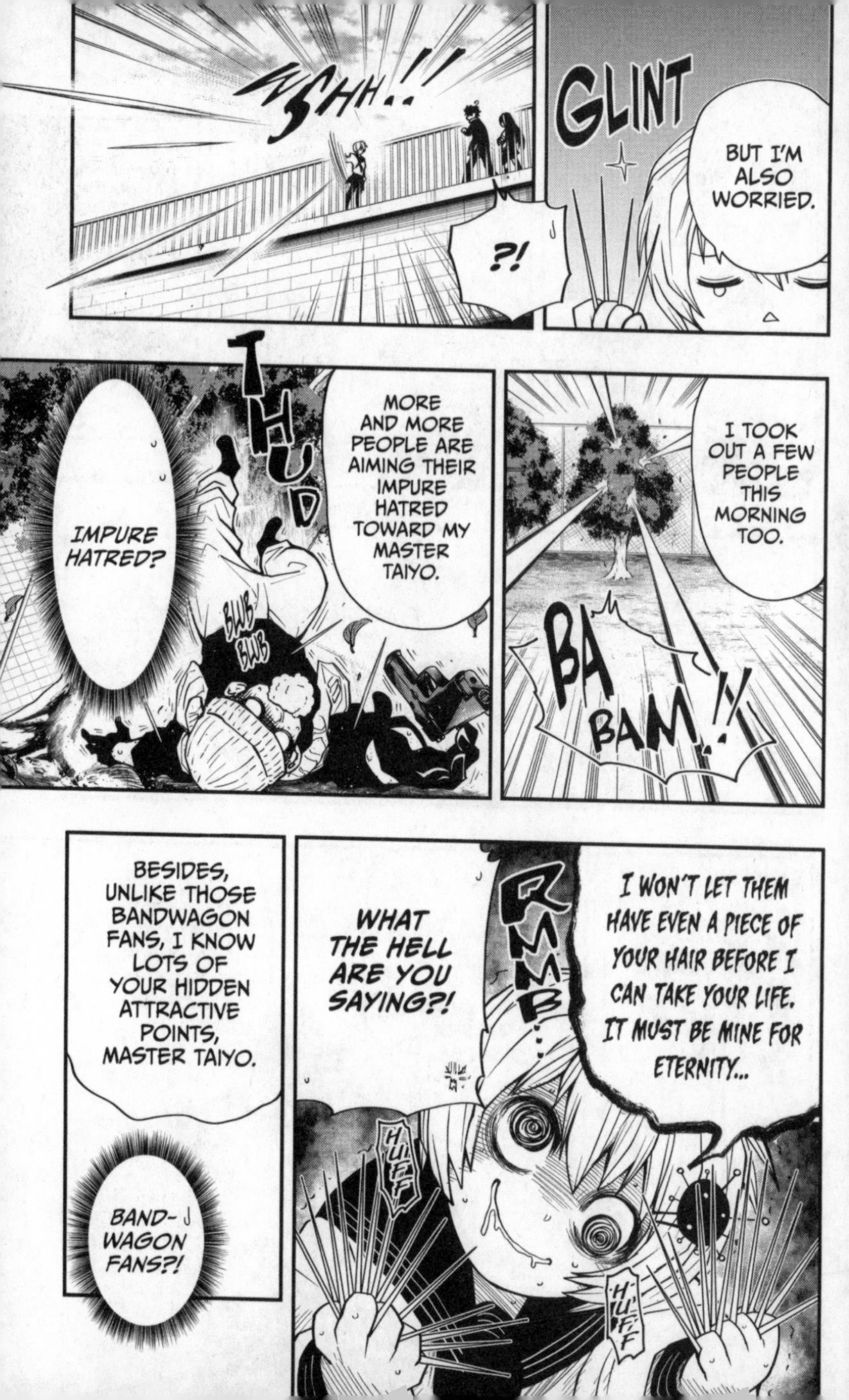
GLINT
BUT I'M ALSO WORRIED.
WSHH..!!
?!
I TOOK OUT A FEW PEOPLE THIS MORNING TOO.
BA BAM!!
MORE AND MORE PEOPLE ARE AIMING THEIR IMPURE HATRED TOWARD MY MASTER TAIYO.
THUD
IMPURE HATRED?
BLUB BLUB
I WON'T LET THEM HAVE EVEN A PIECE OF YOUR HAIR BEFORE I CAN TAKE YOUR LIFE. IT MUST BE MINE FOR ETERNITY...
RMMB...
WHAT THE HELL ARE YOU SAYING?!
HUFF
HUFF
BESIDES, UNLIKE THOSE BANDWAGON FANS, I KNOW LOTS OF YOUR HIDDEN ATTRACTIVE POINTS, MASTER TAIYO.
BAND-WAGON FANS?!

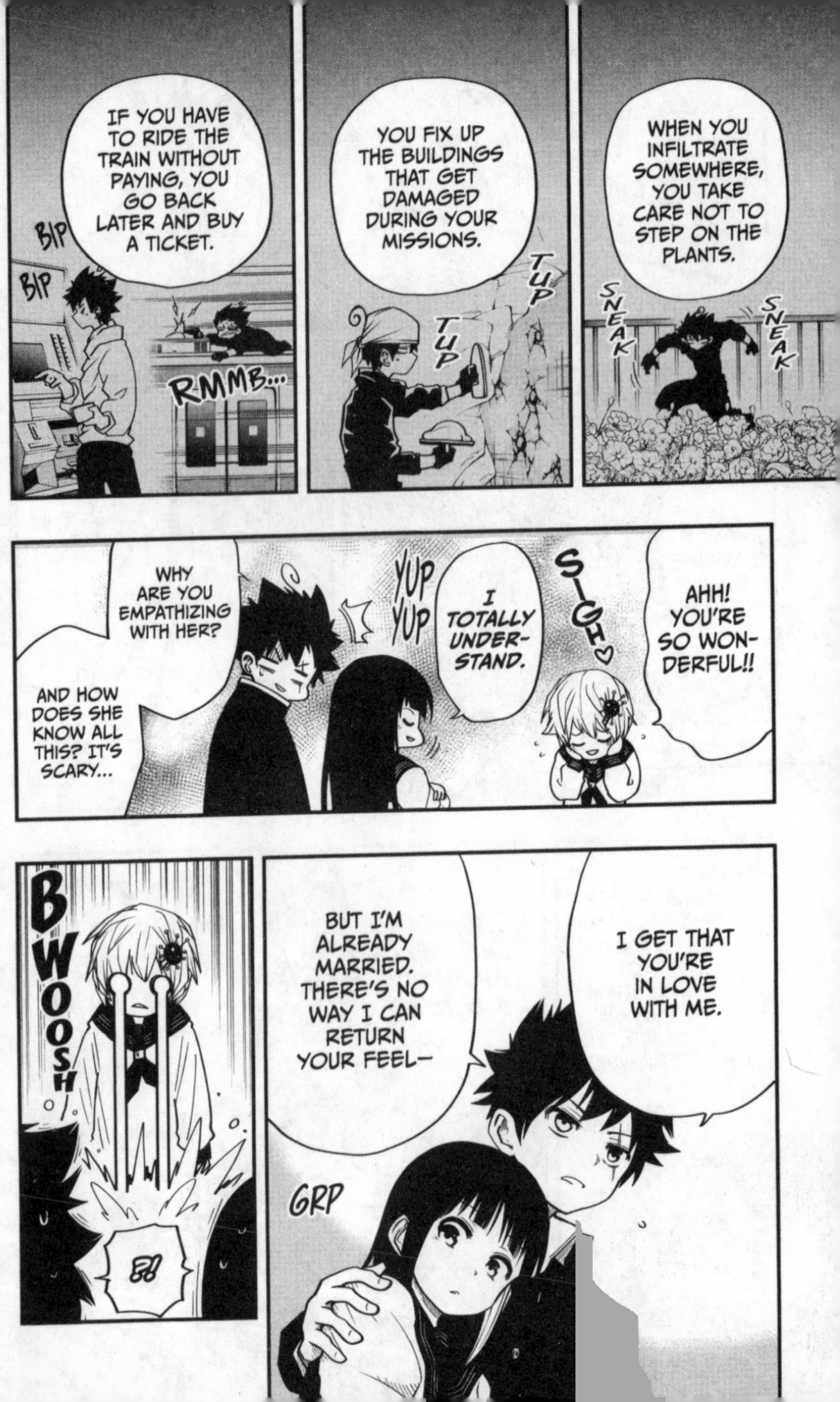
WHEN YOU INFILTRATE SOMEWHERE, YOU TAKE CARE NOT TO STEP ON THE PLANTS.
SNEAK
SNEAK
YOU FIX UP THE BUILDINGS THAT GET DAMAGED DURING YOUR MISSIONS.
TUP
TUP
IF YOU HAVE TO RIDE THE TRAIN WITHOUT PAYING, YOU GO BACK LATER AND BUY A TICKET.
BIP
BIP
RMMB...
AHH! YOU'RE SO WONDERFUL!!
SIGH♥
I TOTALLY UNDERSTAND.
YUP YUP
WHY ARE YOU EMPATHIZING WITH HER?
AND HOW DOES SHE KNOW ALL THIS? IT'S SCARY...
I GET THAT YOU'RE IN LOVE WITH ME.
BUT I'M ALREADY MARRIED. THERE'S NO WAY I CAN RETURN YOUR FEEL—
GRP
BWOOSH
!?

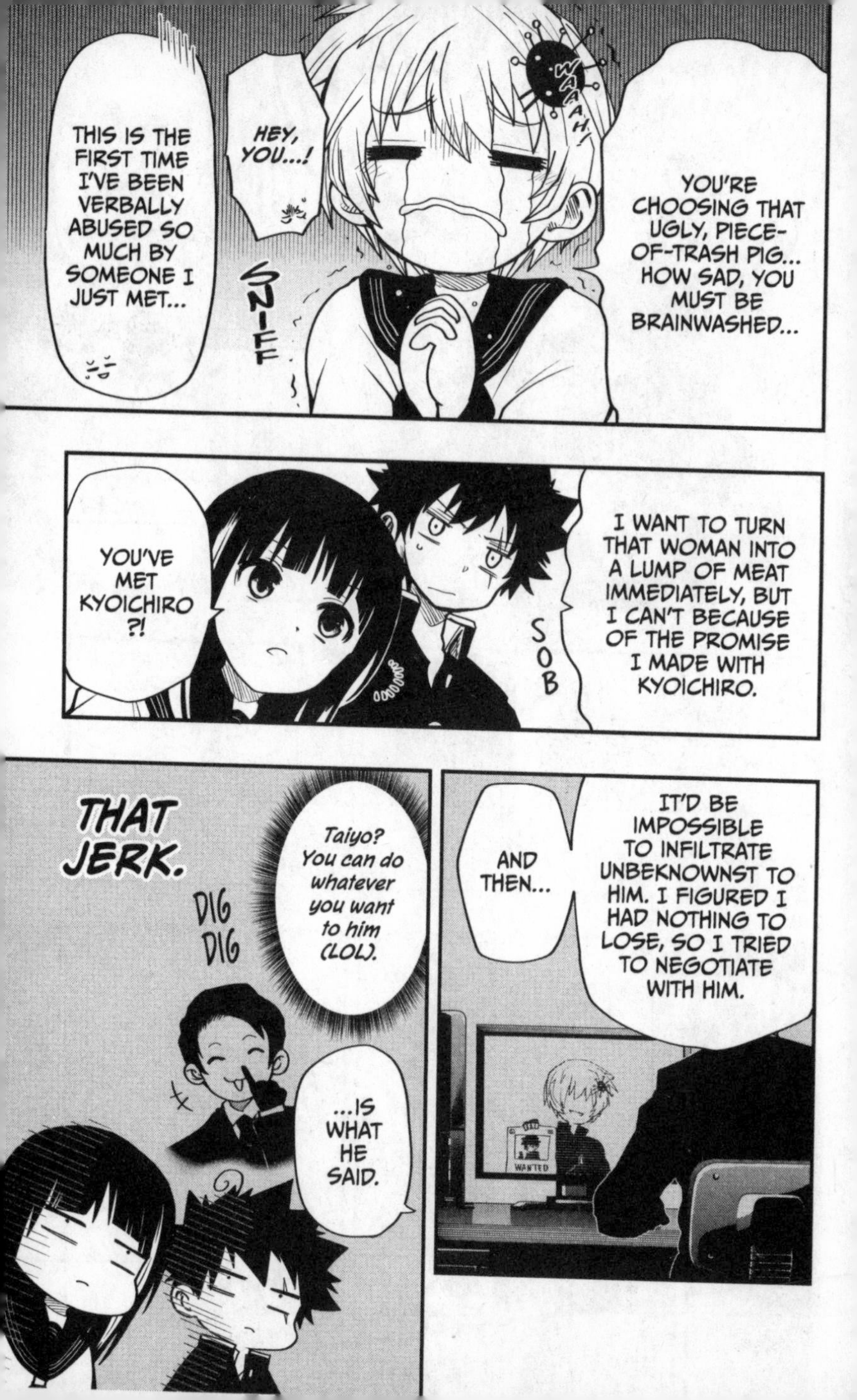
YOU'RE CHOOSING THAT UGLY, PIECE-OF-TRASH PIG... HOW SAD, YOU MUST BE BRAINWASHED...
WAAAH!
HEY, YOU...!
THIS IS THE FIRST TIME I'VE BEEN VERBALLY ABUSED SO MUCH BY SOMEONE I JUST MET...
SNIFF
I WANT TO TURN THAT WOMAN INTO A LUMP OF MEAT IMMEDIATELY, BUT I CAN'T BECAUSE OF THE PROMISE I MADE WITH KYOICHIRO.
SOB
YOU'VE MET KYOICHIRO ?!
IT'D BE IMPOSSIBLE TO INFILTRATE UNBEKNOWNST TO HIM. I FIGURED I HAD NOTHING TO LOSE, SO I TRIED TO NEGOTIATE WITH HIM.
AND THEN...
WANTED
Taiyo? You can do whatever you want to him (LOL).
THAT JERK.
DIG DIG
...IS WHAT HE SAID.

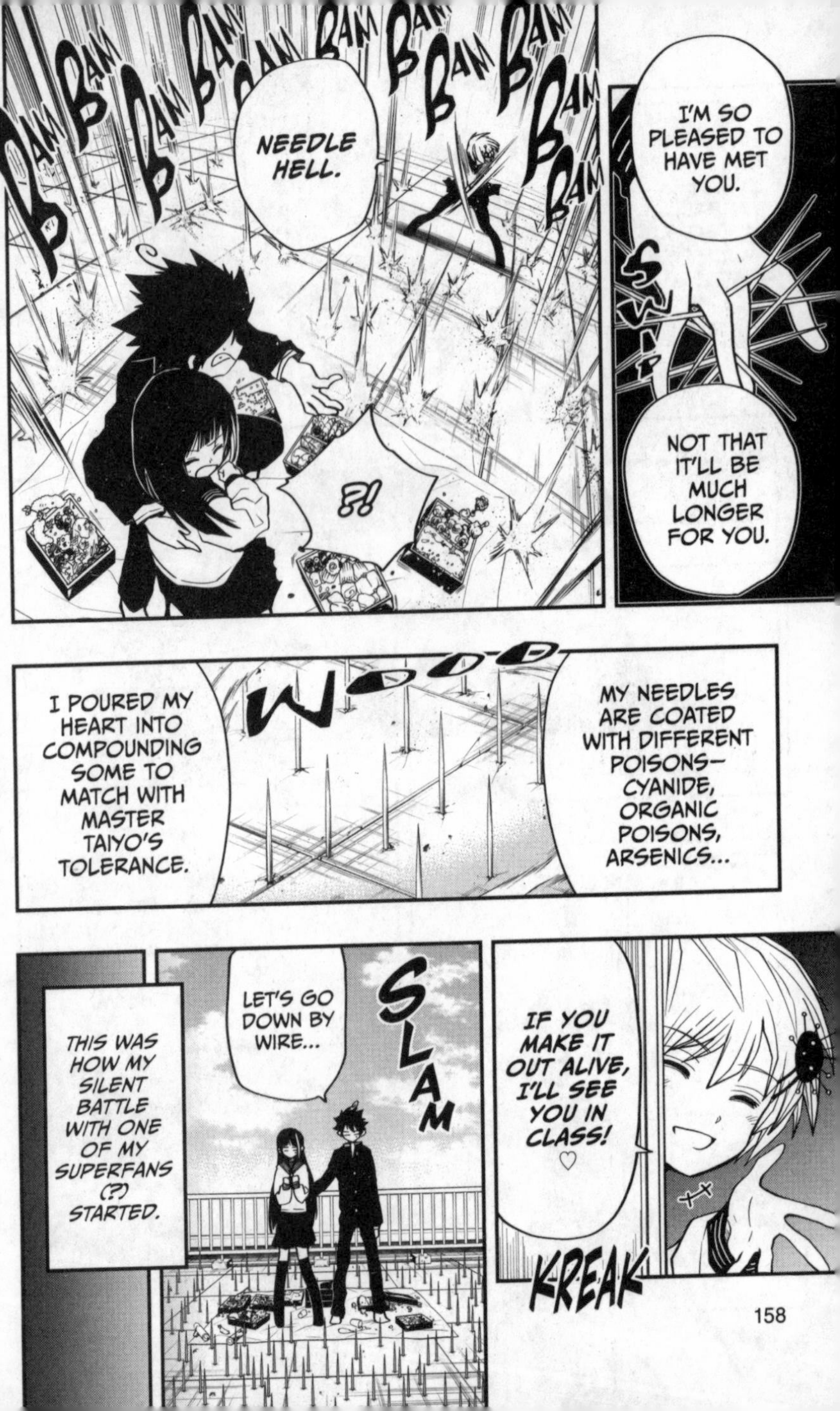
I'M SO PLEASED TO HAVE MET YOU.
SWIP
NOT THAT IT'LL BE MUCH LONGER FOR YOU.
BAM BAM BAM BAM BAM BAM BAM BAM BAM BAM BAM BAM BAM BAM
NEEDLE HELL.
?!
MY NEEDLES ARE COATED WITH DIFFERENT POISONS—CYANIDE, ORGANIC POISONS, ARSENICS...
I POURED MY HEART INTO COMPOUNDING SOME TO MATCH WITH MASTER TAIYO'S TOLERANCE.
IF YOU MAKE IT OUT ALIVE, I'LL SEE YOU IN CLASS! ♡
KREAK
SLAM
LET'S GO DOWN BY WIRE...
THIS WAS HOW MY SILENT BATTLE WITH ONE OF MY SUPERFANS (?) STARTED.

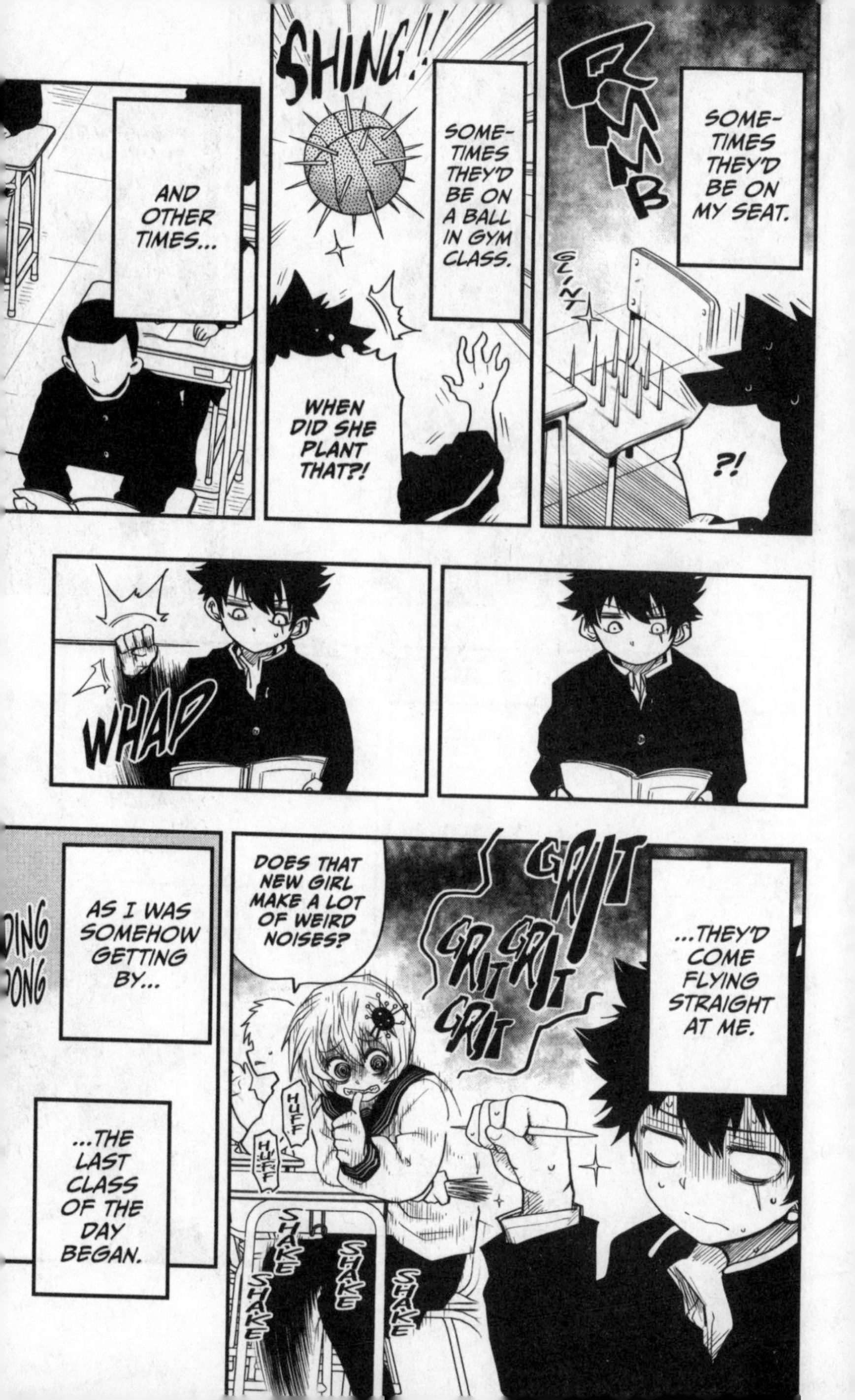
RUMB
SOME-TIMES THEY'D BE ON MY SEAT.
GLINT
?!
SHING!!
SOME-TIMES THEY'D BE ON A BALL IN GYM CLASS.
WHEN DID SHE PLANT THAT?!
AND OTHER TIMES...
WHAP
...THEY'D COME FLYING STRAIGHT AT ME.
GRIT
GRIT GRIT GRIT
DOES THAT NEW GIRL MAKE A LOT OF WEIRD NOISES?
HUFF HUFF
SHAKE SHAKE
SHAKE
SHAKE
DING
ONG
AS I WAS SOMEHOW GETTING BY...
...THE LAST CLASS OF THE DAY BEGAN.

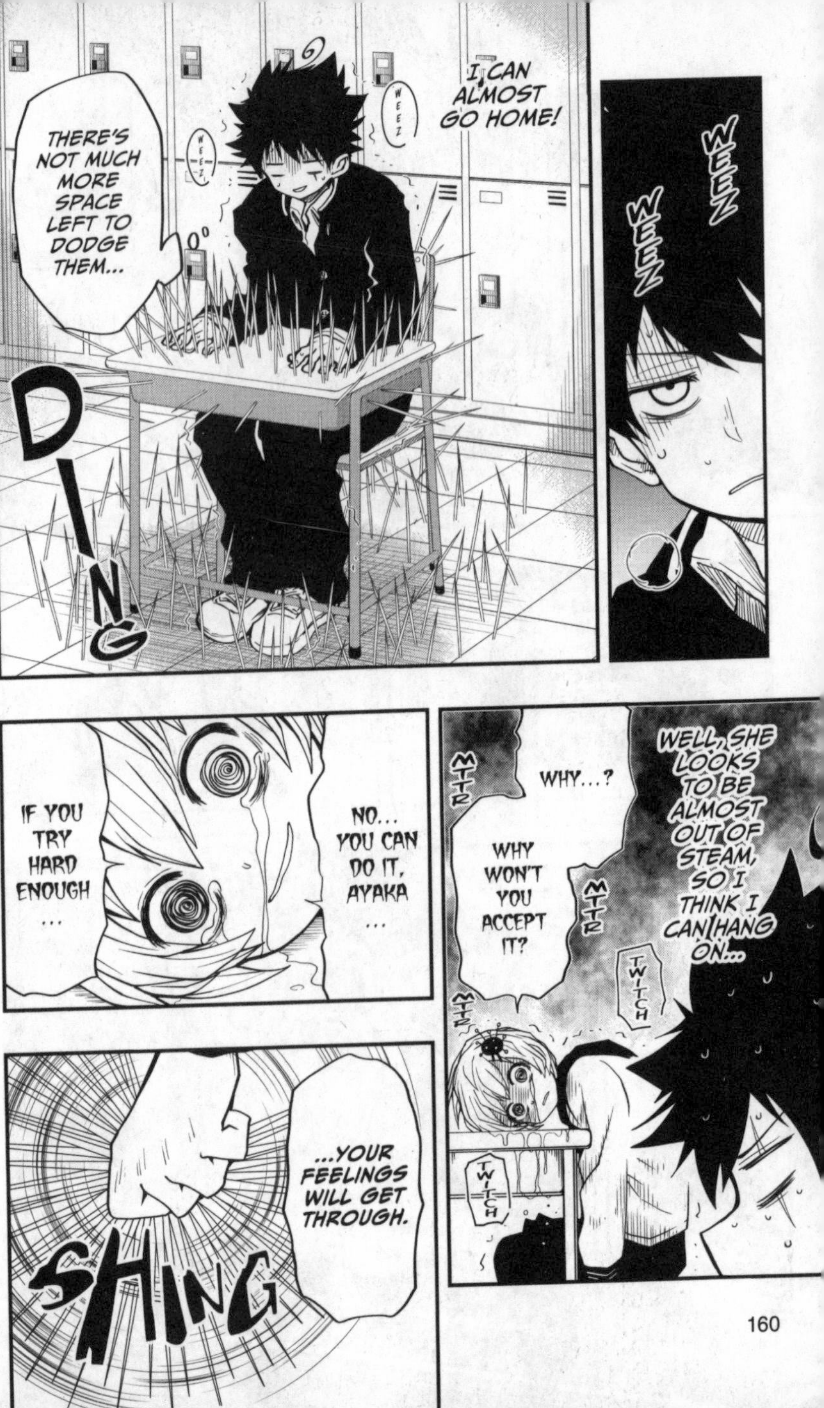
WEEZ
WEEZ
I CAN ALMOST GO HOME!
WEEZ
WEEZ
THERE'S NOT MUCH MORE SPACE LEFT TO DODGE THEM...
DING
WELL, SHE LOOKS TO BE ALMOST OUT OF STEAM, SO I THINK I CAN HANG ON...
MTTR
WHY...?
WHY WON'T YOU ACCEPT IT?
MTTR
MTTR
TWITCH
TWITCH
NO... YOU CAN DO IT, AYAKA...
IF YOU TRY HARD ENOUGH...
...YOUR FEELINGS WILL GET THROUGH.
SHING

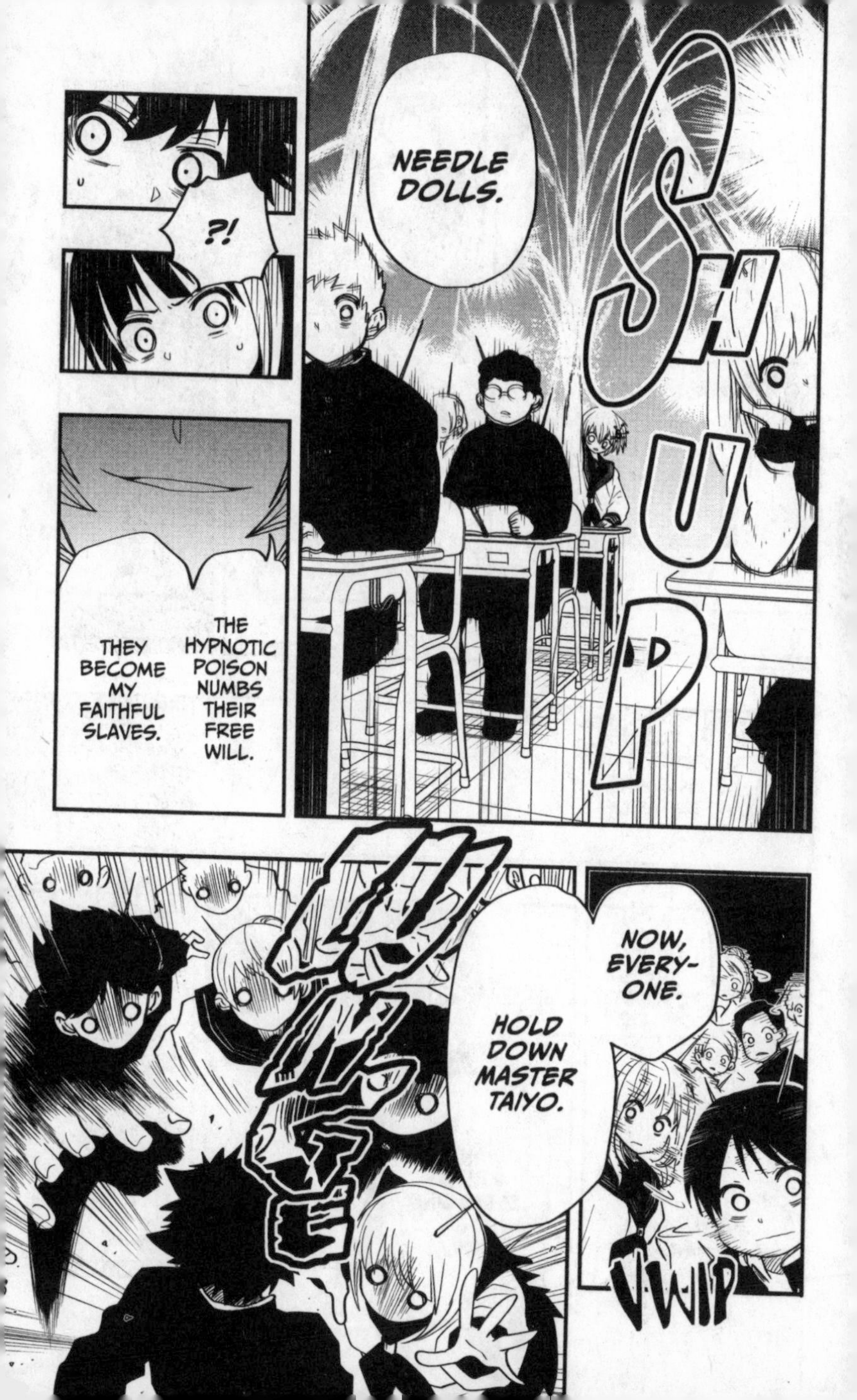
NEEDLE DOLLS.
SHUPP
?!
THE HYPNOTIC POISON NUMBS THEIR FREE WILL.
THEY BECOME MY FAITHFUL SLAVES.
NOW, EVERY-ONE.
HOLD DOWN MASTER TAIYO.
VWIP

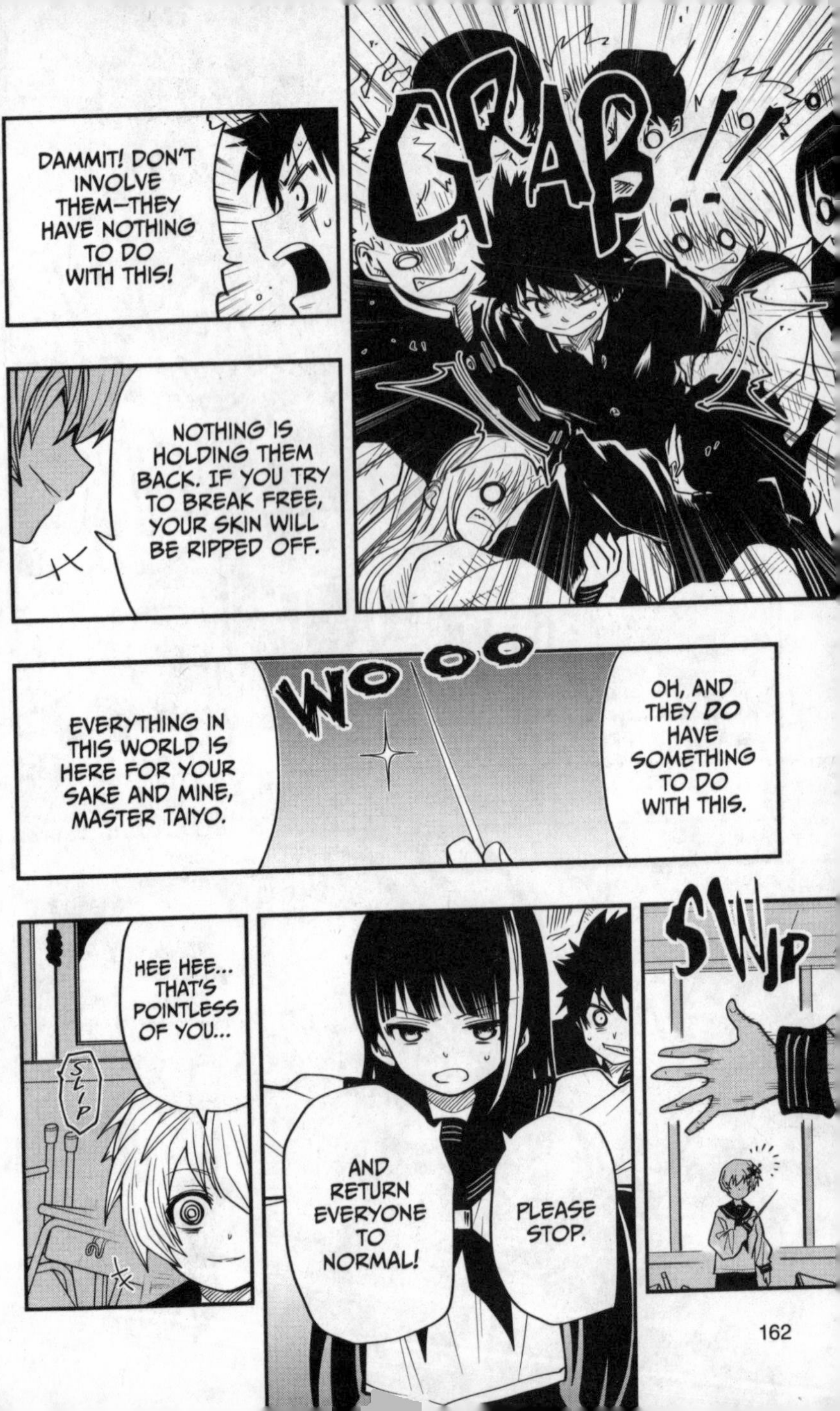
GRAB!!
DAMMIT! DON'T INVOLVE THEM—THEY HAVE NOTHING TO DO WITH THIS!
NOTHING IS HOLDING THEM BACK. IF YOU TRY TO BREAK FREE, YOUR SKIN WILL BE RIPPED OFF.
OH, AND THEY *DO* HAVE SOMETHING TO DO WITH THIS.
WOOO
EVERYTHING IN THIS WORLD IS HERE FOR YOUR SAKE AND MINE, MASTER TAIYO.
SWIP
PLEASE STOP.
AND RETURN EVERYONE TO NORMAL!
HEE HEE... THAT'S POINTLESS OF YOU...
SLIP

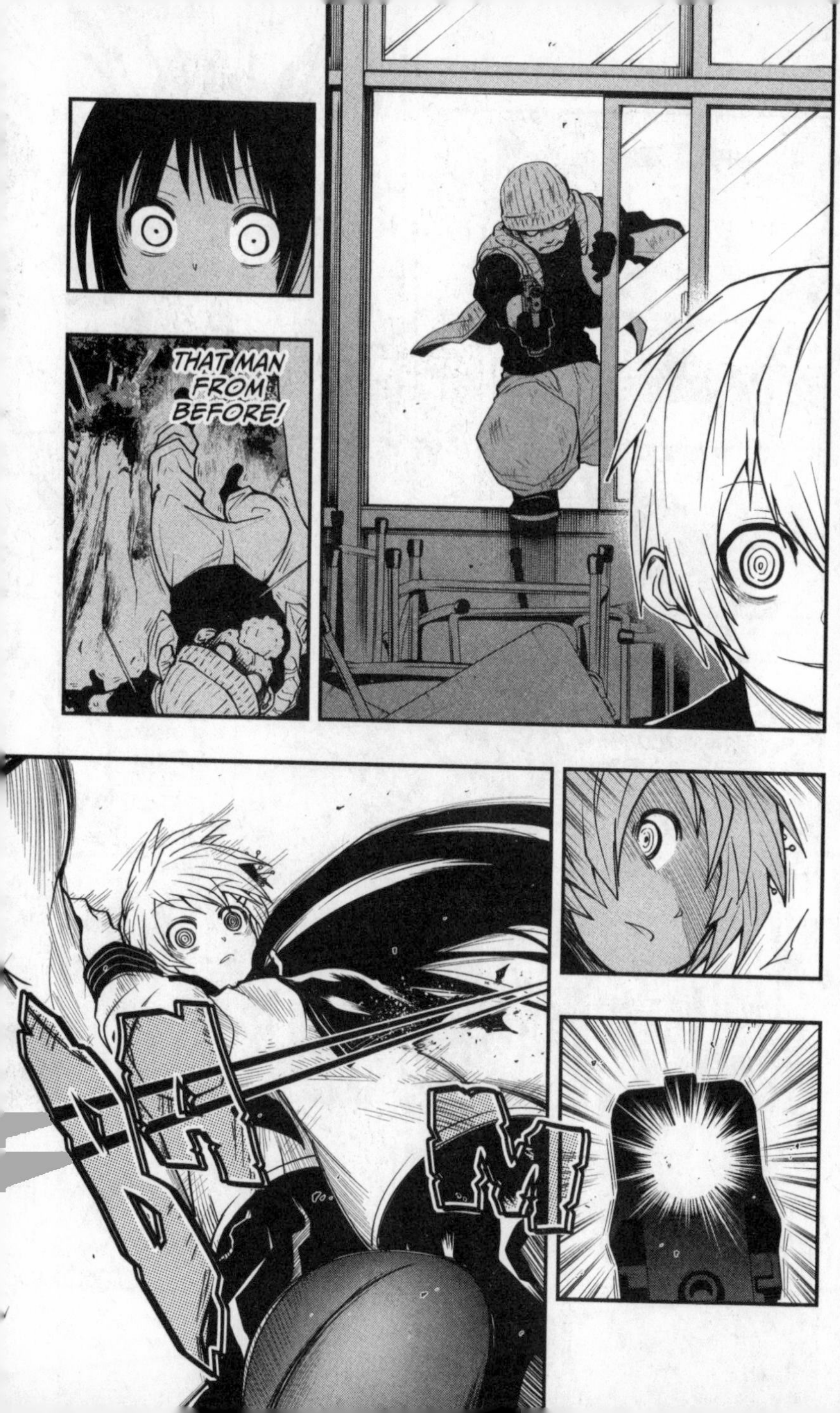
THAT MAN FROM BEFORE!
BAM

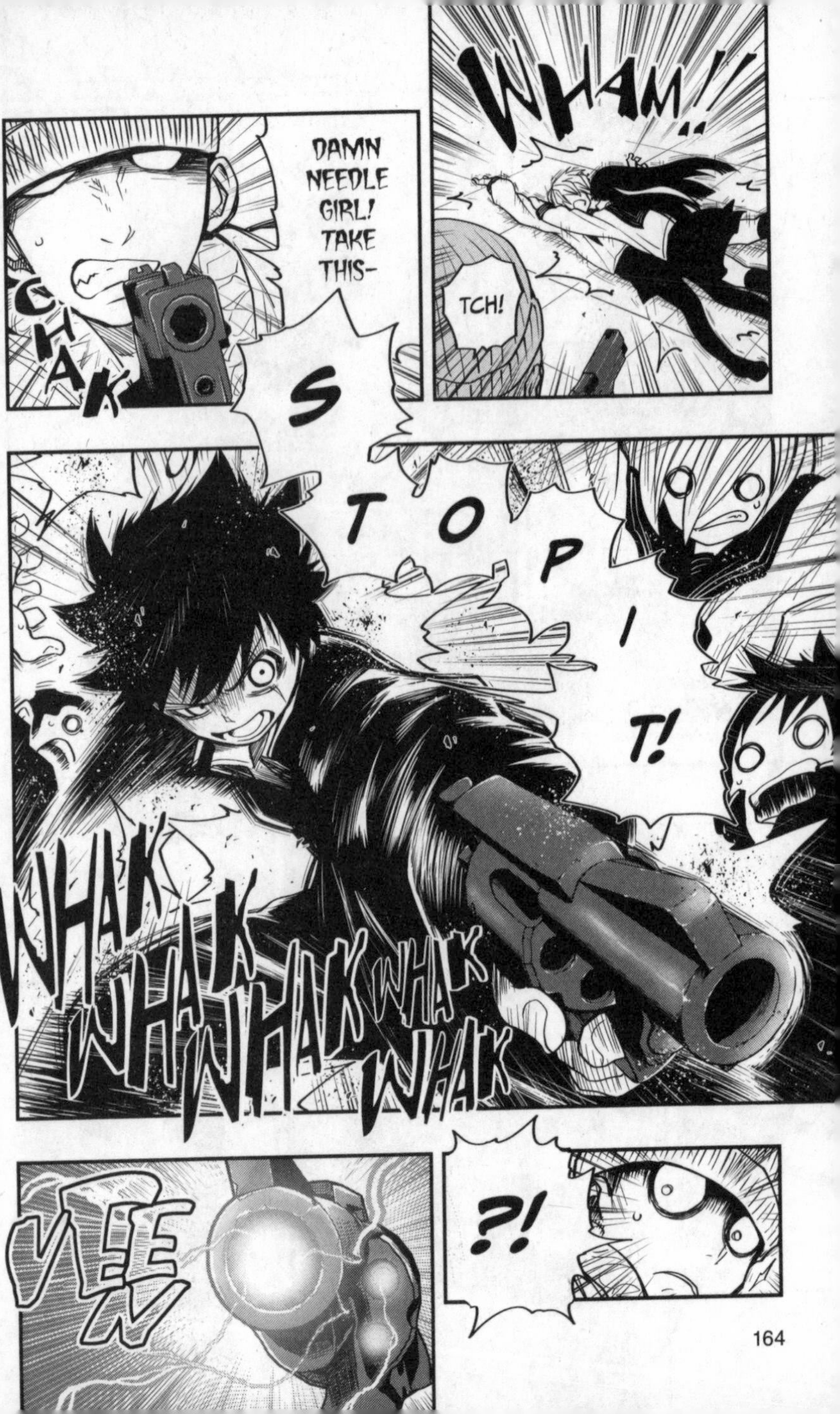
WHAM!!
TCH!
CHAK
DAMN NEEDLE GIRL! TAKE THIS-
STOP IT!
WHAK WHAK WHAK WHAK WHAK
?!
VEEN

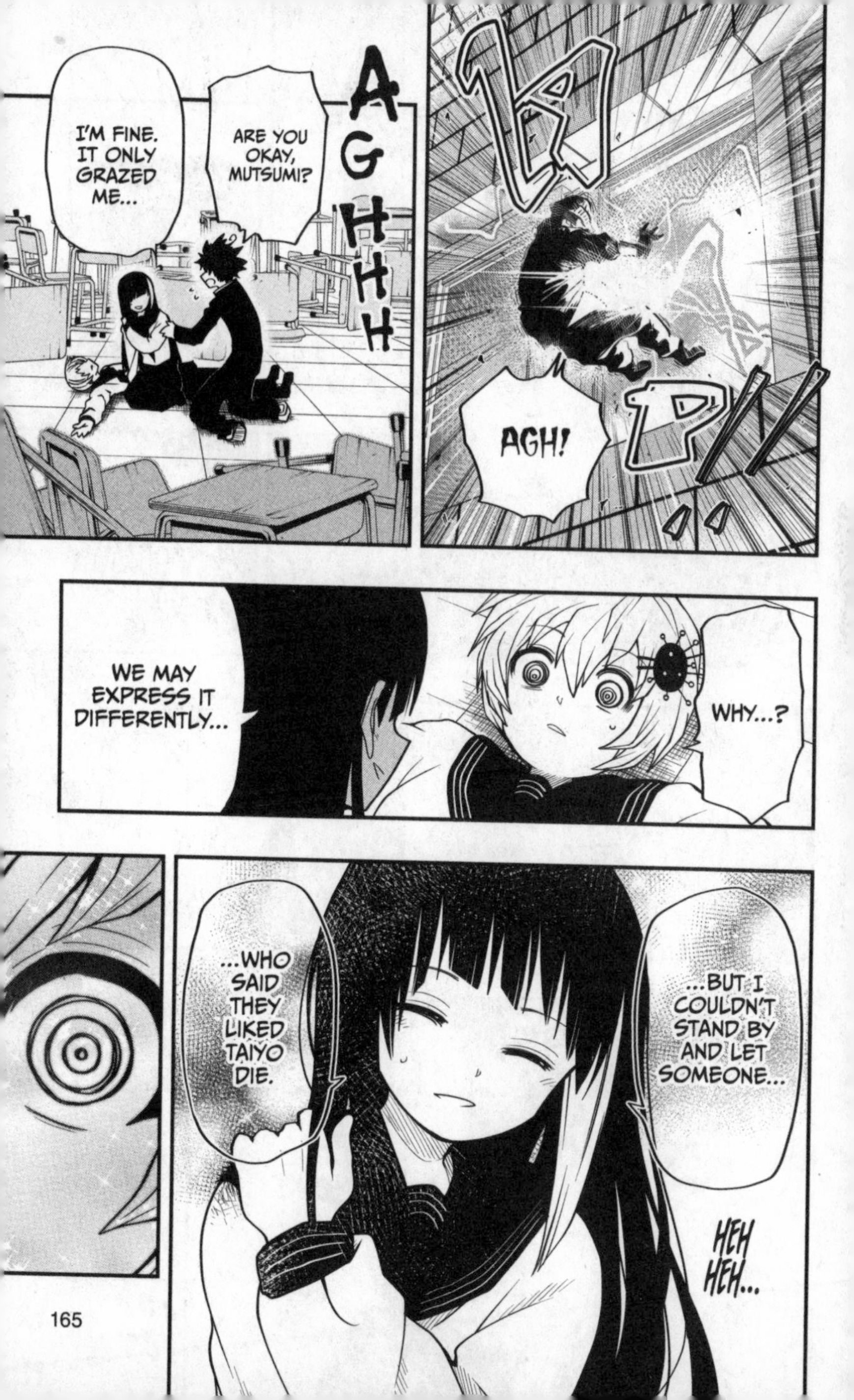
AGH!
AGHHHH
ARE YOU OKAY, MUTSUMI?
I'M FINE. IT ONLY GRAZED ME...
WHY...?
WE MAY EXPRESS IT DIFFERENTLY...
...BUT I COULDN'T STAND BY AND LET SOMEONE...
...WHO SAID THEY LIKED TAIYO DIE.
HEH HEH...

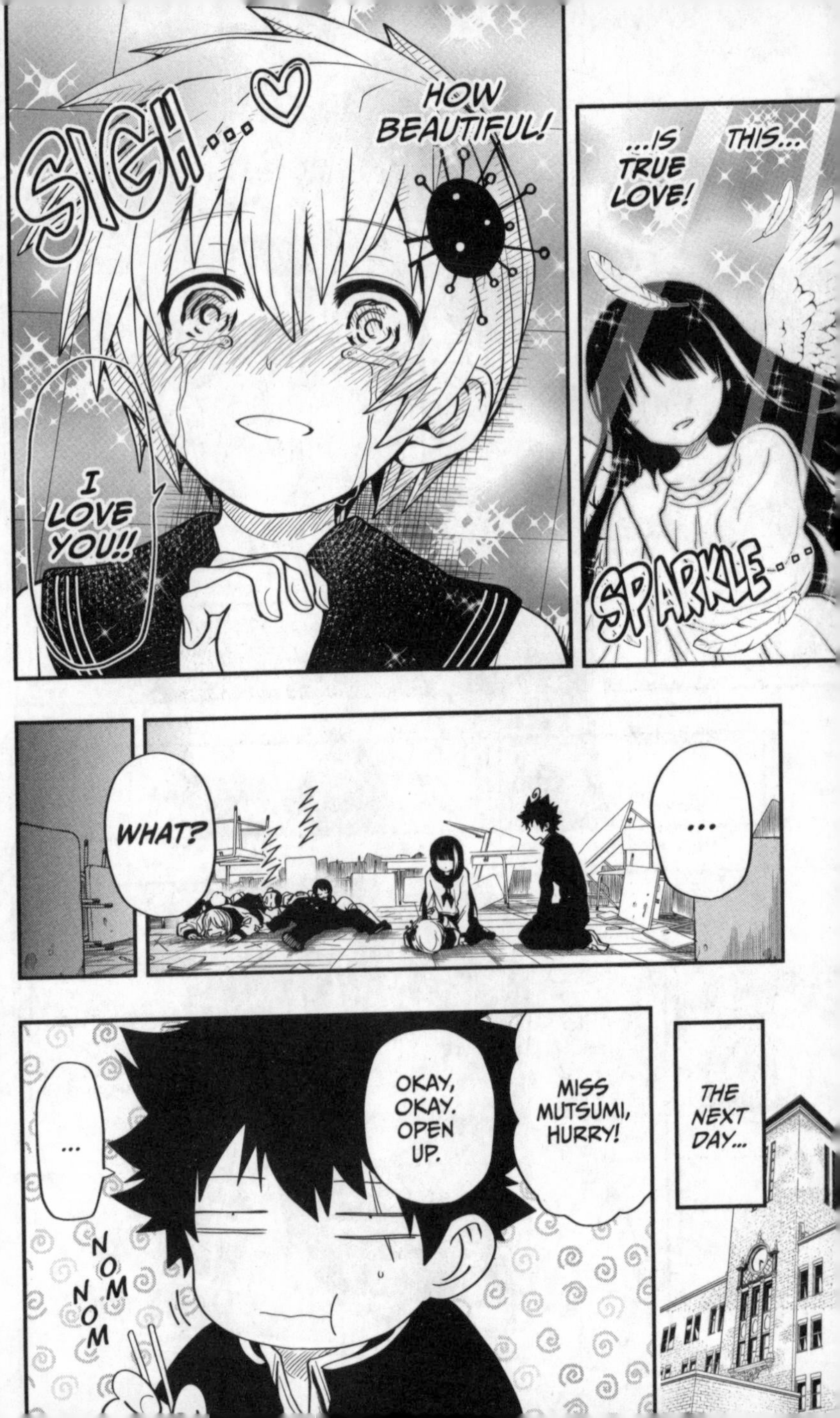
THIS...
...IS TRUE LOVE!
SPARKLE...
HOW BEAUTIFUL!
SIGH...
I LOVE YOU!!
...
ZZZ
WHAT?
THE NEXT DAY...
MISS MUTSUMI, HURRY!
OKAY, OKAY. OPEN UP.
...
NOM NOM

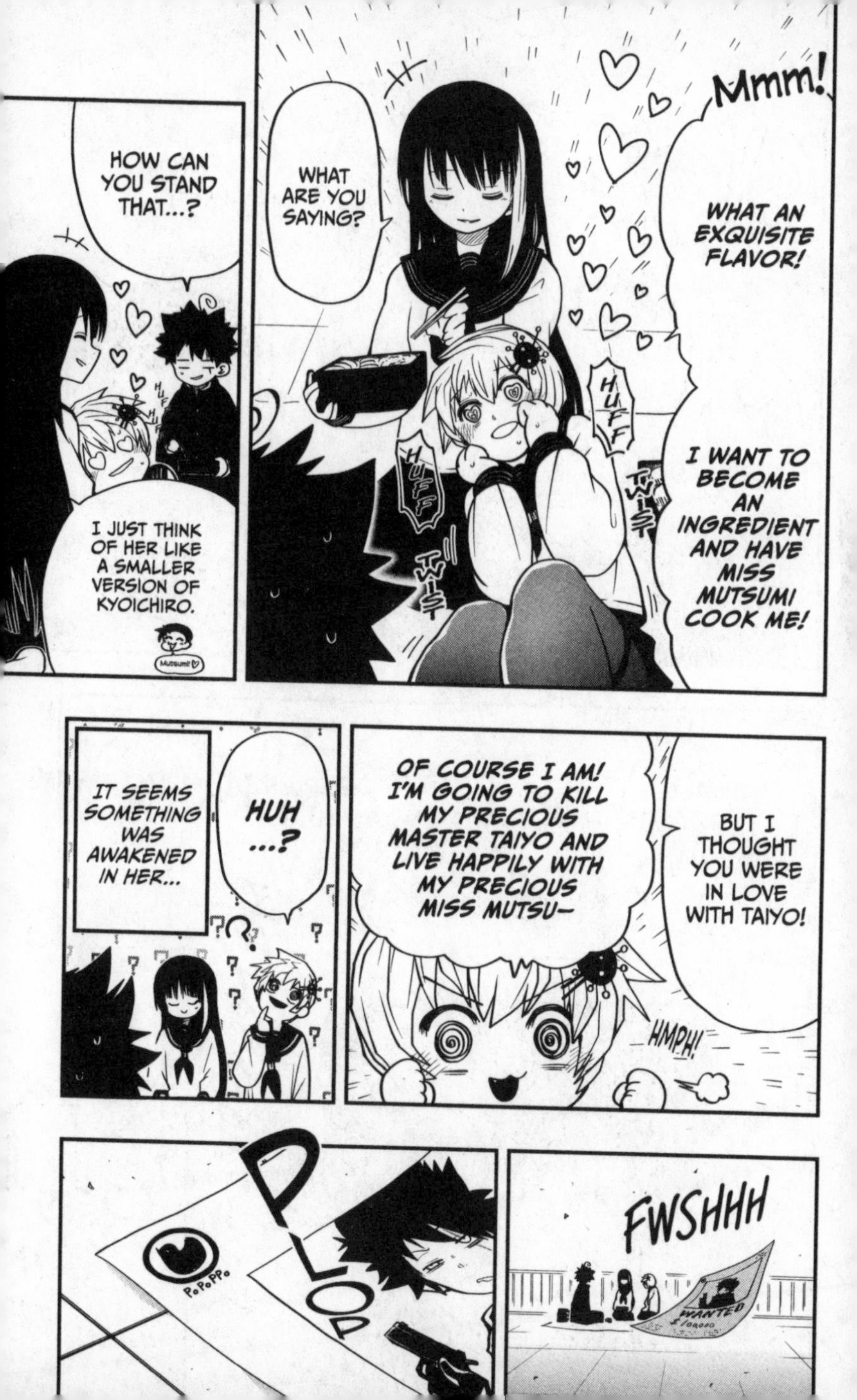
Mmm!
WHAT AN EXQUISITE FLAVOR!
I WANT TO BECOME AN INGREDIENT AND HAVE MISS MUTSUMI COOK ME!
HUFF
HUFF
TWIST
TWIST
WHAT ARE YOU SAYING?
HOW CAN YOU STAND THAT...?
HUFF HUFF
I JUST THINK OF HER LIKE A SMALLER VERSION OF KYOICHIRO.
Mutsumi! ♡
BUT I THOUGHT YOU WERE IN LOVE WITH TAIYO!
OF COURSE I AM! I'M GOING TO KILL MY PRECIOUS MASTER TAIYO AND LIVE HAPPILY WITH MY PRECIOUS MISS MUTSU—
HMPH!
HUH ...?
IT SEEMS SOMETHING WAS AWAKENED IN HER...
FWSHHH
WANTED
PLOP
POPOPPO

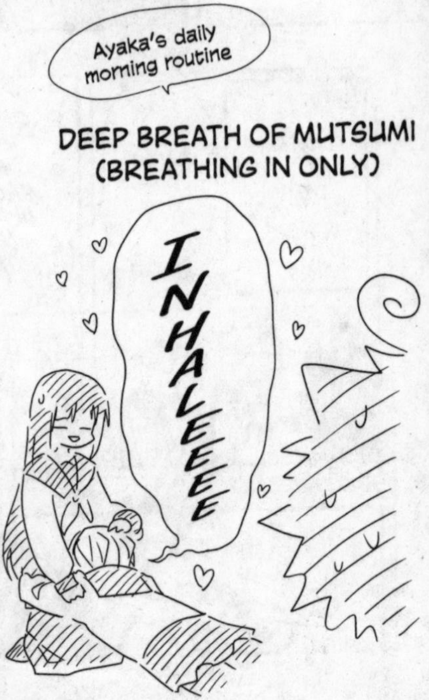
Ayaka's daily morning routine
DEEP BREATH OF MUTSUMI
(BREATHING IN ONLY)
INHALEEEEE

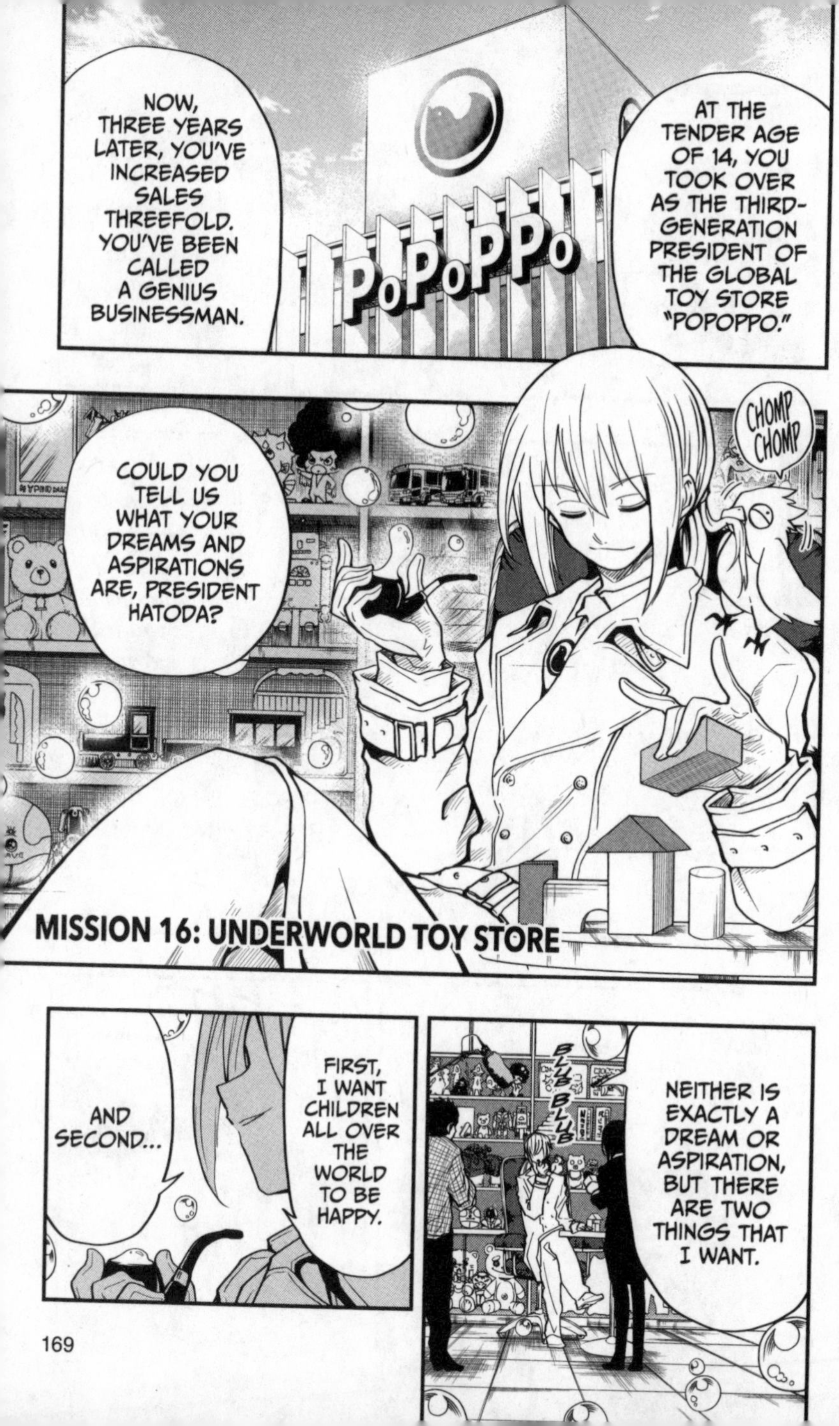
AT THE TENDER AGE OF 14, YOU TOOK OVER AS THE THIRD-GENERATION PRESIDENT OF THE GLOBAL TOY STORE "POPOPPO."
POPOPPO
NOW, THREE YEARS LATER, YOU'VE INCREASED SALES THREEFOLD. YOU'VE BEEN CALLED A GENIUS BUSINESSMAN.
CHOMP CHOMP
COULD YOU TELL US WHAT YOUR DREAMS AND ASPIRATIONS ARE, PRESIDENT HATODA?
MISSION 16: UNDERWORLD TOY STORE
BLUB BLUB
NEITHER IS EXACTLY A DREAM OR ASPIRATION, BUT THERE ARE TWO THINGS THAT I WANT.
FIRST, I WANT CHILDREN ALL OVER THE WORLD TO BE HAPPY.
AND SECOND...

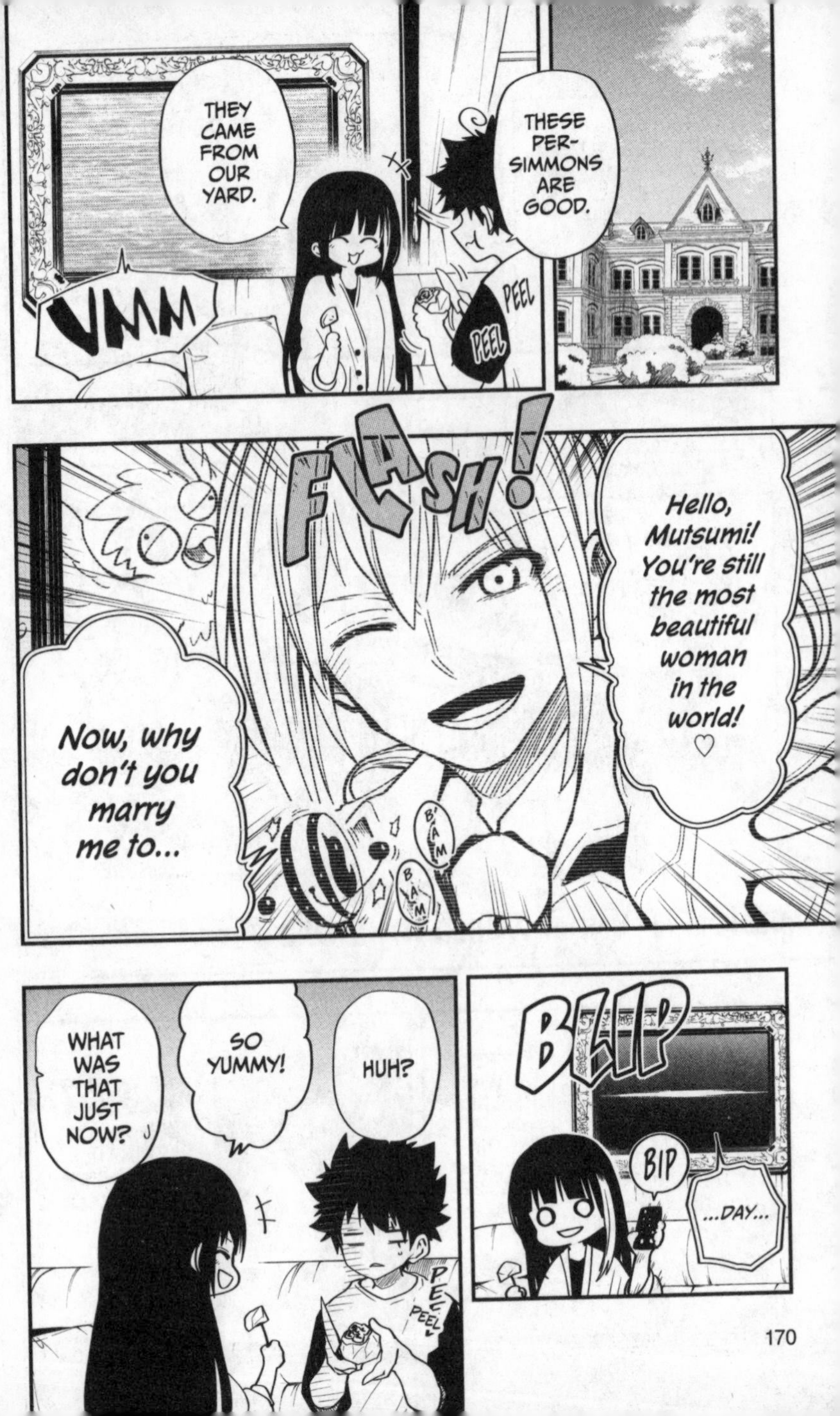
THESE PER-SIMMONS ARE GOOD.
PEEL
PEEL
THEY CAME FROM OUR YARD.
VMM
FLASH!
Hello, Mutsumi! You're still the most beautiful woman in the world! ♡
BAM
BAM
Now, why don't you marry me to...
BLIP
BIP
...DAY...
HUH?
SO YUMMY!
WHAT WAS THAT JUST NOW?
PEEL
PEEL

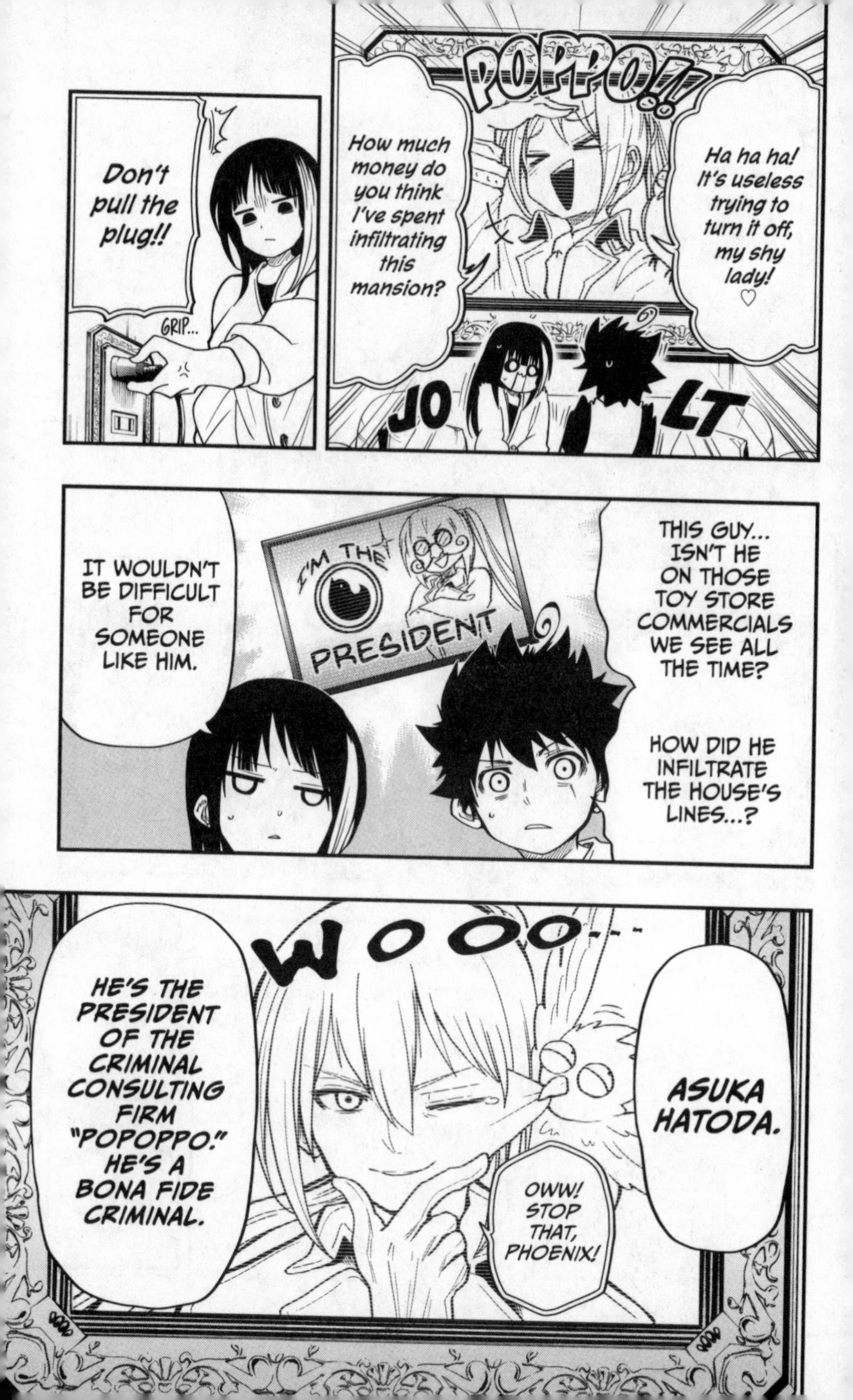
POPPO!!
Ha ha ha! It's useless trying to turn it off, my shy lady! ♡
How much money do you think I've spent infiltrating this mansion?
JOLT
Don't pull the plug!!
GRIP...
THIS GUY... ISN'T HE ON THOSE TOY STORE COMMERCIALS WE SEE ALL THE TIME?
HOW DID HE INFILTRATE THE HOUSE'S LINES...?
I'M THE PRESIDENT
IT WOULDN'T BE DIFFICULT FOR SOMEONE LIKE HIM.
WOOO...
ASUKA HATODA.
OWW! STOP THAT, PHOENIX!
HE'S THE PRESIDENT OF THE CRIMINAL CONSULTING FIRM "POPOPPO." HE'S A BONA FIDE CRIMINAL.

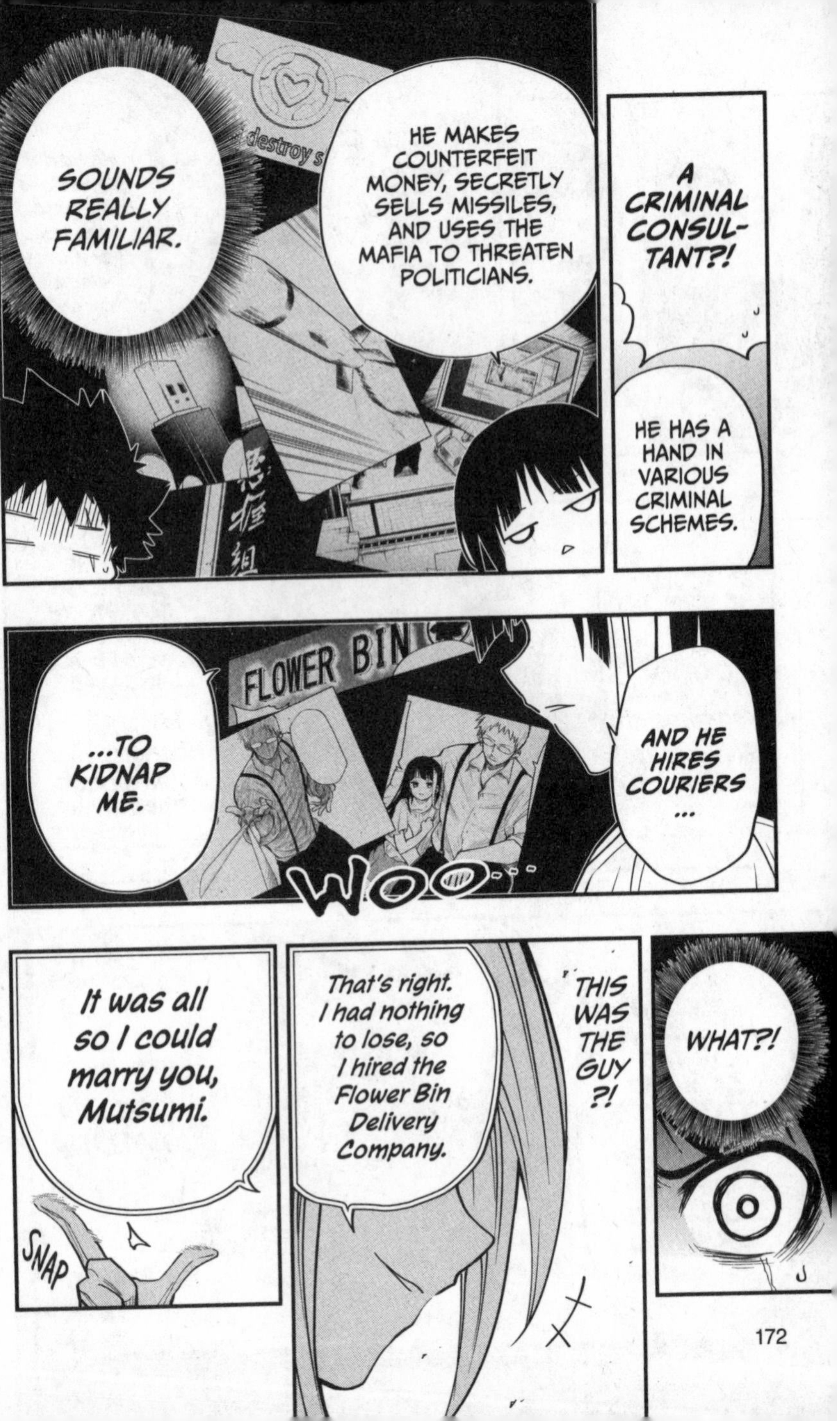
A CRIMINAL CONSULTANT?!
HE HAS A HAND IN VARIOUS CRIMINAL SCHEMES.
HE MAKES COUNTERFEIT MONEY, SECRETLY SELLS MISSILES, AND USES THE MAFIA TO THREATEN POLITICIANS.
SOUNDS REALLY FAMILIAR.
AND HE HIRES COURIERS...
FLOWER BIN
...TO KIDNAP ME.
WOO...
WHAT?!
THIS WAS THE GUY?!
That's right. I had nothing to lose, so I hired the Flower Bin Delivery Company.
It was all so I could marry you, Mutsumi.
SNAP

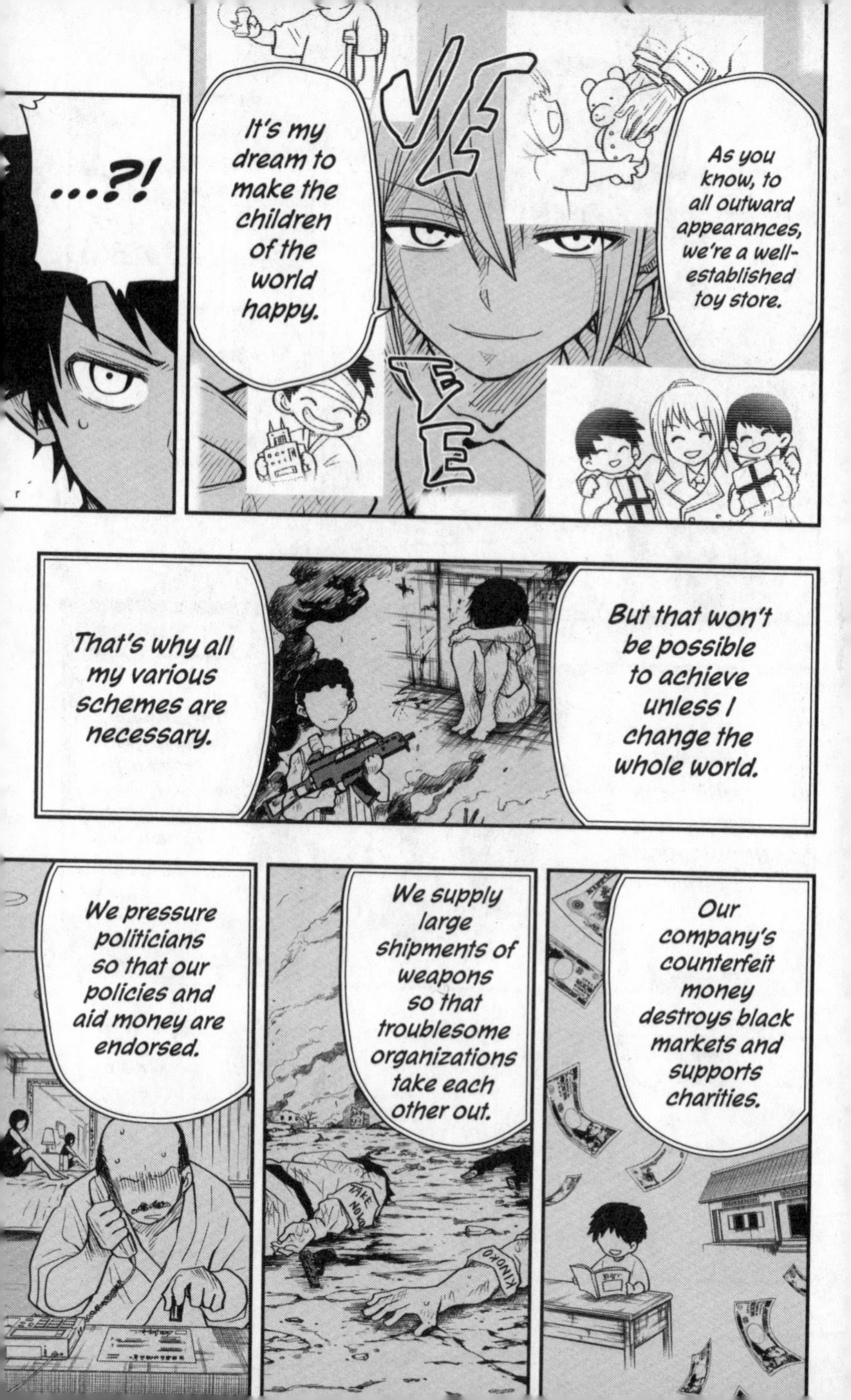
As you know, to all outward appearances, we're a well-established toy store.
It's my dream to make the children of the world happy.
...?!
But that won't be possible to achieve unless I change the whole world.
That's why all my various schemes are necessary.
Our company's counterfeit money destroys black markets and supports charities.
We supply large shipments of weapons so that troublesome organizations take each other out.
TAKE NOKO
KINOKO
We pressure politicians so that our policies and aid money are endorsed.

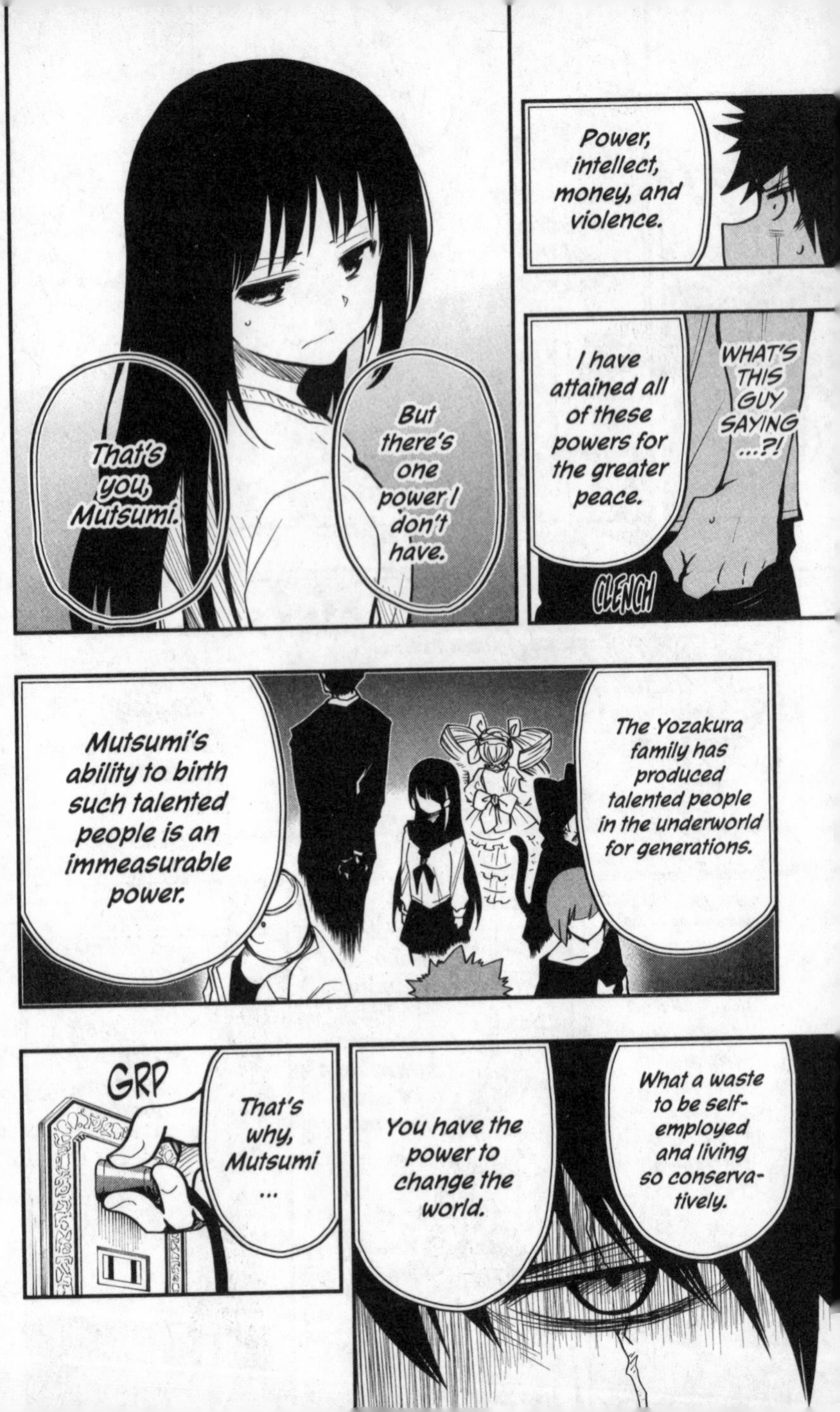
Power, intellect, money, and violence.
I have attained all of these powers for the greater peace.
WHAT'S THIS GUY SAYING ...?!
CLENCH
But there's one power I don't have.
That's you, Mutsumi.
The Yozakura family has produced talented people in the underworld for generations.
Mutsumi's ability to birth such talented people is an immeasurable power.
What a waste to be self-employed and living so conservatively.
You have the power to change the world.
GRP
That's why, Mutsumi ...

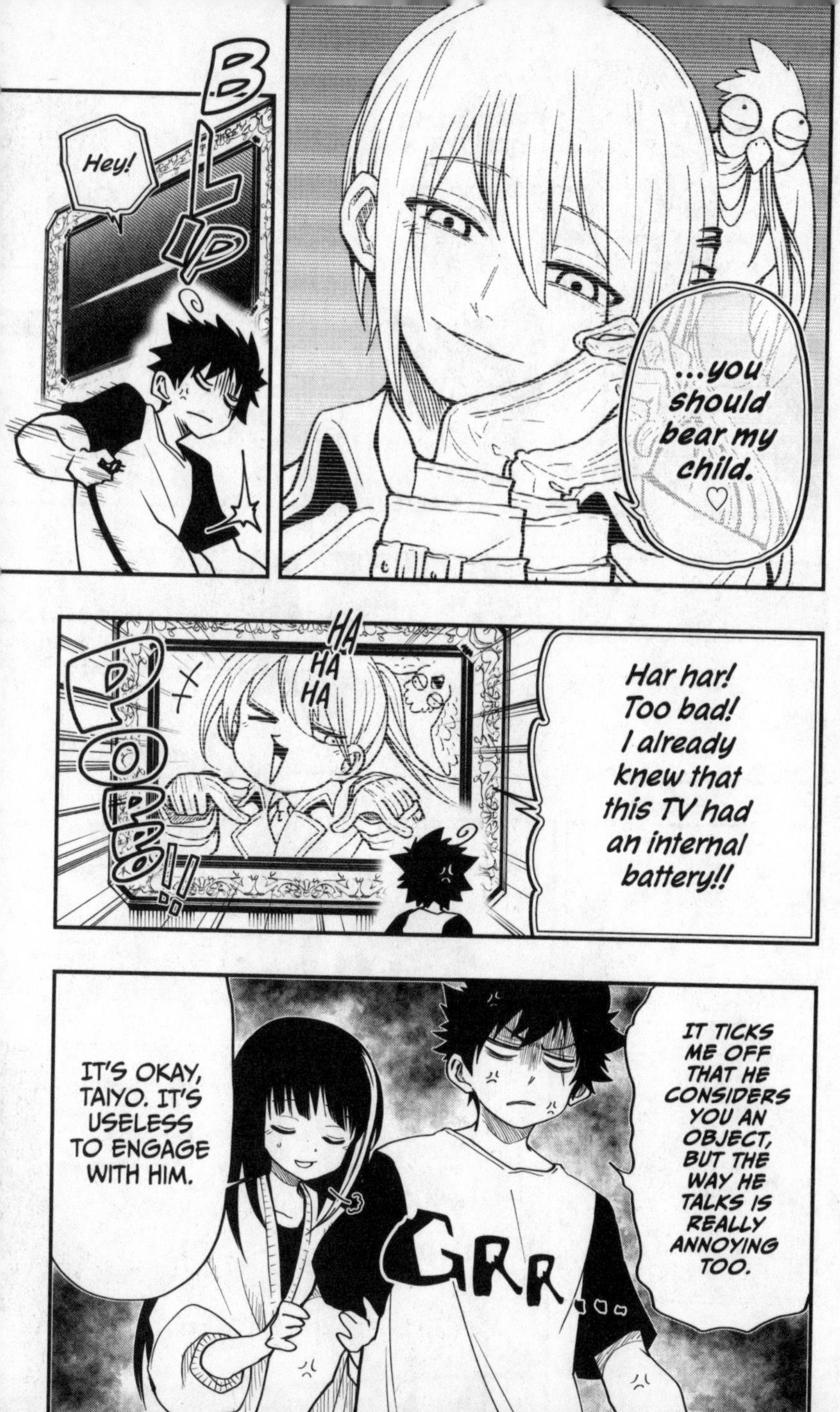
...you should bear my child. ♡
Hey!
B.D.
BLIP!
Har har! Too bad! I already knew that this TV had an internal battery!!
HA HA HA HA
IT TICKS ME OFF THAT HE CONSIDERS YOU AN OBJECT, BUT THE WAY HE TALKS IS REALLY ANNOYING TOO.
IT'S OKAY, TAIYO. IT'S USELESS TO ENGAGE WITH HIM.
GRR...

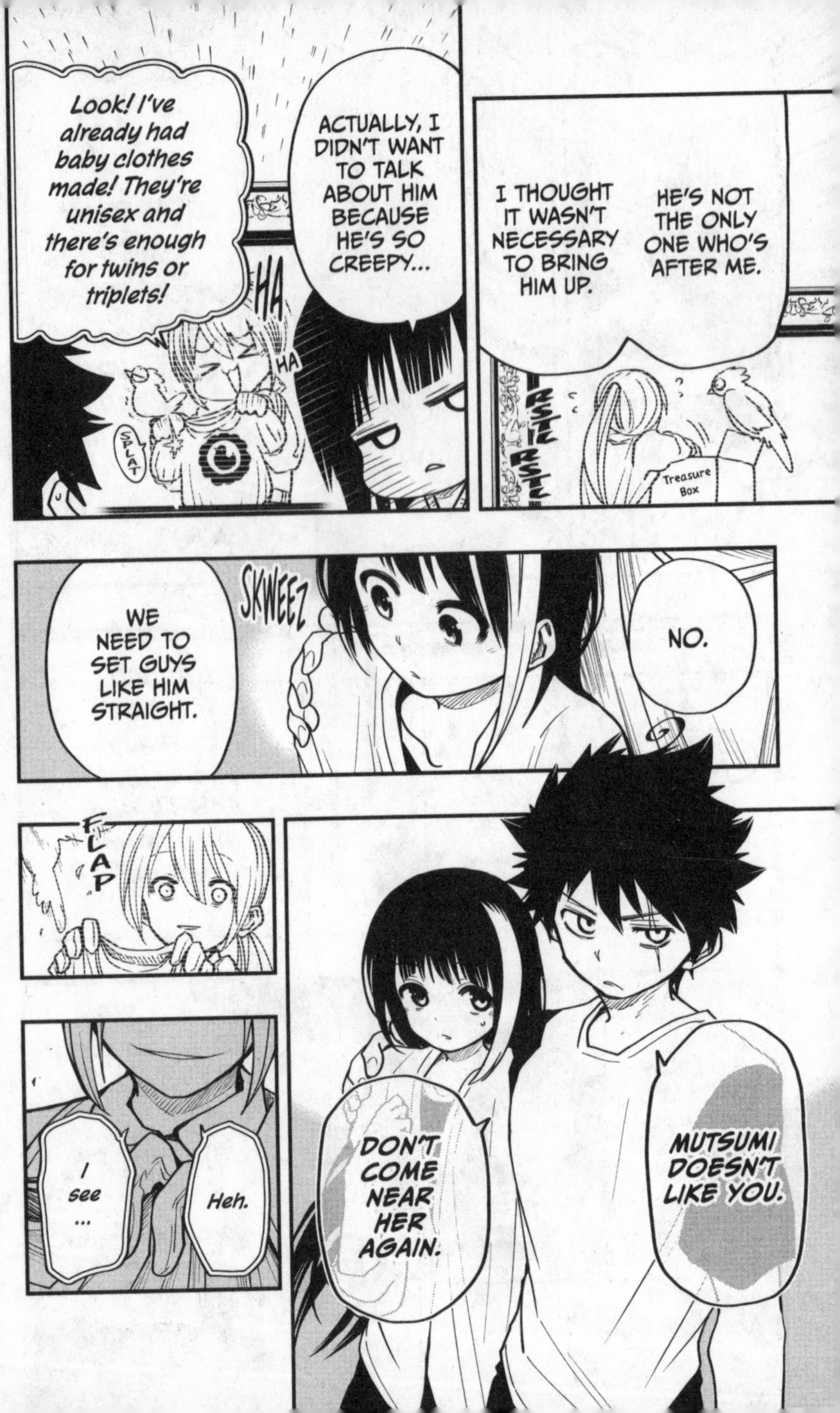
HE'S NOT THE ONLY ONE WHO'S AFTER ME.
I THOUGHT IT WASN'T NECESSARY TO BRING HIM UP.
RSTL RSTL
Treasure Box
ACTUALLY, I DIDN'T WANT TO TALK ABOUT HIM BECAUSE HE'S SO CREEPY...
Look! I've already had baby clothes made! They're unisex and there's enough for twins or triplets!
HA HA
SPLAT
NO.
SKWEEZ
WE NEED TO SET GUYS LIKE HIM STRAIGHT.
MUTSUMI DOESN'T LIKE YOU.
DON'T COME NEAR HER AGAIN.
FLAP
Heh.
I see ...

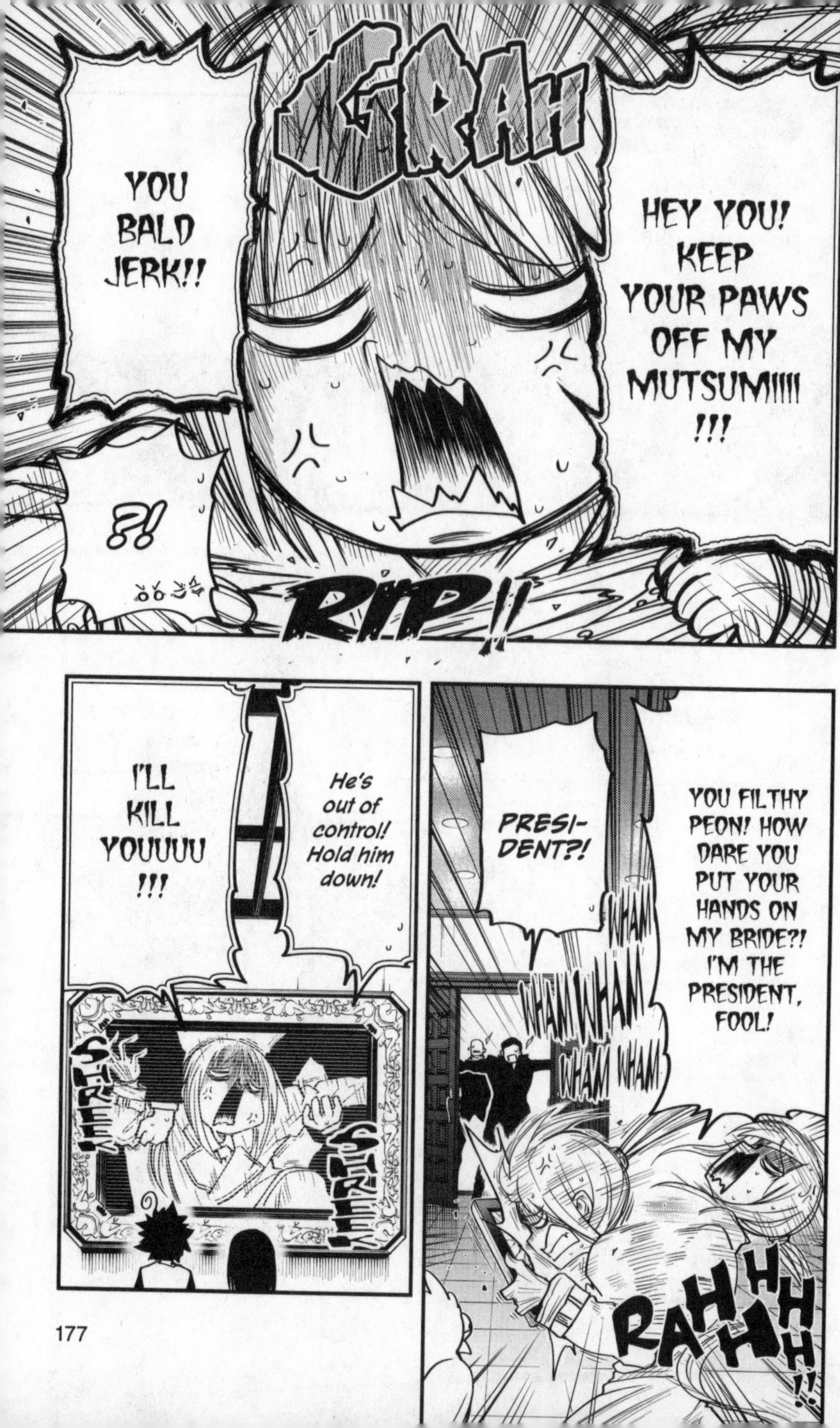
HEY YOU! KEEP YOUR PAWS OFF MY MUTSUMI!!!!! !!!
GRAH
YOU BALD JERK!!
?!
RIP!!
YOU FILTHY PEON! HOW DARE YOU PUT YOUR HANDS ON MY BRIDE?! I'M THE PRESIDENT, FOOL!
PRESI-DENT?!
WHAM
WHAM WHAM
WHAM WHAM
RAHHHHH!!
He's out of control! Hold him down!
I'LL KILL YOUUUU !!!

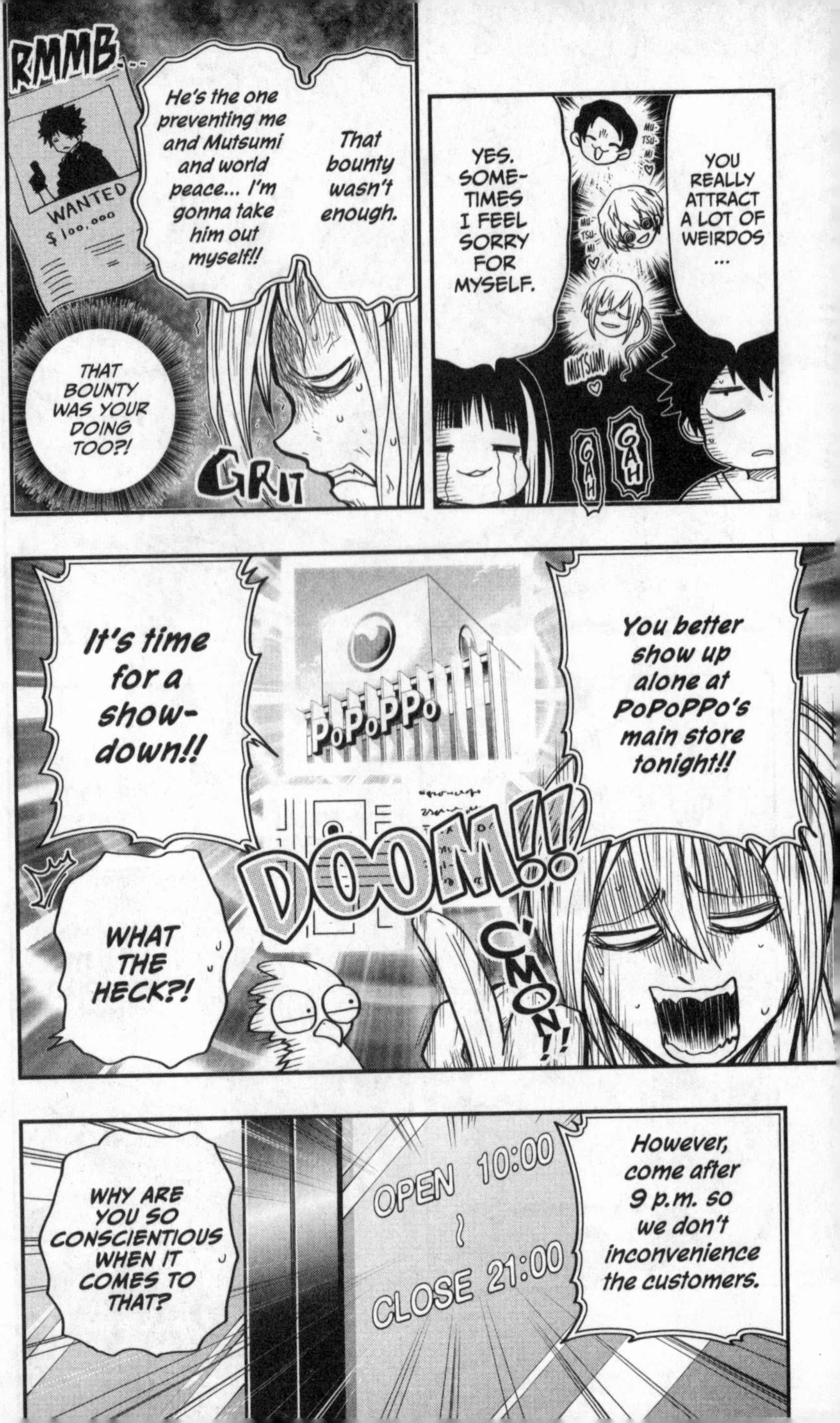
YOU REALLY ATTRACT A LOT OF WEIRDOS ...
MU-TSU-MI
MU-TSU-MI
YES. SOMETIMES I FEEL SORRY FOR MYSELF.
MUTSUMI
GAH GAH
That bounty wasn't enough.
He's the one preventing me and Mutsumi and world peace... I'm gonna take him out myself!!
RMMB...
WANTED $100,000
THAT BOUNTY WAS YOUR DOING TOO?!
GRIT
You better show up alone at PoPoPPo's main store tonight!!
It's time for a showdown!!
PoPoPPo
DOOM!!
C'MON!!
WHAT THE HECK?!
However, come after 9 p.m. so we don't inconvenience the customers.
OPEN 10:00 ~ CLOSE 21:00
WHY ARE YOU SO CONSCIENTIOUS WHEN IT COMES TO THAT?

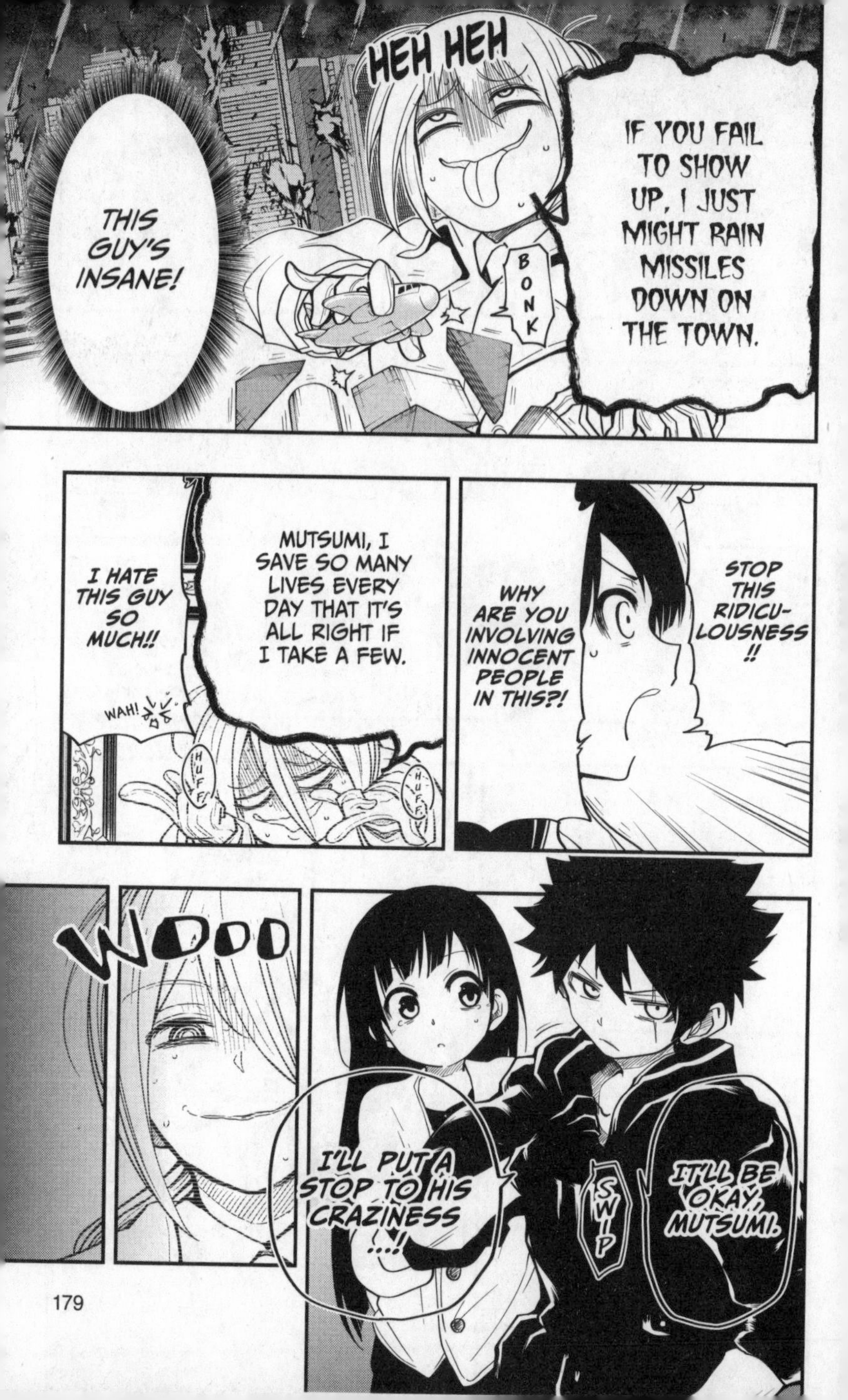
HEH HEH
IF YOU FAIL TO SHOW UP, I JUST MIGHT RAIN MISSILES DOWN ON THE TOWN.
BONK
THIS GUY'S INSANE!
STOP THIS RIDICU-LOUSNESS!!
WHY ARE YOU INVOLVING INNOCENT PEOPLE IN THIS?!
MUTSUMI, I SAVE SO MANY LIVES EVERY DAY THAT IT'S ALL RIGHT IF I TAKE A FEW.
I HATE THIS GUY SO MUCH!!
WAH!
HUFF
HUFF
IT'LL BE OKAY, MUTSUMI.
SWIP
I'LL PUT A STOP TO HIS CRAZINESS ...!
WOOO

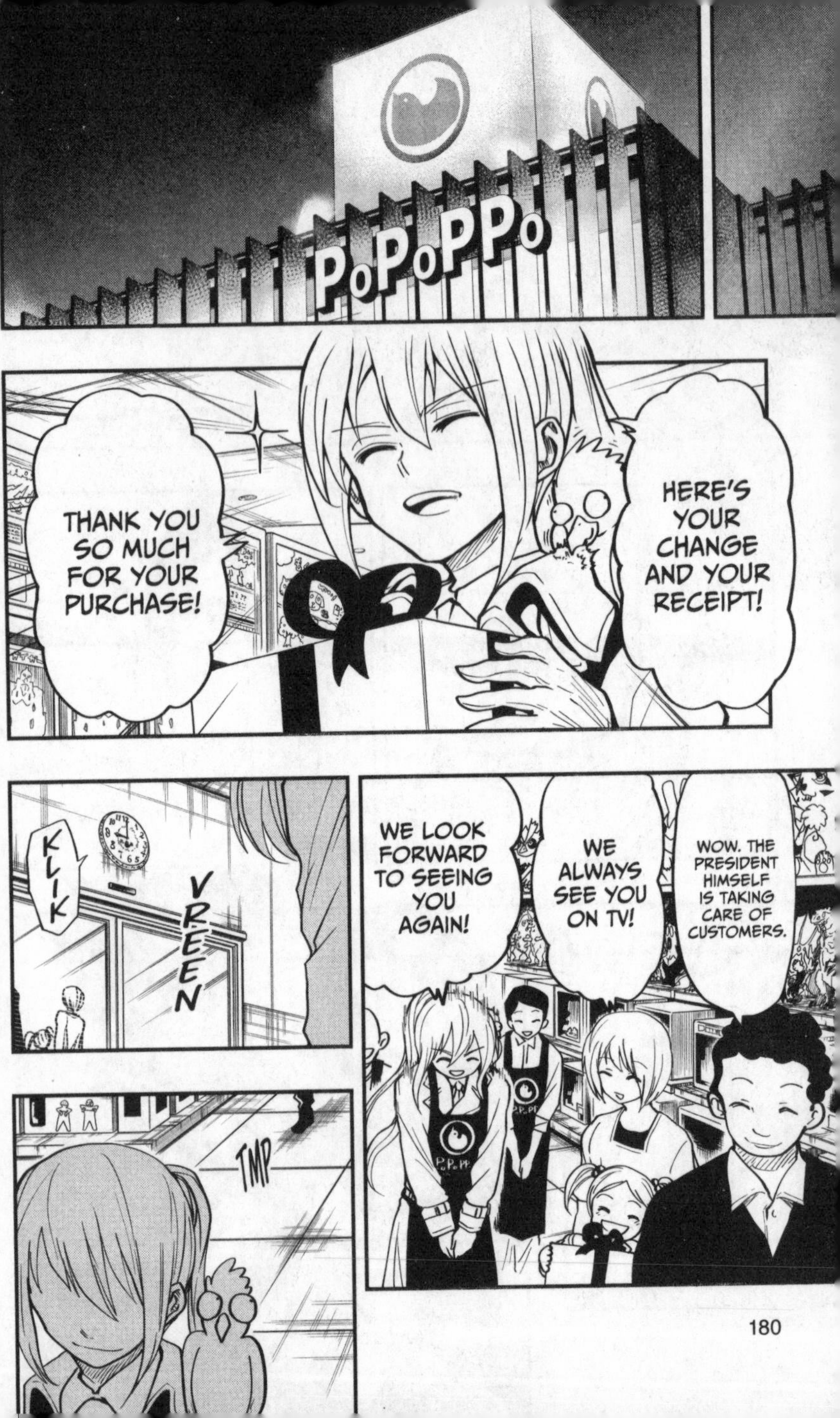
PoPoPPo
HERE'S YOUR CHANGE AND YOUR RECEIPT!
THANK YOU SO MUCH FOR YOUR PURCHASE!
WOW. THE PRESIDENT HIMSELF IS TAKING CARE OF CUSTOMERS.
WE ALWAYS SEE YOU ON TV!
WE LOOK FORWARD TO SEEING YOU AGAIN!
VREEEN
KLIK
TMP

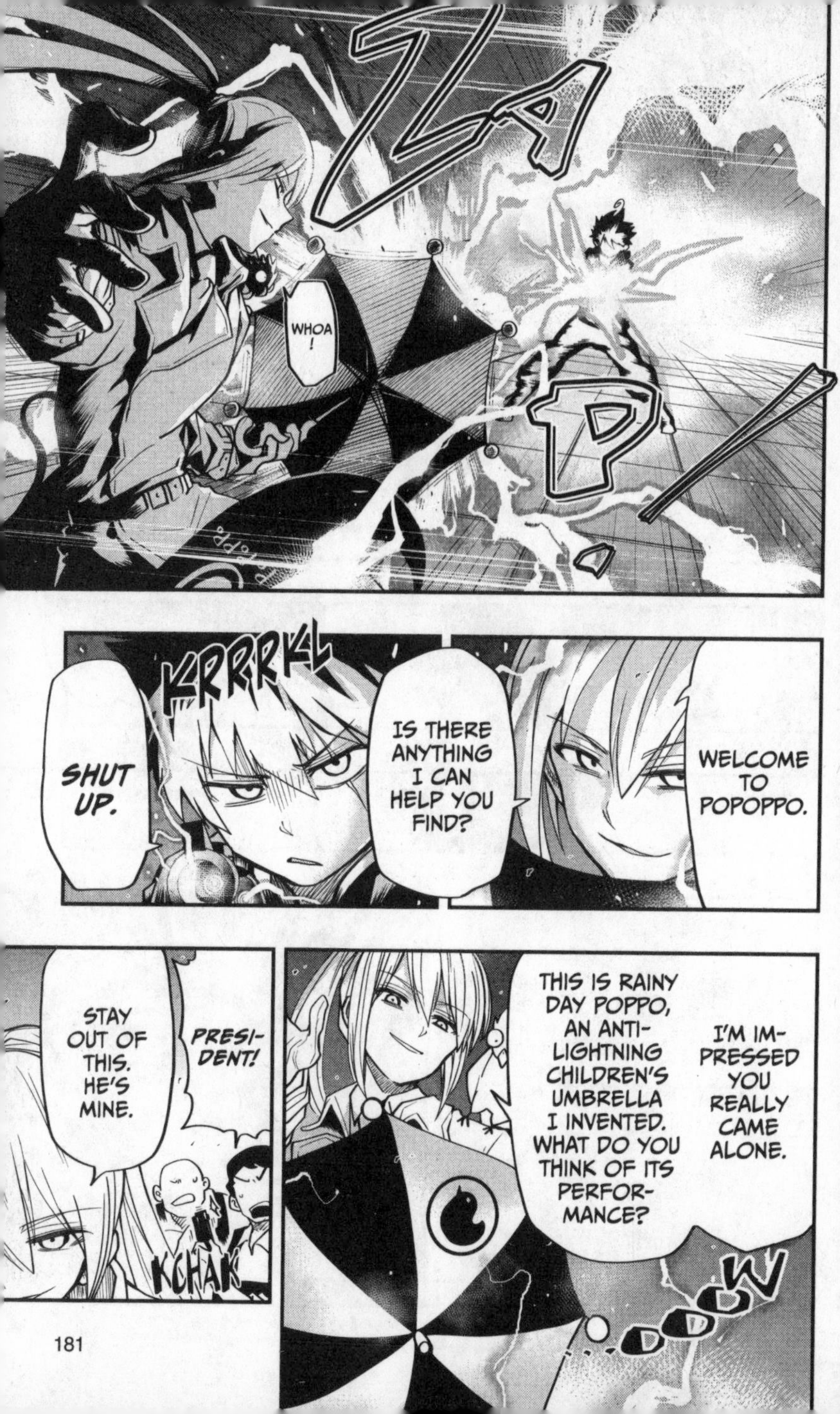
ZZAP!
WHOA!
WELCOME TO POPOPPO.
IS THERE ANYTHING I CAN HELP YOU FIND?
KRRRKL
SHUT UP.
I'M IMPRESSED YOU REALLY CAME ALONE.
THIS IS RAINY DAY POPPO, AN ANTI-LIGHTNING CHILDREN'S UMBRELLA I INVENTED. WHAT DO YOU THINK OF ITS PERFORMANCE?
PRESIDENT!
STAY OUT OF THIS. HE'S MINE.
KCHAK

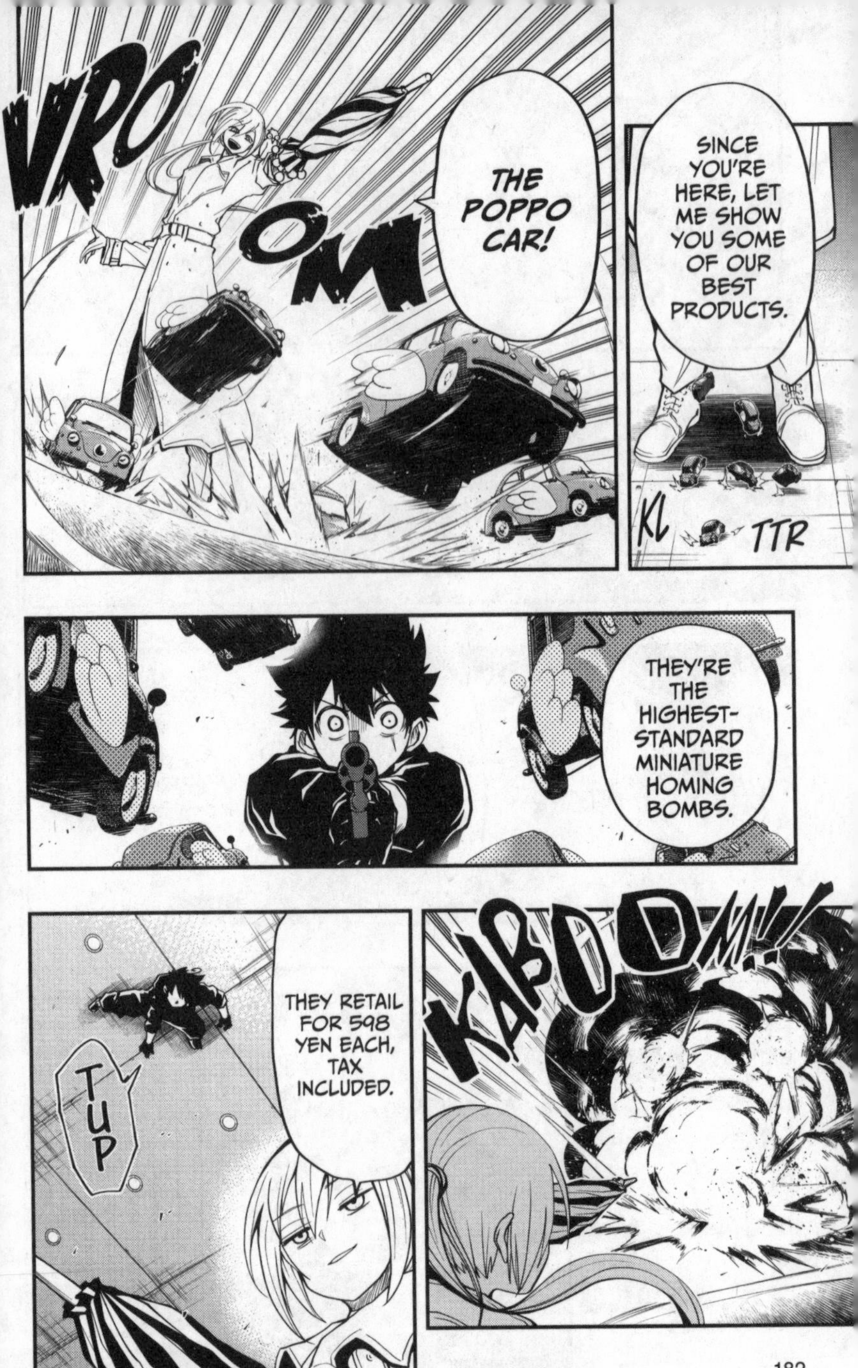
SINCE YOU'RE HERE, LET ME SHOW YOU SOME OF OUR BEST PRODUCTS.
KL
TTR
VROOM
THE POPPO CAR!
THEY'RE THE HIGHEST-STANDARD MINIATURE HOMING BOMBS.
KABOOM!!
THEY RETAIL FOR 598 YEN EACH, TAX INCLUDED.
TUP

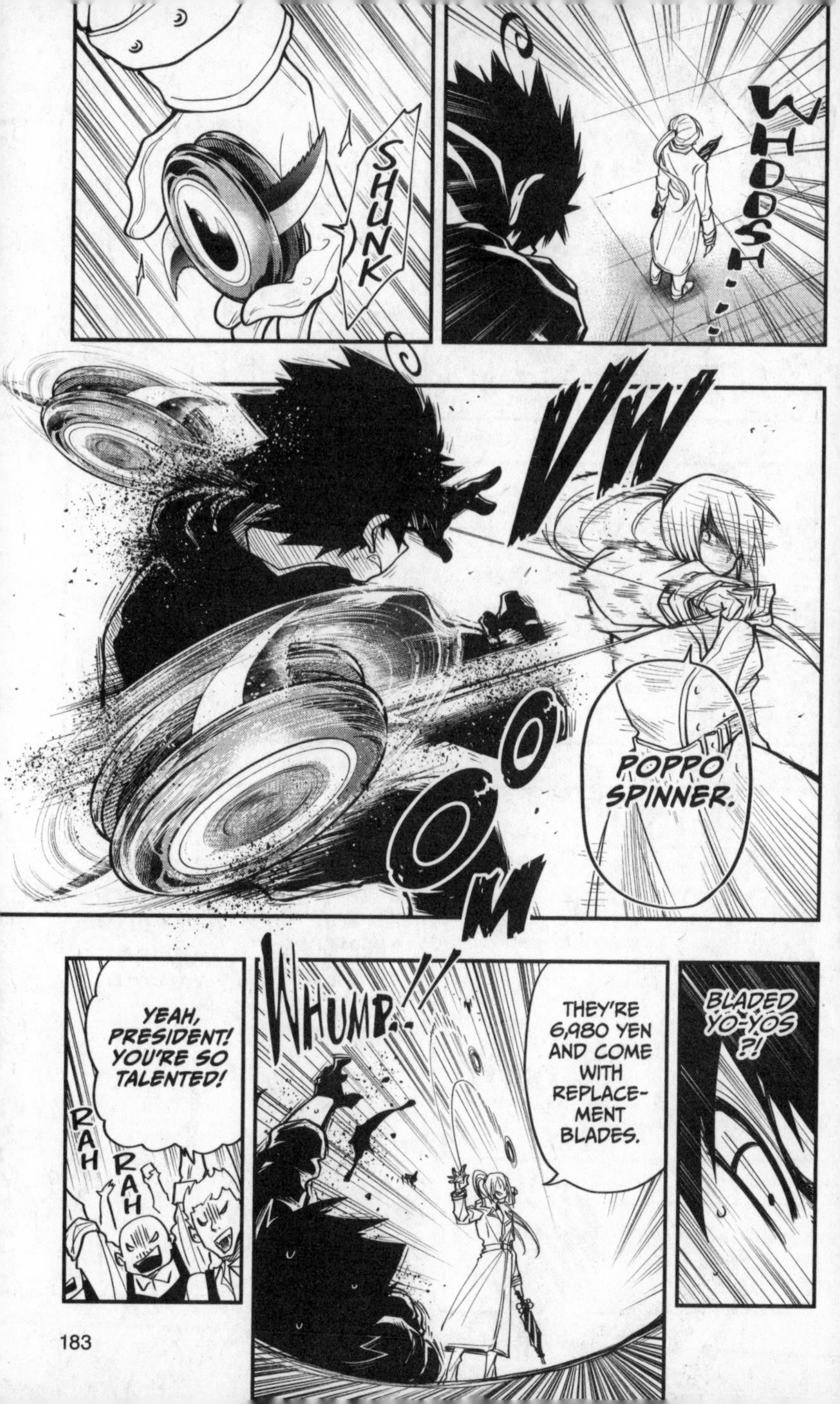
WHOOSH...
SHUNK
VWOOOM
POPPO SPINNER.
BLADED YO-YOS?!
WHUMP!!
THEY'RE 6,980 YEN AND COME WITH REPLACEMENT BLADES.
YEAH, PRESIDENT! YOU'RE SO TALENTED!
RAH RAH

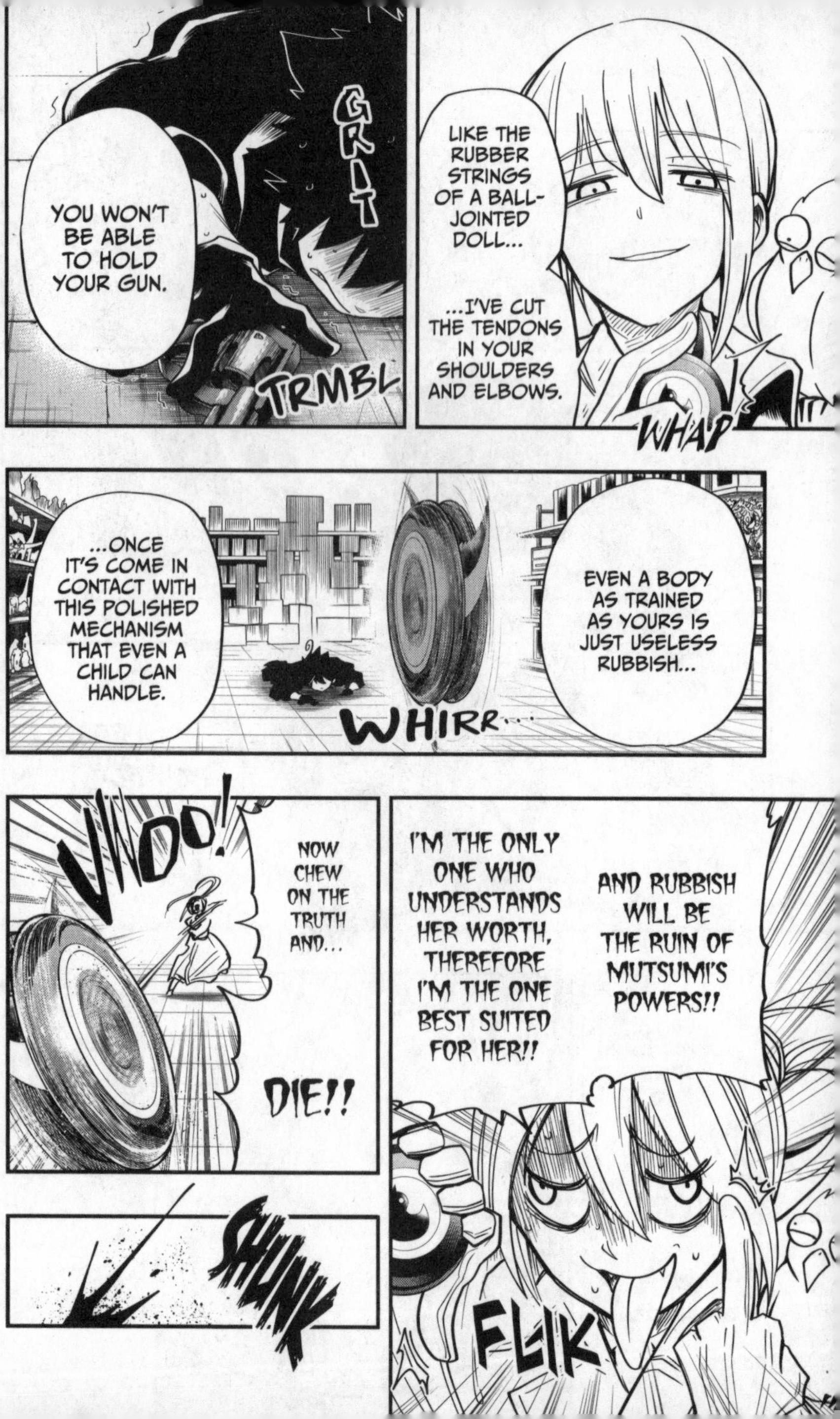
LIKE THE RUBBER STRINGS OF A BALL-JOINTED DOLL...
...I'VE CUT THE TENDONS IN YOUR SHOULDERS AND ELBOWS.
WHAP
GRIT
YOU WON'T BE ABLE TO HOLD YOUR GUN.
TRMBL
EVEN A BODY AS TRAINED AS YOURS IS JUST USELESS RUBBISH...
...ONCE IT'S COME IN CONTACT WITH THIS POLISHED MECHANISM THAT EVEN A CHILD CAN HANDLE.
WHIRR...
AND RUBBISH WILL BE THE RUIN OF MUTSUMI'S POWERS!!
I'M THE ONLY ONE WHO UNDERSTANDS HER WORTH, THEREFORE I'M THE ONE BEST SUITED FOR HER!!
FLIK
VIDO!
NOW CHEW ON THE TRUTH AND...
DIE!!
SHUNK

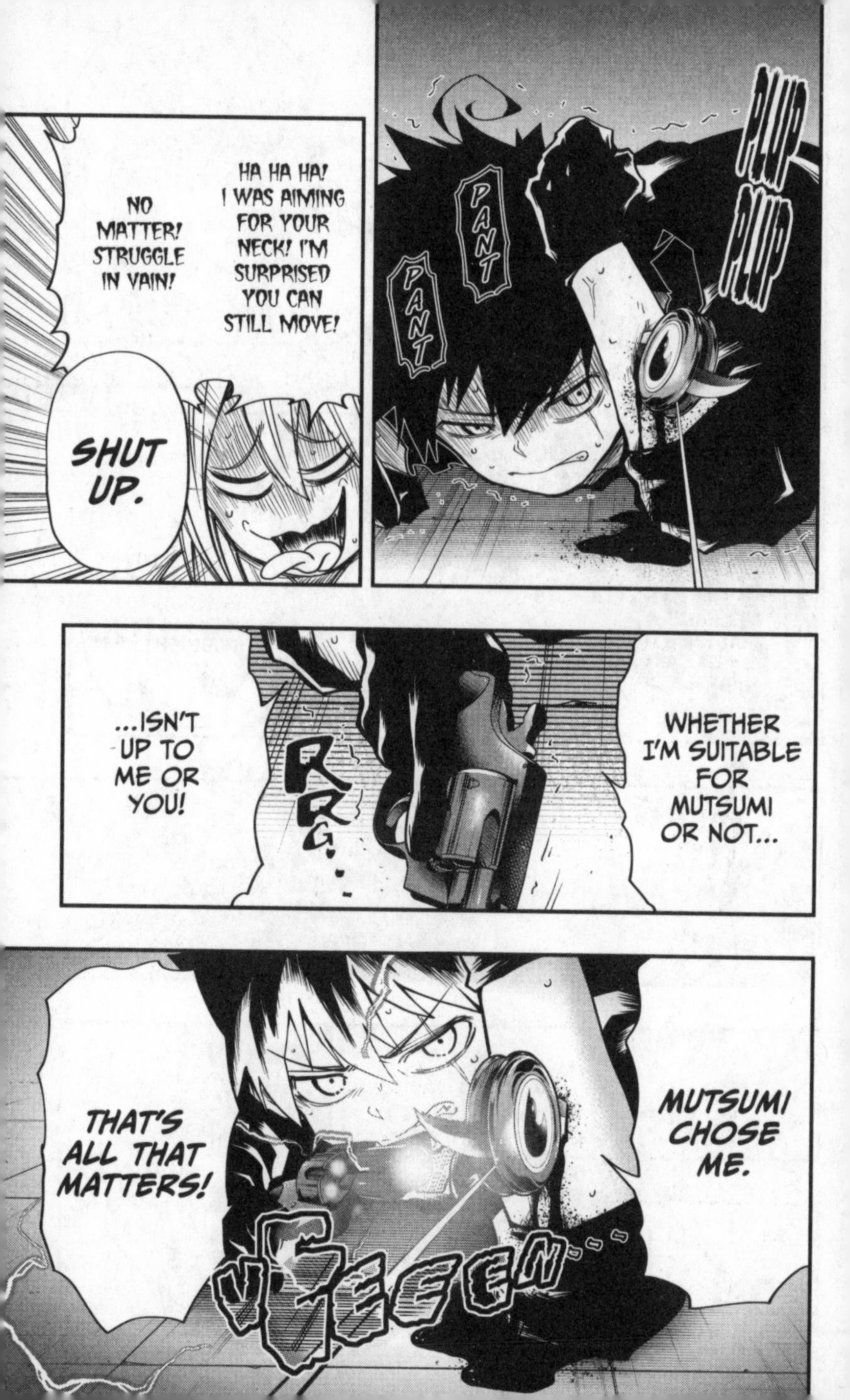
PLUP PLUP
PANT
PANT
HA HA HA! I WAS AIMING FOR YOUR NECK! I'M SURPRISED YOU CAN STILL MOVE!
NO MATTER! STRUGGLE IN VAIN!
SHUT UP.
WHETHER I'M SUITABLE FOR MUTSUMI OR NOT...
RRG...
...ISN'T UP TO ME OR YOU!
MUTSUMI CHOSE ME.
THAT'S ALL THAT MATTERS!

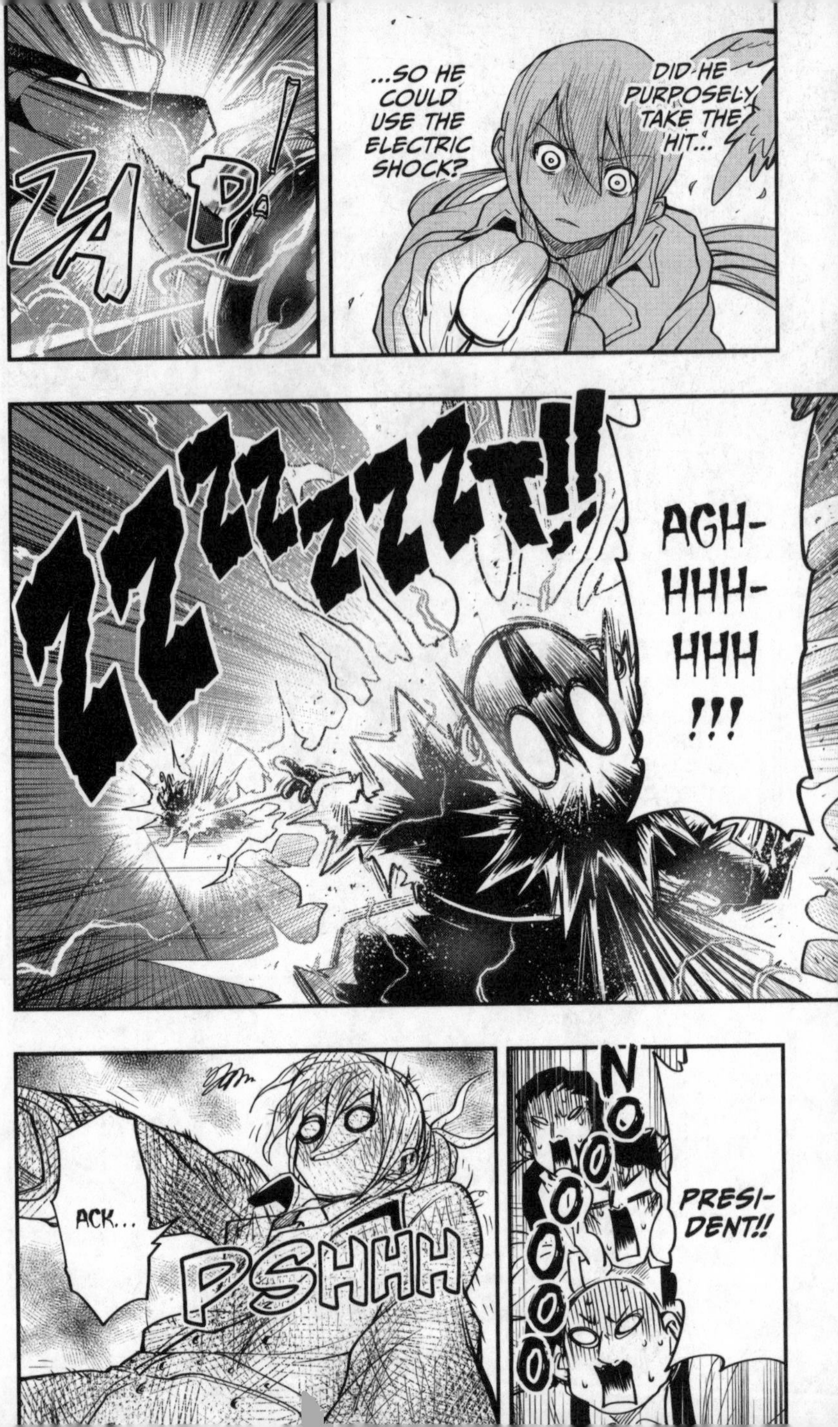
DID HE PURPOSELY TAKE THE HIT...
...SO HE COULD USE THE ELECTRIC SHOCK?
ZAP!
ZZZZ-ZZZT!!
AGH-HHH-HHH!!!
NOOOOOOOOOO
PRESI-DENT!!
ACK...
PSHHH

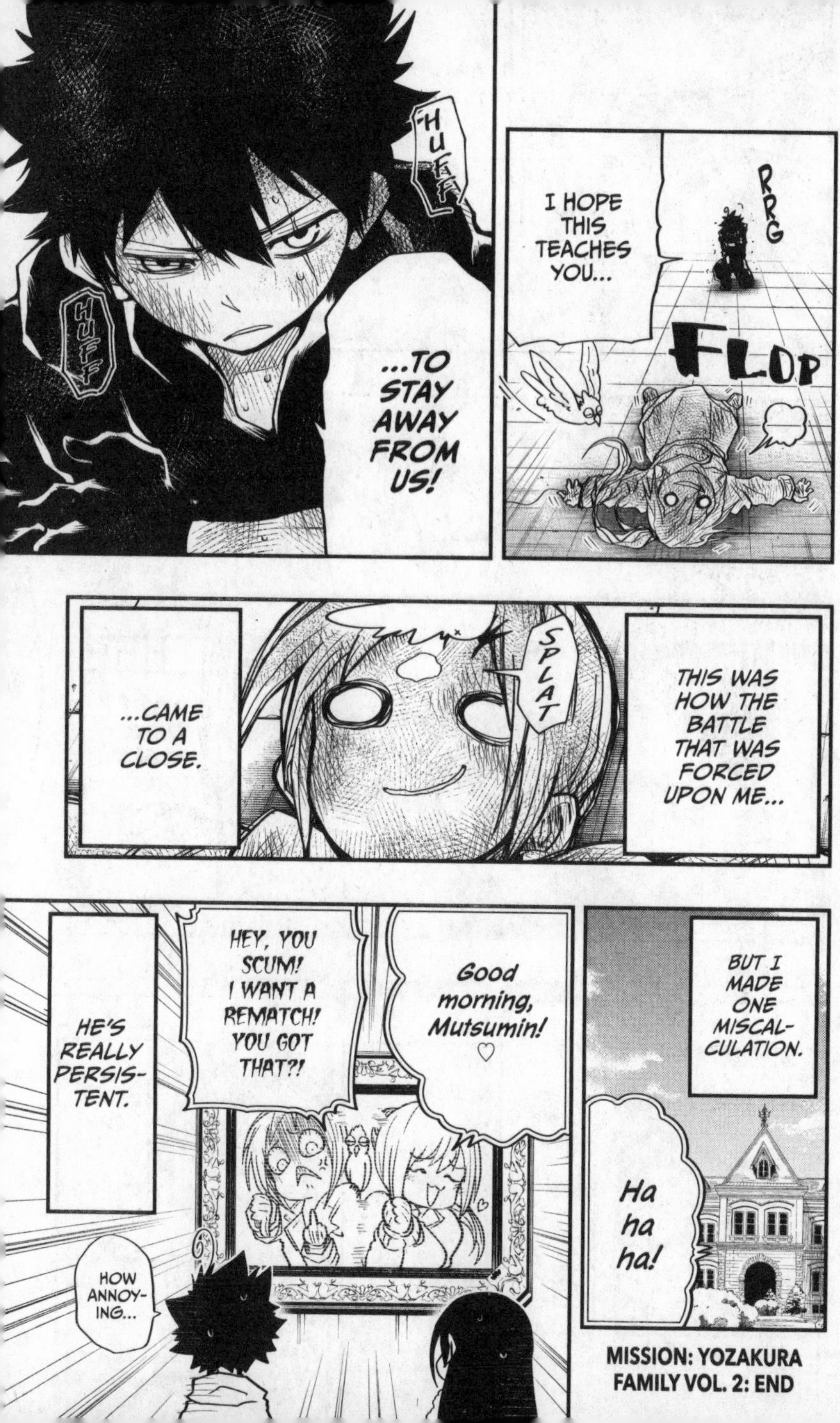
I HOPE THIS TEACHES YOU...
RRG
FLOP
HUFF
HUFF
...TO STAY AWAY FROM US!
THIS WAS HOW THE BATTLE THAT WAS FORCED UPON ME...
SPLAT
...CAME TO A CLOSE.
BUT I MADE ONE MISCAL-CULATION.
Ha ha ha!
Good morning, Mutsumin! ♡
HEY, YOU SCUM! I WANT A REMATCH! YOU GOT THAT?!
HE'S REALLY PERSIS-TENT.
HOW ANNOY-ING...

MISSION: YOZAKURA FAMILY VOL. 2: END

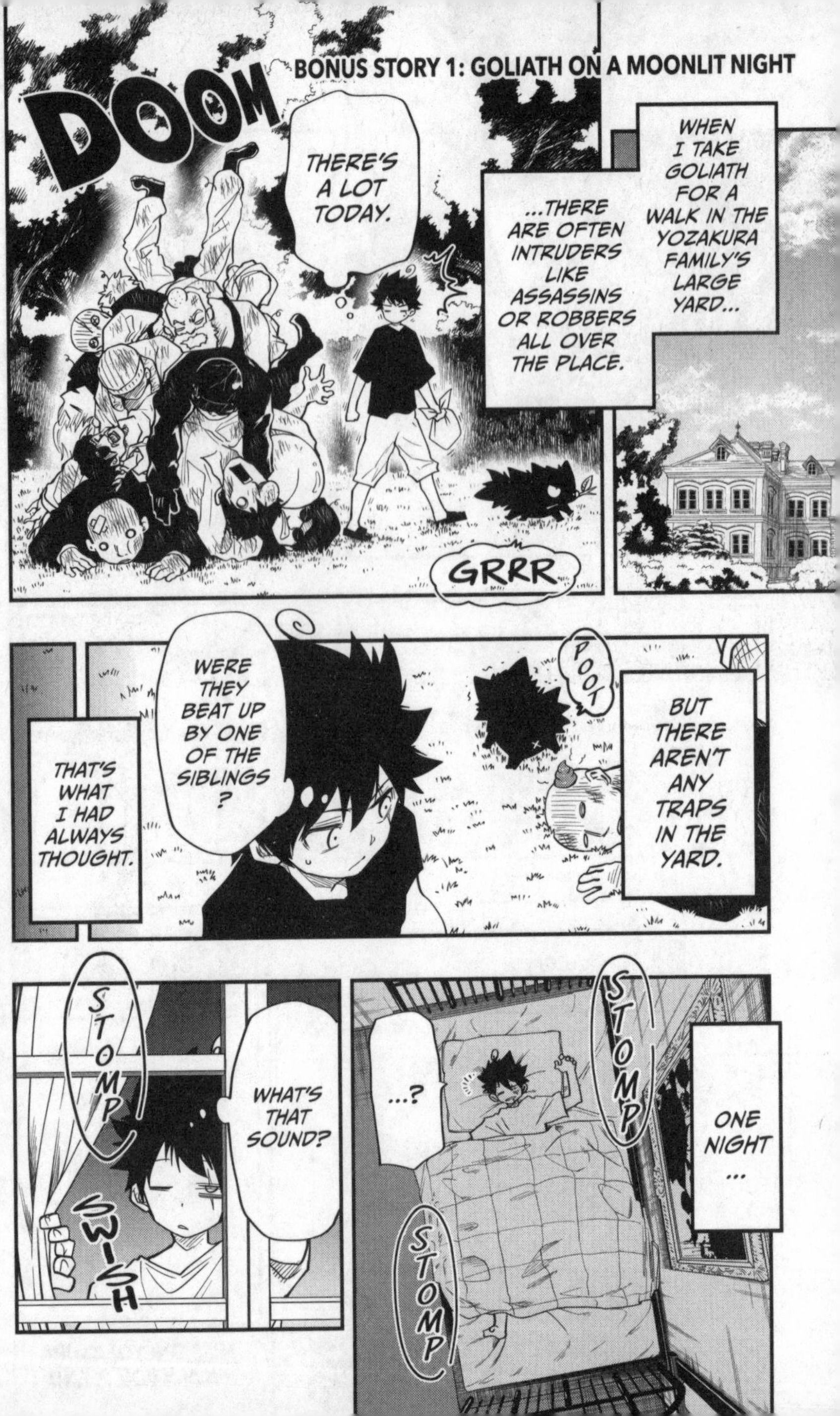
BONUS STORY 1: GOLIATH ON A MOONLIT NIGHT
WHEN I TAKE GOLIATH FOR A WALK IN THE YOZAKURA FAMILY'S LARGE YARD...
...THERE ARE OFTEN INTRUDERS LIKE ASSASSINS OR ROBBERS ALL OVER THE PLACE.
THERE'S A LOT TODAY.
DOOM
GRRR
BUT THERE AREN'T ANY TRAPS IN THE YARD.
POOT
WERE THEY BEAT UP BY ONE OF THE SIBLINGS?
THAT'S WHAT I HAD ALWAYS THOUGHT.
ONE NIGHT...
STOMP
...?
STOMP
STOMP
WHAT'S THAT SOUND?
SWISH

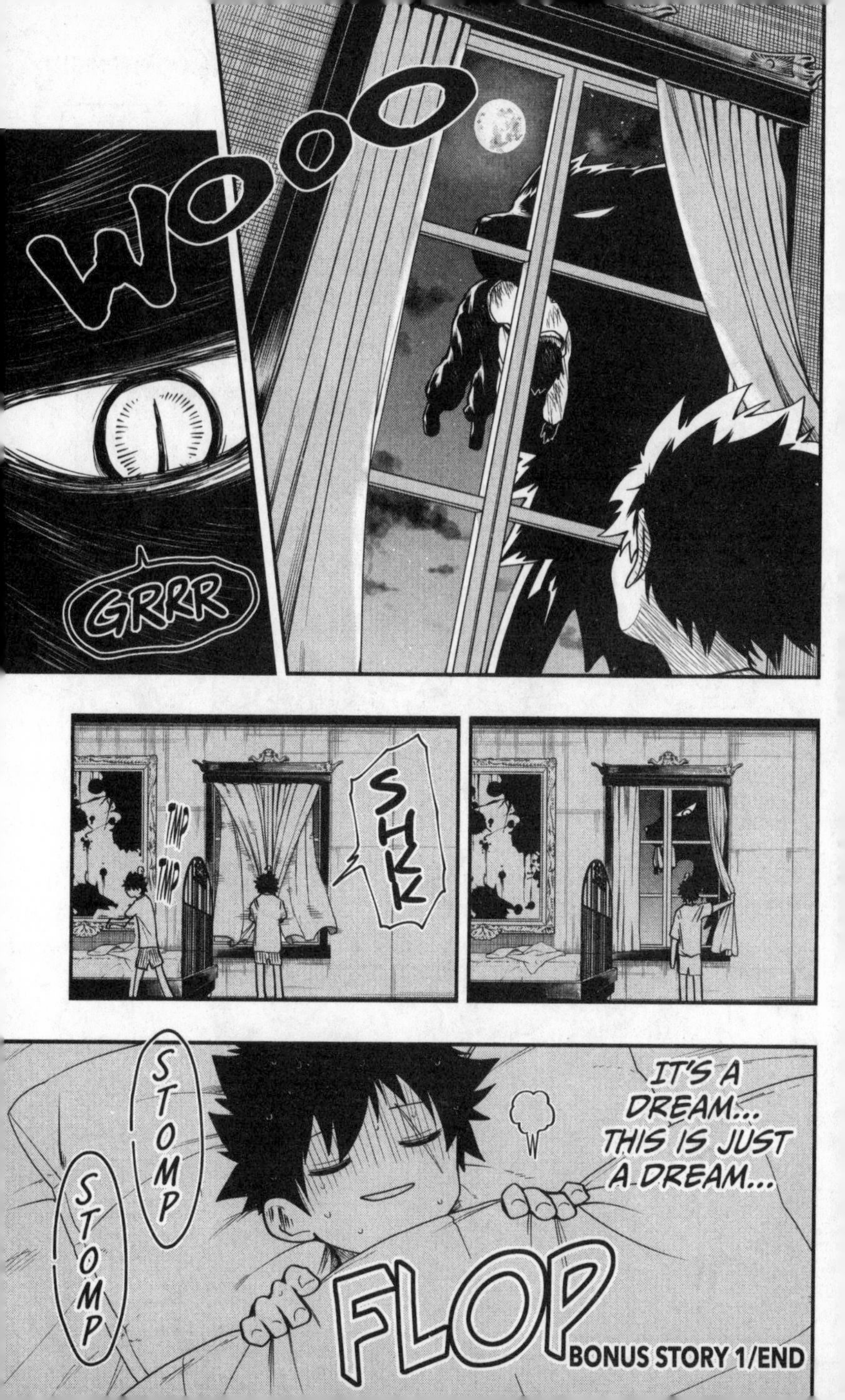
WOOOO
GRRR
SHKK
TMP TMP
IT'S A DREAM... THIS IS JUST A DREAM...
STOMP
STOMP
FLOP
BONUS STORY 1/END

BONUS STORY 2: TEMPLE OFFERING

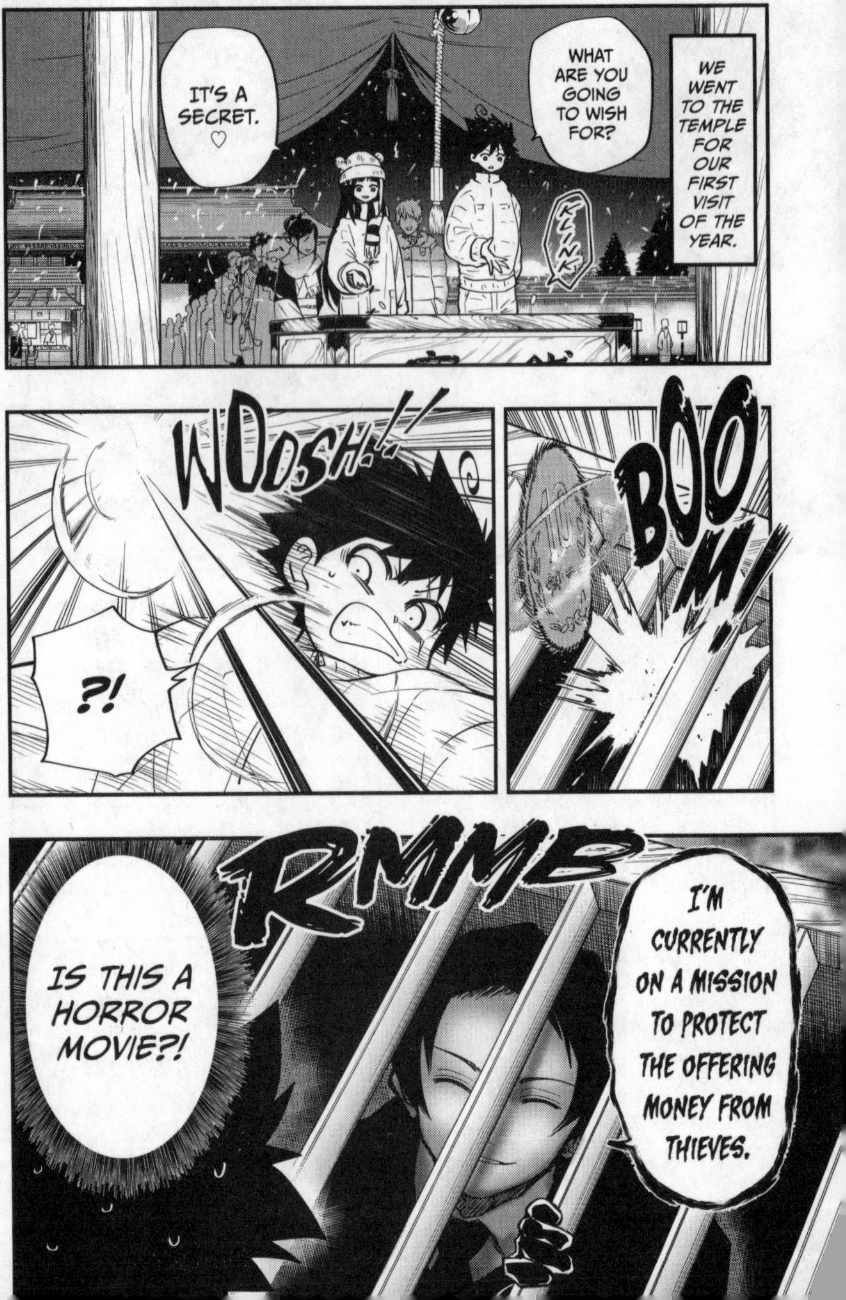
WE WENT TO THE TEMPLE FOR OUR FIRST VISIT OF THE YEAR.
WHAT ARE YOU GOING TO WISH FOR?
KLINK
IT'S A SECRET. ♡
BOOM!
WOOSH!!
?!
RMMB
I'M CURRENTLY ON A MISSION TO PROTECT THE OFFERING MONEY FROM THIEVES.
IS THIS A HORROR MOVIE?!

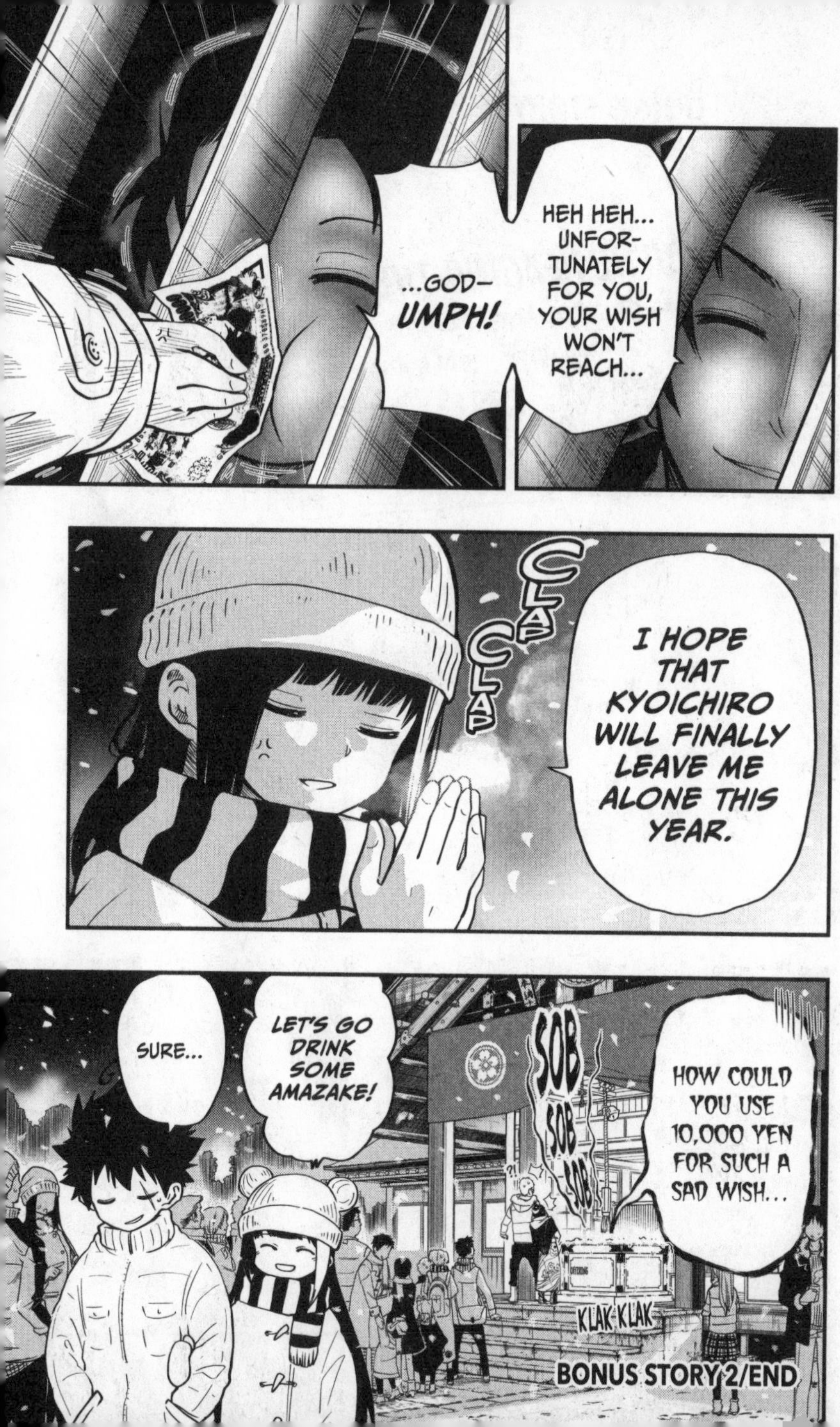
HEH HEH... UNFORTUNATELY FOR YOU, YOUR WISH WON'T REACH...
...GOD— UMPH!
CLAP CLAP
I HOPE THAT KYOICHIRO WILL FINALLY LEAVE ME ALONE THIS YEAR.
HOW COULD YOU USE 10,000 YEN FOR SUCH A SAD WISH...
SOB SOB SOB
LET'S GO DRINK SOME AMAZAKE!
SURE...
KLAK KLAK
BONUS STORY 2/END

YOU'RE READING THE WRONG WAY!

Mission: Yozakura Family reads from right to left, starting in the upper-right corner. Japanese is read from right to left, meaning that action, sound effects, and word-balloon order are completely reversed from English order.

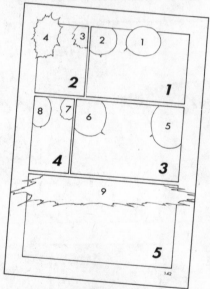

Mission:
Yozakura Family